MAPS OF THE MIND

MAPS OF THE MIND

MACMILLAN PUBLISHING CO., INC.
NEW YORK

To Rollo May for his faith in a humanism that knows
tragedy and in fondest memory of Gregory Bateson
(1904–80). The verse below was a favourite of his and
seems appropriate now:

> Not on sad Stygian shore, nor in clear sheen
> Of far Elysian plain, shall we meet those
> Among the dead whose pupils we have been . . .
> Yet meet we shall, and part, and meet again,
> Where dead men meet, on lips of living men.
> 'Life after death' Samuel Butler

AUTHOR'S NOTE
This book could not have been written but for several fortunate
events which coincided. A Rockefeller Fellowship put me in Britain at
just the right time. A friend, Richard Holme, tipped me off that
Mitchell Beazley had long wanted to create an 'atlas of the mind'.
James Mitchell and Ed Day took the gamble that this 'headlong
assault upon the ineffable' might be feasible after all. They sustained
me with every kind of resource, friendship included, and much of
their own vision went into this book.

It's said that in a good relationship each keeps integrity. Linda
Cole and her assistant Linda Tan, fought tenaciously for the
aesthetics of the visual designs, while I fought for the points I was
trying to make. Our arguments often went several rounds. Francesca
George, my editor, valiantly defended the English language against
the hordes of jargon that infect the social sciences and penetrate my
prose. As a representative of 'the intelligent layperson' she
challenged me to remain intelligible. Avril Cummings typed and
retyped innumerable drafts with great patience. To my wife, Shelley,
and two boys, Michael and Hanbury, I apologize for the long hours I
was shut away from them. Deadlines are remorseless. It only served
to remind me that images of humanity in the abstract are no
substitute for real people.

ILLUSTRATORS
Candida Amsden	pages 72, 73, 75, 77, 82, 85, 87, 90, 95, 109, 157, 167, 175, 179, 201
Beverley Brennan	page 133
Dave Fernandez	pages 21, 65, 69, 101, 113, 115, 121, 141, 153, 171, 187, 195
Suzanne Haines	page 35
Carole Johnson	pages 46–7, 63, 110–1, 112, 122
Stuart Knowles	pages 17, 23, 27, 31, 39, 41, 49, 53, 57, 61, 81, 91, 99, 125, 137, 143, 159, 183, 193, 209
Peter Stevenson	pages 45, 79, 105, 117, 119, 147, 161, 191, 199, 205
Linda Tan	pages 13, 129, 149, 163

Maps of the Mind was edited and designed by Mitchell Beazley
Publishers Limited, Mill House, 87–89 Shaftesbury Avenue, London
W1V 7AD

Typesetting and artwork origination by BAS Printers Limited,
Over Wallop, Hampshire
Printed in the United States of America

Contents

Introduction

'What is the mind?' is a question that has intrigued people from the earliest times – indeed, for as long as man has considered the possibility of mind at all. It is the first truly philosophical question which comes with the dawning of self-consciousness. Yet it stumbles on a vexing question: How can that which knows, know itself? Each representation of the known which lacks the knower is necessarily incomplete.

Maps of the Mind breaks with the notion that the one is prior to the many, that there must be some unitary reality behind multiple appearances. I believe man is his own metaphor, whose self-image fulfills itself in unforeseen ways. Like Proteus we can take many alternate forms but not escape the consequences. This book brings together in visual form numerous ways in which mind has been conceived. Since visuo-spatial imagery of the human is a style of representation largely missing from the dominant schools of psychology and philosophy, there can be no pretence of impartially cataloguing the *status quo*. The image-breakers are still in charge.

This entire book is a plea for the revision of social science, religion and philosophy to stress connectedness, coherence, relationship, organicism and wholeness, as against the fragmenting, reductive and compartmentalizing forces of the prevailing orthodoxies. My belief is that industrial cultures are dangerously overdifferentiated and underintegrated. We compulsively exaggerate our differences while ignoring what we have in common. The maps here are deliberately selected and described with a view to their overall compatibility, complementarity and convergence. W. H. Auden wrote that we must 'love each other or die'. 'Love' is a trifle too ambitious perhaps, but we can understand.

MAP-MAKING

We 'map' with words as well as images but because words come in bits and pieces many people have assumed that the world is in bits and pieces too, with bits corresponding to words. 'Not so,' said Alfred Korzybski, 'the map is not the thing.' Word maps have a fragmentary structure that derives from language itself, not necessarily from what language describes. The idea of linear cause and effect, for example, is inherent in the structure of a sentence, where a subject acts by way of a verb upon an object, but this may be a very inadequate rendering of what is happening, especially of mutual influences. One way to correct this verbal bias is to supplement words with visual maps. If the human mind is to be conceived as a whole as well as parts, we need not just words to convey parts, but patterns, pictures and schemata to convey the whole. Words must also be used

in ways that suggest wholeness. From time immemorial metaphors, symbols and stories have been used to create mental pictures and configurations. To dismiss such forms as ambiguous is to miss the all important function of relating different objects by their similarities. Most of us would regard a photograph of a person as 'true' and an abstract painting as less so, but it depends on whether we are concerned with the separate nature of that person or the relationship between the painter and the person. Also likeness has many aspects.

One day the husband of a woman who was being painted by Picasso called at the artist's studio. 'What do you think?' asked the painter, indicating the nearly finished picture. 'Well . . .' said the husband, trying to be polite, 'it isn't how she really looks.' 'Oh,' said the artist, 'and how does she really look?' The husband decided not to be intimidated. 'Like this!' he said producing a photograph from his wallet. Picasso studied the photograph. 'Mmm . . .' he said, 'small, isn't she?'

MAPS AS SHADOWS

One limitation of maps is that they are usually two dimensional. Verbal explanations suffer the same limitation; to explain meant originally, 'to lay out flat'. To illustrate this, Viktor Frankl invited us to consider the different shadows cast by a cylinder (see illustration). The interesting point about shadow-maps and their limited (but nevertheless 'real') representations is that the same objects can look so different when mapped differently and completely different objects can be mapped so that they look the same. Thus, if one takes a cylinder, a cone and a sphere, the two-dimensional shadows they cast can be identical; but one need only shine the light from another direction and the 'shadow maps' of the same objects become a rectangle, a triangle and a circle respectively.

MAPS VARY ACCORDING TO THE POINT OF VIEW

The problems above arise partly because things normally perceived in three dimensions are being represented in only two. There is also the question of point of view: the shadow depends upon the position of the light – move the light and the shadow changes shape. This visual phenomenon has a verbal counterpart in an old story that has been put into verse. It concerns six wise men, all blind, who came across an elephant, and tried to discern its shape.

> Six wise men of India
> An elephant did find
> And carefully they felt its shape
> (For all of them were blind).

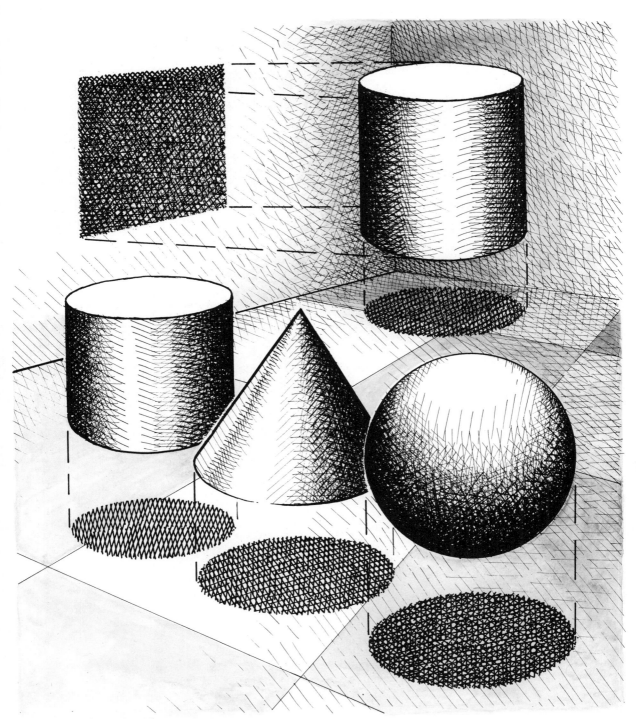

9

The first he felt towards the tusk,
'It does to me appear,
This marvel of an elephant
Is very like a spear.'

The second sensed the creature's side
Extended flat and tall,
'Ahah!' he cried and did conclude,
'This animal's a wall.'

The third had reached towards a leg
And said, 'It's clear to me
What we should all have instead
This creature's like a tree.'

The fourth had come upon the trunk
Which he did seize and shake,
Quoth he, 'This so-called elephant
Is really just a snake.'

The fifth had felt the creature's ear
And fingers o'er it ran,
'I have the answer, never fear,
The creature's like a fan!'

The sixth had come upon the tail
As blindly he did grope,
'Let my conviction now prevail
This creature's like a rope.'

And so these men of missing sight
Each argued loud and long
Though each was partly in the right
They all were in the wrong.

Even the above simplifies our problem by assuming there *is* a lumpy, three-dimensional animal 'out there'; mind is even more elusive because the sensors and the sensed overlap.

MAPS DEPEND ON VALUES
Mapping the mind depends crucially on values and much of this book records these different points of view based on personal preferences. But if perspectives can be reconciled perhaps the values that form their various standpoints can also be integrated and the problems of words and two-dimensionality can be surmounted?

We know that the pupils of eyes expand or contract involuntarily according to our interest. You can distinguish homosexuals from heterosexuals by observing how 'interested' the eye-pupils are in the pictures of naked men or women. When an English economist recently visited Moscow, he found most, but not all, churches missing from his tourist map. 'Those are the living churches,' explained his guide, 'we don't count them.' It is hoped that a multiplicity of maps will reveal such blind spots.

MINDS AT DIFFERENT LEVELS
The story of the blind men and the elephant illustrates an extreme case of 'different points of view'. But it also exemplifies a problem of scientific description. Even if the blind men had agreed on the surface shape of the elephant, this would only have been one level of description. A cross-section of its anatomy, a plan of its ecosystem in Africa or India would also have qualified as 'maps of the territory'.

The approach to mind in this book is structured according to different degrees of inclusivity and moves, with some exceptions, from narrower to broader conceptions of mind, and from earlier to later. For example: mind can be defined as processes interior to the 'deepest' brain (Level 2); as the capacity to combine incoming information creatively (Level 4); as including shared language and relationships (Level 6); or, broader still, as the whole mytho-cultural system (Level 9). Each successive level casts the net wider. There are nine levels of interpretation:

LEVEL 1
Here the human mind is struggling to emancipate itself from servitude to gods, or the laws of Newtonian mechanism which claim mind as just one more response to a determined universe, or from scientists, those Puritan agents of the divine clockmaker.

LEVEL 2
At the psychoanalytic and existential level attempts have been made to comprehend the mind in its deepest recesses and privacy where consciousness shades into preconsciousness and unconsciousness. This level is the one which underlies many differences in human thought and behaviour.

LEVEL 3
At the physiological level of brain functioning crucial discoveries have been made recently which profoundly affect our understanding of mind. These discoveries show that thought and behaviour have a physiological and anatomical basis as well as a psychological one.

LEVEL 4

At the level of the creative mind the capacity to combine, recombine and reorganize received information and mental structures is explored, along with those syntheses which are more than the sum of their parts. The creative mind transcends mechanism.

LEVEL 5

At the level of psychosocial development we study the mind as it learns from, and grows to encompass relationships with others and the environment. In this process earlier levels are subsumed.

LEVEL 6

At the level of communication, language and symbolic interaction we see mind in terms of the structures — linguistic, visual, emotional – that are the basis of mutual understanding. Language and communication are amongst the most highly developed human faculties and the analysis of them has revealed patterns and structures that appear to be common to people of widely different cultures. At this level the mind is seen to be reaching out from the nucleus that consists of the preceding five levels to extend its experience through contact with other minds.

LEVEL 7

At the level of psychobiology mind is studied as a natural organism in terms of the ecology of living systems and examined in the context of the environment. This is also the cybernetic level because any action of the organism will feedback to alter its balance and behaviour.

LEVEL 8

At the paradigmatic level mind is seen to include those a *priori* assumptions about the nature of human intelligence and its relationship to the universe. This is the level of psychology at which the self-consciousness of the preceding levels is subjected to empirical study: which methods and which epistemologies reveal which facts and patterns? How does mind influence discoveries?

LEVEL 9

At its most inclusive mind is seen as inhering in the structure of myth, institutions and cultures. Culture consists of the sharing of mythic patterns, for meaning requires that we complete a picture whether we are certain of its final form or not. Culture is then mind writ large which shapes us unawares unless we develop the understanding to shape culture.

It remains to apologize for the arbitrary nature of inclusions and exclusions in this book. With the exception of the anti-imagists (behaviourists) who exclude themselves, the contents are limited by my own strained comprehension and the gaps in my knowledge and also by my search for an overall coherence which has deterred me from making a mere collection of separate pieces. I confess to finding academic arbiters of who is 'in' and 'out' repellent, and, in a field as embryonic as psychology, both pretentious and blinkered. I have no such ambitions. I have made a start in the process of putting bits and pieces of Humpty-Dumpty together again because it needs to be done and too few are even trying. Should there be a second edition, as literary critics like to say, I would like to find more pieces and make more connections. Those who see pieces of the puzzle that I have missed may care to inform me and see the synthesis grow.

MAP 1

Psyche and Polycentrism:
The view of James Hillman

We get the word psychology from *psyche* and *logos*. *Psyche* means neither brains nor ego, but soul; psychology is thus the logic of the soul and it is this original vision of mind that this book pursues.

The myth of Psyche tells of a beautiful princess, greatly admired from afar, but whom no suitor would embrace or marry. The king, her father, consulted Apollo who told him that Psyche must set herself alone, dressed in mourning, on the summit of a high mountain, from whence a winged serpent would carry her off as his bride. The sorrowing family obeyed and Psyche waited all night in cold and terror, but found herself by morning wafted to a beautiful palace. She was its queen and every night an unseen husband came to make gentle love to her. He asked only that, as a sign of trust, she was never to look at him. But her sisters persuaded her that her husband must be the serpent monster and one night when her husband fell asleep she shone her lamp upon him. There she saw Eros (or Cupid), a man of surpassing beauty, but the lamp awakened him and he fled. In desperation she appealed to his mother, Aphrodite (or Venus), but she was jealous of the girl's beauty and demanded that she first perform several tasks so arduous and dangerous as to make her survival nigh impossible. But Psyche prevailed. Aphrodite then told her that her efforts had left her so ugly that only by using the beauty-charm she offered could she retain the affections of Eros. In fact, the charm contained a potion that put Psyche into a perpetual sleep. But Eros flew through the bars of her castle keep and awoke her with the prick of his arrow. He then went to Zeus and begged him to make Psyche and their marriage immortal, and to this day Love and Soul have never been separated.

What might this myth mean? Half a dozen interpretations occur to one almost at once. That loving involves making oneself vulnerable, that unity grows out of prior separation, that anxieties about serpents and arrows will assail young virgins (what might Freud have made of *this* myth!), that the soul must make a journey into night and prays for some presence in the dark, that the sceptical light of objectivity can kill the relationship between the knower and the known, that feeling and touch are senses equal to sight, that Cupid and Psyche remain child-like till joined, that soul or *psyche* is a form of apprehending that can turn monsters into lovers, and so on.

The Greeks would not, I think, have appreciated our insistence that this story has *one* meaning or message. It has *all* the above meanings and many more besides. It means one thing to a bride, another to a young initiate to adulthood, another to someone recently bereaved and yet another to a person approaching death. It is less an answer than a question. It is there to educe, literally 'to lead out', from us meaning after meaning till the end of time.

The Greeks would have been equally puzzled by our current attempts to produce a monolithic theory of the nature of myths. Are myths inadequate attempts to describe nature, or a protoscience purporting to explain origins? Are they heuristic devices that 'stand in' temporarily for scientific discoveries, giving us a vision that is whole yet tentative? Are they vital forms of social cohesion in a preliterate culture, that allow people to differ within a common framework? Are they, as Malinowski believed, the founding charters for customs and institutions? Edmund Leach has endorsed this idea but added to it the notion that unresolved and irresolvable arguments and issues are also handed down. Mircea Eliade sees myths as evocations of the creative era, designed to re-establish a god-inspired creativity wherein nature works with men. Radcliffe-Brown saw them as the basis of social rituals, for example Greek dramas were rituals based on myths. Cassirer wrote of a world permeated by symbolic forms.

Freud believed that myths help to keep us sane by evoking repressed,

Rollo May has remarked that while the symbol of modern industrial society is the vertical office block, an ascending line of material 'progress', the motif of Ancient Greece was the circle, with soul or 'psyche' as the centre and measure of all things, relating the world to human scale. 'Psyche' was perspective more than substance, a picturing of vital activities, which mediated events and registered their differences. This map shows the polycentric universe of Greek civilization with its pantheon of gods and 'daemons'. Each represented particular human endowments – Truth, Beauty, Persuasion, Justice – but to degrees of immortal perfection, which inspired and drew out from the human personality wide ranges of its finest capacities. The Greeks understood what personality research has laboriously rediscovered, that positive traits of character correlate positively. The Intellect of Apollo, the Justice of Athena, the Passion of Dionysus and the Communication of Hermes interpenetrate like vibration waves. Instead of treating emerging human aspects of personality as complexes and dangerous dissociations to be controlled by a unitary self or monotheistic deity, the Greeks decentralized the personality, creating in Jay Ogilvy's words a 'heterarchy' rather than a hierarchy and a multi-dimensional person. 'Psyche' was a vitalizing relationship and immortal affinity between human beings and lasting monuments to humanized gods.

unconscious feelings and ideas. Kluckholn believed that they help resign human beings to their condition and share the anxieties of finite existence. Jung saw mythic archetypes as clues to the structure of the brain. Lévi-Strauss sees a binary code in myth revealing the structure of mind itself (see Map 58). To such hypotheses the Greeks would have assented. What would have puzzled them, I believe, is our insistence on *one* 'right' theory. The major difference between our Hebrewism and their Hellenism is that we are monotheistic, hence monolithic in our theorizing and monadic in our conceptions. We constantly assume that the many have their origin in the one. But the Athens of Pericles was polycentric, plural in its theorizing and conceived of life in terms of radiating fields and personified relationships. Because we derive the many from the one, we typically conceive of a conscious 'I', an ego or self, or some other unitary explanatory principle like a Systematic Reinforcer who conditions subjects in a behaviour-control laboratory and stands 'above' like god. We conceive of the Christian soul as something carried inside, the condition of which, at the end of our lives, will transport us up or down, and can in the meantime be dedicated to God or bartered with the devil; Descartes identified the soul of man with the pineal gland, a pea-sized object in the brain with no other evident function. It has been well said that 'I' is our only remaining capital letter used to indicate respect, save for some Christians who still write 'He'. Desperate is our narcissism as a consequence. We float like tiny shells of subjectivity amid the flotsam and jetsam of objects, upon a polluted sea of indifference.

How different was the world of the Greeks. They walked with Truth (Apollo) and Beauty (Aphrodite) at their side. They raced with *daemons* of excellence, the spirits of past athletes running beside them, urging them on. They travelled with Hermes, danced and drank with Dionysus, and sailed the seas under the guardianship of Poseidon. They fought for the rights of married women, children and the home with the tenacity of Hera and harvested their crops with Demeter beside them. Even Zeus, the embodiment of might and power, was a first among equals, in no sense were the other gods his satellites. Rather they were to be weighed equally according to the situation, and it is surely no coincidence that Athena the patron goddess of Athens was herself the goddess of Wisdom, Law and Justice, who in the *Oresteia* by Aeschylus asks for the help of mortal men in judging Orestes and arbitrating between Apollo and the Furies (see Map 58). For the Greeks the one was derived from the many, be it the one judgement of Athena, or the one personality of a human being. Polytheism and the polycentric human crowded with god-derived endowments are parts of the same pattern.

Indeed it is as universal pattern, not as encapsulated object that we must understand the Greek concept of *psyche*. Perhaps the legend of Orpheus conveys it best and the Orphics played an important part in the development of sacred verse and music culminating in the *harmónia* of democratic theory and Greek tragedy. Orpheus played so sweetly on his lyre that the creatures, the rivers, even the rocks vibrated in natural sympathy with his strings. When his bride Eurydice was killed by a snake he descended into the Underworld with his lyre singing so beautiful a song that Cerberus was tamed, Ixion's wheel halted, Sisyphus rested, even the Furies wept and Pluto dropped tears of iron.

Soul was for Greeks an unbreakable relationship between men, gods and nature which even encompassed death. The Greek word *chaos* means literally 'gap', a breaching of the imagined perspective that joins up all things to human scale. James Hillman has likened the shrines and temples to receptacles into which human endowments, wrought to the acme of excellence, were offered to the appropriate god to honour Truth, Justice or Workmanship. *Psyche* stretched from

'I do nothing but go about persuading you, young and old alike, not to take thought for your persons or properties but first and chiefly to care about the greatest improvement of the soul. I tell you that virtue is not given by money but that from virtue come money and every other good of man, public as well as private.'
Socrates at his trial,
'The Republic' Plato

'Then weave again for sweet
Eurydice
Life's pattern that was taken from
the loom
Too quickly. See, I ask a little
thing
Only that you will lend, not give
her to me.
She shall be yours when her
year's span is full.'
'Amores' Ovid

'Cromwell's pious Protestants
tore down and smashed images
. . . because to their Puritan minds
images were not Christian.
Because subjectivities can be
made visible images, these were
especially damnable . . .
Personifying was driven out of the
churches into the madhouse . . .
Roundhead minds were more
concrete than the stones they
smashed.'
'Revisioning Psychology'
James Hillman

'We moderns would do well to
reflect on the transformation of
the Trinity of Zeus, Apollo and
Dionysus into their more recently
mythological counterparts, the
superego, ego and id.'
'Many Dimensional Man'
Jay Ogilvy

the immanent to the transcendent like arcs ascending to the sky. Plato described the soul as a winged chariot drawn by two horses representing contrary aspects of human nature, the one straining up the other pulling down.

The concept of *psyche* gave the Greeks their infinite love and delight in nature and an extraordinary courage in exploring it. Into every nook and cranny of the world the spirits of gods or heroes had already ventured. Men crossed the seas in the path of Odysseus, entered labyrinths of mind or nature wherein Theseus had already slain the Minotaur. Hercules had cleared the earth of monsters as Greek civilization eclipsed the monster gods of Egypt and Mesopotamia with their supremacy of the inhuman. Miguel de Unamuno might have been commending Greek humanism when he wrote: 'In order to love everything, in order to pity everything, human and extra-human, living and non-living, you must feel everything within yourself, you must personalize everything . . .' The union of Psyche and Eros is an epistemology of the heart.

But what of the criticism usually made of the Greek world-view. That it is idolatrous, that it projects primitive and animistic ideas upon dead objects by 'anthropomorphic subjectivism' (the attribution of the human to the non-human), and that polytheism is obviously disintegrative of social order? The dangers of idolatory are real, but mainly in the context of monotheism. If there is one God, or mind, with several images of endowments, then it can be disastrous to be obsessed with a single idol, or *idée fixe*, rather than the whole. But if there are many gods, or many potential personalities within the human capacity then multiple images have precisely the opposite effect. They broaden, they qualify, they liberate, and redeem our complexes and compulsions by offering them fuller personalities. The accusation that the Greeks 'projected' their 'inner' nature upon the 'outer' things assumes a *psyche* imprisoned in the head, a Cartesian dualism which the Greeks would certainly have regarded as institutionalized chaos. And what is more disintegrative: psychologies of the kind we have today, with every small clique shrilly insistent upon its monopoly of truth, exercising a single principle imperialism which tries to make all other appear dependent and derivative, or a psychology that acknowledges diversity, a polycentric universe of mind, but seeking always the patterns which connect? Could it be that unity requires a prior separation as Psyche and Eros discovered and every return of the wandering hero attests? We have in short no right to disparage the Greek concept of *psyche*. It is close to modern information theory, cybernetics, phenomenology, general systems, structuralism, much philosophical anthropology and many maps in this book.

And who looking back over twenty-three centuries could deny Psyche her immortality? Has she not penetrated dark ages to find her lover beyond? Petrarch who did more than anyone to fire the Italian Renaissance with the spirit of Ancient Greece could not read the language. Many whose works were inspired by Greek culture were never able to visit that country. They included Racine, Goethe, Hölderlin, Hegel, Heine, Keats and Nietzsche. What can you say of the imaginative power of the world that reaches across centuries, continents, languages and religions to revivify human forms and configurations? When Pericles delivered his famous funeral oration in 430 BC he knew the soul of Athens would never die. 'Mighty indeed are the marks and monuments we have left . . . Future ages will wonder at us, as the present age wonders at us now . . .'

MAP REFERENCES
Circle, see cybernetics, 39, 45–52
Greece, 2, 9, 12, 13, 23, 24, 38,
40, 56–8; Gods, 2, 5, 7, 8, 12, 24,
26, 35, 47, 57–9; Myths, 2, 3, 4,
13, 24, 40, 57–60; Polycentrism,
2, 10, 26, 30, 32, 48, 57, 59.

MAP 2

Grapes Grown from the Twisted Stump:
Dionysus, drama and democracy

The period from 462 to 429 BC is known as the Age of Pericles. It witnessed the height of the Athenian empire, the establishment of democracy, the centralization of the Delian League in Athens, the *Oresteia* of Aeschylus, the poetry of Pindar, the sculpture of Myron, the philosophy of Anaxagoras, the building of the Parthenon, *Antigone* by Sophocles, Phidias's statue of Athena Parthenos, the Thirty Years Peace, *Medea* by Euripides, the medicine of Hippocrates, the history of Herodotus, and the first production of *Oedipus Rex*.

An attempt to 'map' this extraordinary age must look to the logic-in-use among contemporaries, not to the reconstructed logic of Plato's academy, which was out of sympathy with the earlier age, nor even to Aristotle writing after Athens was in decay. What cries out for explanation is how Athenian society cohered at all. Fiercely competitive and individualistic, inventing new distinctions by the day, Athens worshipped gods whose polycentric values pulled outward like a centrifuge and whose own relationships were fraught with infidelity and turmoil. Athenians must have had principles of cohesion as powerful as the forces differentiating that society. What might account for this burst of cultural magnificence, some rare quality of relationship among like minds? It lay, I believe, in the coherent nature of their drama, ethics and democracy.

To understand Greek drama we must lay aside contemporary assumptions about theatre. The plays were state religious festivals, more inclusive of the citizenry than democratic institutions, since women, resident aliens and prisoners were welcomed, the poor received refunds and a public holiday was declared so that attendance among the non-slave urban population was near total. Even the term religious is misleading. The Greeks had a natural theology. The universe had made the gods, as well as man, so that gods personified the force fields in *this* world, not another. Drama was a concerted attempt to elevate the consciousness of a whole community. It was as if in our contemporary culture, theatre, religion, politics and psycho-drama were to fuse in a common social arena of imaginative enactment. Little else that happened to an Athenian could have left so deep an impression. Actors were regarded as interpreters of the gods and were excused military service. A reciter of Homeric poems in one of Plato's dialogues suggests the intensity, 'When I am describing something pitiful my eyes fill with tears . . . and my heart throbs . . . and whenever I look down from the platform at the audience, I see them weeping, with a wild look in their eyes, lost in wonder at the words they hear'. Why?

First we need to understand the whole function of play, in the sense of pretending. It is a major principle of learning in higher animals – by pretending to fight, they learn to do so while avoiding the consequences of fighting in earnest. The so-called 'territorial imperative' is not an example of 'animal capitalism', as popular writers contend, but a mock combative method of distributing members of a species across enough land to support them without starving. Human play, especially tragic drama, is a similar 'early warning system', a way of facing finiteness without neurotic repression, of losing your life in imagination in order to retain it longer in reality, and of studying the consequences of moral choices in dramatic simulation. Hence when the real crisis comes you are innured not to scientific dispassion but to the emotional resilience and moral courage demanded by life.

The structure of Greek tragedy is inherent in the dual aspects of Dionysus, the god of wine, joy and plenitude, symbolized by the lush harvest of the vines in late summer, and the god of *agón*, compassion, but also emotional excess, torn in pieces by the Titans, and symbolized by the pruned and twisted stumps of the vine in winter. Repeatedly the tragic dramas show this cycle of the seasons: Orestes magnificent in avenging his father's death, then driven by the Furies till he collapses

Greek dramatic art grew out of the worship of Dionysus, with contributions from Orphism, Eleusis and initiation rites in general. What began as choral recitations culminated by the 5th century BC in the City Dionysia spring festival, presenting five days of mostly tragic drama before audiences of 17,000.

Dionysus, youngest of the gods, was born of Zeus out of a mortal mother whom he fetched from Hades, so saving her soul. Almost alone among gods, Dionysus suffered 'agón' and shared human distress. The Greeks identified Dionysus with the radical pruning of vines in winter, when they resemble black and amputated stumps twisted in pain, and the lush intoxicating harvest of grapes, bringing joy and dance. Dionysus was dismembered by Titans, whom Zeus then reduced to ashes with his thunderbolts. But from these ashes mingled with the blood of Dionysus, grew mortal men with their immortal 'psyches', their evil and good and the shifting balance of contrasting capacities.

In the cyclic seasons of Dionysus and the lyre of Orpheus, the Greeks sought rhythm in mind and nature. While later philosophers defended slavery and advocated oligarchy, the tragic dramatists attacked slavery, protested against imperialism and gave to the harmony and justice of opposites its sacred, democratic expression. 'It is by the power of persuading one another', wrote Isocrates, 'that we have raised ourselves above the level of beasts . . . laid down laws, and discovered arts'.

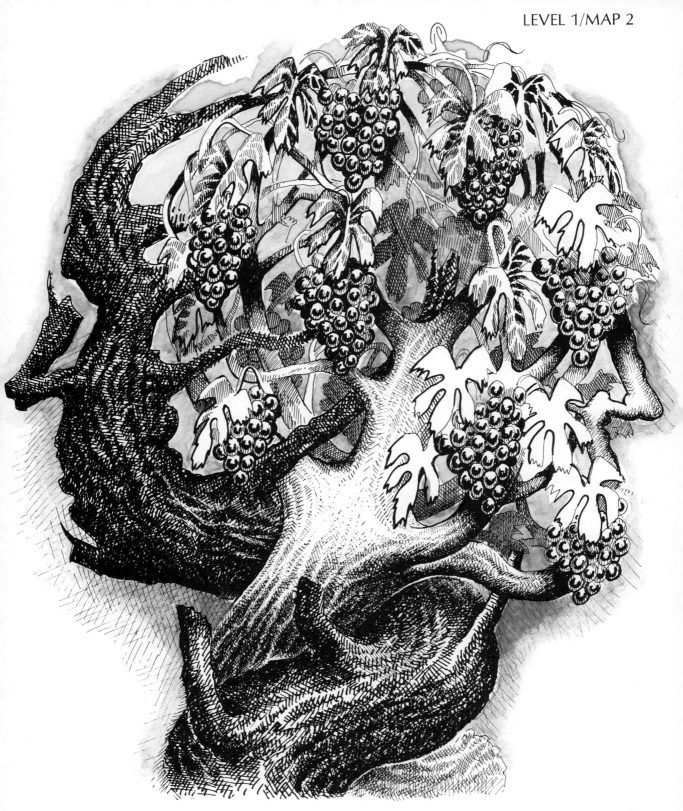

exhausted before the shrine of Apollo; Oedipus, the King of Thebes, the city dedicated to Dionysus, moves from a stump riveted to the earth to glorious kingship and back to a stump cut back from its roots and cast away. Yet the gods bless Oedipus, as the citizens of Athens uphold Orestes, for in the rhythm of the seasons is the secret of the immortal soul reborn in the springtime of the Dionysian tragic festival, held in March–April of each year.

However, if the Greeks believed in a rhythmic universe of contrasting joys and pains, they also deplored excess, as the failure to realize that every pride must ebb and anger subside. Hence disaster results from breaking the principle of *sophrosýne*, 'nothing to excess'. Originally Zeus had hurled thunderbolts at mortal *hubris*, but by the fifth century BC, the principle of *peripéteia* held that when *sophrosýne* failed the actor would achieve, in Aristotle's words, 'the transformation of his action into its opposite'. This was essentially similar to the older Heraclitean notion of *emantiodromia*, 'the return swing of the pendulum'. In short, the finest human ideals, honed to god-like perfection, swing to and fro, in dynamic opposition. It was a frightening vision, which the Greeks used drama to exaggerate. Why did they insist upon it?

First, the mind is magnified in conflict. If you are seeking to delineate the human *psyche*, then its values loom large and are sharply contrasted in states of *agón* or struggle, while in synthesis the same values are not only indistinguishable, their 'just proportions' are unique to situations. It is easier to teach by negative example that every situation requires the rock of Apollo, the whirlpool of the Furies and, as in the *Oresteia*, the justice of Athena to mediate between them. Error can be universally dramatized. Virtue requires each person to steer between intellect and impulse. Human folly is thus less a consequence of badness in people or values than of misjudgement in combining values. The tragic hero triumphs, over-learns the winning value combination, and employs it in new circumstances with disastrous results. Such insights give Greek tragedy its compassion and emotional range – Medea abandoned in a foreign land by a husband for whom she has given everything, moves with terrible logic to punish him. She, Iphigenia, Orestes all stand for lesser human conflicts as well: for every child deadened by marital strife, endangered for military glory, or asserting independence from his mother. In each case a single element in the value system grows 'cancerously' to kill the whole. We hate the crime but not the perpetrators.

Another function of Greek tragedy was the presentation of anomalies that called forth a creative response. If we agree with theories of creativity that two or more matrices of thought must be 'bisociated' (see Map 27), that the blocking of 'vertical thinking' by frustration, induces 'lateral thinking' (see Map 29), that disintegration must precede reintegration and only the greatest resilience in the face of anxiety can achieve this (see Map 13); if we accept that higher levels of moral awareness are born out of a frustrating dialectical clash between opposed moral positions, each inadequate to the dilemma presented (see Map 38), then the presentation of tragedy makes brilliant sense. Essentially tragedy imposes a Dionysian/Christ-like 'crucifixion' between polar ideals upon an entire audience, while much Christian practice persuades us that Christ agonized to save us for fundamentalism!

Yet we must not imagine that tragedy spells unmitigated misery. The principle of *peripéteia* works here too, as the trough of tragedy yields to a wave of elation. If the Greeks depicted disintegration on the stage, this had the effect of fostering reintegration around the stage as thousands wept as one for the entombment of Antigone, for Iphigenia the bride of death. These great waves of intoxicating emotion, accompanied doubtless by clasping and weeping in each other's arms

'Health consists in the enjoyment by the powers – the wet and the dry, the hot and the cold, the bitter and the sweet . . . of equal rights, while the monarchy of one or the other is conducive to sickness.'

Alkmaion of Kroton

' "Harmónia" is an atunement of opposites, a unification of the many, a reconciliation of dissentients . . . '

Theon of Smyrna

'In the seasons, in plants, in the body and above all in civil society, excessive action results in violent transformation into its opposite.'

'The Republic' Plato

'The evershifting interplay of conflicting moods is like an elaborate piece of counterpoint, in which two themes, continually varied, are played in two long crescendoes one against the other.'

George Thomson discussing the 'Oresteia' in 'Aeschylus and Athens'

affirmed the vitality of the moment, the infinite preciousness of human lives, poised on the edge of an abyss. For the joys of life, as Tillich and May (see Map 13) have argued, are found in its contrast with death, attachments are strengthened in beholding abandonment, and it takes genius, surely, to encounter imaginary death in a way that celebrates real life.

A psychological experiment by Leonard Berkowitz suggests the effects of tragic drama. Two groups were shown an identical excerpt from a violent film. The first group were provided with a story context that justified the punishment visited on the protagonist. The second group witnessed grave injustice to a tragic hero. When members of both groups were subsequently invited to punish an incompetent assistant, the witnesses to tragedy were three times less punitive than the rejoicers in righteous wrath. Tragedy gentles, then. Few wish to add one iota to human pain, rather they feel drawn, participatively and democratically, into an unjust scene to set it aright.

Greek drama and democracy, viewed as wholes, were celebrations of *harmónia* (harmony) and *symphrónasis* (reconciliation and symphony), terms employed by the mathematician and democratic theorist Pythagoras. Pythagoras defined social, civil and personal harmony in the image of the tetrachord lyre, and the four fixed notes of the octave, represented by the numerical series 6-8-9-12, corresponding to the relative lengths of the strings. Harmony was not some persistent harping on a single mean, but the play of the instrument *around* the mean. Similarly Greek tragedy shows scant respect for the equable temperaments of Ismene in *Antigone* or Crysothemis in *Electra*. Both are too slavish to be aroused by injustice. The ideal is *both* the attainment of heroic extremes *and* the realization that harmony requires one extreme to yield to its opposite, in the rhythm of verse, plot and music. What is heroic about Oedipus is his *anagnórisis*, his painful change from ignorance to knowledge, based on Orphic rites of initiation and purification. The gods bless the state (Athens) that sheltered Oedipus at Colonnus because he had accepted and learned from the extremities of human experience, freedom–determinism, vigilance–blindness, sovereignty–exile.

It remained for Anaxagoras, teacher of Pericles and Socrates, to propose that mind pervaded a patterned universe, wherein every value contained the seeds of its opposite, where democratic debate, like theatre, staged conflict in order to contain it. Pericles was surely echoing his teacher in the funeral oration: 'We are capable at the same time of taking risks and estimating them beforehand. Others are brave out of ignorance . . . But the man who can most truly be accounted brave is he who best knows the meaning of what is sweet in life and what is terrible, and then goes out undeterred to meet what is to come.' Therein lay the moral strength of Socrates that scorned to flee. He died not for a Courage that conquers Caution, nor even for an Individual Conscience that defies the State, but for the Virtue that grows from its opposite. He knew that the twisted old vine of Socrates would flower as long as the human mind endured, that loyalty was the harvest of dissent, truth of scepticism.

MAP 3

The Yin and the Yang: The philosophy of T'ai Chi

One day Confucius and his pupils were walking by a turbulent river. They saw an old man playing in the raging waters around the rocks. Suddenly he disappeared from view, and Confucius sent his pupils racing to the rescue, but the old man as suddenly emerged by the bank. Confucius asked him how he could survive the torrents. He answered: 'Oh, I know how to go in with the descending vortex, and come out with the ascending one.' He knew the *Tao*.

The *Tao* (literally the Way of the Universe) originated in the poetic and paradoxical writings of Lao Tsu, an older contemporary of Confucius, in the sixth century BC. It was not until two centuries later that we find the first recorded depictions of the *Yin-Yang*, which together comprise *T'ai Chi* (diagram of the Supreme Ultimate). This diagram appears in the 'appended explanations' to the *I Ching* (*The Book of Changes*).

Yin and Yang mean literally 'the dark and sunny side of the hill', but in their profound influence on Chinese philosophy, religion, government, art, medicine, nutrition, sexuality and social custom they have come to stand for two complementary principles, alternating in space and time, throughout the myriad forms of nature. Yin, the dark side, has been taken to represent female, earth, valley, stream, night, yielding, absorbing, rest, autumn–winter, and many associations therefrom. Yang, the light side, has been taken to symbolize male, heaven, mountains, rock, day, forcing, penetrating, movement, spring–summer and similar associations. They are said to have originated from one primordial breath, *Chi*, which divided into a lighter mountain mist, and a darker earth vapour.

In art, writing and symbolism Yin is represented in even numbers, in broken lines, in colours such as orange, and by fungi, cows, turtles, snakes, peaches, blossoms, waves and clouds. Yang is represented by odd numbers, in solid lines, in colours such as azure, and by dragons, stallions, Feng-birds, rams, cocks, horned beasts, jade and mountains. But the symbolism is less polarized than unified. Life is a rhythmic movement among opposites, a timeless ebb and flow in vibrating wave patterns. The story of Confucius and the raging waters is a gentle reproach against those who strive *against* rather than *with* nature. The old man knew the secret of the vortices, the ever-cycling *Chi*, and went with the flow of things. The Taoists were originally opposed to the Confucians, to their set rules of etiquette and the practicality, but the *T'ai Chi* was invoked by scholars of both schools and appears to have partly reconciled them.

While the Yin–Yang is not specifically a map of the mind, it is so by implication, since human wisdom, perfection and immortality were to be gained by becoming one with the *Tao*. We cannot understand Chinese art unless we see it as *moral* symbolism, an unceasing persuasion towards harmony, aestheticism, fusion, complementarity, permeability and interpenetration. The erotic relationships of couples exchanging essences were favourite devices as were numerous metaphors for positions in sexual union: 'seagull's wings over the cliff-edge', 'hovering butterfly', and 'bamboos near the altar'.

We can no longer dismiss the *T'ai Chi* as mysticism. Principles of complementarity and theories of relativity in physics, double helices in biology, field theories, systems in equilibrium, and ecological perspectives, all remind us that for certain purposes patterns and relationships must be considered as prior to the 'things' being organized. Personality is a whole, life itself a coded pattern, interdependence a principle of survival. Fritjof Capra in *The Tao of Physics* makes a persuasive case for the *Tao* as a paradigm for sub-atomic physics; no less a celebrity than Niels Bohr, the Danish physicist, used it for his coat of arms. Unless our values interpenetrate and our 'maps' mingle, the human species could be doomed.

The Yin (dark side) and the Yang (light side) are intertwined, ever-cycling polarities. Take any phenomenon or human value to its logical extremity and it will yield to its opposite, as the large, fiery sun sinks into night.

Moreover the end of any polarity contains within itself the seed of its opposite, as man and woman contain the seeds of both sexes and as each season contains the seeds of the next.

The schema works well for human characteristics. A woman is humble . . . more still . . . then famed for her humility? A man is confident . . . more still . . . then supremely confident. Is there not some doubt pushing that confidence to excess?

Yin–Yang anticipates the whole modern concern in psychology with gestalt, binary constructs, figure–ground relationships, and contexts in which behaviours occur. It uses, as does much of Chinese arts and letters, an essential ambiguity to suggest the unity of its possible meanings, as well as to educe new interpretations: a cycle, a vortex, a winding path, an embrace of lovers, a golden mean, a balance wheel, fertility, aestheticism. It is our earliest known symbol of integrity . . . 'only connect . . .'

MAP 4
The Tree with Poisoned Fruit: Saint Augustine and others

The story of Adam and Eve is myth, and myth is often regarded as something untrue by definition. The view taken here is that the human mind seeks meaning. Meaning involves wholeness and coherence of vision; yet whole explanations may suggest that nothing remains to be discovered. Myth is thus a mediator between the known and the unknown, a non-dogmatic vision ever open to individual reinterpretations, yet a touch-stone around which an entire culture may cohere. Like all great teaching stories the myth of the Garden of Eden has given rise to innumerable interpretations. It is an overarching metaphor lending unity to diversity. Nor should we consider such interpretations as right or wrong. Like branches on the Tree of Knowledge itself, they are derivatives, free associations upon what Rudolph Bultmann calls the *Kerygma*, the deeper human meaning embodied within.

We know that the world did not evolve in the manner described by Genesis, but what if the book is describing a dawning awareness of the world? The anthropologist Edmund Leach has argued that the 'bit' or binary digit is the basic unit of pre-logical communication. Genesis is a sprouting of 'bits', ie elementary binary distinctions, along with mediating categories like serpents. Hence God divides the light from the darkness, water from earth, heaven from the firmament, grass and trees from bare earth, the sun, stars and moon from the sky and the seasons from one another. Then fish are distinguished from the seas, animals from grass and trees, man from animals and woman from man. By resting on the seventh day, God distinguishes rest from work. So far, this Tree of Life is not problematical. Like many animal organisms, Adam and Eve learned and survived by increasing the elaboration of simple discriminations. But there was a second tree near the centre of the garden: the Tree of the Knowledge of Good and Evil. The Lord had forbidden Adam to eat of this tree, 'For in the day that thou eatest thereof thou shalt surely die'. Again this must mean awareness of impending death, since Adam ate and did not die within the compass of the story. That the knowledge of good and evil is different to other kinds of knowledge is surely undeniable. Physics and biology, for example, are light years ahead of our ethical self-understandings. Scientists have until recently got away with the pronouncement that their work was 'value free', perhaps the most innocent (or serpentine) opinion ever perpetrated by associations of grown persons.

It was St Augustine in *The City of God* who provided the general interpretation of the Eden story, which most other scholars have taken as their point of departure. The Garden represents the innocence of man's primal unity with God. Adam was the pure subject of divine contemplation, while material creation was subject to Adam's reason, and hence God's. Adam's fall was a collapse of these relationships into division and disharmony, '. . . and just as Adam's soul was divided against itself by sin, so all men were divided against one another by selfishness'. Adam prized knowledge above unity and this lets loose the demon. ('They are called demons from the Greek word meaning knowledge. The demons have knowledge without charity . . .') To redeem the Adam in man, God bade his Son take on a human body and live among men. In the words of St Paul, He was 'in Christ reconciling Himself to the world'. The cross symbolized the original Tree of Knowledge and Christ's crucifixion was a healing of the division between God and Adam, and an end to the death sentence pronounced upon him, 'Dust thou art, and unto dust shalt thou return'.

The Tree of Knowledge finds many branches in this book. For as Paul Tillich asserted, an 'ultimate concern' for our 'being or not being' unites those scholars who think deeply, whatever their 'preliminary concern' or discipline. For Søren Kierkegaard (see Map 12) the Tree symbolized that man is a union of opposites. He

The Tree of the Knowledge of Good and Evil was but one tree in the Garden of Eden. In modern terminology we may call it a 'decision tree', one sub-assembly of thought and action in the midst of an ecological network and balanced environment of the Garden. Whenever man acts purposively, one part of the total system is arbitrarily made into a subject and other parts into objects or means for satisfying desire (or reaching fruit). This has an inherent tendency to upset the balance of the whole. The ecology of animal and plant life is 'innocent' in the sense that equilibrium appears to be maintained by automatic reflex and instinct, which may even be a part of our genetic endowment (Map 46). Our self-conscious-ness frees us also to discover, understand and restore it.

The Tree of the Knowledge of Good and Evil has many branches in this book. For example, the human nervous system and brain organization abound with analogues of trees (Maps 20, 21, 23); language takes the form of a tree (Map 41) and much of it, especially 'the knowledge of good and evil', appears to have a lethal structure that traps us in deadly disputes (Map 43). Some have suggested that the serpent represents one-dimensional thought and evaluation, the dominance in our culture of a technical 'either/or' over an ecological 'both . . . and'.

is self-conscious within a physical body, the only animal capable of reflecting on his condition. Transcendent over nature like the branches of a tree, he is yet rooted to the earth and destined to return thence. Man's fall into self-consciousness brings him to dread, or anxiety, fear and trembling and sickness unto death. 'If man were beast or angel, he would not be able to be in dread. Since he is a synthesis he can be in dread. . .' trapped between 'soulish and bodily' existence, 'The spirit cannot do away with itself . . . Neither can man sink down into the vegetative life'. Perhaps he cannot, but Tillich among others has insisted that he tries, and here lie the roots of sin. Man finds himself painfully stretched between finite and infinite poles of existence, a form of psychic crucifixion which H. A. Williams has elaborated upon (see Map 5). The contradiction and anxiety are so intense that human beings over-emphasize the either/or of living, and either commit themselves to the transcendent, the imaginative and the ideal, listening to the promise of the serpent, 'Ye shall be as God', or they become obsessed with the finite, the corporeal and the real. War, exploitation, violence and perversion are invariably dedicated to *one* branch of the Tree, with a boasting, a vainglory and a pride in the finite or in the infinite. Hence human history is witness both to the naive and disastrous idealism of a Children's Crusade and to the bodily backlash of a Marquis de Sade and his imitators, who try to subjugate sexual anxiety in sado-masochism, and to sodomize the conventional, spiritual virtues of the day.

Tillich saw the Garden of Eden as fulfilled in the experience of Protestant Christianity. Cast out of monasteries and from feudal society, itinerant monks found themselves exiles from the Great Chain of Being, taking refuge in Calvin's Geneva, and moving from gardens to cities to ply their trade. Later, many were cast out of the Old World into the New, trekking across the American continent in search of freedom. It was the Protestant poet Milton who suggested in *Paradise Lost* that Adam and Eve's exile was as much opportunity as sorrow:

> Some natural tears they dropped, but wiped them soon,
> The world was all before them, there to choose. . .

David Bakan describes the Garden of Eden as prophetic of the schism between Roman Catholicism and Protestantism. The first chose communion with an ever present God, the second chose to become the agents of a more distant God, and uncover His works through their own (see Map 8). Tillich's interpretation (see Map 13) is strictly Protestant. The 'dreaming innocence' of Adam before the Fall was less a state of perfection than of unfulfilled potential. The actualization of human potential involves self-differentiation, disobedience, trial, error and, hence, sin. Eve's acceptance of the serpent's argument gives Adam a second birth, one in which man is perpetually torn between the anxiety of losing himself through not fulfilling his potential and losing himself through errors involved in the attempt to fulfill it. This is essentially similar to Otto Rank's death fear versus life fear (see Map 15) and to Freud and Jung's notion that the split between conscious and unconscious minds must be healed (see Maps 9, 10). Freud spoke of playing 'the devil's advocate' to find repressed alternatives to conscious decisions.

Erich Fromm (see Map 11) goes so far as to suggest that contradiction is man's essence. The sin of Adam was the first step towards a self-conscious differentiation which in turn facilitates loving integration at higher levels. Plants and animals in the biology symbolized by the Tree of Life do this unwittingly, man living by the Tree of Knowledge must consciously practise the arts of reasoning and loving. How foolish, says Fromm, to believe that Adam and Eve cover their nakedness through motives of Victorian prudery. They realized that they were different from each other and

'O Sacred, Wise and Wisdom-
giving Plant,
Mother of Science, Now I feel thy
power,
Within me clear, not only to
discern
Things in their Causes, but to
trace the ways
Of highest Agents, deemed
however wise.'
The serpent in 'Paradise Lost'
John Milton

They saw 'that they were naked and they were ashamed . . . while recognizing their separateness, they remain strangers, because they have not yet learned to love each other. . . The awareness of human separation without reunion by love – is the source of shame . . . of guilt and of anxiety.'
'The Art of Loving' Erich Fromm

'There was once a Garden. It contained many hundreds of species . . . there were two anthropoids who were more intelligent than the other animals . . . On one of the trees there was a fruit very high up . . . so they began to think. That was a mistake . . . to think purposively . . . The he ape . . . Adam . . . went and got an empty box and put it under the tree . . . a second box and put it on top of the first . . . and finally he got the apple. Adam and Eve then became almost drunk with excitement. This was the way to do things. Make a plan, ABC and you get D. They then began to specialize in doing things the planned way. In effect, they cast out from the Garden the concept of their own total systemic nature and of its total systemic nature . . . Pretty soon the topsoil disappeared. After that several species of plant became "weeds" and some animals became "pests", and Adam found gardening much harder work. He said, "It's a vengeful God, I should never have eaten the apple". Eve . . . heard a voice say, "In pain shalt thou bring forth . . ." '
    'Conscious Purpose versus Nature' from 'Steps to an Ecology of Mind' by Gregory Bateson

from the Lord walking in the Garden. They realized that they had come into the world alone and would leave it alone, and must now learn to cross the gulf between them and live in spite of death. This 'in spite of' is the theme of existentialism (see Maps 12, 14), while creativity (see Maps 26–31) combines different modes, planes and matrices.

Further illumination of the Adam and Eve myth is provided by the physiology of the human brain and nervous system (see Maps 18–25). We can, it seems, process information in two opposed ways, by unifying it or by separating it, with the right or left brain hemispheres respectively (see Map 23) – precisely the choice and the fateful consequences faced by Adam and Eve. Julian Jaynes (see Map 24) argues that our earliest human ancestors were not conscious in the way we are. The Heroes of the *Iliad* experienced themselves, like Adam, as being 'commanded by gods' – a phenomenon produced by the right hemisphere of the brain acting independently of the left. In this event the Eden story may symbolize the birth of consciousness as we know it.

The most intriguing interpretation of the Genesis story is by the anthropologist Gregory Bateson (see Map 50). He coined the word schismogenesis to describe a growing split of lethal consequences in the structure of ideas and relationships. For Bateson, 'God' is the name we give to the larger ecological and environmental pattern of which we are a part. There is a necessary unity between Mind and Nature which we divide dangerously whenever we act with conscious purpose (see margin). Holy sacraments are one way in which we honour our interdependence. We will continue to pollute, ravage and despoil our environment until we acknowledge oneness with the ground of our being. Bateson likes to quote the Lord answering Job out of the whirlwind:

'Who is this that darkeneth counsel by words without knowledge? . . . Where was thou when I laid the foundations of the earth? Declare if thou hast understanding . . .'

MAP 5

The Cross and the Prison: The psychotheology of H. A. Williams

St Luke relates how the Pharisees demanded that Jesus show them 'The Kingdom of God'. Christ answered that, 'the Kingdom of God cometh not with observation . . . [it is] . . . within you'.

H. A. Williams has dedicated much of his life to the Kingdom of God within. He is both an orthodox New Testament theologian and a student of depth psychology who believes that it is possible for individuals to identify psychologically with the experience of the historical Jesus. Wilderness, passion, crucifixion, resurrection are not early biblical terms but feelings of what it is like to be fully alive today, participants in Christ's death and rebirth. I have chosen to present him here because he does for theology what I only aspire to do for mind, that is, stand at the cross-roads of different systems and viewpoints and constantly relate rather than isolate ideas. Williams' vision of the cross-symbol is a place where minds and bodies, thoughts and feelings, absolute truth and our relative images of conveying it, can meet and become whole.

Williams starts with the proposition that conflict is life. From the smallest atomic particle to the poles of the earth itself, positive and negative charges pervade reality. To the mind which opens itself to this world inner conflicts and tensions are necessary, healthy and creative. These are minor intimations and imitations of Christ's sufferings upon the cross of human choice. There is continual tension in our lives between competing truths: 'This is the case, but this is also the case'. We must allow ourselves to be torn, to be stretched upon psychic poles to the limits of endurance, in the effort to reconcile these poles and so resurrect the life within us.

Williams takes from psychoanalytic theory the idea that we habitually repress those parts of our experience which seem to conflict with other parts. This repression may push the unwanted ideas into the unconscious, or it may lock them away in the dungeon of the mind, wherein they grow ugly and savage like prisoners who, for that very savagery, remain imprisoned. Some well-known cultural and personal conflicts are illustrated below, with the first in each polarity and the second in each polarity forming parallel 'bars' as if on the door or prison, thus:

1				
mind	determinism	autonomy	objectivity	thinking

2 vs	vs	vs	vs	vs
body	freedom	dependence	subjectivity	feeling

3				
finiteness	dispassion	reason	scepticism	action

4 vs	vs	vs	vs	vs
infinite	passion	imagination	faith	contemplation

An exponent of the 'scientific world-view' for example, might imprison bars 2 and 4 beneath 1 and 3. It is 'good' to be cerebral, deterministic, to give autonomy to the scientist (if not his subjects) and to think objectively and dispassionately about finite quantities subjected to sceptical reason. Williams would not object to these values, only the *division* between these values and the ignored values of the deeper, 'unknown self' which the 'known self' shuts away. Those conflicting values we repress will, if we reach down to them, form a larger pattern of totality which is God, within us, the ground of our being. When we push these deeper strata into unconsciousness, or when the conscious mind uses its body like a slave, curbs its imagination, mocks its

'The root of sin', writes H. A. Williams, '. . . is the identification of my total self with the self of which I am aware. Two consequences follow from this identification. First . . . the known self is too narrow to be satisfying to me and is felt in its constriction to be intolerable. Secondly, the unknown self which, for mistaken reasons of security, I keep imprisoned and in exile, becomes a savage as a result, like a man locked for life in a dark dungeon seeing nobody.'

Behind the 'bars' of a mental prison (in the lower part of map) we lock our unknown self, which can escape only by way of Calvary (the top part). Here the unknown self ascends from the unconscious, like the vertical bar of the cross, to engage, struggle and ultimately be reconciled with, the known self, or horizontal bar. This is why Christ spoke in parables, so that ultimate truth would elude us and we would never cease our search for Him. For God cannot be grasped by discursive reasoning alone or by objective research, by obeying laws or similar prideful displays. Through prayer (as through psychotherapy), through communion with God and our neighbours, through worship and, above all, through faith, we surrender to a deeper awareness that we are more than we can possibly know. That 'more' is God, the ground of our being. The surrender to Him does not conquer the known self, but renews, heals and makes us partners in His death and resurrection and so whole persons.

MAP REFERENCES
Binary constructs, 2–4, 9–16, 22, 28–30; Crucifixion, see also schismogenesis, splitting, 2, 4, 10, 12, 15, 27, 30, 56, 59; Mind–Body, 6, 14–15, 18, 21, 55, 59, 60; Prison, 6, 12, 14, 59; Resurrection, see synergy, 42, 55, 60.

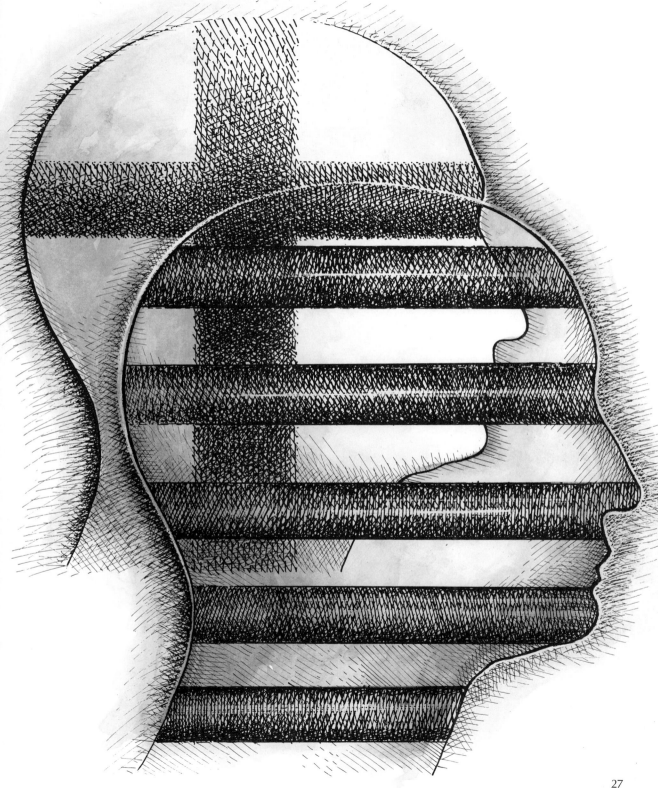

faith, there is loss of the life within us Christ came to make more abundant; we become partial zombies.

However, Williams is no priest of Dionysus or guru of the counter-culture. He quickly pointed out that flaunted bodies, cults of feeling, freedom and subjectivity and the credulous faiths that swept Western cultures in the sixties were only evidences that the 'slave' had been given a half holiday. The 'revolution' had been precisely that, a revolving of dominant and subordinate values to show that the puritan was a pornographer beneath. But feeling without thought, body without mind were only different forms of imprisonment, equal and opposite repressions. The mental divisions remained.

We find the symptoms in neuroses and bigotry, the sensation of deadness, repetition and role playing, the grim certainties born of doubt, the zeal fired by anxieties, the violence employed to coerce our recognition, the doctrines clung to like personal possessions. 'In the realm of knowledge, as elsewhere, to be invulnerable is not to be immortal. It is only to be dead.' The only exit from this interior prison of deadness is to accept the whole of ourselves, so that deeper layers of mind can ascend, like the vertical axes of crosses which in *agón* or struggle meet in dialogue and reconciliation with the horizontal axes. This is for all of us an exceedingly painful, frightening, psychic process, but can be achieved in the context of a loving environment with joy as the culmination. Christ's crucifixion is replete with images of splitting and coming apart. The Veil of the Temple rent in twain, the piercing of His side, the darkness at noon, the blood and water running out as separated elements. He showed that we must risk coming apart to be reintegrated, lose our life to save it.

The crosses in the margin illustrate the structure of our personal salvation. The endurance of these tensions, the descent into hell to release the prisoner, will threaten to tear us apart, and yet it is the only way. The deeper our neuroses and the longer the imprisonment, the greater will be the pains of repentance. Not just our personal repressions afflict us, but the schismatic hatreds of whole communities can become the cross of the person alone, as utter *isolation* ascends to struggle with *love*. 'My God, my God why hast Thou forsaken me?' Williams, of course, is concerned with the *structure* of conflicting values, less than with their specific contents. There are many additional examples of content, absolute versus relative, inner versus outer, and the 'Father' of Protestant theology with the 'Mother' of Roman Catholic. The Trinity is for Williams the fusion of the different faces of God, the Holy Ghost that unites Father, Son (and Mother).

For me, a moving moment of psychic crucifixion occurs near the end of Nathanial Hawthorne's *The Scarlet Letter*, as light breaks into the prison that Puritanism has become. Standing before the community in the market place, its revered minister, Dimmesdale, bares his chest to reveal a letter A, burned into his flesh. The seducer and adulterer, long sought by the townspeople, has unmasked himself. In a state of nervous collapse he reaches out for Hester and for Pearl, the disgraced mother and daughter he has long disowned as he disowned the passion of his own body. But Pearl has always refused to kiss or to touch him in their furtive meetings in the forest. She has become a shallow, wilful child, the letter A incarnate. Now, forlorn, he begs her to kiss him. 'Pearl kissed his lips. A spell was broken. The great scene of grief in which the wild infant bore a part, had developed all her sympathies; and as her tears fell upon her father's cheek, they were the pledge that she would grow up amid human joy and sorrow, nor forever do battle with the world, but be a woman in it. Towards her mother too, Pearl's errand as a messenger of anguish was all fulfilled.' This passage reminds us that there is no cheap grace. The poor minister could not physically survive this torment. His silence had been too

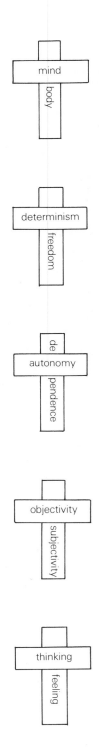

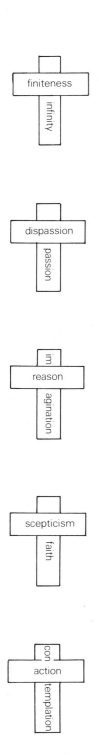

long, his stature too high, his guilt too great. He was the victim both of his own hypocrisy and of his community's desperate pathological desire for a purity of conception. Yet his passion at the last gave life to those he loved and reunited mother and daughter with their community, with each other and within themselves. Pearl now had a past and so she could have a future. In reaching out to her father she had reached down into the depth of her own being and found the self she had never before experienced. This was *True Resurrection* for all concerned, or as Williams puts it: 'All that separates, injures and destroys has been overcome by what unites, heals and creates. Death has been swallowed up by life.'

How do we recognize this mysterious power of resurrection that comes to those who do not shirk their cross? Williams gives us several examples, some minor in themselves but all speaking of a creative combination of mind and body. Consider the tennis player who has ordered his reluctant body to obey him, and felt his body fight back in pain and fatigue. Then, after hours or days of struggle, mind and body combine in fluent, graceful power. Consider the artist who suddenly finds that his hand has surpassed even the beautiful conception in his mind's eye. Then there was George, raised to hate his impulses and his sexuality, who later revenges himself on his parents by bringing home provocative women on whom he flaunts his promiscuity. Later he meets Margaret, and suddenly the earlier innocence of youth is one with the sexual experience of recent years, transforming mind and body and resurrecting the slave within him into a joyful eroticism.

Williams entitles these stories the 'resurrection of the body' but mind is resurrected too. We are resurrected by the realization that knowing and not knowing are in perpetual tension. We can know God 'absolutely' only in analogy and through metaphor, so that the language of worship changes with the times. There is no immaculate perception of theological truth, but a knowledge about God that must meet a knowledge of God in prayer and communion. Our images of God are like scientific theories, the best human construction that we are able to place upon our spiritual experiences. They are limited, inadequate and always open to revision, which is why Christ spoke in parables, 'that in seeing they may not see . . .'

Williams puzzles over the problem of evil in the presence of a good God. He quotes Rilke, 'If my devils were to leave me, I am afraid my angels will take flight as well.' But the answer lies in Williams' basic approach. It is in vain that we search for an *essential* difference between good and evil, for their constituents are the same. The crucial distinction lies in the structure, ie the manner in which the pieces are assembled. Evil is disintegration, an angry juxtaposition of alienated opposites, with parts always striving to repress other parts. Good is the synthesis and reconciliation of those *same* pieces. To permit evil forces to crucify one is the first perilous step in the conscious internalization of conflicts usually blamed on others (or on oneself by others). As we let these conflicts tear us, we become painfully aware of the values involved and of our responsibility for the quality and disproportion of those contending forces. Hence there lies within our agony the priceless opportunity to reconcile the values in exactly those just proportions that will resurrect the whole body of those values. The good, then, is inherent in our capacity to make 'evil pieces' whole. Sanctus is Satan reconciled, the house no longer divided against itself . . .

MAP 6

The Broken Image: Floyd Matson's view of Descartes, Newton and Darwin

How can the historical section of this book justify the telescoping of the two and a half centuries from René Descartes who died in 1650, to Charles Darwin who died in 1882? The answer is that the image of mind was so reduced, reified, phantomized, mechanized, boxed and beheaded in this period, that no 'map' worthy of the name emerged. The empiricists seemed to be determined to shave all *a priori* constructs with Occam's razor until barely a shadow remained. To assume that the mind was nothing, or at most an empty box, a clean slate or a retinal mirror, was supposed to reduce 'bias', as if a blank between our ears was not a massive presupposition! Floyd Matson has most ably chronicled this desiccation of mind in *The Broken Image* to which this account is much indebted.

By the time of René Descartes, the image of man had already been dislodged from the centre of the universe by Copernicus and Galileo, it was for Descartes to divide that image, mind from body, subject from object, knower from known in a lethal split which has yet to heal. The motive was probably reverential, a deep religious respect for the immortality of the human soul. The Church was the proper guardian of that soul and of scientists themselves. The stuff of science was *res extensa*, ostensible objects located in public space. *Res cogitans*, things of thought, were located in private space, known only to each person in the privacy of relationship to God. 'I think therefore I am' Descartes had proclaimed, and, with that, further discussion of the observer's status was closed.

The vision of nature conceived by Descartes and perfected by Newton was that of a vast perpetual-motion machine, objective in the sense that no human act qualified its behaviour. God was the clockmaker, who had wound His creation and left it to tick on. It followed that uncovering the Divine Plan was a calling compatible with Protestant theology. Astronomy was the leading science of this time and its vision was bleak indeed. It had reduced man, as E. A. Burtt expressed it, 'to a puny, irrelevant spectator . . . imprisoned in a dark room. The world that people had thought themselves living in – a world rich in colour and sound, redolent with fragrance . . . speaking everywhere of purposive harmony and creative ideals – was crowded now into minute corners in the brains of scattered organic beings. The really important world outside was a world hard, cold, colourless, silent and dead . . .' After Newton, no image of man or nature could be too pessimistic. The tough-mindedness of dispassionate reason and scepticism became the prevailing orthodoxy, with calamitous consequences for the concept of mind. For while the science of mechanism now developed apace, culminating in the Industrial Revolution, the Observing Mind remained apart, locked in its private cubicle, an Unknown Self (see Map 5), and the captive of religious authority. In the words of Gilbert Ryle, it became 'a ghost haunting a machine'.

The immunity of mind from being investigated as yet another object in the universe was not to last long. Thomas Hobbes studied Descartes' *Meditations* and at once communicated his objections to the author. Human thought, Hobbes argued, was no exception to universal mechanism, but was reducible to material causes. 'This mind will be nothing but the motions in certain parts of the organic body.' A few years later Spinoza fulminated against those who regarded mind as, 'a kingdom within a kingdom . . . [which] disturbs rather than follows nature's orders'. He would regard mind 'in exactly the same manner as though I were concerned with lines, planes and solids'. It remained for John Locke to anticipate the direction of twentieth-century mechanistic psychology.: the human mind was a *tabula rasa* upon which irresistible external forces inscribed themselves. The simple, the molecular, the external, the visible and the developmentally earlier were all of more fundamental reality than the complex, the whole, the internal, the less visible and

In the two and a half centuries between the deaths of Descartes and Darwin the image of mind was so shattered and reduced by scientists and philosophers that no coherent map emerged. This assault on the mind has continued into the twentieth century and today psychology is still mostly in pieces, broken bits of affect, intelligence, attention, response, memory, behaviour, attitude, belief, and anxiety, scattered through innumerable sectarian journals. No one can put Humpty Dumpty together again, and so long as the 'machine analogy' survives no one ever will, for the principle of cohesion has been destroyed by the very process of analysing. No wonder, then, that experimental psychology is full of data on inflicting pain, prejudice, obedience, conformity, cheating, aggression and scapegoating. Rarely are there experiments on independence, affection or moral decision. When we look closely at these few, we see that the 'affectionate monkeys' in Henry Harlow's experiments were those left alone and not deprived of their mothers; that independent subjects defy the experimenter (Map 13); and that the morally enlightened break out of experimentally induced dilemmas (Map 38). It is anti-social subjects who prove predictable and controllable. These are not just problems of professional ethics. How we use atomic energy may not be a problem in physics, but the capacity of 'scientific methods' to generate selectively the unethical side of human beings is a problem of psychology.

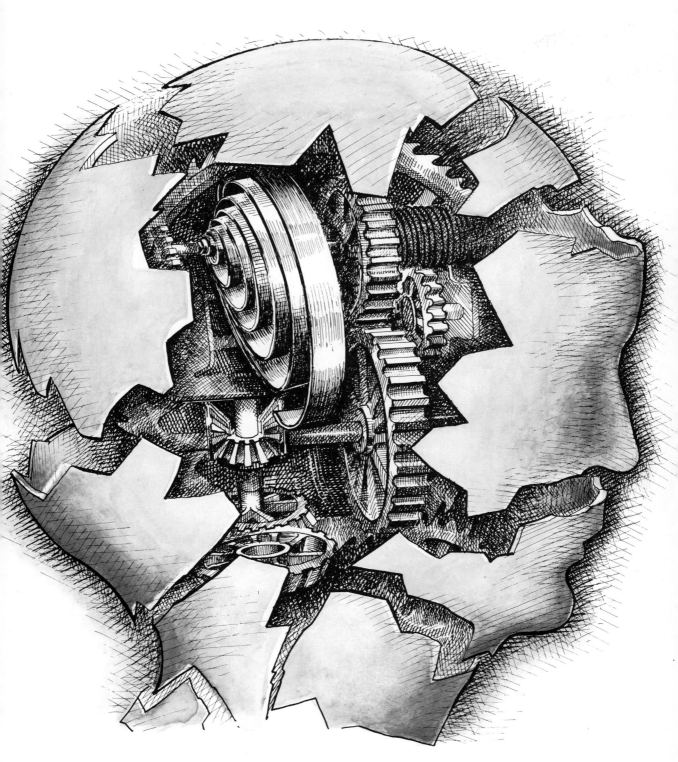

the developmentally later. Mind was also comparable to an empty box into which Newtonian particles were dropped by external agents.

To this point, mechanism was still being dedicated to God. It was His chosen instrument of control. But the march of the Enlightenment and particularly of the 'Left Cartesianism' of the French *philosophes* soon disposed of God as an invisible and unnecessary construct. 'Let us conclude boldly, then,' said La Mettrie, 'that man is a machine, and that there is only one substance differently modified in the whole world . . . what will the weak reeds of divinity and metaphysic . . . avail against this firm and solid oak?' When the Emperor Napoleon asked Laplace where God came into his System of the Worlds, Laplace replied, 'I have no need of that hypothesis'. Carl Becker commented of this revolutionary period that 'having denatured God, they deified nature'.

The human mind thus became a kind of football of those who believed that their science could propel it. The social physics of Saint-Simon and Auguste Comte would attempt to put Reason at the helm of revolution and the common good, while across the Channel, James Mill and Jeremy Bentham used the Associationism of David Hartley to develop a Felicific Calculus in which individuals were social atoms seeking pleasure, avoiding pain and benevolently controllable by arithmetic. The idea of Economic Man as some kind of ambulatory cash-register is still with us.

Into this arena was now introduced the theory of natural selection advanced by Charles Darwin and after a brief, if furious, debate it swept all before it. It is not difficult to see why. It was a creature of the prevailing scientific *zeitgeist*. Natural selection was seen to operate when random mutation of the genes (triggered by radiation, chemicals etc) produced accidental changes in animal and human organisms. Such changes would occasionally improve the fit between organism and its environment, so that 'fitter' organisms were 'selected by nature' to survive, while the 'unfit' perished. Once again the bleakest of visions had won. The human mind had been routed and a new theory of natural mechanism enthroned, while religion and romanticism were driven from their last defensible positions in natural theology. If industrial capitalism selectively rewarded those most fit to survive while eliminating the others, then an invisible hand was merely imitating natural selection to elevate the industrious and the competent. Social Darwinism in Britain and the United States and the *Darwinismus* of Ludwig Gumplowicz on the Continent, elevated the individual and group respectively to the status of externally guided and sanctioned predators.

But it was in twentieth-century America that the long assault on mind reached its zenith with the advent of behaviourism, and it is only in the last two decades that its force has begun to recede. In 1902 Pavlov had introduced the concept of the conditioned reflex. He had warned against generalizing from salivating dogs to human beings, but John B. Watson, psychologist and advertising executive, was not so cautious. 'Give me the baby and my world to bring it up in . . .', he cried, 'and I'll make it climb and use its hands . . . I'll make it a thief, a gunman, or a dope-fiend. The possibility of shaping in any direction is almost endless.' Psychology was a totally objective branch of natural science, he stated, and must 'sweep aside mediaeval conception . . . sensation, perception, image, desire, purpose, thinking and emotion . . . The measuring rod . . . always, is can I describe this bit of behaviour I see in terms of stimulus and response?' Man was 'an assembled organic machine ready to run'.

There could be no map of such a mind because its response was nothing but a dependent variable, the effect of stimuli occurring in certain environmental conditions. 'Mentalism', 'consciousness', 'subjectivism' were epiphenomena, a kind of side-show for the liberal arts but of no scientific significance. Clark Hull continued

[the] new philosophy calls all in doubt
The Element of fire is quite put out;
The Sun is lost, and th'earth, and no man's wit
Can well direct him where to look for it . . .
'Tis all in peeces, all cohaerence gone;
All just supply, and all Relation.'
'An Anatomie of the World'
John Donne

'I seek to destroy the illusion of psychical activity, to reduce everything to constant and in some sort mechanical relationship between elements which should be as simple as possible.'
'Analysis of the Phenomena of the Human Mind'
James Mill

'The drunkard searched for his lost wallet beneath the lamp post because the light was better.'
'The Conduct of Inquiry'
Abraham Kaplan

'Herbert Butterfield tells of the learned professor who diced a piece of cheese with a kitchen gadget and then wrote a learned dissertation on the cubic nature of cheese.'
'The Conduct of Inquiry'

Watson's warning against 'anthropomorphic subjectivism', the tendency to project human characteristics upon psychological science. He counselled a concentration 'on sub-human organisms', but since even these could be imbued with human sympathy, it was safest of all to regard 'the behaving organism as a *completely self-maintaining robot*'. The torch in this curious crusade has now passed to B. F. Skinner with his periodic attacks on 'The Literature of Freedom'. 'The hypothesis that man is not free is essential to the application of the scientific method to human behaviour.' All this was being said at a time when physicists, themselves the objects of 'scientific' emulation, were busy dismantling the Newtonian world view. The field theories of electromagnetism with their invisible and irreducible wholes, the quantum revolution showing energy rather than mass at the sub-atomic level, and principles of complementarity and uncertainty made psychologists look like *petit bourgeoisie* out of touch with their betters.

How could it have happened that doctrines so consistently reductive, manipulative and dismissive of human endowments could have persisted through these centuries? Above all how do we account for the triumph of behaviourism in the United States, the world's foremost exponent of human rights and individual liberties? For an answer we must return to the essential contradiction at the heart of Cartesian dualism, where there are always *two* minds, that of the knower and that of the known. This segregation at the centre of psychological science is no more 'separate and equal' than racial segregation. For knowers and known are in reciprocal relationships. If the known human objects of psychological experiments are the 'dependent variables' publicly exposed, scientifically reduced and rendered powerless and empty, then those who conduct these experiments become the beneficiaries. They, the knowers, are 'independent variables', privately protected, scientifically enhanced with the power to fill the empty with knowledge. The lure of Newtonian mechanism is the whisper of the serpent in the Garden of Eden, 'Ye shall be as God'. The so-called dismal sciences are not so dismal for their adherents, whose enthusiasms remind us of Bernard Shaw's dictum that 'all professions are a conspiracy against the laity'. That the freedoms of Western democracies have generally expanded in this period, is due to the fact that the rights claimed by knowers have proved more realizable than their ambitions to subordinate the known to scientism. It is the image of man that has been the chief victim of predatory paradigms, but these scientisms remain dangerous ambitions disintegrating a unitary vision of mind and society.

And it is all unnecessary. For as Gilbert Ryle explained, Cartesian dualism is a 'category mistake'. Imagine a visitor to a university who is shown lecture halls, laboratories and libraries, only to ask, 'But where is the university?' Mind, like university, is in all the things seen, and in seeing itself. It unites the knower and known, subject and object and all relationships thereto. We are not *either* free or determined, but *both*, since mind through language has multiple levels, B. F. Skinner, in a television debate with me, claimed he could 'shape creative responses by reward and punishment'. I at once agreed, 'But to shape persons to be creative is not to shape *what they will create* since "creativity" is a logically higher category of language than the unique outcomes to which it refers.' We can be determined at one level and free at another, in a freedom within the law. (For the development of this point see Map 40.)

MAP 7

Protestantism, Scientism, Capitalism: Max Weber and religious character

In his famous essay, *The Protestant Ethic and the Spirit of Capitalism* published in 1905, Max Weber, the German sociologist, proposed that the 'ideal type' of virtuous individual expounded in Calvinist and Puritan doctrines had facilitated the rise of industrial capitalism. Weber disagreed with Karl Marx that economic organization was necessarily the prime shaper of personal character and moral beliefs. The opposite, he argued, was also true. A type of New Man shaped by Calvinist ideology had preceded industrial development in many European countries and in the United States of America; there was a strong relationship between Protestant religion and later economic development. Three major studies have borne Weber out: R. H. Tawney's *Religion and the Rise of Capitalism* (1926) has furnished a mass of historical detail connecting Puritanism with economic activity; David McClelland's psychological classic *The Achieving Society* (1958) has correlated the rise in cultural 'achievement imagery' with major surges of Protestant zeal that led a generation later to equivalent surges of industrial growth and development; finally Gerhard Lenski's *The Religious Factor* (1961) found major differences in Protestant and Catholic groups in the United States on attitudes to religion and work.

How did the 'ideal person' as conceived by the Puritan revolution differ from the older ideals of Anglicanism and Catholicism? Below, the insights of Weber have been supplemented by those of Michael Walzer in *The Revolution of the Saints* (1970) and of David Bakan in *The Duality of Human Existence* (1966).

ANGLO-CATHOLIC ORGANICISM
The person is part of an organic hierarchy, a Great Chain of Being, rooted in kinship, feudal loyalties, neighbourhood, animals and land.

COMMUNAL, MEDIATED RELATIONSHIPS
Salvation is in communal faith, with access to God mediated by kings, bishops, judges and lords.

INTERCESSIONIST GOD
God is ever-present, interceding in human affairs in miraculous and supernatural ways.

SALVATION THROUGH COMMUNION
Man is saved less by his own efforts than by faith and partaking of the passion, mercy, forgiveness and indulgence of the crucified God in the family of believers.

GOD EXPERIENCED WITH MANY SENSES
God is experienced as mystery in many dimensions, in ritual, community, sacrament, awe, asceticism, and participation, by way of Mary and the saints.

v PURITAN, ATOMISTIC INDIVIDUALISM
The person is alone, a saintly outcast from corrupt feudalism, but can enter holy leagues or covenants with other upright persons.

v PRIVATE, DIRECT RELATIONSHIPS
Salvation is a private matter between God and His agents on earth, who have direct access to His will.

v DELEGATING GOD
God is distant and delegates his power to chosen human instruments and the laws of nature.

v SALVATION THROUGH WORK
God is the task-master to his earthly agents, a state of grace they can demonstrate but not alter. Interpersonal emotions are indulgences of a corrupt order.

v THE WORD READ, HEARD, ENACTED
God gives unambiguous instructions to man's reason by way of His Objective Words. Mystery, magic and speculation are vain, when compared with active obedience.

For the Calvinist the Bible was regarded as unmistakable instructions in God's will, a written memorandum from an absentee director to his saintly executives on political action in this world. The Word was 'objective' to those purged of personal vanity and conceit, sufficiently separated from the corrupt social order and imbued with godly habits, who must therefore agree upon its correct implementation, or doubt their saintly calling. The Word overruled residual loyalties to kings and bishops and rendered their mediation unnecessary. The Word's objectivity could be further proven by actively creating visible entities, leagues, covenants, pamphlets, parliaments, administrative units and, later, commercial products and pieces of scientific data, all aimed at establishing that Nature's objective order was a state of obedience to God.

Modern behavioural science is thoroughly infused with Puritan ethics, for example: the idea of the scientist, as a predicting and controlling agent for scientific determinism; the 'dogma of immaculate perception'; a preference for the abstract, the methodological, for visible activity publicly verifiable, and the 'godly discipline' of rigorous experimental minutiae. There is the same rejection of 'speculative questions', of the private imaginings of subjective personality, of the human image, emotional relationships and reconciling schema in general.

And unto one he gave five talents, to another two, to another one to each according to his several ability: and he went on his journey. Straightway he that received the five talents, went and traded with them, and made other five talents ◖ In like manner he also that received the two gained other two ◖ But he that received the one went and digged in the earth, and hid his lord's money ◖ Now after a long time the lord of those servants cometh and maketh a reckoning with them ◖ And he that received the five talents came and brought other five talents, saying, Lord, thou deliveredst unto me five talents: lo, I have gained other five talents ◖ His lord said unto him: Thou hast been faithful over a few things, I will set thee over many things: enter thou into the joy of the lord

OTHER-WORLDLINESS	v	THIS-WORLDLINESS
In this vale of tears the greatest respect belongs to those who prepare us for the world to come.		God's Kingdom will be founded in this world by the Saints doing the work to which God calls them.

HUMAN PERSONALITY CULTIVATED	v	PERSONALITY SUBMERGED IN WORK
Virtue is personified by self-cultivation, courtliness, wit, charm and the flamboyant manners of the Cavalier.		Virtue is achieved by self-effacement, and becoming the mere agent of God's objective order (eg the Roundhead).

. . . for the kissing of the hand as if he were licking his fingers, bending down the head as if his neck were out of joint . . . or leering aside like a wench after her sweetheart, or winking with one eye as if he were levying at a woodcock, and such apish tricks as come out of the land of Petito . . . we allow none of that.'
'The Court and Country'
Nicholas Breton

Weber argued that while in theory the Calvinists and Puritans were in an unalterable state of grace and predestined to salvation, in practice it was only possible to remain certain of this belief if continued evidence was provided which fellow Saints could scrutinize and confirm. This evidence was objectified by ceaseless work and in the building of institutes and organizations which gave public visibility to private concern. Weber credits these early associations of godly men with legitimizing the delegation of authority, the division of labour, the idea of contractual relationships, the separation of instrumental organizations from the primary groups of hearth and home, and with the systemization and methodical practices which later came to characterize organizations and bureaucracy. By preaching the virtues of productivity combined with asceticism and thrift, and by eschewing sociability, the Puritan generated a surplus from his business that was reinvested in greater works, rather than in increased consumption or enjoyment. His was a peculiarly abstract ideology relying on words, acts and objective indices, precisely the kind of information necessary to run a business.

'We shall not indulge curiosity . . . should not speak, or think, or even desire to know, concerning obscure subjects, anything beyond the information given in the Divine Word.'
'Institutes of Christian Religion'
John Calvin

But even more important from the viewpoint of this book was the influence of Protestantism, especially Calvinism, upon the growth of Newtonian science. In Map 6 we saw that the universe of Newton was a vast perpetual-motion machine, wound by a divine clockmaker, and left to tick on by the laws of natural mechanism in a world 'hard, cold, colourless, silent and dead'. This was a Puritan vision, *par excellence*, with physical scientists deputed by God to uncover his predestined holy order and works, whose nature, like the Scriptures, was determined, objective and unambiguous to a sufficiently dispassionate observer. Even the word 'law', as used in science to characterize the regularities of the physical universe, originates in the notion of obedience to authority. For God, like His chosen agents, was to be known by His works. These included Nature along with human instruments of inquiry. The respect traditionally shown to God was now transferred to physics. As Weber pointed out, physics was the favourite science of all Puritan, Baptist or Pietist Christianity.

The Puritan insistence on submerging the personality of the scientist in the God-fearing authority of data, helps to explain the otherwise extraordinary reluctance to make maps of the mind. This virtual prohibition comes from the same root as objections to 'speculative' image-making and the portrayal of 'idolatrous' human figures of saints and virgins. It is my contention that modern doctrines of scientism, positivism and behaviourism, so far from having escaped from religion, 'super-stition' and *a priori* beliefs, are steeped in Calvinistic ideology, having borrowed even its most objectionable characteristic, a devastating lack of self-awareness. The characteristics of the two doctrinal sets are compared below; the correspondence, covering more than three centuries, is so close that it has to be more than coincidence.

'Whereof one cannot speak, thereof one must be silent.'
  'Tractatus' Ludwig Wittgenstein

In 'Janus: A Summing Up', Arthur Koestler points out how closely behaviourism follows Darwinism, and both, of course, derive from Calvinism. 'Calvinist ideology: Fallen man – God's election – Eternal life Biological evaluation: Chance mutation – Natural selection – Survival Behavioural learning: Random tries – Selective reinforcement – Survival'.

CALVINIST AND PURITAN IDEOLOGY

Religious freedom is the means by which the Elect show proofs that they are predestined by God.

The individual is primarily alone before God and only through a common subjection does he learn to associate himself.

The visible world is prior to and of greater salience than the invisible. Self-objectification through visible works is the best evidence of God's grace.

The human personality should efface itself for the benefit of manifest, orderly and disciplined habits of work.

The individual's relation to God is strictly private and should not be confessed to mediators. Justification being through works, picturesque images are false.

The objective word of God is unambiguously rendered in the Bible and in activity based thereon. The public scrutiny of sober men will lead to agreement.

Attention to method, details and the minutiae of daily life will lead to human self-discipline and perfectibility.

There is a permanent inescapable estrangement of man from God, for which the answer is the obedience and total subjection of man to become an instrument of God's will.

'Forsake unprofitable speculation; avoid mysteries that haveth no daily use.'

BEHAVIOURISM, POSITIVISM, SCIENTISM

'Academic freedom' is the means by which behavioural scientists demonstrate strict psychological determinism.

The operant learns by atomistic responses elicited by his trainer and so learns to form associations and bonds.

Scientific data must be demonstrable and located in public space. Self-objectification through observable behaviours are the building blocks of science.

The 'mentalism' and 'consciousness' of the person should be ignored in favour of his systematic response and reflexive habits.

'Mental events' are private and inaccessible to science. Mutual understanding should not be confused with scientific exploration. Humunculi and 'maps' are mistaken.

An objective science of behaviour is unambiguously rendered in responses to stimuli under schedules of reinforcement. A consensus of dispassionate and disciplined observers will naturally result.

Careful methodology, rigorous testing, and painstaking precision will lead to perfect systems of prediction and control.

There is a permanent dualism between knower and known, for which the answer is that the known must become a part of the knower's behaviour-control technology.

Theories, models and non-operational concepts are unscientific.

MAP REFERENCES
Capitalism, 6, 8, 18, 20, 27, 60; Behaviourism, 6, 8, 18, 20, 27, 60; Fall, 4, 24, 35, 54, 56, 60; God, 1–2, 4–6, 8, 12, 24, 35, 48, 58–60; Protestantism, 6, 8, 12, 26, 43–4, 52, 60.

None of the foregoing discredits the very real contributions made by Newtonian, Darwinian or behavioural sciences. It only shows the impossibility of escaping from presuppositions and how those who zealously eschew 'religion', fall deeper in its debt. Images of the person and maps of the mind fly in the face of Puritan prohibitions, not of science *per se.*

MAP 8

Psychology and the Image of Satan: The views of Henry Murray and David Bakan

One way of characterizing the schism between Catholicism and Protestantism according to David Bakan, a psychologist at York University, Canada, is that Catholicism stressed *community* and Protestantism stressed *agency*. Each has historically become haunted by the surfeit of its preferred value. The Puritan Saints, earthly agents of God's will, placed no limit on the zeal or thoroughness of its exercise and extension. It followed that the heirs of Calvinism – capitalism, positivism, scientism – have likewise displayed overweening agentic powers, repressing that concern with community which might have qualified their runaway technologies.

Since human agency running amok was so common an occurrence, the Puritan ethic conceived of a rival task-master, Satan, who willed his own agents to do battle with the Saints. In fact, Bakan argues, 'Satan is a projection in which the agentic in the human psyche is personified . . .' When frantic efforts at mastery reach the limits of their effectiveness, driving the agent to despair, the individual ejects his agentic function and attributes it to a projected image of Satan whose separate existence and utterly alien nature is illusory.

Power without charity is a persistent Satanic theme. Early Christian fathers have varied explanations for Satan being cast from heaven. Besides the sin of pride Prudentius wrote that Satan claimed to have made himself, and St Gregory and St Thomas agreed that Satan denied his relationship to God and sought to derive happiness from himself alone. Satan is prince of *this* world and tempted Christ in the wilderness with earthly kingdoms and powers. Freud wrote that Satan shared with Oedipus the mission to be father of himself, in short, agency without community. St Augustine's *Confessions* introduce Faust to us as a Manichee, 'exquisitely skilled in the liberal sciences'. Goethe's *Faust* yields at once to temptations on a high mountain, aspiring to reclaim land (probably Holland) from the sea. He proceeds by steps to ever greater agentic obsession. 'In the beginning was the Word . . . the Thought! . . . the Power! . . . the Deed!' He seeks and obtains loveless power over women. Another characteristic of Satan was the contract, the veritable shadow of the Saint's covenant, save that this was for life's term, and the immortal soul was forfeit. Christopher Marlowe's Dr Faustus enjoys enhanced temporal powers until Mephistopholes comes to collect; Luther, Calvin, Knox and Milton were all haunted by agentic devils; while classic Protestant literature illustrates the runaway powers of agency – Roger Chillingworth in *The Scarlet Letter* using pagan medical arts to destroy, Captain Ahab in obsessive pursuit in *Moby Dick* and Mr Hyde periodically escaping from Dr Jekyll's control.

Has this overemphasis upon agency spilled over into modern scientism and behavioural psychology, which, as we saw in Map 7, are still cast in the Calvinist mode? This was Henry Murray's contention in his 1962 address to the American Psychological Association. 'And here is where our psychology comes in with the bulk of its theories . . . and images of man, obviously in league with the nihilistic Satanic spirit. Man is a computer, an animal, an infant. His destiny is completely determined by genes, instincts, accidents, early conditionings and reinforcements, cultural and social forces. Love is a secondary drive based on hunger and oral sensation, *or* a reaction formation to underlying hate . . . There are no provisions for creativity, no admitted margins of freedom . . . no fitting recognitions of the power of ideals, no bases for selfless action, no ground at all for any hope that the human race can save itself from the fatality that now confronts it. . .'

From the struggle of the human mind to emancipate itself from servitude to gods, the laws of Newtonian mechanism and from scientists covered in these first eight maps, we turn in the following eight (Maps 9–16) to explore psychoanalytic and existential attempts to comprehend the mind in its deepest recesses and privacy.

Map 8 illustrates the Puritan Devil, the counterpart to the Puritan God. God was the clockmaker of the universe who had sent His Saints to earth to act as divine agents in uncovering his predetermined plan. It is this mentality that gives technological science and its most zealous imitator, psychological behaviourism, their distinctive characters. The concern with learned response to external programmes, with control, habits, order and technique in a determined universe has neglected community, creativity, freedom, personality and affections. But the problem with serving some external power and with demanding freedom the better to show that one was predetermined all along is that one is left with fearful doubts when one's efforts go wrong. The Puritan Saints would attribute such disasters to the devil. This devil came more and more to resemble a critique of Puritanism itself, that the doctrine sanctioned an exaggerated agentic power and was liable to runaway escalation. Today the behavioural sciences are replete with 'devilish' research findings on obedience, aggression, alienation, authoritarianism, anomie and cheating. Does this mean, as the Puritans, now joined by the behaviourist B. F. Skinner, insisted, that man must subject himself further to behaviour control? Or could it be that the devil we keep 'finding' is but the cloven hoof-print of our controlling, all-determining god?

MAP REFERENCES

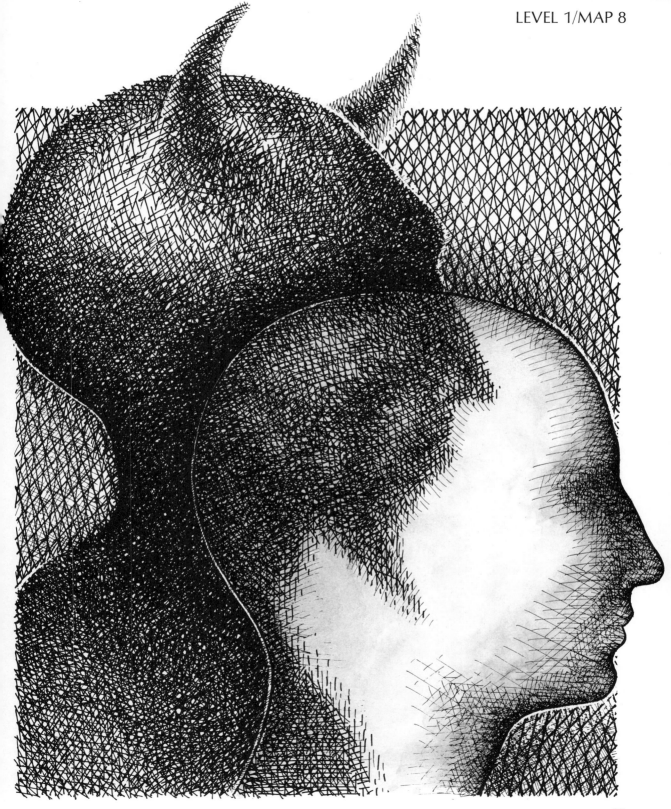

MAP 9
The Limited Energy Model of Sigmund Freud

Freud's contribution to our understanding of mind began with the puzzle that we 'know' more than that of which we are consciously aware. Why, for example, do we 'forget' so selectively, make 'Freudian slips' of the tongue, feel guilt about acts we have justified perfectly, suffer phobic dreads and anxieties, and recall buried memories under hypnosis or drugs, all despite conscious determination not to feel or behave in these ways?

Other thinkers had presupposed an unconscious, but Freud insisted he could demonstrate its effects on conscious processes. Laboratory experiments tend to bear him out. When subjects were read a seemingly random list of words and were administered a mild but uncomfortable electric shock four words after the word 'barn' had been read out, then fewer than a quarter could consciously work out that 'barn' had preceded the shocks. Yet three-quarters of the subjects showed an increase in their level of anxiety (as measured by electric skin conductance) as soon as 'barn' was uttered, while nearly a third had unconsciously generalized that anxiety to all rural words in the list, eg 'hay', 'plough', 'field'. Clearly such feelings of pervasive unease are intelligent, as is our sense of inner excitement which tells of the imminent solution of a problem.

Freud conceived of the human personality as having an abstract structure of contrasting functions. The conscious and the unconscious mind were also divided between the unconscious *id* (agent of the Pleasure Principle) and the partly conscious *ego* (agent of the Reality Principle). The id and ego come directly from Latin and mean literally, the 'it' and the 'I'. We normally speak as if we were ego controlled, eg 'I cook a meal', but when beset by impulses we often refer to id forces 'It makes me mad', 'The "It" Girl', etc. The id consists of instinctual energies and drives which are without rationale or inhibition, but clamour to be satiated, eg hunger, thirst, assertion, the general category of aggressive instincts, and the sexual instincts. The ego usually functions intelligently to serve the id. Hence the ego would know that a tin contained food and how to open it. The id would know only the hunger that demanded satisfaction.

The id, embodying the instincts, serves The Pleasure Principle, by way of primary process thinking, eg the visualization of food or sexual encounter. It is typically heedless of realistic obstacles, like a child demanding to go to the lavatory in a crowded lift. The ego, in contrast, must work on the Reality Principle and attempts to engage the environment so as to satisfy the id, using secondary process thinking to calculate means to ends. The ego can find itself swamped by id demands. In an experiment with very hungry chickens, it was discovered that they were unable to take their eyes off the sight of food on the other side of a wire fence long enough to go round the fence, while the moderately hungry chickens were able to do so.

The peril of being overwhelmed by impulses is met by learning to satisfy the id, learning to postpone gratification, and by erecting emotional barriers of automatic control called *ego defence mechanisms*. These include *repression*, the pushing down of unwanted impulses (and later unwanted ideas and thoughts) into the unconscious; *projection*, the attribution of unacceptable impulses within oneself to other persons (eg 'Black people are sexually active.'); *displacement*, the shifting of impulses aroused by one person or situation on to a safer target (eg losing your job and beating your son); *intellectualization*, the elaborate rationalization of a naked impulse (eg 'I visit brothels to redeem fallen women.'); *regression*, behaviour appropriate to an earlier childhood stage which seeks to reduce demands made on the ego – the same result is achieved by *fixation* at a particular stage; *denial*, the conscious refusal to acknowledge an impulse-evoking fact, feeling or memory; *reaction-formation*, the conversion of one feeling into its opposite, typically hate

The mind is divided between consciousness (light) and unconsciousness (dark), and between ego, id and superego, meaning literally 'the I', 'the it', and 'that above the I'. Note that the id, a reservoir of basic, raw and undifferentiated impulses is entirely unconscious and remains so. The ego, the rational, mediating centre of the psyche, which balances the other internal elements with the demands of the environment, is partly conscious and partly unconscious. The same applies to the superego, the locus of inner moral standards taken from parents and authorities and internalized.

For example, the ego's defence mechanisms are automatic and involuntary and act to shut out and push away overly demanding impulses arising from the id, which are inconsistent with the realities pursued by the ego or the moralities pursued by the superego. Not the impulses alone, but painful memories and traumas suffused with anxiety are also pushed back into the unconscious. The superego's prohibitions are also partly unconscious, so that people feel guilty for transgressing a reasonable moral boundary, but also for surviving a concentration camp, or demanding those rights which conscious political conviction tells them are theirs.

The preconscious lying between conscious and unconscious refers to those mental events recallable by act of will or remembering. For deeper exploration psychoanalysis is prescribed.

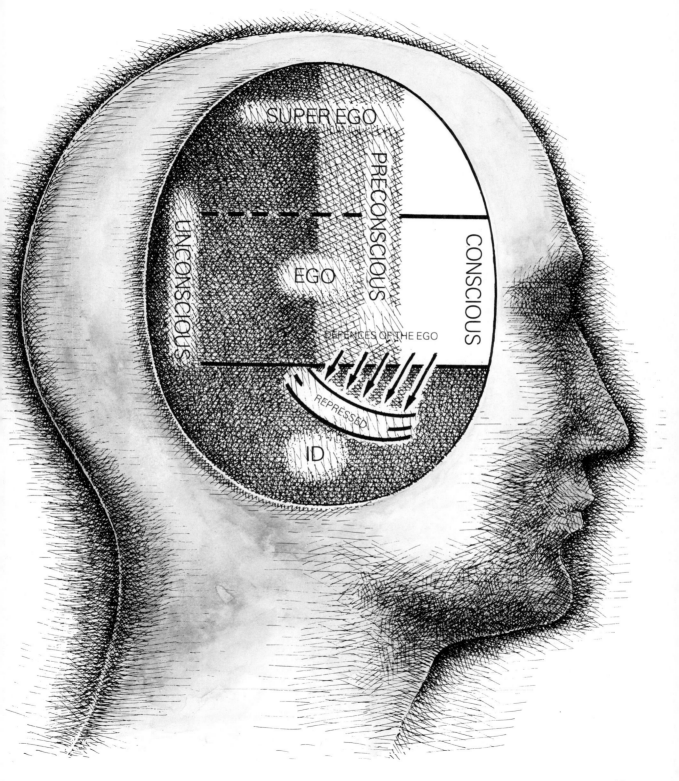

into love or *vice versa*; and *sublimation*, the channelling of unacceptable impulses into acceptable and refined social forms. While the ego is partly conscious, the mechanisms of defence and other aspects remain unconscious.

Although ego defence is necessary up to a point, a constant need to defend against a cauldron of unconscious elements places great strain upon the ego's energies, with resulting exhaustion. The ego besieged, as it were, from within and without, suffers from anxieties about coping while containing frustrated impulses. Freud's entire concept of motivation hinged on the idea of tension reduction. The psyche having a limited amount of energy finds this sapped by excessive inner conflict so that tension reduction becomes a rational objective.

Freud likened repression to debarring noisy students from a lecture hall. Although unseen they pound upon the door to gain admittance, but can no longer be recognized or assuaged. Repressed impulses may, however, return disguised as *neurotic symptoms*. Thus Elizabeth Barrett Browning became hysterically 'ill' in order to regress to an earlier stage of development, to intellectualize her father's tyranny into a solicitude for the sick, to deny and ward-off his aggressive sexuality and to sublimate her misery into the romantic expressions of a dying poetess.

Such symptoms constitute a disguise which tends to defeat the gratification of the real, underlying impulses. Neurotic symptoms typically repeat themselves in vicious circles of frustration: the compulsive hand-washing that never cleans; the phobia never overcome because its object is avoided; the defensiveness which, by anticipating disapproval, actually recreates it. Early memories 'haunt' the conscious mind so that it wrestles constantly with phantoms.

An important way in which repressed ideas, wishes and instincts seek substitute satisfaction is through our dreams and waking fantasies. In sleep, when the ego and Reality Principle are 'off duty', fantasies can seem vividly real, while in neurotic and psychotic states the weakened ego finds itself trapped in nightmares without end. Dreams are an important avenue for tapping the unconscious, as is free association and the analysis of resistance during psychoanalysis.

The ego is constrained not only by the demands for pleasure and the exigencies of reality, but also by whether the possible is also permissible by internalized moral standards. This inner conscience is called the *superego* and includes both the rules and precepts handed down by parents and other authorities, and the 'ego ideal' fashioned by the individual, ie the kind of person he or she aspires to become. For example, I am deterred from finishing off a blackberry-and-apple pie before my family returns home, neither by impulse (id) nor by feasibility (ego) but by my aspiration to be more than a selfish slob who grows only in his middle. Like the ego, the superego is but partly conscious, so that rationally articulated rules must contend with deeper taboos and prohibitions. Our moralities show a stubborn resistance to modification by even the most devastating critiques.

It is during the earlier years that the divisions of the psyche grow. The id is present at birth, the ego starts to emerge at six months, but the ego defences and the superego emerge between the ages of three and six as a consequence of what Freud calls the Oedipus and Electra conflicts.

The child is at first entirely dependent on a crucial relationship with its mother – she can gratify every whim or she can withold herself. The child will normally grow through oral, anal and phallic stages of development during which sensations of pleasure are concentrated in these areas. Until the phallic stage is reached, around the age of three, the mother is barely distinguished by the infant as a separate person, but is loved as 'a life support system'. With the dawning awareness of the mother's separate existence an emotion akin to sexual love begins to replace infant

'Shall we follow the hint given us by the poet-philosopher and venture upon the hypothesis that living substance at the time of coming to life was torn apart into small particles, which have ever since endeavoured to reunite through the sexual instincts?'
'Beyond the Pleasure Principle'
Sigmund Freud

42

narcissism. It is at this point that boys feel rivalry, even hatred, for their fathers who share their mothers' attentions. Boys believe, usually erroneously, that since they feel animosity towards their fathers, this must be reciprocated to the extent that fathers seek to punish the phallic impulses of their sons with castration.

In the course of growing up through the latency period (6 years to 12) and into the genital stage (12 years to maturity) the Oedipal conflict will usually be resolved. This resolution requires that the child introjects (internalizes) parental prohibition against sexual unity with his or her partner, and replaces sexuality with tender affection. But notice that the defence mechanisms and the superego are thereby being exercised and formed. There is first a projection of the aggression within the child onto the parent of the same sex, the resulting fear of punishment produces a repression of phallic impulses, an identification with father's/mother's prohibition, and consequent sublimation of sexuality into affection. This leaves the child with an embryo superego. The identification of boys with their fathers and girls with their mothers is the process that transmits masculine and feminine characteristics. Just as the original King Oedipus, in the drama by Sophocles, was ordained by fate to be the unwitting murderer of his father and seducer of his mother, so is the human child shadowed by the fantasy of unconscious murder and incest, suffering a conscious guilt for an unconscious urge.

The resolution of the Oedipal conflict is a pattern for the development of personality. Freud was pessimistic about human perfectability but suggested ameliorations. He advised that the conscious ego should reclaim as much territory as possible from the id and the unconscious, that the ego should maintain an equilibrium between id, superego and external demands and that the instincts of Eros and Thanatos (his later terms for sex and aggression) should be channelled into loving and working.

During the course of psychoanalysis the patient is likely to develop *transference*, the process by which strong positive or negative feelings, along with neurotic symptoms, are transferred from the person in the patient's life who occasioned them, to the psychoanalyst. This enables the neuroses to be worked on directly in the relationship of analyst and client. Freudian analysts traditionally use the methods of *free association* wherein the patient, lying on a couch, verbalizes whatever thoughts come to mind. *Dream interpretation* is another method, while *analysis of resistance* shows the client the manner in which his defence mechanisms and other strategems are currently operating to impede the therapeutic relationship.

MAP 10

The Dynamic Unities of Carl G. Jung

Carl Gustav Jung is often described as a mere disciple of Freud (see Map 9). In fact, he had pioneered word association tests, received an honorary degree from Clark University and earned himself an international reputation before he met Freud in 1907. Their intellectual relationship was intense, if short. Jung published his major dissent from Freud's position just five years after their first meeting.

Jung borrowed from Freud the conception of conscious and unconscious spheres, of a mind mediated by a defended ego, a source of psychic energy called the libido, and a mission to reclaim territory from the unconscious. Beyond these similarities their differences were profound; while Freud's model tended to be mechanistic, analytic and reductive to basic causes, Jung's was more organic, expansive, and unfolding to purposive ends. The son of a clergyman, Jung never subscribed to the supposition of his age, that science and religion were incompatible.

The circle motif dominated all Jung's thinking and symbolizes the wholeness of the psyche, within which he distinguished *four functions* (see diagram 1). Thinking–feeling and sensation–intuition are forms of psychic activity, independent of content. Hence one could look at a picture of the Madonna and Child and *think* consciously 'are they true or false depictions of historic persons?' Or, one could *feel* for the picture an acceptance/rejection, liking/disliking (of unconscious origins). Likewise one could realistically examine the painting at the level of *sensation* in description, eg 'oil on canvas, figure seated, child held in left arm'. Or, one could try to *intuit* its deeper meaning, eg 'the sacred bond of earth and mother with new life'. The thinking–feeling axis involves a ratio of judgement. The sensation–intuition axis involves different modes of perception. The poles are opposites in the sense that one end obviates the other at single moments of time, although both can be used in alternation as 'either *and* or'.

Most persons have a general habitus, ie a preferred function with at least one auxiliary. Hence the empiricist would use mostly thinking about sensations; the theorist, thinking about intuitions; the aesthete, feeling about intuitions and the sensualist, feeling about sensations. While the clients who came for therapy varied widely in the balance of these functions, Jung had a general diagnosis for Western culture. It was overly dominant in its *thinking* function. Technological man had gained the whole world and lost his soul. Jung saw Freud's approach in this context. It was useful for those patients, often younger persons, who were still concerned to engage the world for practical advantage, and with minimum inner disturbance, but the task of middle and later age was the achievement of insight, wholeness and spiritual depth. The rounding out of the psyche followed the 'inner way' of the *T'ai Chi* (see Map 3), from thinking to intuition to sensing to feeling, a serpent winding to the heart of darkness, to the very depth of the unconscious where lies the knowledge of good and evil (see diagram 2).

Jung's concept of the unconscious was much more elaborate than Freud's. There was a *personal unconscious* of dimmed memories and repressed materials, a *collective unconscious* at a deeper level, evidenced by emotions and visions erupting from its depth and a fathomless part beyond. By collective unconscious Jung meant 'the inherited possibility of psychical functioning . . . namely . . . the brain structure'. This shared human heritage was quite unlike the dark chaos of impulse which Freud had assumed. Jung's unconscious has a primordial structure and coherence, like a burial chamber of priceless antiquities which are lustrously revealed by the light of consciousness probing the darkness of the tomb.

While we cannot directly observe the unconscious mind, there are persistent hints of its archetypal structure. The term archetype was used by St Augustine to

The circle motif represents psychic totality which the human mind, pulsating with libidinous energy, is conceived as striving to attain.

The ego mediates the relationships of psyche with the external world, and of the conscious mind with the unconscious. The latter is divided into a personal unconscious, of dimming memories and repressed experience, and a collective unconscious, the structural patterning of the brain itself, but comprehensible only through the metaphors and symbols of our dreams, world cultures and religions.

The persona, or façade, grows upon the face which the ego presents to the world. At best it is a malleable mask facilitating social encounters. Behind the ego lies the shadow, deep and dark in proportion to the degree in which aspects of the ego have been split off and repressed. This unrealized potential hauntingly reproaches the ego for its incompleteness.

Beneath the shadow lies the soul-image, an anima, or female spirit, within men; an animus, or male spirit, in women. Romantic 'love' is often an infatuation with one's own soul-image, a craving for inner balance and completion.

The self emerges only in those who explore their depths and reach fullest maturation. It is both the nucleus of the whole psyche and the expression of that whole. It is represented in many of the unifying symbols of antiquity: the mandala, the cross, the 'T'ai Chi'.

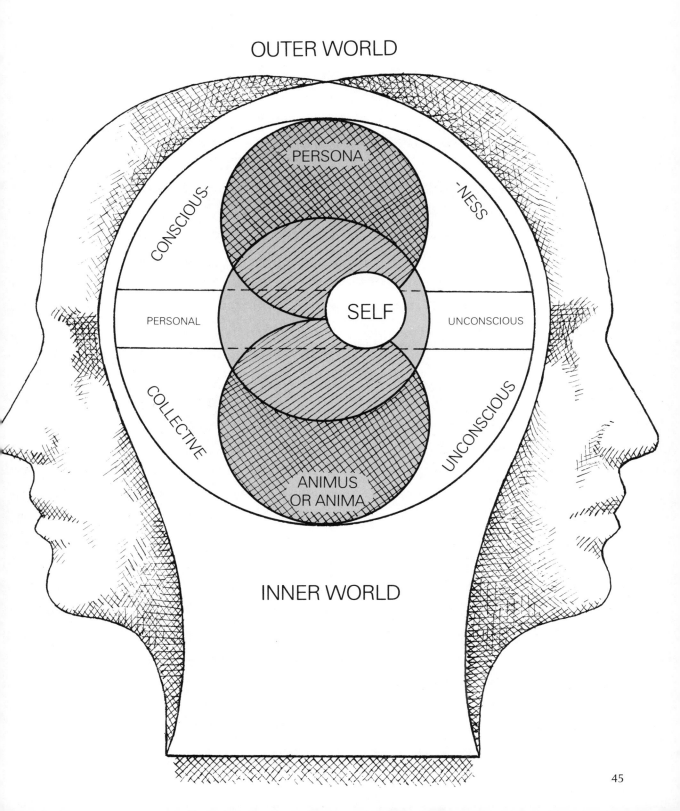

OUTER WORLD

PERSONA

CONSCIOUS-

-NESS

PERSONAL

SELF

UNCONSCIOUS

COLLECTIVE

UNCONSCIOUS

ANIMUS
OR ANIMA

INNER WORLD

designate the principle ideas of human culture. For Jung they were primordial psychic processes transformed into images, where consciousness can grasp them, but only elusively via symbol and metaphor. Archetypes are 'self-portraits of the instincts', which lie in something resembling a transparent medium of aqueous solution, which hardens to form a crystalline structure with multiple axes and facets. For example, the archetype 'father' is on the opposite pole to the 'mother', but mother is part of the axis Virgin–Mother, and is also polarized into Good Mother–Kali (the destroying mother). Hence mother is like the point on a crystal with axes converging from several directions.

The archetypal structuring of the unconscious pulls the experience and memories which sink from the conscious mind into polar forms, as if drawn by magnets (see diagram 3). Because extreme human situations leave deeper and sharper memory traces, and because lesser extremes can be conceptualized within the greater, the archetypal unconscious seethes with heroes and villains, cowardly betrayals and steadfast loyalties, endless odysseys and eternal returns. The high contrast forms 'a world of opposing forces in equilibrium' and an 'a priori form of psychic ordering'.

The conscious and unconscious parts of the psyche are not only divided among the four functions but are polarized between two attitudes, extraversion and introversion. The extravert is characterized by a more positive relation to external objects, eg garrulous and outgoing; the introvert by a more positive relationship to internal objects, eg meditative and withdrawn. The functions of thinking–feeling, sensation–intuition may thus be introverted or extraverted in their attitude (see diagram 4). Unconsciousness is generally in a compensatory relationship to consciousness, so that a quiet, intuitive introvert will have a noisy, sensational extravert latent within him, who may burst out in vexatious circumstances. Such conscious onesidedness greatly limits the capacity of persons to adapt themselves to new circumstances.

When the ego uses a dominant function to engage the environment it will typically develop a *persona* at its outward edge. This public relations façade is 'a compromise between the ego as it aspires to be, the social functions demanded of it, and the inherent limitations of the life situation'. Unless a balance of these elements is attained the persona rigidifies into some stereotyped mask, say, rebel, mass man or fatalist. Ideally the persona is a supple protective coating that facilitates daily encounters. Only a brittle façade will crack, as did the waxen face of the villain in the film *The House of Wax*, to reveal his mutilated visage beneath.

As the ego has its persona in front, it has its *shadow* behind. Real shadows split away from our bodies joining us, as if hinged, at the feet. Similarly, the shadow is the split-off part of the ego, which the latter has repressed or rejected, the dark brother. Examples abound in literature: Dr Frankenstein and his monster, Cain and Abel, Dante and Virgil, Dr Jekyll and Mr Hyde. Their characteristics are contrapuntal, the monster being as full of pathos and savagery as Dr Frankenstein is cerebral and 'civilized'. To confront your shadow is to encounter your own unrealized potential, the missing arcs of the circle, the functions never developed, which grow dark by their exclusion. The shadow, therefore, personifies both the evil of isolation and the hope of reconciliation. Shadows can also be collective, an entire cultural *zeitgeist* shadowed by its antithesis as the Nazis' Triumph of the Will was shadowed by a mass annihilation of wills in the Götterdämmerung, and our consumer society is seemingly shadowed by failing production.

Beyond the shadow in the journey 'inwards' to the unconscious lies the *soul-image*. In men it is the anima, or female spirit, in women the animus, or male spirit,

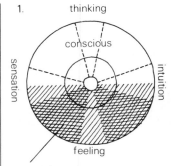

1.

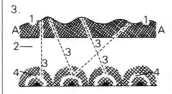

1. The four functions.

2.

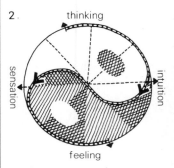

2. The 'inner way' of Jungian analysis from thinking to intuition to sensation to feeling.

3.

3. Images (2) sink down from the mind's conscious surface (1), and drawn, as if by magnets (3), assume archetypal order (4).

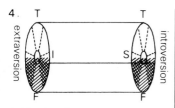

4. *The four functions on an introversion–extraversion axis.*

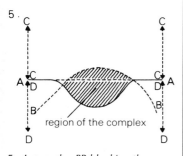

region of the complex

5. *A complex BB blocking the threshhold AA between consciousness CC and unconsciousness DD.*

for the soul-image is the contrasexual archetype of the ego. In romantic love we tend to fall for our soul-image, blind to the real nature of the other, we are in love with the idea of love, with our own inner craving for completeness and balance. In the film *The Blue Angel* the professor's feeling and intuitions were so poorly developed that he fell for a strumpet. His poor internal differentiation was as one with his poor external discrimination. Yet the soul-image can also be known, and act as a guiding spirit, as Socrates knew his daemon.

The psyche's structure is animated by the energy of the *libido*, a life force which in high intensities energizes will, affect and performance and in lower intensities energizes attitudes, interests and possibilities. Energy shifts ceaselessly to and fro along the structural axes in dialectical patterns, governed by the principle of *emantiodromia*, literally 'the returning swing of the pendulum'. The ego can intensify the energy flow towards one value polarity, but consciously or unconsciously it must flow back – tension–relaxation, openness–closure, evaluation–decision. In dynamic balance the psyche moves progressively (external adaptations) and regressively (internal adaptation).

Jung's definition of a symptom is 'that which blocks the flow of psychic energy'. Symptoms form complexes, encapsulated nuclei of symptoms which rise from the unconscious and block the downward path from consciousness (see diagram 5). As a result, the level of consciousness sags, making the psyche liable to passive seizure, eg faith is suddenly assailed by doubt, love by jealousy or some other incompatible, unassimilable emotion. The encapsulation of the disturbing symptoms is often triggered by trauma. A soldier may not have merely supressed his emotional response to the screams of a dying friend, he may have repressed awareness of the screams, but now, years later, the complex rises to haunt him, for the feeling function will out.

Jung accepted Freud's view of clamorous natural instincts, but believed these to be balanced by a spiritual instinct, in an equilibrium of nature and spirit. The mind was not just caused, but strove purposefully towards finality. Jung puzzled over an acausal principle he called *synchronicity*, an *effectance through synthesis*. How could it be, he asked, that we experience so many inner forebodings or realized hopes concerning outward events? We must have some archetypal inner model and be guided by the wisdom of the ages. Syncronicity is often mediated by symbols – the word symbol means literally 'to throw together'. The Virgin Mother, for example, is a throwing together of two sequential stages of womanhood, just as the self-devouring snake symbolizes life in the midst of death, the eternal paradox.

We develop by a process of internal differentiation of the parts of the psyche, which is essential to their integration. Jung calls the differentiation *individuation* and applies it both to the mind and to human relationships. Only the individuated person can relate effectively to another. In the fullness of maturation there can rise the *self*, which is both a nuclear element integrating the psyche and the totality of that psyche. It reconciles all the various faces of the mind and represents the self-realization that the Kingdom of God is within you. This is why the highest symbols are the unifying ones, the *coincidentia oppositorum*, the crucifix, the mandala, the wheel, the flower, the Uroborus, the *T'ai Chi*. There is no imprint on the mind without an imprinter, who reveals the way to salvation through death and resurrection.

MAP REFERENCES

Archetypes, see also split brain, 23–4; Collective unconscious: as brain structure 20–5; as language 40–4; Persona, soul image, shadow, see catastrophe theory, 56; Synchronicity, see also creativity, synergy, 26–31, 42–3, 60.

MAP 11

'Therefore Choose Life': The psychoethics of Erich Fromm

Erich Fromm was trained as a psychoanalyst and as a social psychologist in Germany, but had to flee to America from Nazi persecution. There, in 1941, he published his first book, *Escape from Freedom*, the first major psychological explanation of fascism. Within months America entered World War II. The book is committed, passionate and urgently conceived in the path of the holocaust. Fromm has continued to write as if human survival depended upon the speed of his and our comprehensions. He does not build carefully and respectfully on Freud and Marx, deferring to their other interpreters, but speaks directly to his large public audience with highly personal interpretations, hastily assembled to combat the monsters of our age. And if his writings are occasionally moralistic and sweeping, at least he has been consistently ahead of his time, on fascism in the forties, on post-war existentialism, on the bland conformity of the fifties, on the deadly technocratic consciousness that led to Vietnam, and on the need for rapprochement with China. He was an ego psychologist and an unrepentant Marxist humanist more than a decade before these positions became academically respectable. While in the boldness of his parallels between personal growth (ontogenesis) and the growth of whole communities (phylogenesis) he anticipates modern structuralism. Fromm also swept aside the norm of value neutrality in social science at a time when others could only breach it with lengthy apologetics. Humanistic ethics, Fromm stated, was an applied science, the art of living and loving. As such these depended on a theoretical science of mankind, and this science was psychology. Human beings do what they *ought*, by becoming more fully what they *can* be, a process that includes evoking greater potentials from all members of their community.

Fromm starts with the idea of contradiction, man is 'the freak of the universe', a veritable sphinx as Oedipus understood when he confronted her. We are part nature and subject to her laws, yet we also transcend nature through culture, language and symbolism. We are set apart from each other, as Adam and Eve realized in their nakedness, yet we yearn for the harmony from which we are cast out. We plan and try to empower ourselves, yet we were thrown accidentally into this world and will be pulled inexorably out of it. We have vast potentials, yet in the course of our short span on earth we can hope to realize but a fraction of our endowments. Reason is then our blessing and our curse, enabling us to solve the more superficial issues until we reach the impasse beyond. Our man-made contradictions are soluble, he believes, by forms of socialist humanism, but this will leave us still with the ultimate anomalies. The unanswerable questions posed by existence do, however, evoke from us our vitality, the arts of loving, creating and producing. Faced by the growing chasms of modernity we continually strive to reunite ourselves with others, if only for a moment. In this endeavour we use our love and reason to replace the biological innocence of the instinctual animal behaviours left behind in Eden.

One fatal reaction to being stretched upon the existential poles of finitude and transcendence is that human reason consciously opts for one and tries to negate the other. Yet the negated pole creeps back into the equation, the more dangerous for being unrecognized. Nations dazzle themselves with idols, glowing images of transcendence, yet in reality the idols are dead. 'They have mouths and speak not, eyes have they and see not ... They that make them shall be like unto them.' Others are obsessed with death itself, sexuality, sadism and earthly pleasures in a celebration of finitude, and may ironically earn themselves a place in the annals of morbid fascination. This capacity to hold finitude and transcendence in balance distinguishes the growth of the *productive personality* from the regression of the *non-productive*:

The human being can reach up to realize more of his or her potential, or crouch down (literally or figuratively) in abasement, fear, and foetal postures of regression. It is the choice between actively giving and fulfilling one's potential, or the preponderantly receiving, taking, hoarding and marketing features of our political economy that shrink us backward into death. By 'active' Fromm does not mean busyness. The meditator may be more active in consciousness than the salesman of kitsch.

Each one of us must grow from the bottom of the map upwards developing on the three dimensions, so as to engage the social world with liveliness and love. While these dimensions may seem like simple linearities, some subtleties may be noted. In the centre and on the right are two dimensions, narcissism–love of neighbour and incestuous symbiosis–independence. By growing up these dimensions, that which provides for separateness in infancy (narcissism) provides for relationship in maturity (love), while that which provides for relationship in infancy (incestuous symbiosis) provides for separateness in maturity (freedom).

Such is the modern world that it accelerates our separateness, whether or not we experience this as freedom. We must therefore learn (and soon!) to unify ourselves by developing that which is uniquely human, our reason and love.

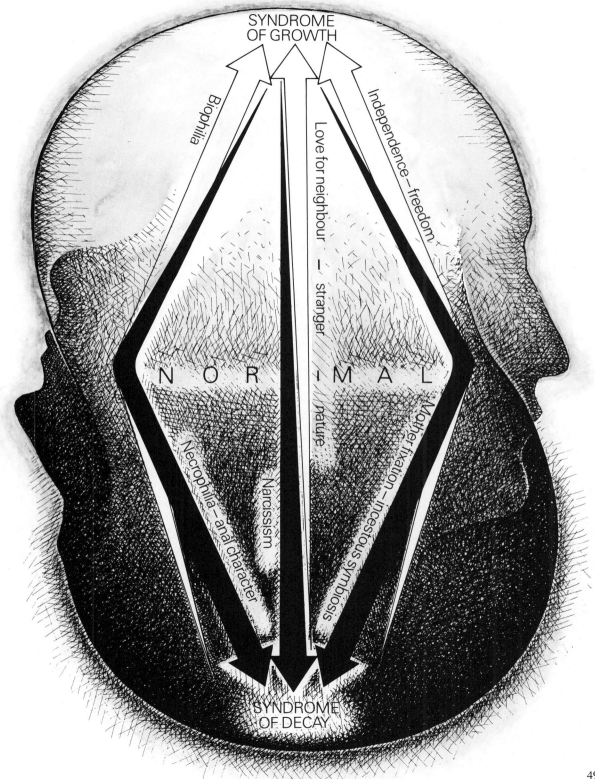

SYNDROME
OF GROWTH

Biophilia

Independence – freedom

Love for neighbour

I

stranger

N O R   M A L

nature

Mother fixation – incestuous symbiosis

Necrophilia – anal character

Narcissism

SYNDROME
OF DECAY

TYPE OF PERSON	FREUDIAN CATEGORY	RELATIONSHIP TO THINGS	RELATIONSHIP TO PERSONS
Productive personality (active)	genital	creative work	art of loving with care, respect, responsibility, knowledge
Non-productive personality (passive)	pre-genital (anal/ oral/ phallic)	receiving, exploiting, hoarding, marketing,	masochistic loyalty, sadistic authority, destructive assertion, indifferent fairness

'I have set before you life and death, blessing and cursing: Therefore choose life, both that thou and thy seed may live.'
Deuteronomy XXX, 19

'In the act of loving, of giving myself, in the act of penetrating the other person, I find myself, I discover myself, I discover us both, I discover man.'
'The Art of Loving' Erich Fromm

'The necessity to find ever-new solutions for the contradictions in his existence, to find ever-higher forms of unity with nature, his fellow men and himself, is the source of all psychic forces which motivate man, all of his passions, affects and anxieties.'
'The Sane Society' Erich Fromm

It is difficult to think of a more unfortunate choice of word than 'productive' to describe what Fromm means. His critics have had a field-day. But such wilful misrepresentations aside, 'productive' means the creative synthesis of human powers in an active flowing out from the person. Hence when human labour is not alienated, the worker moves from conception through action to completion of his product. This is analogous, but not reducible, to Freud's genital phase of development (see Map 9). Productive persons relate to things creatively and to people through the art of loving. Loving is unified separateness. We can love others as equals only because they are different from us, not because they are the same. Equality is the balancing of differentiations and integration by which we grow. Loving is less 'having' or 'falling' than giving in a way that creates mutual abundance, as when Romeo says to Juliet 'The more I give you the more I have.' Loving contains four elements, care, responsibility, respect and knowledge: care is an active concern for the life and growth of the other; responsibility the desire (not duty) to respond to the other's needs; respect, from *respicere* 'to look at', is to recognize the other's uniqueness; knowledge combines objective knowing with that which is revealed through participation and intimate identification.

But Fromm is perhaps best known for his social critiques of Western society. He does not agree with Freud that child-rearing practices shape social character. Rather societies choose to work in a certain manner and so influence parents to raise their children in this mould. Our modern society, culminating in the present alienation of labour, evolved first the *receiving* character, with a masochistic loyalty to outside directives. (This was evidenced in Calvinism, Lutheranism and early Puritanism.) Later came the *exploiting* character with sadistic authority over others; this type also regards value as external but must achieve it and subordinates others in the process. (Nineteenth-century commercial adventurers were typical exploiters.) Thirdly there is the *hoarding* character which has an obsession with holding and retaining values, conceived as being within; Soames Forsyte *The Man of Property* exemplified this conservative phase of bourgeois respectability, and would assert himself destructively to hold his own. Modern consumer capitalism has brought us the *marketing* personality with its ethic of indifferent fairness. So called love relationships in this society tend to deteriorate into mere exchanges of mutually profitable personality packages, sex objects fabricated to popular taste. *Homo consumens* is the ingestor of sight, sounds, drink, smoke, foods, opinions and drugs and makes of himself a commodity, essentially uniform, and only marginally differentiated like a 'personalized' bath towel.

In *The Heart of Man* Fromm presented the schema of which Map 11 is an elaboration. The overlapping ascending–descending arrows in the centre and on the right represent the duality of separation and union. We ascend from infant

'Self-awareness, reason and imagination have disrupted the "harmony" which characterizes animal existence. Their emergence has made man into an anomaly, into the freak of the universe . . . Reason, man's blessing, is also his curse; it forces him to cope everlastingly with the task of solving an insoluble dichotomy . . . in a state of constant unavoidable disequilibrium.'

'Man For Himself' Erich Fromm

'The modern market is no longer a meeting place but a mechanism characterized by abstract and impersonal demand.'

'Man for Himself'

narcissism to increasing capacities for loving and relating to neighbours, strangers and nature itself. This 'love' of strangers is an imaginative identification with them, as reason universalizes our experiences of intimates. We similarly ascend from an 'incestuous' clinging to maternal bonds to increasing capacities for freedom. Note that maturation accomplishes a metamorphosis, primitive individuality (narcissism) changes into mature relation, while primitive relation (symbiosis) changes into mature freedom. These qualitative changes mean we can never go home again, that active social relationships *must* go forward to alter primitive harmonies, and that to regress permanently to earlier patterns is to die within ourselves.

The unfolding capacities for freedom and relationship converge at the top of the map towards a *syndrome of growth*, while a regression into narcissism and incestuous fixation converge at the bottom towards a *syndrome of decay*. Since both growth and decay constitute themselves from strivings for unity and separation it becomes crucial to distinguish the ascent from the descent. Since whole nations have marched back into the Dark Ages with flags flying and drums beating, how can we discern when the devil is quoting Scripture?

Here it is necessary to interpret Fromm because he tends to illustrate rather than explain. The structure of separation and unity in growth relationships transforms, integrates and is mutually enhancing. Each lover offers a beloved self to form a unity with the other. Not just the persons but their values 'embrace'. But the structure of separation and unity in decaying relationships is fixated, segregated and mutually conflicting. There is an 'alienation from the self' in the very centre of the personality, similar to R. D. Laing's sense of 'schizoid organization' (see Map 14). The narcissist is consumed by self-love and so, unable to relate to a genuinely independent person, is bound hand and foot to some incestuous object, whether a mother, a gang or a totalitarian state. This 'mother' is needed but resented, worshipped yet feared. Like the sphinx she becomes a nurturer–destroyer, both binding her subjects and unleashing them in sanctioned savagery. There is a *coincidentia oppositorum* (coincidence of opposites) in the decaying syndrome with a destructive tension gathering between the poles of unity and separation with oscillating extremes of both. Fromm assumes that distinguishing growth from decay is non-problematic. The growing exude *biophilia*, the love of life. They personify spontaneity, pleasure and vivacity. The decaying are *necrophilic*, in the sense of being morbidly preoccupied by death, destruction and putrefaction. Fromm cites the Death's Head legions, the Spanish General who cried 'Long live death!' and the parents of soldiers killed in battle who lamented that they had no other sons to sacrifice for the Fatherland. He cites also the obvious patterns of self-destruction among addicts and the 'death-like' regressions of psychotics.

I question whether the biophilia/necrophilia distinction is usually that easy. We have known since the counter-culture that biophilia can be faked and Positive Mental Health can celebrate itself in a new idolatory. Not all those who cry 'Fromm, Fromm', shall enter the kingdom of biophilia. The letters home from German soldiers trapped in Stalingrad seem more genuine and moving than hip Polyannas. Whether a person is risking his life to save it or to lose it can be difficult to judge. It is on such ambiguities that Fromm is weakest. Whole chapters of his more polemical works read as if a Manichee were trying to get out with angelic and devilish homunculi fighting for the mind of man. I have summarized his more balanced views; in other moods he has it in for the early, the primitive, the childlike, the technological, the conservative and the religious whom he treats as 'gremlins of regression'. Even sadness is described as bad, because the biophilic person does not think of death! . . . And so a new cycle of repression starts.

MAP 12
The Solitary Solidary:
Existentialism from Kierkegaard to Camus

Existentialism is neither an agreed system nor philosophical school, but a general premise that persons exist. The word, from Latin, means *ex-istere* 'to stand out'. The English verb, unlike the French and German, is intransitive and connotes the passivity of 'mere existence'. The idea is better conveyed by saying that persons are centres radiating or exuding meaning. While existentialists recognize objects, they deny that the human being is just an object among others. Rather he or she defines objects into structured fields of meaning. I can say of that man on the hospital bed, that he is male, Caucasian, 75 years old and admitted for observation, or that there lies my father who conveys meaning to me. Both viewpoints are valid, but existentialists insist that *existence precedes essence,* ie that before the doctor or I came along, my father had already defined himself. Since there is no attention without intention the objectifying of my father is an act of intending that chooses to ignore his intending.

Existentialism emerged as a protest against the displacement of individual consciousness from the centre of life's stage by a depersonalized nature, a transcendent deity, and/or the collectivized state. Three centuries of rapid advance and compartmentalization of sciences, based on Newtonian mechanism, had shattered the human image (see Map 6). Rival authorities claimed to control the personality. Existentialism is usually traced to Søren Kierkegaard, the Danish philosopher of the early nineteenth century, but is also anticipated in Melville, Dostoevsky and Nietzsche. But it took the disasters of the early twentieth century, war, depression, Stalinism, fascism before total disenchantment with systems external to the individual engulfed Western cultures. In a world where Christianity, progress and enlightenment had countenanced Auschwitz it seemed necessary to start again, with the only ideals still untarnished – the personal values proclaimed by writers, prisoners and resistance fighters, evoking anguished memories of lost friends and moments of tenderness grasped in the lull between battles. Anyone who had loved anyone for precious moments had fared better than the corporate worlds of 'abstractions, of bureaus and machines of absolute ideas and crude messianisms', the churches bent on institutional survival and collaborating businesses.

So it was that existentialism came to stand for an entire range of missing elements in Western culture. Where advanced industrialism had stressed the static, the abstract, the objective, the logically rational and unambiguous and the dispassionate universalism of systems detached from the knower, existentialists stressed the dynamic, the concrete, the inter-subjective, consensually validated experiences however ambiguous, and the passionate uniqueness of the engaged participant.

Søren Kierkegaard anticipated Freud with a brilliant exploration of psychological inwardness. We identify, said Kierkegaard, with universal objective systems, concerning which our knowledge has increased vastly, yet our personal sense of certitude diminishes rather than increases. We feel at one and the same time infinitely great because we are a part of those systems and utterly lost in nothingness, because we must separate from systems and die. This, then, is the contradiction at the centre of our being, which we can deny only at the cost of a creeping despair. For man is a union of opposites, 'soulish and bodily . . . half angel and half beast', transcendent and immortal in spirit, yet possessed by an animal finiteness that is doomed. To ignore this contradiction and live by logical alternatives is to suffer 'a demonic shut-upness' which imprisons one side of the equation or the other, leaves us 'in a half obscurity about our condition' and allows 'the elasticity of freedom' by which an indefinable self is stretched between worlds,

Map 12 illustrates the contradiction at the centre of human existence, as seen by Søren Kierkegaard and later existentialists. Man on the right of the map finds himself immersed in nature, guaranteed by her laws, filled with miraculous machinery and crowded around by people chattering cheerfully about forms, patterns and discoveries. Yet he is also poised on the edge of the abyss, doomed irrevocably to death, to aloneness and to 'fear and trembling' at this prospect . . . although each scientific cause can be calculated, the ultimate purpose of it all eludes comprehension. The dread in one half of his being supports the shut-away dogmatics in the other half.

Albert Camus' solution to the contradictions portrayed in this map involved a rebellion by the 'lone left' being in the picture, followed by dialogue with its other half; so as to contend but to trust in the midst of contending, and so respect that which is rebelled against. The failure of revolutionaries to respect their adversaries is what leads to new tyranny. Like Kierkegaard, Camus attacked the Aristotelean logic of either/or that will tolerate no contradiction and may finally kill rather than face other views. We should look not for rules but for images of the human that have the breath of life.

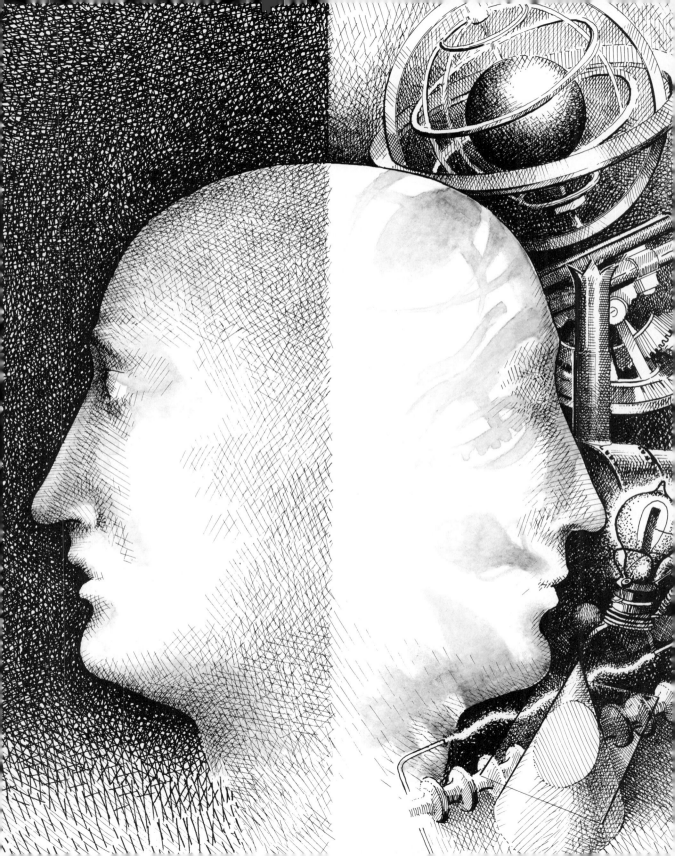

to shrink to a rigidity of mind. We sacrifice self-knowledge in a desperate identification with universals and crowds who 'with their loud-voiced enterprises keep lonely thoughts away'.

To accept the 'absurd' opposition at the centre of being is to know dread or anxiety and the sheer ambiguity of our powerlessness to remove this dread. We must live with the perpetual tension of 'the infinite expanding factor of the self' struggling with 'the finite limiting factor of the self', for 'without dread there is only dogmatics'. 'Dread is the dizziness of freedom' which 'gazes down into its own possibility, grasping at finiteness to sustain itself'. It follows that freedom is as great as one's tolerance for ambiguity and anxiety.

The Garden of Eden, says Kierkegaard, is an outward image of inner reality and re-enacts the dilemma of the self or soul, which must mediate between the heavenly innocence of aesthetic human potentials and the mundane guilt of actual ethical accomplishments. We inevitably fall into sin and guilt whenever lofty possibility meets earthly limitations. The knowledge of good and evil which follows upon action comes too late to redeem error. Yet not to venture, to try to escape the crucifix of finite−infinite brings us only 'a sickness unto death'. The person who declines to embrace ambiguity or to make the existential leap from aesthetic vision to ethical action will sicken from unrealized potentials. So each must choose and fall in 'fear and trembling' since 'each person becomes great in proportion to his expectation' and must commit himself despite anxiety. To will to be ourselves is our true vocation to which God calls us. Only by passion of thought and action can we bridge the divide at the centre of being. Madness and despair, said Kierkegaard with astonishing insight into psychoses, derive from runaway possibility or runaway necessity. The lunatic weaves endless cocoons of lofty metaphor and abstraction, and/or hugs his body to himself in seeming terror of its departure.

Kierkegaard's description of the human condition seems inspired, yet he never really reconciles the oppositions he confronts. His 'knight of faith' leaps again, this time from ethical action to obedience to God's command, despite ethical dilemma. Thus Abraham commanded to sacrifice his only son, obeys God and through faith has his son restored. Kierkegaard's ultimate solution was thus a lonely leap made in hope of divine miracle. To this end he subordinated human relationships, sacrificing his own engagement in order to more nearly approach God, who alone could resolve the rending of his soul.

Existentialists in general have proved better advocates of the immeasurable fires of subjectivity, than exponents of how such passionate private experience might re-engage the world of objects and events. With Martin Buber (see Map 36) and the later Camus some embryo resolutions emerge. Unlike Kierkegaard Albert Camus believed that one must live without appeal to God. 'I will always refuse to love a creation in which children are tortured.' Absurdity lay in man's relationship to the universe, the yearning for justice and unity amid palpable injustice and fragmentation and 'the wild longing for clarity whose call echoes in the human heart'. And yet, as he so lyrically put it, 'History appears to be in the grip of blind and deaf forces which will heed neither cries of warning, nor advice, nor entreaties. The years we have gone through have killed . . . the old confidence man had in himself, which led him to believe that he could always elicit human reactions from another man if he spoke to him in the language of common humanity. We have seen men lie, degrade, kill, deport, torture − and each time it was not possible to persuade them not to do these things because they were sure of themselves and because one cannot appeal to an abstraction, ie the representative of an ideology.'

Ideological abstractions in polarized conflict were what Camus most abhorred.

' "Behold the days are coming", says the Lord God, "when I will send a famine on the land: not a famine of bread, nor a thirst for water, but of hearing the words of the Lord." '
Amos VIII, 11

'. . . take high abstracted man alone; and he seems a wonder, a grandeur and a woe. But from the same point, take mankind in the mass, and for the most part, they seem a mob of unnecessary duplicates . . .'
'Moby Dick' Herman Melville

'A tremendous remark rings out: "Despite so many ordeals, my advanced age and the nobility of my soul make me conclude that all is well". Sophocles' Oedipus, like Dostoevsky's Kirilov, thus gives the recipe for the absurd victory . . . and that remark is sacred.'
'The Myth of Sisyphus' Albert Camus

'The metaphysical rebel . . . attacks a shattered world in order to demand unity from it. He opposes the principle of justice which he finds in himself to the principle of injustice which he sees being applied in the world . . . Metaphysical rebellion is a claim, motivated by the concept of complete unity, against the suffering of life and death and a protest against the human condition for its incompleteness.'
'The Rebel' Albert Camus

'The climax of every tragedy lies in the deafness of its heroes.'
'The Rebel'

'We live in terror because persuasion is no longer possible . . . because [man] can no longer tap that part of his nature, as real as the historical part, which he recaptures in contemplating the beauty of nature and of human faces . . . We suffocate among people who think they are absolutely right, whether in their machines or their ideas. And for all those who can live only in an atmosphere of human dialogue . . . This silence is the end of the world.
'Neither Victims nor Executioners'
Albert Camus

'Neither hatred nor amnesty' he said on the subject of French collaborators, and later, 'neither victims nor executioners', 'neither masters nor slaves'. He would not side with Spain against Russia nor with Algerian rebels against his mother's people. He had portrayed Caligula, 'within an abyss of silence, a pool of stagnant water and rotting weeds', as in mad pursuit of abstract principle cut off from concrete sufferings. The real struggle of life was to break through and sustain others with an authentic understanding. His hero was Sisyphus, the Titan condemned by Zeus to roll a rock for ever up a hill. It is in the process of struggle, without tangible rewards, that man affirms himself, 'a blind man eager to see, who knows the night has no end'. It is a rebellion that snatches meaning from 'the whirlpool's shrieking face'.

Yet the later Camus found in the process of human dialogue a morality 'which, far from obeying abstract principles, discovers them only in the heat of the battle and in the incessant movement of contradiction'. Note the word 'discovered', rather than Sartre's 'invented'. 'A human nature does exist, as the Greeks believed', Camus wrote. If so, existence must encounter essence.

The consistent theme running through Camus' later writings is that life-enhancing values carry their contraries within them. Consider rebellion. 'In order to exist, man must rebel, but rebellion must respect the limits it discovers in itself – a limit where minds meet and, in meeting, begin to exist.' Camus is saying that rebellion as a process contains its opposite, loyalty. The rebel is loyal to dialogue, to justice, and to the other's humanity. As in Letters to a German Friend, the content is anger, the context is friendship. In Camus' short story 'The Artist at Work', the protagonist falls ill with the pains of creation. One morning his friends find a scrawled word in the middle of the canvas. Is it 'solitary' or 'solidary'? Camus wants us to understand that the two are one. In the solitary act of Socratic rebellion lies the principle of solidarity that could reconcile mankind. All individuality must carry cooperativeness within or be doomed to abstraction. All cooperation must confirm human individuality or become ideologically lethal. This was why Camus detested the death penalty. He was not against punishment. For how can compassion come to brutal persons save as punishing repentance? He abhorred final punishment, total condemnation beyond recall, with compassion as victim and punishment as executioner. The guillotine was the knife of abstraction severing mind from body. To refuse to struggle against our universal death sentence is ultimate abdication. Since our hope lies in dialogue, indeed dialectically joined, our enemies are unmistakable; monologue, tyranny, injustice, silence, solitude, severance and the logical precision of either/or.

It is in the contrast between, and in the artistic synthesis of, rebellion and loyalty, solitary and solidarity, life and death, that human existence may be fully savoured. Martin Luther King took Camus' The Rebel with him to prison. I do not believe that American culture has ever been closer to civic virtue than in those campaigns. There lay 'naked suffering intermingling its roots with stubborn hope' (see Map 59).

MAP 13

The Face of Crumpled Linen:
Rollo May, Paul Tillich and anxiety

There is a ghost story by M. R. James,' 'Oh whistle and I'll come to you, my lad'. The protagonist is a Professor Parkins, neat, precise, methodical, humourless, hen-like, a caricature of logical positivism. Parkins does some amateur archaeology during his vacation and discovers an ancient whistle. He blows it and there comes to his call a 'creature' with a face of crumpled linen. Sheer anxiety and perplexity would have driven Parkins mad, had the creature not subsided into a heap of sheets as mysteriously as it arose.

What *is* anxiety? The phenomenon has been intensely studied by Rollo May, the writer and humanist psychotherapist. He was a student of the existential theologian Paul Tillich, in whom several of his ideas are grounded. May has given us an excellent summary of anxiety theories, together with his own synthesis. His conclusions follow.

Anxiety must first be distinguished from fear. Anxiety is an indefinite, pervasive, objectless apprehension which, unlike fear, lacks a logically identifiable source. It combines a feeling of being vaguely menaced from without, with feelings of being subtly subverted from within. Hence Parkins is in a catastrophic condition. The face of crumpled linen threatens him somehow from 'out there' while 'in here' his entire scientific paradigm and his basic values as an academic are being undermined by a supernatural phenomenon. Anxiety attacks the whole pattern of his being, the very core of his beliefs and personality and his continued relationship to an environment on which his life depends. He no longer has a perception of himself as distinct from the world. Is he dead, alive, or dreaming?

Anxiety, says May, arises from being torn between your expectations and discrepant realities. It grows from the apprehension of social dilemmas and irresolvable contradictions. Typically one threat is juxtaposed to another, so that dealing with either one will expose you to the other. Consider Parkins' 'horrid perplexity'. A sheet cannot be alive, and if alive not a sheet. It is blind yet 'sees'. It is utterly mundane and proximate to the sleeper yet how unearthly and remote that 'face'. Parkins finds it repellent, yet it wants to snuggle up with him! His scream of fear reveals his position and only confounds his predicament, for the creature homes in upon his mental anguish and a vicious circle forms.

There are two general approaches to such situations. The first claims that anxiety is neurotic, and stems from what Spinoza called 'a weakness of the mind'. The second approach proposed by May and Tillich is that anxiety is basic, normal and necessary, although it also has neurotic forms. Let us first consider neurotic anxiety. According to the conventional view, men mystify each other with irrational ideas of which ghost stories are a notorious example. 'The sleep of reason brings forth monsters.' Had Parkins only persevered in his rationality the face of crumpled linen would have proved a trick of the imagination, a dream, an hallucination or perhaps a hoax. Freud at first believed that anxiety was caused by repressed libido, hence Parkins, a generally 'anal' and over-controlled character, is being haunted perhaps by the very imagination he has repressed. Jung would say that his collective unconscious is trying to reach him. A. T. Jersild studied the imaginings of children and found that while they were occasionally endangered by accidents they were anxious about lions, ghosts and witches from which little harm could be expected! They had used storybook images to objectify general anxiety about their relationships to parents. In this view Parkins might be haunted by some enforced intimacy with a parent long ago.

Alfred Adler saw anxiety in the striving of those with inferiority feelings to be superior, although this strains social bonds which alone can relieve inferiority feelings. Parkins, an opinionated academic recluse, seems a good candidate for this

Anxiety is the experience of being confronted with non-being, with one's death in the midst of life, of feeling trapped in the paradox of freedom and finiteness. Anxiety is evoked by contradictions threatening us simultaneously from both sides, or inside outside. In Map 13, we see the vision of death which confronts Professor Parkins with meaninglessness and disintegrates that 'scientific world view' which structures his personality. The paradoxical 'face' seems both dead and alive, random in movement yet with its own order. Neither an objective sheet nor a subjective person it gropes blindly yet 'sees', in a manner between feeling and thinking. Parkins the bold searcher is suddenly the searched for, the known. Assuming that ghosts are illusory, could Parkins have brought this neurotic fantasy upon himself? We know that he shunned the poles on the left side of the map; he preferred the observing and knowing of alien and ordered objects. Could this 'ghost' be the clamour of his repressions, intimate feelings wanting/dreading to be known before death comes? To integrate by encompassing reason all poles of these constructs requires a courageous tolerance for existential anxiety. Those who hide from the pains of paradox and in the name of technical reason reduce anxiety by habitually subordinating one pole to the other, will find themselves visited by neurosis and nightmare.

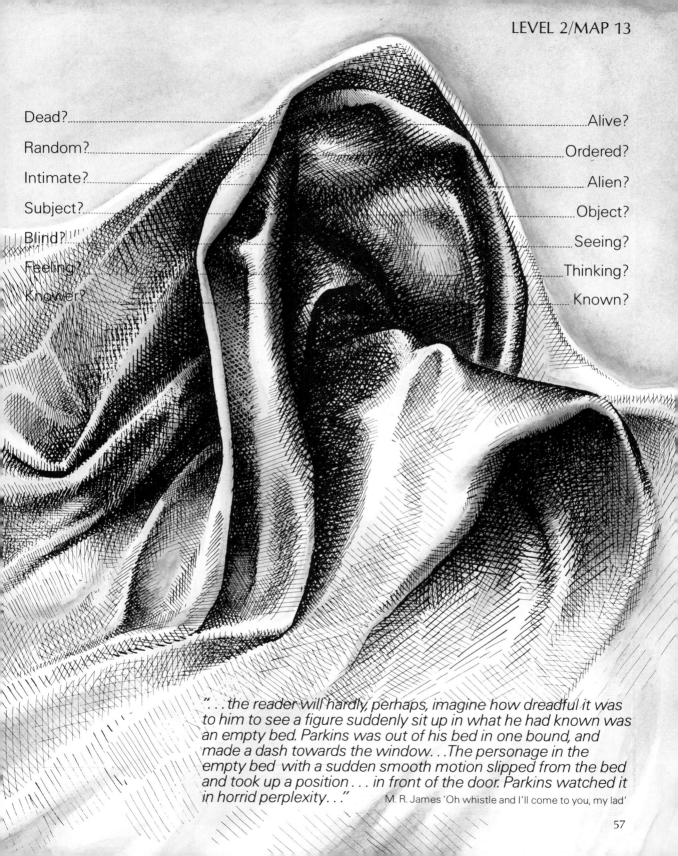

Dead? .... Alive?

Random? .... Ordered?

Intimate? .... Alien?

Subject? .... Object?

Blind? .... Seeing?

Feeling? .... Thinking?

Knower? .... Known?

*". . . the reader will hardly, perhaps, imagine how dreadful it was
to him to see a figure suddenly sit up in what he had known was
an empty bed. Parkins was out of his bed in one bound, and
made a dash towards the window. . .The personage in the
empty bed with a sudden smooth motion slipped from the bed
and took up a position . . . in front of the door. Parkins watched it
in horrid perplexity. . ."* M. R. James 'Oh whistle and I'll come to you, my lad'

theory. Henry Stack Sullivan saw anxiety arising from an empathic anticipation of disapproval from others. The self is formed by attempts to control such anxiety. The ghost story relates that Parkins had always avoided socially those persons in his college who used ambiguous language or ideas. Perhaps these all came for him in one night! Finally May, himself, traces much neurotic anxiety in Western culture to the disjunction between competitive individualism and the experience of community. Parkins overdid his eccentric individualism, perhaps.

This view of anxiety-as-neurosis would trace Parkins' catastrophic experiences to poorly processed information and/or social relationships so badly disturbed that reality was distorted. May studied a sample of unmarried mothers. Those who could accept that their own mothers had rejected them, could live with this reality with relatively low anxiety. It was those who, steeped in middle-class morality, refused to countenance this rejection and whose mothers also disguised their rejection, who found themselves perpetually anxious.

Surely, then, Spinoza was right? Parkins' 'weak mind' became deluded or hallucinated. By separating his subjectivity from objective reality, he would have found either a disturbance in the former or some prankster at work in the latter. The irrational spectre of 'life-in-death' would have been reduced to nothing but life or nothing but death. The 'animated linen' might have changed to mere appearance with a real person beneath.

This is the triumphant view of the enlightenment which has swept all superstition before it. It follows that anxiety is a reaction to the irrational, a child-like perturbation calmed by educated reason. It is reasonable to fear, since certain objects are dangerous, and fear girds us – for fight or flight. But states of diffuse and pervading anxiety are consequences, surely, of failure to pinpoint dangers accurately? They are vestiges of unreason.

Not quite . . . The first error comes from confusing the final clarity of some ideal theory with the perplexity and ambiguity of creating it. The final answer to a problem may be a clear 'yes' or 'no' to a simple either/or, but what Abraham Kaplan called reconstructed logic is not the same as the logic of discovery. A famous psychological experiment illustrates the point. Richard Crutchfield asked a group of people to estimate the relative length of two lines and similar tests of visual discrimination. The group's individual answers relayed by a signalling system, were so contrived that every subject believed his own estimate to be contradicted by everyone else in the room, so each believed himself alone. Rarely in psychology does one get a perfect correlation of 1. But in this case *everyone* showed a marked increase in physiological measures of anxiety. Those who then conformed with the bogus group consensus, denying the evidence of their own senses, lowered their anxiety. Those who called it as they saw it, and dissented, kept their anxiety high. They lived with anomaly, dilemma and seeming contradiction. They confronted the possibility that their eyesight or minds were failing, exposed themselves to ridicule in order to know themselves and came through anxiety to vindication. This is what Tillich called 'the courage to be'. Scientists, writers, artists and creators of every kind go through uncertainty, anomaly and meaninglessness in the faith of some reconciling powers.

But there is a second error in discounting anxiety as 'irrational'. Can we always assume that, at the end of some struggle to comprehend, there is a final solution, similar to choosing the longer line? Ghosts are, I believe, rightly subject to scepticism and dissolve before reductive explanations, but can we say the same about that harsh reality which ghosts symbolize? Ghosts represent a life which knows it will die, a being in the words of Pascal, 'engulfed in the immensity of spaces

'For if I have ventured amiss – very well, then life helps me by its punishment. But if I have not ventured at all – who then helps me? And, moreover, if by not venturing at all in the highest sense . . . (to become conscious of oneself) . . . I have gained all earthly advantages . . . and lose myself! What of that?'
'Sickness unto Death'
Søren Kierkegaard

'Man is only a reed, the feeblest reed in nature, but he is a thinking reed . . . were the universe to crush him, man would still be more noble than that which slays him, because he knows that he dies, and the advantage the universe has over him; of this the universe knows nothing.'
'Penseés' Blaise Pascal

'Courage does not remove anxiety. Since anxiety is existential it cannot be removed. But courage takes anxiety of non-being into itself . . . He who does not succeed in taking his anxiety courageously upon himself can succeed in avoiding . . . despair only by escaping into neurosis . . . Neurosis is the way of avoiding non-being by avoiding being.'
'The Courage to Be' Paul Tillich

'Now it began to move, in a stooping posture, and all at once the spectator realized, with some horror and some relief, that it must be blind, for it seemed to feel about it with muffled arms in groping and random fashion . . . it suddenly became conscious of the bed he had just left, and darted towards it and bent and felt over the pillows in a way that made Parkins shudder . . . then moving into the area of light facing the window it showed for the first time what manner of thing it was.

. . . I gathered that what Parkins chiefly remembers about it is a horrible, an intensely horrible, face of crumpled linen . . . that the face went nigh to maddening him is certain . . . as the creature groped and moved, one corner of the draperies swept across Parkins' face. He could not . . . keep back a cry of disgust and this gave the searcher an instant clue. It leapt towards him upon the instant, and the next moment he was half-way through the window, backwards, uttering cry upon cry at the utmost pitch of his voice, as the linen face was thrust close into his own . . .'

'Oh whistle and I'll come to you my lad'   M. R. James

which I know not and which know not me . . .' The psychological experience which juxtaposes being with non-being, our worldly ambitions with nothingness, are the intimations of an animal who is aware that he will turn to dust. Now physical science has taught us that there can be no contradictions in perceptual space, an organism must be physically dead or alive, but psychologically we continually contrast our existence with non-existence. Ghosts symbolize this fusion of present with approaching realities, and while we can exorcize ghosts we cannot exorcize what they stand for.

It is not just the sleep of reason that brings forth monsters. At the opposite extreme, the dream of reason brings forth monsters too, in the shape of Final Solutions. How so? Because, says Tillich, we have failed to distinguish *technical reason* from *encompassing reason*. Technical reason is that kind of means–ends rationality that gives yes/no answers to either/or questions. It abolishes contradiction, cuts through anomaly, and permits vague anxieties to be replaced by definite fears which can supposedly be mastered. But the ethical social, and existential issues of ultimate concern require a totally different kind of reasoning, a kind that encompasses several alternatives, and which answers not in terms of either/or, but of both/and. Should we be individualists, standing boldly for our own values against the crowd, or communitarians determined to confer social benefit? May would answer 'both'. Love *and* will, power *and* innocence, all must be encompassed as *freedom from* finds fulfilment in *freedom for*. The dissenters in Crutchfield's experiment encompassed responsibility to their group through responsibility to themselves. While they solved finally the question of the longer line, they (or we) never solve finally the questions of individual versus social responsibility. These questions arise repeatedly in that crucible of anxiety which lies between persons, and the dilemmas must be repeatedly joined in the changing patterns and proportions that solve particular problems. Existential anxiety is basic to this process, the shadow of the intellect, essential to those who, like Sophocles, 'see life steadily and see it whole'. It is by evading anxiety that we convert it, unawares, to neurotic forms, which return to haunt us.

For it is disastrous to use technical reason with encompassing problems and so convert multi-dimensional anxiety into shrunken, uni-dimensional fear. Communism, we are told, is dangerous, so arm, deter it and master fear! But is it just danger we face, or a ghost-like dilemma? Russia could attack us 'aggressively' because our weakness tempts her, or 'defensively' because our strength alarms her. As the might of both countries escalates, we are trapped in an ever narrowing cleft between these two ever more contrasting interpretations. Both countries are now so 'strong' that they are 'weak' and could 'defend' themselves only by 'attacking' and destroying everyone concerned. Have we reached the stage foreseen in Kierkegaard wherein fear and desire lock horns in an impotence that brings 'sickness into death'? With Parkins we are caught by the Kierkegaardian contradiction of either/or, trapped in a Cartesian dualism wherein the ghost-like mind haunts the mindless machine.

At the roots of the Cold War are the anxiety-reducing, technical responses given by Western and Eastern blocs to the eternal dilemma of human rights versus social responsibility. West has said yes/no, East no/yes. Now each reproaches the other's incompleteness. Each feels subverted by an alien dimension, and the anxiety engendered by confrontation has become neurotic. It could be our last mistake.

MAP 14

The Divided Self:
Jean-Paul Sartre to R. D. Laing

R. D. Laing advances the existential position of Jean-Paul Sartre, that persons experience *being-for-themselves* and seek to enhance this. Existential being refers to a continuous dynamic flow of *consciousness-through-action* (praxis) which issues from human beings out into their social environments. Yet when we behold others we tend to see them as *beings-in-themselves*, as objects located in our own purposive vision. For Sartre interpersonal relationships were a perpetual struggle to assert the fluidity of our own existence against persistent attempts to objectify us by others.

Now the 'scientific world view' is overwhelmingly objectifying. This view of the detached observer seeks to explain us further by analytic reasoning which reduces us to parts. There is psychological violence in this stony gaze and disintegrative thinking. Sartre opts for his own brand of dialectical reasoning wherein the convictions of any persons or group will be 'depassed', ie encompassed into the larger configuration of another's convictions. No conviction should therefore masquerade as a moral absolute or objective determination.

R. D. Laing regards contemporary psychiatry as having made a false objectification of psychic states. Freud descended into the 'underworld' of stark terrors wielding his theory like Medusa's head which turned these terrors to stone. We must learn to understand psychotics without petrifying them. Laing is not claiming that Freud's theories are 'wrong'. They may, indeed, accord with observable evidence. His point is that facts can be measured and communicated in a manner that increases their salience! Patients seeking help because they feel like dead and shattered objects find themselves further petrified by the viewpoints of psychiatry. The very data which symptoms constitute are in reality *capta*, pieces torn and abstracted from the fabric of lived experience.

Laing's view of the process of becoming schizophrenic begins with split or schizoid functioning. Persons ontologically insecure, that is those who have not been allowed to experience themselves as continuously related to the world by moral action, may split themselves into two systems, a system of false selves presented as a mask to the world, and an inner self of authentic experience not revealed to others.

Schizoid organization is a question of degree. We all recall as children the discovery that we could hide our knowledge from detection by parents. It is when the false self becomes habitual that splitting can become a permanent characteristic. The advantage being sought by splitting is the reduction of anxiety. When I offer my true, embodied self to others for acceptance or rejection there is existential anxiety in the anticipation of their response. Such anxiety may be excruciating for those much rejected and poorly socialized in their past lives. They seek relief in the fabrication of false selves designed to gain acceptance. Should such a self be rejected, the pain is considerably less.

Yet this immediate relief can spell later disaster. If the true self is never committed to others, it can neither confirm itself nor learn from experience, while the false self can only be confirmed in its falsity, so that even success is like crowning a dummy. Social skills will atrophy and neurotic anxieties consequent on gauche behaviour soon replace the existential anxiety. There is, claims Sartre, 'no exit' from the vicious circle (*Huis Clos*) of proffering in 'bad faith' false versions of ourselves. We will become tormented by mutal objectification in a world where 'hell is other people'. Schizoid behaviour does not lead directly to schizophrenia, rather it intensifies psychological violence so that some win the struggle to define others as objects, and others lose this struggle. It is among victims and losers that the drift to psychosis is likely to occur.

The patient (left) is being viewed by the psychiatrist (right) through a screen of theory which divides the patient into so many 'signs of illness' and objective categories. Such a psychiatrist may understand everything about schizophrenia without understanding a single schizophrenic. Ironically the patient has come to seek help because of feelings of disintegration, feelings to which the psychiatrist adds by the very process of reductive analysis. Sanity is judged in our society by the degree of conjunction between two persons, the certifier and certified, when the first is sane by common consent. Patients are typically those whose relatives or friends have pinned objective determinations of sickness upon them, persuaded them to seek help, which then furthers their disintegration. The patient unintentionally facilitates his own psychoses by fabricating a 'false self' which inauthentically complies with the demands of a hostile environment, while an inner 'true self' resorts to fantasies of freedom and compensatory dreams of revenge. While the false self accumulates onerous experiences, the true self feels progressively isolated and unreal. It dreads being swallowed by the false-self system, now seething with introjected critics and inconsistent attributions . . . So the person who says he is a machine is mad, while many of those who say men are machines are considered great scientists!

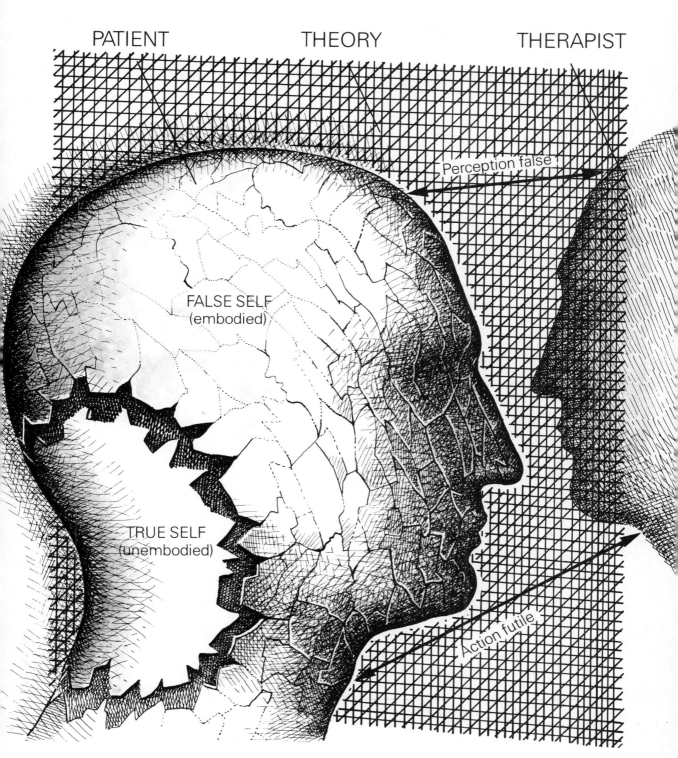

PATIENT   THEORY   THERAPIST

Perception false

FALSE SELF
(embodied)

TRUE SELF
(unembodied)

Action futile

These dynamics are illustrated in the map. The patient (left) has split off a system of false selves designed to conform to others' expectations. These are deployed in defence of an inner self, which suffers in Kierkegaard's phrase, 'a demonic shutinness'. Yet the psychiatrist (right) has his own 'false self', in the shape of theory, by which the patient is objectified and analysed. Just as parents or spouses won 'the politics of experience' and persuaded the patient to be their 'sick object', so the therapist now confirms the diagnosis. By a vocabulary of denigration, whether moral or medical, one schizoid system labels the other as mad, each wearing a 'death mask' that mirrors the others falsity. The patient is likely to agree with psychiatric suggestions, while the psychiatrist delights in the self-fulfilling powers of his theory. Why even the patient's dreams oblige!

This victory of authorities over patients accelerates their psychoses. The false self becomes an increasingly brittle façade crowded by a collage of inconsistent attributions and increasingly mocked and hated by the true self, which develops compensatory values. The more craven, defeated and bounded the false self becomes, the more dauntless, victorious and free grows the true self. There are, after all, no limits to the imaginings of a phantom locked away from the world. Steadily the paradox becomes sharper, that the true self is equally threatened by continual imprisonment *and* by letting in the external reality.

The psychotic break is usually signalled by changes in language. Near the borderline a patient may say that he does not really make love to his wife. Over the borderline he may say that the woman he makes love to is not his real wife. Yet the transition is understandable. A two-way conversation has yielded to one between four or more entities. The false self, by now so invaded by relatives and psychiatrists, has become indistinguishable from them. They are it and it is them, while the true self has opted for the fantasy wife. The original conflict between the patient and others has been pushed by objectification within him, so that his selves literally mock and caricature each other.

With the onset of schizophrenia in early adolescence there are often three sequential descriptions of the patient by parents, 'goodness, then badness, then madness' (see diagrams). Typical was the case of Julie, 'the ghost in the weed garden'. She 'never made trouble' was always 'sweet, obedient and clean'. Since real children are not in the least like this, Julie's 'perfect self' was clearly false, with a true self seething behind the mask. As the psychotic break approached, Julie made a frantic bid to save herself. This was her 'badness phase'. She suddenly accused her mother of never leaving her alone, of smothering her. Desperate truths, but naturally her parents were aghast. How could their darling harbour such sentiments? We can imagine the ferocity of their shock and disapproval. It therefore came as a relief to her parents (and as a surrender signal from Julie) when she said that her mother had murdered a child and the police must be informed. Julie was ill! Her badness could be explained by madness. She had not meant what she said.

Sartre and Laing would agree with Marcuse (see Map 53) that Julie is the victim of one-dimensional judgements. The moral absolutes of her parents – obedience, cleanliness, quiet – leave no room for the other ends of the dialectic process – rebellion, dirtiness and noise. Even medical science was one-dimensional in insisting on the sanity of her false self and the insanity of her true experience. Moralism and positivism joined to smash those values which appeared to negate their being. But it is a fallacy of momentous proportions to regard obedience as *good* and rebellion as *bad*, to insist on yielding and not assertion. The real disease lies in the *splitting* of these values, so that the false self seems docile and dead and

'In short we have an already shattered Humpty Dumpty who cannot be put together again by any number of hyphenated or compound words: psycho-physical, psycho-somatic, psycho-biological, psycho-pathological, psycho-social, etc . . .'
'The Divided Self' Ronald Laing

. . . We shall be concerned specifically with people who experience themselves as automata, as robots, as bits of machinery, or even as animals. Yet why do we not regard a theory that seeks to transmute persons into automata or animals as equally crazy?'
'The Divided Self'

'Patients kick and scream and fight when they aren't sure the doctor can see them. It's a most terrifying feeling to realize that the doctor can't see the real you, that he can't understand what you feel, and that he's just going ahead with his own ideas.'
'The Divided Self'

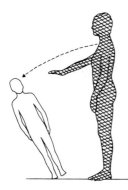

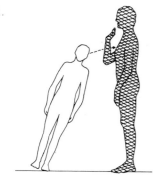

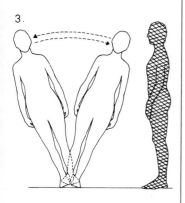

Three phases of schizophrenia in early adolescence:
1. A 'good', obedient child
2. A 'bad', rebellious child
3. A 'mad' child oscillating between the extremes of 'good' (false self) and 'bad' (true self).

the true self wildly animated. The pattern we observe in psychosis is an oscillation between extremes, with no moderation or mutual restraint between absolutes.

Laing's views were championed by the counter-culture of the sixties and grossly simplified. The media presented him in an increasingly bizarre light, in seeming sympathy with patients who were conceived of as having mystical experiences – the veritable odyssey and return of the hero. I believe, however, that we can distinguish the profundity of Laing's work from its later extravagance by making a single important distinction. Laing took Sartre's 'real self' and 'imaginary self' and altered these to read *false self* and *true self*. He did not, he now insists, intend to convey that the true self in its split-off, phantomized condition was an enviable state of superior sanity, only that it was truly experienced. Patients can be helped back to a fusion of their subjective experiences with the social realities seen by others, only if these true selves are first accepted as legitimate bases to build upon. In this way their rebellion is respected along with their obedience, their assertion with their yielding and the entire range of behaviours between.

It was Laing's popularizers, not he, who tried to define whole as one polarity upon the continuum subjective whole–objective part. The principle of unity cannot be applied at only one level of language (see Map 40), but must logically refer to the whole continuum, which includes objectivity and parts in a widened context. When the continua of whole–part, subject–object, separation–relationship are cloven in a divided self, then all split-off ends are pathological, mutually excitatory, and wildly oscillating, the turned-on hippie and the buttoned-down automaton alike, and both can only be healed by the integration of their extremities. If Laing has emphasized the subjective end, it was because too many others had de-emphasized it. The necessary one-sidedness of his tactics have been confused with the vital balance of his goal.

In the light of such models as catastrophe theory (see Map 56), Laing's work takes on renewed importance and the concept of a widening, catastrophic splitting in mind and behaviour, with jumps or oscillations between, becomes much more than a metaphor and is capable of mathematical expression and three-dimensional representation. Essentially the schizophrenic is crucified by the subject–object split of Cartesian dualism (see Map 6). He (or she) *is* 'the broken image' as Laing puts it. The risk consists in this: if one experiences the other as a free agent, one is open to experiencing oneself as an object of his experience and thereby of feeling one's own subjectivity drained away. One is threatened with the possibility of becoming no more than a thing in the world of the other, without any life for oneself, without any being for oneself. In terms of such anxiety, the very act of experiencing the other as a person is felt as virtually suicidal. Sartre discusses this experience brilliantly . . .

MAP 15

The Death-Denying Mind:
Otto Rank and Ernest Becker

Otto Rank was a close pupil of Freud (see Map 9), who encouraged the former to attend university and helped pay for his studies. Rank later dissented from his master, but his reformulation remains respectful yet profoundly original. In 1974 the sociologist Ernest Becker won a Pulitzer Prize for his rehabilitation and elaboration of Rank in *The Denial of Death*. The book had a special poignancy, for Becker was himself dying of cancer.

Rank and Becker take as their point of departure that the human being is unique in the animal kingdom. We alone are alive while consciously aware that we shall die. Our symbolizing capacities provide endless food for thought, yet our bodies will be food for worms. It is vain to search for a 'basic essence' of humanity to attempt to reduce mind to a unitary source, for we are suspended in paradox, seething with vitality against the back-drop of obliteration. We exist between the *life fear* and the *death fear*, of feeling overwhelmed by potential and excitement, and of feeling abandoned to limitation and lassitude.

It was Freud who noted that the unconscious and id impulses seem not to know of death and time. In our inner recesses we feel immortal and like Narcissus see the world as reflections of ourselves. It is the ego and the reality principle which warn us we are doomed, and while we believe this of others, our private impulses cry out against the sentence of death and will, in the words of Dylan Thomas, 'Rage, rage against the dying of the light'.

An entirely fresh understanding is thrown upon Freud's insights if we assume that what is being repressed is not sexuality so much as the terror of death. For example, the anxiety aroused by sex, nakedness, bodily functions, etc, is now seen as an unwelcome reminder of mortality. Oral, anal and phallic stages of development are infantile attempts to swallow, expel and penetrate a 'world' shrunk to manageable size. The young child has no direct knowledge of death, but has many experiences of paradox, which has the same structure as death. For example, the child may feel omnipotent since by the simple act of yelling nurturance comes at his command. Then comes the dawning realization that his 'power' is a tribute paid to impotence. The baby's very life hangs upon the thread of parental solicitude. 'Castration fear' is thus focused on the mother, not the father. The boy yearns to be independent yet fears to be alone and rejected. The mother, like the legendary sphinx, has a paradoxical aspect, she can nurture through dependence, yet destroy through overdependence. The cradle, seemingly so warm and safe, rocks upon a dark ocean. This paradox of infancy yields to the larger paradox of adult existence itself, in which another encapsulated shell rocks on another ocean. The child has no means of articulating this fear of paradox, save by symbols close at hand, hence the fear of long-legged beasties and things that go bump in the night.

The Oedipal complex becomes, in this view, the project of attempted self-creation. Oedipus sought to confound death by becoming the father of himself, the motive and sin for which the gods cast him down (and for which Satan was expelled from heaven). Oedipus had grown to manhood by solving the riddle of the sphinx, that 'man' emerges from the conflict between nurturance and destruction. But that solution had been verbal and symbolic only, so that Oedipus then stumbled into the greater paradox, that which lies between the symbolizing power of heroes and kings and the underlying limitations of mortal flesh. He knew 'everything' save the origin and fate of his own body.

Mankind has sought numerous solutions to the paradox that 'in life we are in the midst of death'. Rank and Becker have distinguished religious, heroic, romantic, philistine and creative solutions, without which we become neurotic or even psychotic and end up as 'psychological man', continually in therapy. All these

In the process of human perception we usually distinguish 'figure' from 'ground' (or background). Although we select a figure to focus on automatically, this choice is arbitrarily governed by our motives or expectations and is not given by the object itself. Otto Rank and Ernest Becker proposed that we deny death to rid ourselves of the painful paradox of life-in-death. Accordingly we focus obsessively on 'the white angel of life' while repressing 'the black devil of death' deep into the recesses of unconsciousness. We invent immortality systems, which stress Heaven, Heroism, Romanticism, Corporatism, the State and Revolutionary Immortality. The cruel reality is that during our natural lives the dark background is moving inexorably forward. We cannot stand this and so create symbolic visions of 'all whiteness', which so swathe the ground in miasmic mist that we literally stumble into the abyss to ultimate deaths. 'We give birth astride a grave, the light gleams an instant and it's night once more.'

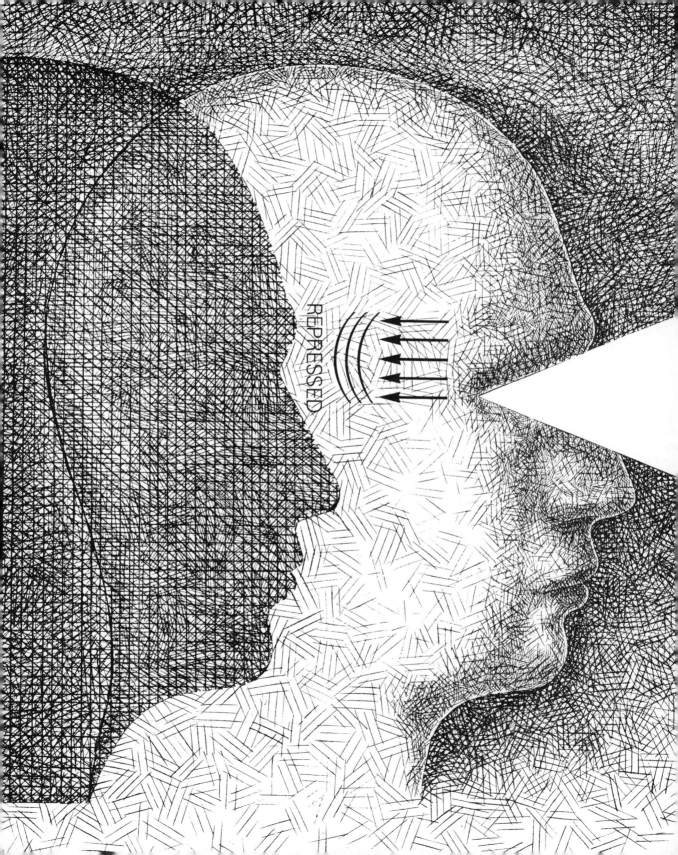

solutions attempt to create a universe of symbols woven like illusions around cadaverous reality. 'For man,' says Rank, 'is a theological being.'

The historic solution appealed to 'other worldly' religion. What is this brutish existence of ours, this vale of tears compared with life and joy everlasting amid angels (who, as St Augustine reminded us, have *no* fundamental orifices!)? The Eastern traditions similarly invite us to dissolve paradox by mystic selflessness and ceasing to strive. The whole world of oppositions recedes into the realm of no-mind, save that here the concentration is on the concrete, eg the breathing of one's own body. The result is the same: the sensation of timelessness and transcendence, an immortal oneness with the universe. Death is put aside awhile and the paradox of the koan (a verse riddle) is used to anaesthetize us against the larger paradox of existence.

Heroism also promises immortality. Traditionally the hero faced death and conquered it by killing his country's foes. He left on long odysseys, as if dead, and returned with life-enhancing knowledge or substance. Those who partake of the hero's aura will share his apparent immunity to death as he survives miraculously amid the slaughter. To be stronger than enemies who wish your death is to be stronger than death itself. We are still today under the spell cast by persons, whether holy warriors or the newer breed of pop-stars, gurus and daredevils. Millions seek to be pulled into cloud-cuckoo land on the coat-tails of Fred Astaire or the wall-to-wall noise of rock bands.

The romantic solution attempts to make a religion of love relationships. Romanticism, the tradition of courtly love, historically challenged the institution of Christian (arranged) marriage with a passionate 'cosmology of two'. The love object is celestial, sublime, perfect, and because she accepts me, I am redeemed from death by her grace. Of course I must avoid her body and the relaxation that comes from consummated love. That is why romanticism feeds on frustration, why it sings to the lady within the castle wall of unrequited love, and leaves a symbolic rose upon the battlements. To encounter a real woman would be a profound anticlimax, a dangerous mingling of heaven with halitosis. Jonathan Swift, who was tortured by such anomalies, laments:

> 'No wonder that I lost my wits
> For Caelia, Caelia, Caelia shits!'

The philistine solution finds refuge in compromise, mediocrity and shrinking the world to bite-sized pieces. The bourgeois aspires to becoming deputy supervisor in charge of yogurt at the office of his grocery chain. Rank called this 'partialization', the reduction of human existence to manageable objectives. In sexual relationships it becomes a fetish, a whole woman reduced to boots or suspenders. It is the adult's equivalent to the child's oral and anal fixation.

Rank placed most of his hope in the creative resolution of the life—death paradox through the work of artists. Freud, he noted, was an agnostic, desperately warning his disciples against straying into 'the occult', but then creativity was Freud's private religion. When reproving his followers for straying from the fold, he would be subject to fainting fits. His own immortality was at stake! Creative persons are more comfortable with paradox because they tend to see life itself as a problem or question that evokes a personal synthesis. Art is the attempted objectification of our subjective yearning for immortality. For the act of creation is never really completed, the artist must await in desperate vulnerability for the answer to his offering. Nor will popular acceptance suffice. Since creativity aspires to immortality, it craves the acknowledgement of immortal authorities, be they god, culture or

'Let sanguine healthy-mindedness do its best with its strange power of living for the moment and ignoring and forgetting . . . the skull will grin at the banquet'.
'Varieties of Religious Experience'
William James

'For life is at the start a chaos in which one is lost. The individual suspects this, but he is frightened of finding himself face to face with this terrible reality, and tries to cover it over with a curtain of fantasy, where everything is clear. It does not worry him that his ideas are not true, he uses them as trenches for the defence of his existence, as scarecrows to frighten away reality.'
'The Revolt of the Masses'
Ortega E. Gasset

'What will become of my whole life? . . . Is there any meaning in my life that the inevitable death awaiting me does not destroy?'
'Confession' Leo Tolstoy

'The history of mankind divides into two great periods, one existed from time immemorial . . . and was characterized by the ritualist view of nature. The second began with . . . the modern machine age. . . . In both periods men wanted to control life and death, but in the first they had to rely on non-machine technology . . . by building a ritual altar and making that the locus of the transfer and renewal of life-power.'
'Escape from Evil' Ernest Becker

posterity. The true creator must combine the highest level of self-expression with total self-surrender, Eros married to Agape. Rank would have agreed with Ingmar Bergman that the world's greatest art was offered to god. The modern cult of the creative person takes its theme from Norman Mailer's *Advertisements for Myself*; this overly self-conscious creativity inflates its self-importance as it elbows to gain precedence at the pearly gates.

Rank saw the symptoms of neuroses and psychoses as breakdowns in the capacity to deny death. These people were 'artistes manqué', tortured by the paradoxes they could not resolve and confronted by death-in-life. This accounted for typical neurotic symptoms, ambivalence, hesitation, stammering, anxiety, inner conflict, chronic indecision, with intimate relationships equally conflicted. Often there was an underlying disgust with the mortal coil, evidenced by depression, rituals of decontamination, rage turned inwards or outwards, with extremes of hyperactivity or nervous prostration. The psychotic has totally split the death fear from the life fear, babbling to himself in a symbolic world divorced from social reality, or suffering beneath the weight of his body in rigid, foetal and immobile postures.

Before he died Becker came close to a major contribution to our comprehension of genocidal man. His last, unfinished, book, *Escape for Evil*, reveals the lethal consequences of immortality systems. Religious dogmas rigidify and become so emotionally charged in their futile battles with death that they fall upon each other in religious wars. Human sacrifices, warlordism and the ritual slaughter of captives are public demonstrations of the hero's power *over* death. Armies, tribes and hordes seek immersion in the aura that surrounds their leaders or in the revolutionary immortality of collective purpose. Romantic lovers like Tristan and Isolde, Romeo and Juliet escalate their passion as the forces frustrating it escalate too. In a grand climax they prove the immortality of their love by dying for it. The idol 'love' is venerated, only the people perish! Before death can come for us we rush to lay our lives at the feet of idols, History, Providence, God, Romance, The Party, Patriotism, LSD. But as Aldous Huxley warned, 'All idols, sooner or later, become Molochs hungry for human sacrifice'.

The mounting tolls of war sharpen the pains of paradox, and human beings typically respond with even more powerful repressions. For example, in the Great War, we refused to countenance that thousands of young men could be cut down in their prime. 'Youth wasted' was a paradox too sharp to bear. We had to give it meaning. 'The war to end all wars' we said to ourselves; 'Greater love hath no man than this, that a man lay down his life for his friends.' Yet it is absurd to pretend that such elevated and improbable sentiments were crossing the minds of ordinary soldiers as bullets struck them. Such rhetoric is for *us*, the survivors, who are threatened by our own mortality and the meaninglessness of existence. As we comfort the bereaved and ourselves by gathering around war memorials, are we not laying the foundations for the next slaughter, readying another generation to charge 'heroically' into the jaws of paradox?

The different forms of death denial share a common structure. The life-in-death paradox is converted into life-and-after-life, an altogether more comfortable and consistent proposition, but one that dangerously obscures the choice of living out our span in *this* life. We shall survive death, we say, in heaven, on war memorials, in the annals of romantic love, in the future of the corporation, in some final 'fix', in deathless art or prose. But death denied by abstract ideals will come upon us in concrete reality, as we perish sooner rather than later, and earn for the human species its reputation as the most murderous animal the world has known. 'Man,' as Eli Wiesel said, 'is not human.'

MAP 16

Left, Right and Centre:
The view of Silvan Tomkins

Ideology, says Silvan Tomkins of Princeton, New Jersey, is a basic dimension of personality, analogous to the notion of paradigm. He defines ideology as any organized set of ideas about which human beings are at once both articulate and passionate and about which they are least certain. Ideology in the form of working hypotheses and assumptions lies at the very centre of an individual's logic of discovery. These assumptions constitute the foundation of mathematics, the philosophy of science, metaphysics, theology, epistemology (the path to knowledge), the theory of values, ethics, politics, educational theory and child rearing. No matter how large an accumulation of facts we have made, ideology and its uncertainty lie at the base of this edifice. We cannot be sure of our pre-suppositions because they are self-fulfilling, so that we find that the variable we have isolated to be isolated fact. Shifts at the base of our discipline threaten us, and are fiercely defended against. Ideologies are Left, Right or Centre.

Tomkins makes the following distinctions between Left and Right. *Left*: Is Man the measure, an end in himself, an active, creative, thinking, desiring, loving force in nature? or *Right*: Must Man realize himself, attain his full stature only through struggle towards, participation in and conformity to, a norm, a measure, and an ideal essence basically independent of Man?

It will be clear at once that this definition does not principally distinguish between rival forms of capitalist and communist economic organization. To the extent that either of these blocs calls upon their citizens to be worthy of their economic system, Tomkins would regard them as ideologically right-wing, so that Soviet and Free Market orthodoxies are both conservative, while the Prague Spring of Alexander Dubcek in 1969 and the anti-war presidential campaign of George McGovern were both left-wing in trying to modify the *status quo* with the ideals of liberal humanism. While this definition of ideological polarity does not cover every sense in which these terms are loosely used, it has the advantage of being a reconcilable definition. Hence parliamentary democracies who define Left and Right in this fashion, as well as learned societies, can evolve consensually by combining the contributions of each polarity.

Consider now, how this polarity runs through domains of different disciplines. In mathematics we have Jules Poincaré on the Left arguing that mathematics is the finest type of human play, a personal delight constructed by the imagination. For the textbook authors of *What is Mathematics?* such views are caprice. 'Only under the discipline of responsibility to the organic whole can the free mind achieve results of scientific value.'

In the philosophy of science we have Einstein on the Left stating that 'the formulation of a problem is often more essential than its solution, which is merely a matter of mathematics and experimental skill … Physical concepts are free creations of the human mind and are not, however it may seem, uniquely determined by the external world.' As against this, there are the many philosophers who have stressed that concepts must correspond with reality and with facts. Careful measurement and exact methods are necessary to control wild fancy and loose inferences.

In metaphysics we have Plato on the Right, planting his Eternal Forms on ground cleared by the radical scepticism of Socrates. Men and nature are but pale copies of ideas and essences, which exist prior to, and independently of Man. In contrast Johann Fichte and William Berkeley on the Left saw the world itself as the projection of mind, while Alfred North Whitehead chided poets for celebrating nature rather than themselves. 'Nature is a dull affair, soundless, scentless, colourless; merely the hurrying of material, endlessly, meaninglessly.'

Left- and Right-wing ideologies are a basic dimension of personality. Ideology consists of a 'love affair between a loosely organized set of feelings and a highly organized and articulate set of ideas'. These resonating ideas and feelings are mapped by the individual upon whole families of related issues, politics, sexual relationships, education, crime-control, child-rearing and the frontiers of particular disciplines.

Since ideology precedes any dealing with problems, the nature of such problems can become reactions to ideology. The Left typically solves any conflict between expressed human desires and existing standards by extolling the human, 'Man is the measure' (see left of map). If black Americans score poorly on IQ tests, look to the 'racist', 'biased' tests! The Right tends to resolve any conflict in precisely the opposite manner. Human beings habitually fall short of standards of excellence, so blacks and others should shape up instead of abusing intelligence! 'The measure is independent of Man' (see right of map).

Seen in this light, extreme Left and Right ideologies involve the crippling of personality by stereotyped reactions to any dissonance between expectation and experience. The Left can always blame the residual influence of out-moded values for the postponement of millenia. The Right can always insist that its values remain untarnished, only Man is vile. It is the Centre, which, by interweaving change with continuity and by measuring up to values it has humanized, permits democratic processes to learn from experience.

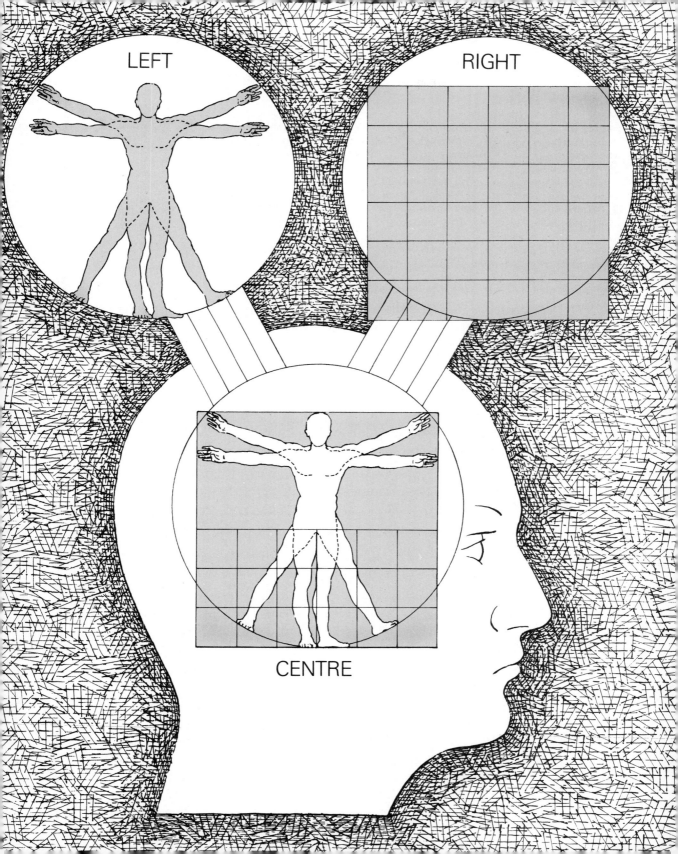

LEFT

RIGHT

CENTRE

In psychology we find humanistic psychology on the Left insisting that the whole person, growing and bursting with immeasurable enthusiasms must be the true stuff of psychology, no matter what difficulties this imposes on scientific methodology. Even further left we have Fritz Perls teaching the incantation 'I am not in this world to live up to your expectations . . .' a sentiment that swiftly earned him a following of persons who had never lived up to anyone's expectations, and were in no danger of doing so. The Right, in contrast, will admit to the discipline only those eye-blinks, reflexes and unambiguous behaviours that allow for strict measurement and definition. The consciousness of what it means to be human is too vague and emotional to deserve a place in psychology! The far Right would object to any map of the mind at all, since the mind is properly subject to external forces which write upon the tabula rasa.

In art there is the recurrent polarity between romanticism on the Left, with its emphasis on the felt, the irrational and the personal, and the classical on the Right, with its emphasis on control, restraint and reason. The mind is seen as either a lamp illuminating darkness or a mirror reflecting the world. In theology, the Left, typified by John Robinson in Honest to God, declared that our image of God 'as an old man in the sky' was outmoded. We had 'come of age' and God was 'the ground of our being' coextensive with our growth and unfolding. The Right rebuked the bishop, complained that the faithful were 'bewildered' and urged renewed supplication to an external Father.

Educational theory pits 'unstructured' progressive education, believed to draw out the healthy curiosity, natural cooperation and learning potential from the child, against structured and formal education, believed to fill the child's mind like a container and drill, exhort and challenge it to learn. Progressive teachers are friendly, non-judgemental and nurturant. Traditional teachers define 'high standards' and encourage compliance. In child rearing the Left tends to regard the child 'as a beautiful flower opening to the sunlight'. Delinquency testifies to lack of love and understanding which are then prescribed in large doses. The Right condemns this as indulging bad behaviour, which deserves rebuke and punishment.

The basic ideological cleavage between, Man is a valuable end in himself (Left) and The valuable exists independent of Man, who should conform to it (Right), can be used to generate several derivative propositions. On the Left, whatever perpetuates Man's existence is valuable or whatever threatens and harms it is wrong. On the Right, such threat or harm is neutral. All depends on whether Man's errant behaviour is thereby changed to more nearly approximate the Good. The Left tends to assume Man's inherent goodness. Evil has usually been induced by coercion, repression or restraint and the lack of unconditional love. The Right suspects innate depravity and prescribes ceaseless efforts to overcome this. Only the worthy should be loved.

The Left is more comfortable in the realm of feeling, especially interpersonal affections which are the roots of fraternity and equality. The Right fears that affection among people might hinder norm attainment, but generally approves of feelings when expressed towards objects symbolizing the norm, hence reverence for the flag, wonder for the cross, awe for the trappings of authority. The Left sees reason as part of Man's glory, but as a 'brother' of feeling. The Right distrusts reason in its overweening challenge to authority, but approves of reason when it governs affections and passions.

Although these distinctions seem elegant and consistent, political scientists such as S. M. Lipset and Daniel Bell have warned of the trap of ideology. In states of crises,

'And the great principle and foundation of all virtue and worth is placed in this: that a man is able to deny himself his own desires, cross his own inclinations, and purely follow what reason directs as best, although appetite leans the other way.'
'Some Thoughts Concerning Education' John Locke

'A thousand ancient fears obstruct the road to happiness and freedom. But love can conquer fear, and if we love our children nothing can make us withhold the great gift which it is in our power to bestow.'
'On Education' Bertrand Russell

anxiety and social breakdown rival ideologists will see each other as 'the cause'. When the Left sees living beings sacrificed to the Holy Inquisition, Law and Order, or the Thousand Year Reich, they proclaim that the external norm or essence of conservatism has become an idol hungry for human sacrifice. When the Right sees rioting, looting, anarchy, violence and lust it cries, 'See what happens when people place their impulse above authority, law and conventional decencies!'

The irony is that both are correct but see only opposite halves of the contradiction. A disintegrating social order such as Nazi Germany includes *both* rigid adherence to external idols *and* huge excesses of uncontrollable emotion, the first triggers the second which triggers the first, and so around in a vortex of escalating intensities. Thus the Nazis were classic in their pseudo-Roman order and regimentation, yet romantic in their flaming torches, seething passions and Wagnerian crescendoes. Everything about the regime was a juxtaposition of opposites, legal anarchy, radical rightism, national socialism, even the fasces themselves, ultra-individual rods bound tightly together in the brotherhood of the scourge (see also Map 50).

It is therefore necessary to ask whether Left or Right ideologies are a sufficient basis for political life or learned disciplines, liable as they are to mutual recrimination. Tomkins suggests that the ideological centre may be the true repository of creative change-plus-continuity. He cites Kant who reconciled the subjective with the objective, rebellion with authority, and passion with discipline. The individual should act he said, if necessary, rebelliously and passionately, but that action should be capable of being universalized to become a norm or formal essence, by which others can learn to live. Be yourself, find morality within but externalize that moral example.

The Centre, so defined, would not be a faint-hearted compromise between Left and Right, nor a hostile juxtaposition of extremities which goad one another, but a movement between the poles which encompasses their extremities while reconciling both within a single process. For surely mathematics is playful imagination *and* discipline. Education must provide the freedom to formulate questions and the discipline to answer them. 'I love you but . . .' is the key to raising children, by which the whole child is held in the context of affection while specific behaviours are criticized and modified.

We learn, then, by discovering which of our human reasons, impulses and imaginings can be trusted and which let us down, and we encode both successes and failures so that each generation need not repeat the same moves. These external norms and essences are like bannisters on a staircase, to guide us, to be touched lightly and, in emergencies, grasped.

If we wish to see Left–Right syntheses at work, perhaps the best models are parliamentary democracies where conflict exists within the context of cooperation, dissent within loyalty, private conscience within public accountability, open persuasion within secret balloting, freedom within the law, and Left-wing changes within Right-wing continuities (see Map 58). Man is the measure that must also measure up. It is a process of learning which moves from outer to inner in a cycle of eternal return. Ideologists should beware lest they become obsessed with one arc of a circle, having failed to appreciate the whole.

MAP 17

The Great Ravelled Knot:
The anatomy of the brain

Our understanding of the mind has been profoundly affected by crucial discoveries which have been made recently in the physiology of the brain. These discoveries (see Maps 18–25) show that thought and behaviour have a physiological and anatomical basis as well as a psychological one; however, before turning to these, it is important to grasp the basic anatomical make-up of what Sir Charles Sherrington called 'that great ravelled knot'.

Like all vertebrate brains, the human brain is divided anatomically into three sections: the forebrain, the midbrain and the hindbrain (see small diagram). The forebrain consists of the neocortex (the thinking cap), the limbic lobe (mood and memory, see Map 22), the hypothalamus (basic drives such as hunger, thirst, sex, sleep and emotions), the thalamus (which is thought to act as a relay station sending information from the sensory organs to the neocortex) and the pituitary gland (which secretes hormones that regulate metabolism, body growth and sexual maturation). The midbrain consists of the top part of the brain stem; the hindbrain of the lower part of the brain stem (the pons and the medulla) and the cerebellum. The brain stem monitors incoming sensory signals via the millions of neurones which make up the reticular formation (see Maps 19, 20), while the cerebellum is concerned with balance and muscle coordination.

The human brain can also be seen in terms of the three distinct brains which have developed in the course of evolution from fish to man – the reptilian, the paleomammalian and the neomammalian brains (see Map 21). In humans, the reptilian brain is situated at the top of the brain stem and consists of much of the reticular formation, the medulla, the pons and the basal ganglia; the paleomammalian brain consists of the limbic system situated deep in the valley between the two hemispheres; and the neomammalian brain of the neocortex or grey mantle which wraps almost the entire brain. In species such as the snake, the grey mantle forms only a small segment but in man it folds itself into great wrinkles and convolutions to squeeze into the skull (see page 82). The neocortex is divided longitudinally into two hemispheres – the left and the right – linked by a mass of nerve fibres called the corpus callosum; these hemispheres are of approximately equal size but are bilaterally specialized (see Map 23). Each hemisphere is also subdivided by grooves called fissures and sulci, and folds known as gyri, into four lobes – the temporal (hearing and smell), the occipital (vision) and the parietal (skin, touch and body position) – which lie in the temples, the lower and higher back of the skull respectively, and the frontal lobe (speech, personality and abstract thought). The frontal lobe is divided from the three others by the central gyrus running from the top centre of the neocortex to a point just above the ears, and by the Sylvian fissure which curves upwards and backwards past the base of the central gyrus. Above and to the right of the central gyrus is the precentral gyrus containing the motor cortex, while the postcentral gyrus below and to the left contains the sensory cortex. The motor cortex sends signals that activate hands, legs, eyes, jaw and tongue; the sensory cortex receives sights, sounds, touch and other signals from the sense organs (see Map 18).

The structure of the brain and of its physiology have been mapped in a variety of ways including the direct stimulation of the brain with low-voltage electric current, the placing of electrodes within the brain or on the scalp to record the reaction of nerve cells to specific bodily stimuli, the systematic removal of different cells in the brains of monkeys to note relative impairment and the medical records of human surgery and brain damage. These experiments have yielded a number of results which are invaluable to the psychological interpretation of the mind and it is to these we now turn.

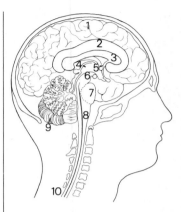

The small map above illustrates a cross-section of the left-hand side or left hemisphere of the human brain showing: 1. left cerebral hemisphere; 2. cingulate gyrus; 3. corpus callosum; 4. position of thalamus; 5. hypothalamus; 6. midbrain; 7. pons; 8. medulla; 9. cerebellum; 10. spinal cord.

The main map illustrates the right cerebral hemisphere enveloped in the neocortex or 'thinking cap'. This convoluted ravelled knot of grey matter is intersected by two large fissures, the Sylvian fissure and the central sulcus, and by smaller grooves (sulci) between folds (gyri) which divide it up into four specialized lobes (see text for functions). The precentral gyrus above and to the right of the central gyrus contains the motor cortex, while the postcentral gyrus below and to the left contains the sensory cortex. Both left and right hemispheres have identical structures but specialized functions (Map 23).

MAP REFERENCES
Brain research, 18, 21–5, 60;
Limbic system, 21, 23, 60;
Motor–sensory cortex, 18, 19, 25;
Neocortex, 18–19, 21, 23, 25;
Three brains, 21–2, 27, 47; Two hemispheres, 23–4, 29, 55, 60.

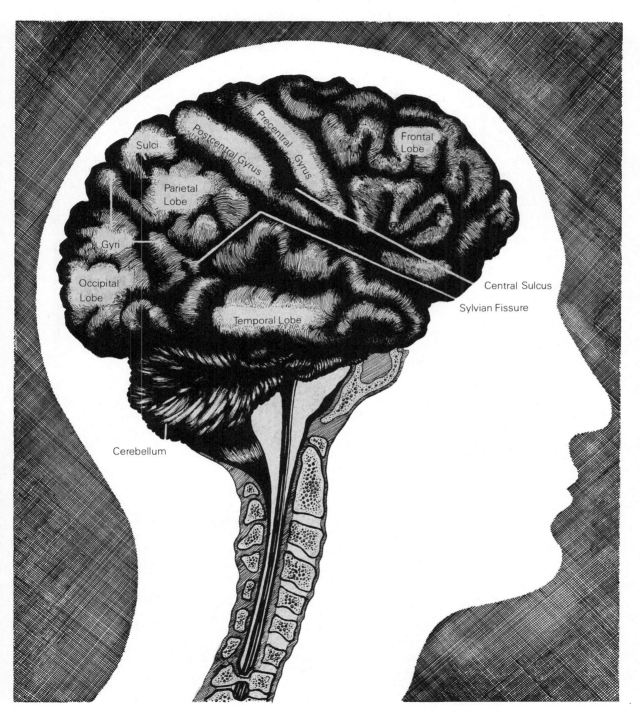

MAP 18

The Motor–Sensory Homunculus: The research of Wilder Penfield

The motor cortex and the sensory cortex lie immediately in front and behind the central fissure. It was Hughlings Jackson in the nineteenth century who first observed the connection between irritated areas in the sensory and motor cortex and the uncontrollable sensations and seizures in epileptic patients. More recently Wilder Penfield and colleagues in Montreal used electrical brain recordings to connect bodily stimuli with selective activity in different parts of the sensory cortex. Because of the seemingly simple one-to-one relationship between both cortical areas and touch or movement in various parts of the body, these areas of the brain are probably the most accurately mapped of any. They are known as 'projection areas' in contrast to three-quarters of the human cortex known as 'association areas'. The sensory cortex receives touch sensations before they are associated in other brain areas. The motor cortex transmits 'final' instructions for movement, received from the pre-motor cortex, after these have been associated. The images so projected are that of a little man, or homunculus, with those parts of his body which are most crucial for sensing or moving, vastly enlarged. Movement and sensation depend largely upon their source in the human brain, as opposed to their physical manifestation in the body. Hence one receives more sensation from the small lip area than from the large trunk area, an amputated limb may still tingle because the receptors remain in the brain, and those with diseases of the nervous system can sometimes 'smell', 'taste' or 'see' symptoms belonging to quite other senses.

Wilder Penfield's map of the motor–sensory cortex has been interpreted in various ways. The dominant view is that the motor–sensory cortex is mechanical, ie that the activity in the cortex signals the movement of muscles; Colin Blakemore recently referred to the motor cortex as 'a keyboard instrument, whose strings are muscles, which finally plays the melody of movement'. However, this view is being increasingly challenged by evidence that suggests it is the end states or purposes which are coded in the motor–sensory cortex and it is these which are transmitted. For example, different movements have been created by varying the density of stimulation, by varying the initial position of a limb, the cybernetic feedback from joints, and the overall state of the organism. The pattern of activity in the motor cortex is not, it now appears, a function of the muscles used, but of the *amount of force* required to complete an action. Karl Pribram (see Map 25) and some colleagues trained monkeys to open a complex latch box to obtain a peanut within. They then removed all or parts of the motor cortex in these animals. Slow-motion films showed the monkeys as able to move every muscle necessary to complete the task: the impairment was to the task itself, that is to actions necessary to achieve the outcome. Pribram believes that it is these completed movements which are coded in the cortex, and that the method of directly stimulating the brain by electric current produced only gross approximations of these signals.

This coding would help explain our motor equivalences. For example, we can crudely write 'Constantinople' with left hand, teeth, or toes, despite never having done it before; chimpanzees can build a facsimile of their nests out of newspaper and by unaccustomed methods if they must. The Swedish neuro-physiologist Ragnar Granit has recently amassed considerable evidence of this kind in *The Purposive Brain*. There are, it seems, high degrees of freedom and indeterminacy in the composition of an action, since it is the *overall purpose* or intentionality which is encoded. Recent studies of Soviet marksmen showed that they did not stand unusually still, rather their bodies were in a moving tension which held their guns still. The principle involved appears to be cybernetic, with the cortical area signalling a desired outcome of an organism–environmental relationship.

The map shows, left, a right hemisphere section of the sensory cortex and, right, a left hemisphere section of the motor cortex. The sensory cortex is the brain's main projection area for sensations of touch, heat, cold and pressure. The motor cortex despatches directions for movement to the body, which are synthesized in the pre-motor area directly in front of the cortex.

Note that both the sensory and motor cortex run in bands across both brain hemispheres, between the two fissures of Sylvian. The motor cortex is in front of the central fissure and faces the sensory cortex behind, hence their alternate names, the precentral and postcentral gyri. Just as this fissure divides receipt from despatch, so the division between the hemispheres allows independence to each arm, leg, and side of the body, which is controlled by the cortex opposite.

Wilder Penfield mapped both cortices by electrical recordings and stimulations. He found that the number of nerve fibres running from each was not proportionate to the size of limbs, organs or skin area, but to their use in sensing, and to the need for a fine coordination in movement. Hence a disproportionate area of the sensory cortex is given over to lips, fingers, hands, face and tongue, while the trunk and arms are greatly under-represented. Similarly a disproportionate area of the motor cortex is given over to jaws, eyes, ankles and toes. The result is the rather repellent homunculus on the left of the map.

MAP REFERENCES

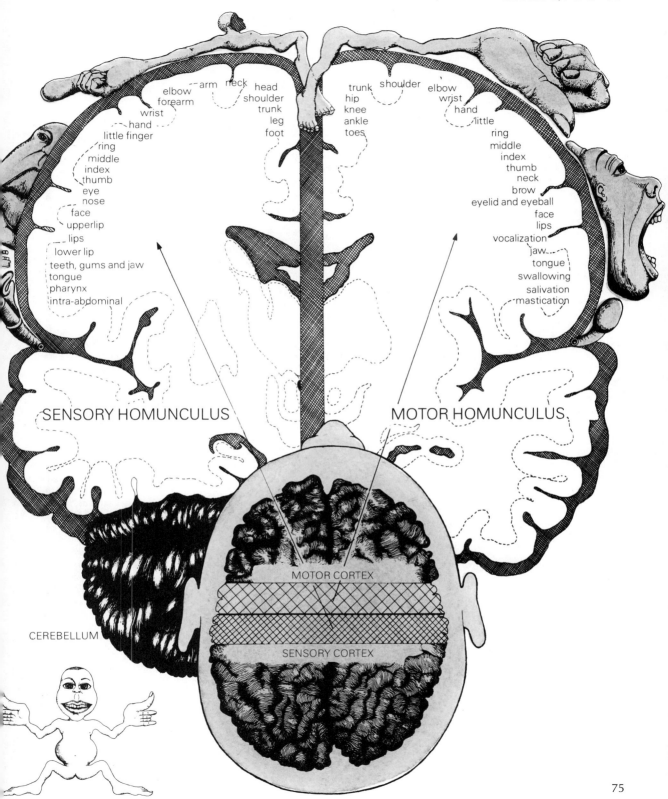

SENSORY HOMUNCULUS

MOTOR HOMUNCULUS

CEREBELLUM

MAP 19

The Reticular Activating System

More researchers are agreed on the crucial nature of the Reticular Activating System (RAS) than on how it is so crucial. It is generally agreed that the RAS is 'the alarm bell of the brain' without which we would remain comatose. Impulses travelling up the sensory nerve column to the cortex cannot be projected there unless the cortex is first aroused. The brush-like interconnections which feed from the sensory nerve column into the ascending reticular function assure that the brain is awakened to receive 'mainline' messages. Opposite lies the descending reticular function which similarly diverts impulses travelling from the motor cortex to limbs and muscles. Less is known about its working, but movements become jerky when the descending function is damaged. The RAS appears to adjust itself to personal requirements, thus a mother is alerted by the faint crying of her baby, and her elder child by the distant chimes of the icecream van.

The importance of the RAS to psychology lies in the facilitating and inhibiting functions located in the upper and lower parts of the system respectively. Stimulants such as amphetamines decrease inhibition and facilitate alertness, while sedatives have the opposite effect. H. J. Eysenck (see Map 20) has collected evidence which points to the greater inhibition of sensory input by extraverted personalities and the greater facilitation of these inputs by introverts. Stimulants will typically make the extravert more introverted by lowering his inhibition. Inhibition tends to accumulate during periods of focused attention upon stimuli, which is why the 'high inhibiting' extravert will periodically break off his attention and re-engage the environment in altered ways. He is 'stimulus hungry' yet needs to chop and change stimuli. The introvert lets in more sensation, seems absorbed in processing it, and is more suggestible. The RAS also affects the sympathetic and parasympathetic divisions of the autonomic nervous system. The first acts as an emergency reaction, the second as a calming, stabilizing response. We know that tranquilizers strengthen the parasympathetic division by way of the reticular formation. Hence the RAS must influence the dimensions stability–instability (or neuroticism) as well as introversion–extraversion. Questionnaires can be designed to measure these traits and the mean scores for deviant groups plotted to show that introverts tend to be teachable while extraverts inhibit incoming advice and are more likely to end in prison.

The Reticular Activating System (RAS), shown here as the cross-hatched area, is a net- or lattice-work of short-fibred nerve cells no larger than a finger, which lead from the spinal cord through the pons, to the base of the thalamus (the brain's relay station) and the hypothalamus (emotions and drives), see Map 17. From this point the RAS splays its impulses in all directions (dotted lines) like a general alarm that impartially awakens the entire cortex and its interconnections. The main sensory nerve column ascends along the (right) side of the RAS on its way to the sensory cortex, while the motor nerve column descends from the motor cortex along the other (left) side. Nevertheless both sensory and motor trunks have brush-like branches that feed into the RAS from either side to form the ascending reticular function and the descending reticular function, respectively. Nerve impulses which bypass the RAS cannot by themselves arouse 'the sleeping cortex', so that persons in whom the RAS fails to function fall into comas and permanent vegetative states. The upper portions of the system have been found to have facilitative effects which amplify and excite sensory and motor impulses. The lower portion of the system has inhibitory effects which reduce and calm such impulses. Mental balance may be vitally involved in the functions of the RAS. Neurotics appear to suffer from over-arousal of the sensory cortex, criminals from a mixture of under-arousal and stimulus hunger.

MAP REFERENCES
Mental balance, 20, 22, 30, 45–51; Motor–sensory cortex, 18; RAS, see also: central nervous system, 20, 22; extraversion–introversion, 10, 20; limbic system, 22; reptilian brain, 21; sympathetic–para-sympathetic systems, 20, 22.

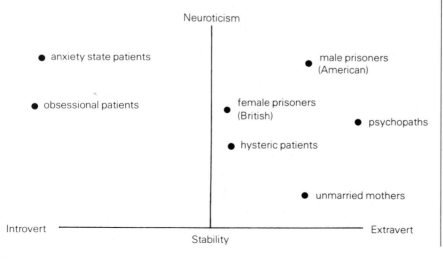

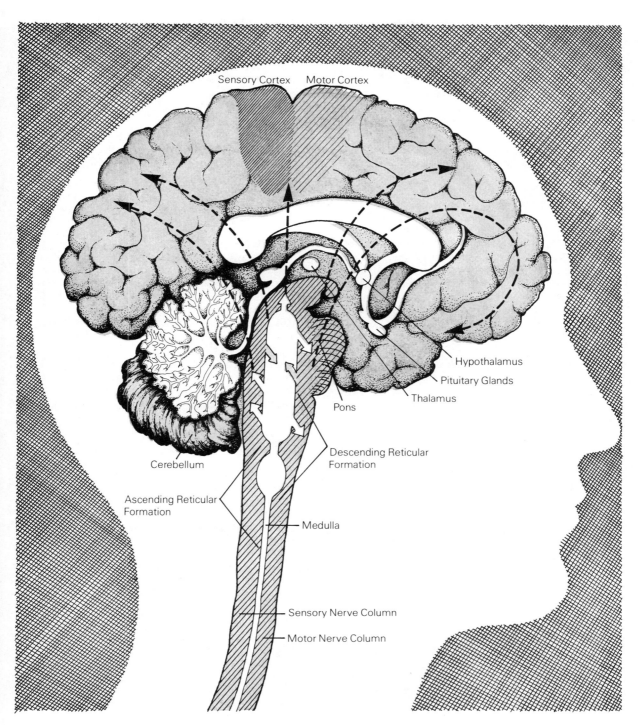

Sensory Cortex   Motor Cortex

Hypothalamus

Pituitary Glands

Thalamus

Pons

Descending Reticular
Formation

Cerebellum

Ascending Reticular
Formation

Medulla

Sensory Nerve Column

Motor Nerve Column

MAP 20

Eysenck's Demon:
Heredity and behaviour control

The viewpoints of most behaviourists are necessarily underrepresented in this book. This is because they generally disapprove of maps, models and schema being presented in advance of collecting sufficient evidence. A *logos* of the psyche will emerge, they argue, from the results of many more controlled experiments, rather like an archaeologist who searches for fragments and reassembles them. Those who rush to judgement are no friends of science. H. J. Eysenck is that rare exception, a map-making behaviourist. This is because he focuses on the inherited physiological factors of mental functioning upon which external stimuli impinge. For him the mind is not, therefore, the black box bequeathed us by Locke or the behaviourists J. B. Watson and B. F. Skinner, but contains inherent predispositions to over- and underreact in crucial ways. Eysenck also uses factor analysis to 'map' the personality of different individuals on dual-axis diagrams using the axes stability–instability and introversion–extraversion. As Eysenck puts it with his usual modesty, '. . . future research will undoubtedly uncover many more [variables] although it may be surmised that they will be of rather less generality and importance than the ones discussed here.'

Eysenck has chosen these two axes because it is known that both stability–instability and extraversion–introversion are functions of balance within the body's central nervous system. Stability–instability is a characteristic of the parasympathetic–sympathetic balance within the autonomic nervous system which controls heart-beat, respiration, tension and heat within the body. The sympathetic part of the autonomic system controls emergency reactions, by which we are aroused to deal with threat and anxiety so that our muscles are tense, more air is taken in, and blood is pumped faster around the body. The parasympathetic part has just the opposite effect. It lowers heart-beat and respiration, relaxes the muscles and induces states of calm. Persons vary considerably on this dimension of emotional reactivity. Those with relatively dominant sympathetic systems will be touchy, volatile, and excitable, which in stronger manifestations is called neurotic. The dimension introversion–extraversion has been traced to the ascending reticular formation (the place where the neural pathways of the central nervous system join the lower parts of the hindbrain) which has an amplifying–inhibiting function. Its precise mechanism is not yet known but Eysenck calls it his 'demon' (after Maxwell's demon), a symbolic 'creature' that regulates the amount of excitation reaching the brain by way of the reticular formation. According to Eysenck, extraverts inhibit this excitation and wrest the initiative, as it were, away from incoming messages, while introverts let in much more stimuli by way of their nervous systems and seem preoccupied by its internalization. Hence introverts will condition more easily, while extraverts resist the process, constantly shifting their attention and blocking the flow. By dint of superimposing his dual-axis grid over the diagram of the Four Humours (see map opposite), Eysenck has been able to coordinate his theories of physiology with the numerous human characteristics researchers have discovered over the last two decades; these characteristics correlate, in different degrees, with the stable–unstable, extravert–introvert coordinates.

A major vindication of Eysenck's approach has been the success enjoyed by Joseph Wolpe and other behaviour therapists in the treatment of 'unstable' anxiety reactions. By teaching relaxation techniques to bring emotional reactivity under the control of a learned, parasympathetic relaxation response, such therapists have enabled patients to relax in the presence of anxiety-inducing situations and to 'teach their bodies' that their former anxiety was groundless (see also Martin Luther King, Map 59).

To map his theory of heredity and behaviour, H. J. Eysenck has borrowed from Galen, the famed physician of Ancient Greece, the diagram of the Four Humours – Choleric (angry), Sanguine (cheerful), Phlegmatic (cool and self-possessed) and Melancholic (sad) – and placed them among the cross axes of two major physiological dimensions of inherited mental predispositions, unstable–stable and introverted –extraverted. He has then summarized more than two decades of American and British questionnaire research and personality inventories and has plotted those characteristics found to correlate in different degrees with his two major dimensions. Hence such words as 'passive', 'reserved', 'impulsive' and 'carefree' are points plotted on a graph, between the coordinates unstable–stable, introverted–extraverted. This procedure permits Eysenck to locate numerous kinds of persons. Male criminals, for example, tend to be unstable extraverts as do pyschopathic patients; they have conduct problems. Obsessional neurotics are unstable introverts as are those with general anxiety states; they have personality problems.

It is interesting to note how similar this map is to many others, despite Eysenck's habit of consigning pyschiatry to the categories of 'fiction', 'abuse' and 'nonsense'. Those who start with 'facts' and assemble them and those who employ intuitions of the whole seem to be converging.

MAP REFERENCES
Anxiety, 9, 13, 34, 49–50, 56, 59;
Ascending reticular function, 19;
Autonomic nervous system, 19, 22; Factor analysis, 31;
Introversion–extraversion, 10;
Relaxation response, 59.

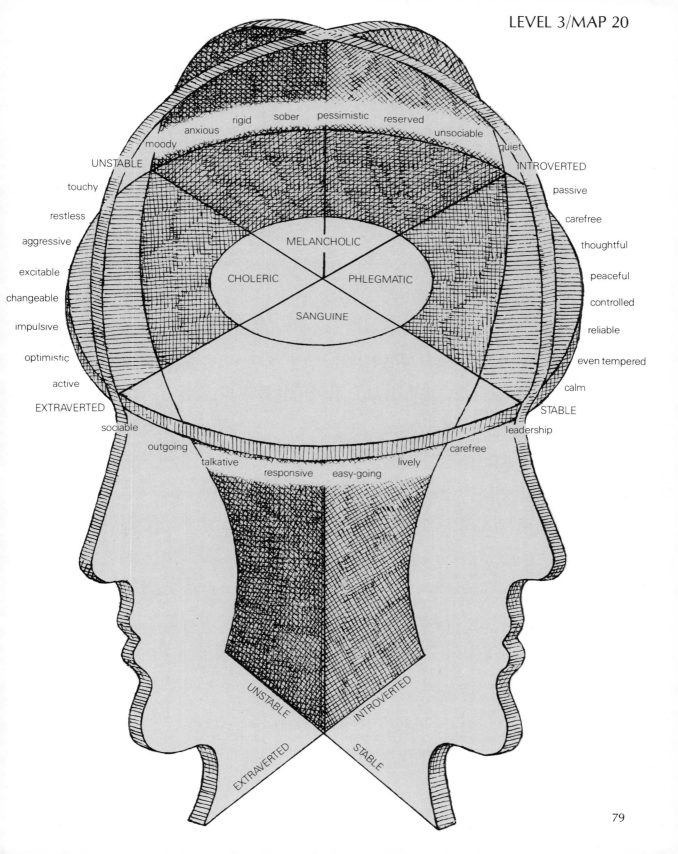

MAP 21

Lying down with a Horse and a Crocodile: The Papez–MacLean theory of brain evolution

Paul D. MacLean is head of the Laboratory for Brain Evolution and Behavior at the National Institutes for Mental Health near Washington, DC. Building on the earlier work of James W. Papez, MacLean has identified three distinct evolutionary stages in the development of the human brain. There is an ancient, basically reptilian brain, hardly touched by evolution, and found in prehistoric reptiles as well as in turtles, alligators and lizards today. In humans, this brain is located at and near the top of the brain stem. Encircling it is the old mammalian brain, consisting of the limbic system. We share this with lower mammals in general – rats, rabbits, kangaroos, horses, etc – whether monotremes (egg-laying), marsupials (pouch-bearing) or the more common placentals. Finally there is the new mammalian brain or neocortex, which is highly developed in primates, most especially *homo sapiens*. This wraps itself around the mammalian brain in a pattern of brain-within-brain. 'Speaking allegorically . . .' says MacLean, 'we might imagine that when a psychiatrist bids the patient to lie on the couch, he is asking him to stretch out alongside a horse and a crocodile'.

These three 'biological computers' are noticeably distinct in their structure and chemistry, which is revealed by the Golgi method of staining brain tissues. While the functions they perform are duplicate and overlap, they differ markedly in style. For the purpose of this comparison the two old brains will be amalgamated and compared to the neocortex.

The older brains seem involved in the ancestral lore of the species, ie hierarchies of dominance–submission, sexual courtship and display, follow-my-leader rituals, mass migration, ganging-up on the weak and the new, defending territory, hunting, hoarding, bonding, nesting, greeting, flocking and playing. The neocortex, in contrast, seems more adept at learning new ways to cope and adapt. If the limbic system is removed from monkeys, they do not seem incapable of any specific movements, rather they cease to resemble monkeys in their behaviour. The whole capacity to imitate the 'monkeyish style' is lost; all rituals cease. They will try to eat garbage, even burning matches, and to copulate with chickens. Jung would say they have lost their 'collective unconscious' (see Map 10).

While these older brains learn, remember and trigger motor activities, they seem 'id like' in their strivings, less unconscious than unable to verbalize their meaning beyond emotive expressions. The limbic cortex registers basic affects, hunger, thirst, etc, specific affects, pain, shock, repugnance, and general affects, those not tied closely to specific stimuli but motivating behaviours such as searching, aggression, protecting, caressing, rejoicing and sorrowing. These persist long after circumstances that incited them. In short, the limbic system has some 'intelligence of feeling'. If the limbic cortex is irritated by epilepsy, rabies infection, or experimentally stimulated, sudden gusts of rage, panic, pleasure or 'Eureka!' sensations can sweep over the organism, which may snarl, salivate, attack, or become addicted to pleasurable self-stimualtion. Such areas seem almost exclusive to the older brains, which also mediate the autonomic nervous system, the body's involuntary internal responses. In contrast the neocortex deals much more with voluntary movements, and with external and environmental events.

These three brains appear to have been successively *superimposed* upon one another. Unlike the claws that evolved into hands and the gills which evolved into lungs, each brain appears to have made some 'new starts' and replicated older functions. For example, the anencephalic monster is a baby born without a neocortex, yet strangely some have lived as long as four years, waking, sleeping, cooing, crying, digesting and smiling, sensate creatures which respond 'intelligently' to kindness and cruelty.

The human brain is in reality three brains, the reptilian, the old or paleomammalian and the neomammalian or neocortex, each successively superimposed over the earlier in a pattern of brains-within-brains. The structure of these older brains is part of a shared inheritance from the crocodile and the horse (or reptiles and mammals generally). The reptilian brain consists of the matrix of the brain stem, the midbrain, the basal ganglia and much of the hypothalamus and reticular activating system. It shows greatly enlarged furrowed structures and turns green in dye tests because of large amounts of dopamine, a transmitter substance. This brain is a slave to precedent and seems to contain the ancestral lore of the species.

The old mammalian brain consists of the limbic system and comprises two nearly concentric rings, one for each hemisphere, folded in upon a central core. Limbic means 'hemming in' or 'bordering around'. The whole is enclosed by the cingulate gyrus above and the parahippocampal gyrus beneath. The limbic brain registers rewards and punishments, is the seat of a variety of emotions and controls the body's autonomic nervous system. Over the limbic or mammalian brain lies the neocortex or 'thinking cap', a convoluted mass of grey matter which, spread out, reaches the size of a hearthrug. It is this latter brain, which, evolving with extraordinary rapidity, produced homo sapiens. Perhaps like the antlers of the Irish Elk or the shells of some turtles we are 'top heavy'. Is there chronic dissociation between our brains?

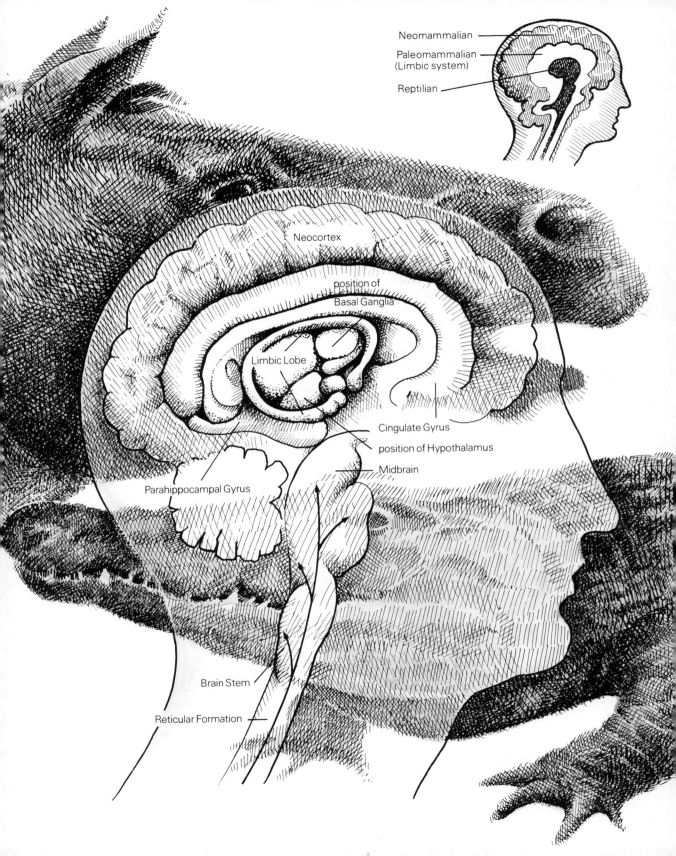

Neomammalian

Paleomammalian
(Limbic system)

Reptilian

Neocortex

position of
Basal Ganglia

Limbic Lobe

Cingulate Gyrus

position of Hypothalamus

Midbrain

Parahippocampal Gyrus

Brain Stem

Reticular Formation

MacLean's thesis, ably elaborated and supported by Arthur Koestler (see Map 27), is that the human brain as a whole suffers from a lethal 'design error', a quasi-schizophrenic split between reason and emotion, precipitated by inadequate coordination between the neocortex and the two older brains. Such error consists less in falling short of some arbitrarily imposed ideal, than of the recognition, common in evolutionary biology, of those impasses and dilemmas which have halted the evolution of whole species and doomed some to extinction. For example, spiders, scorpions and other arthropods developed their brains around their gullets, and so confront a dilemma. Their brains cannot grow without impeding their capacity to swallow, yet they need brains to find food. This conflict has led to the compromise, not reconciliation, of sucking blood or other fluids, a form of 'phylogenetic senility'. Similarly the koala bear, like other marsupials, lacks a corpus callosum, the nerve fibre which joins the left and right hemispheres of most mammalian brains. The koala, a victim of inadequate cerebral integration, has yielded before countless rivals, and survives only in Australia where he is left, in Koestler's words, 'clinging to his eucalyptus like a discarded hypothesis'.

The human brain is well integrated laterally by the great cerebral commisure which joins its hemispheres, but can the same be said for its vertical integration between the two older brains and the neocortex? This neocortex started to grow prodigiously in the second half of the Pleistocene age, that is about half a million years ago, an unprecedented rapidity and degree of evolutionary change, that could well have thrown the brain out of balance. We suffer, MacLean believes, from 'schizophysiology', a constitutional dissociation between newer and older brains. MacLean argues from studies of limbic epilepsy where seizures confine themselves to the limbic system. Just as epileptic seizures do not cross from one brain hemisphere to another when the corpus callosum is cut, so the mammalian brain appears to contain its disturbances as if cut off. Seizures induced by irritating the limbic cortex of monkeys have confirmed this. Anatomically, MacLean has shown the vertical connections between the limbic systems and the neocortex are relatively few, indirect and slow to react.

If MacLean were correct about this dissociation between our outer cerebral thinking-cap and our inner visceral awareness, would not Dissociated Man know his environment better than himself, and haunt his own body like the ghost in the machine? The growth curve for science and technology would grow exponentially; while ethics remained with Confucius, Buddha or Christ. Two major religions might share a myth of ethical harmony and innocence until a fatal choice was made by Representative Man using *reason* instead of *ethical sensibility*, an 'original sin' that dooms posterity to persistent error (see Map 4). Tradition in this culture might locate precise thoughts in the mind, but vague emotions in the heart, breast, bowels, blood, nerves or viscera (which are indeed controlled by the limbic or mammalian brain). Famous psychoanalysts might rightly insist that deep within us is a quite different, dumb, dark yet powerful mind, binding us to some ancestral superego, and which, full of resistances, fastens tenaciously on symbols which express its feelings. Such a culture might be split between cerebral conceptions of science and the expressive arts, the two barely on speaking terms. The first would dismiss as 'not meaningful' all emotive utterances, the second would boast of 'intellectuals', a term excluding Albert Einstein, and which appeared to consist of deathless prose mounted precariously upon passionate premises. Plausibly this culture might divide itself internationally into political blocs, the first celebrating the either/or of individual choice between empirical propositions, the second espousing the dialectical movement of conflicting values. All the confident

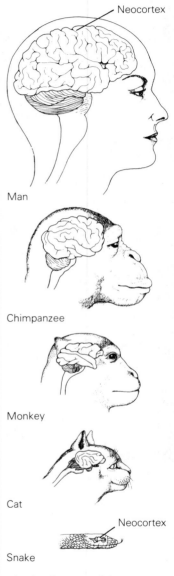

Man

Chimpanzee

Monkey

Cat

Snake

The development of the neocortex or 'thinking cap'.

'Let the biologists go as far as they can and let us go as far as we can. Some day the two will meet.'
'The Origins of Psychoanalysis'
Sigmund Freud

'Gay Talese in "The Kingdom and the Power" pointed out that where one sits in the "New York Times' newsroom is never a casual matter . . . How did these highly educated people learn to behave this way – from reading Llewellyn Evans' description of a hierarchical struggle of black lizards living on a cemetery wall?'
'Evolutionary Trends of the Triune Brain' Paul D. MacLean

promises that Reason and Enlightenment would for ever banish superstition, mysticism and residual religious beliefs would stumble over that other quality in the depth of the human mind, that 'heart' which, in the words of Pascal, 'has its own reasons, of which reason knows not'.

To a considerable extent it would be a war of metaphors, between the straight line of progress, the linearity of causes and effects, and the conception of a circle, cycle, mandala, a meeting of Alpha and Omega. This is powerfully suggested by comparing the motor–sensory cortex (see Map 19) wherein the genitals keep a respectable distance from the head, face and tongue, with the limbic (mammalian) system where the anal–genital, oral and olfactory areas come nearly full circle into close proximity, reminding more than one investigator of Uroboros, the self-devouring snake of paradox (see Map 22). But it is important not to fall into the ancient error of positing a demon within, or even the Victorian nightmare of the beast in man. It only compounds error to consider either the inner brains or the outer cortex as 'savage' or 'repressive' respectively. Animals are, in any case, far less lethal and genocidal than human beings, and they respect surrender signals from their own species while humans kill already vanquished fellows in cold blood. We have to bring the brains together, a process MacLean sees as involved in creativity, wherein dissociated brains are bisociated (see Map 27).

If the answer is to combine the brains, then championing Natural or Cerebral Man is one more symptom of the original pathology. This pathology starts with free-floating anxieties and accumulating affects which the rational neocortex is helpless to control, since ultimate concerns are insoluble by technical reason. Anxieties and incohate yearnings cannot find objects and outlets for their own discharge, but turn instead to pseudo targets falsely concretized, like Jews blamed for the Great Depression. 'Better a terrible end than an endless terror', as the Brownshirts used to say. But paranoid vindictiveness, scapegoating and obsessional rituals only add guilt and frustration to incubating rage. If technical reason were enough, could not those with phobias and obsessions calm the mounting panic in their own nervous systems when the dreaded objects approached? As it is their bodies won't obey. The ultimate holocaust is reached when such absurd hypotheses as the genetic inferiority of Jews, join with the technologizing and organizing powers of the neocortex to make the incredible true by systematic murder. We have reached the point where we are powerful enough to 'redeem' visceral prejudices by mutilating society to fit them.

But *is* MacLean right? I prefer to think of anatomy as tendency rather than destiny. If we can but discover a logic of emotions, the few connections between the neocortex and the older brains may yet prove enough. To this we now turn.

MAP REFERENCES
Creativity, 26–31; Genocidal man, 15, 22, 50, 56–8; Hierarchical view, 33, 38, 41, 47, 55; Limbic lobe, 22; Older brains: as holarchies, 47; as unconscious, 9, 10, 15; Splitting, 6, 12, 23–4, 48–50.

MAP 22
Runaway in the Limbic System

The limbic system is concerned with attention, emotion, learning and resulting memories. It mediates messages received from the outer environment on their way to the neocortex, suffusing these with moods ranging from rose-coloured anticipation to dark disappointment, as when an anxious mother meeting a train sees her son's resemblance in every passing boy. Despite many problems in isolating functions within the limbic system there is general agreement upon its homeostatic and equilibriating principles of operation. Investigators have tentatively identified areas mediating between rage–fear, fight–flight, pleasure–pain, expectation–actuality, tension–relaxation, etc. For example, when the upper limbic ring is stimulated in monkeys, grooming, courtship, sexual and affectionate responses occur, while stimulating the lower limbic ring evokes revulsion and antagonism. But the chief concern here is with mounting evidence that the limbic system can 'oscillate' or 'run away'. These terms are borrowed from cybernetics and general systems theory, and refer to a mode of pathological feedback by which the system instead of regulating itself as through a thermostat progressively destabilizes and disintegrates itself instead (see Map 45).

If we take just two dimensions from Map 22 and draw a feedback loop thus.

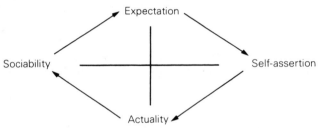

The expectation which I assert changes the social actualities which changes my expectations . . . Normally the poles of expectation–actuality, self-assertion –sociability are mutually restraining and in complementarity. But suppose I joined a gang in which my popularity (or sociability) depended on how mercilessly I clubbed old women who frustrated my expectations of snatching their purses. In this event sociability–self-assertion as a single dimension of my system goes into 'runaway'. Within the limbic system Karl Pribram found a capacity for 'rebound' or 'answering effect', while E. Gellhorn found that in disturbed states one division of the autonomic system could trigger responses in its opposite. This is essentially similar to the oscillations between 'true' and 'false' selves (see Map 14). We have only to consider the other dimensions of limbic equilibria described on the map opposite, and we could characterize most known forms of psychological and social pathology as oscillations which cause different dimensions to 'run away'.

Whence the origin of such disturbances? Is it the anatomical dissociation between the limbic system and the neocortex discussed in Map 21? Perhaps, but clearly the two brains operate on quite different principles, which are more than the differences between 'reason' and 'emotion'. By habit, not necessity, we think in linear terms of cause and effect, subjects-acting-on-objects, and the exclusive options of the computer's on/off switches. In contrast, the limbic system is in dialectical balance and operates on cybernetic principals which encompass all variables involved in a rational–emotional synthesis. The Triumph of the Will, Classless Millenias, Eternal Vigilance and being stronger-than-the-bottle are all symptoms of linear, neocortical excess that sends the limbic system into 'runaway'. 'The heart has its own reasons . . .' which Reason sends haywire.

The limbic system is equivalent to the old mammalian brain, bounded above by the cingulate gyrus (Map 21). Here seen in exploded view, the upper and lower rings of the limbic lobe clutch the thalamus like a claw. Across this 'cellar of the brain' has been superimposed eight of the dimensions which various investigators believe that the limbic system holds in balance, to maintain an equilibrium of mood and emotion. These include rage–fear, thought to be mediated by the amygdaloid bodies, fight–flight, which has been precipitated by stimulating the rear areas of the hypothalamus and pleasure (reward)–pain (punishment) located in the septum pelcidum and certain areas of the lower limbic ring respectively. The hippocampus has been found to mediate differences between expectation–actuality. So long as these differences remain minor the hippocampus inhibits the reticular activating system (Map 19), but no sooner do major differences emerge than the RAS is released to awaken the entire cortex to these discrepancies, thereby influencing tension–relaxation.

1. Septum Pelucidum
2. Mammillary Bodies
3. Fornix
4. Hippocampus
5. Parahippocampal Gyrus
6. Amygdaloid Bodies

MAP REFERENCES
Dialectics, 3, 22–3, 53–5, 57–60; Runaway, see: catastrophe theory, 56; 'infernal dialectics', 47; oscillation, 14, 22, 34, 43, 48–51, 56–8, 60; schismogenesis, 48–50, 57–60.

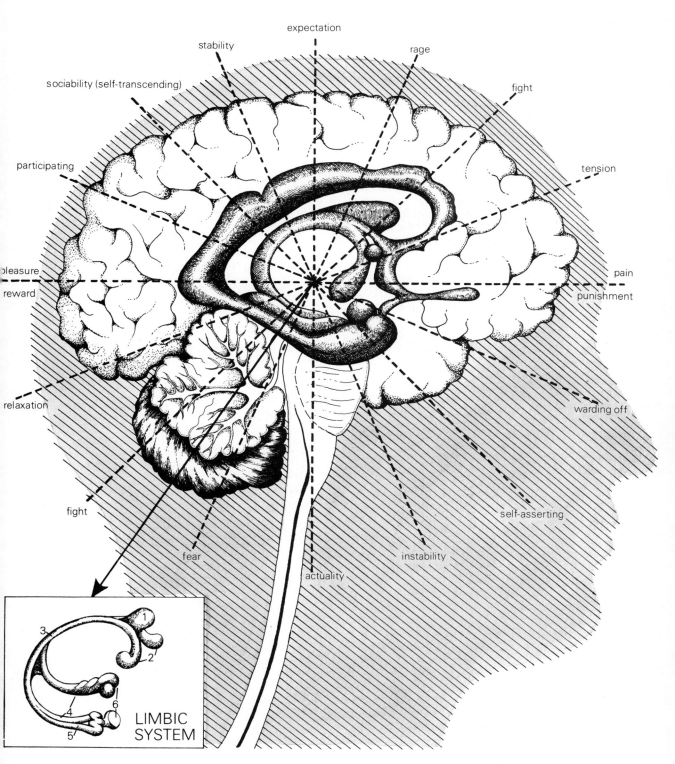

expectation

stability

rage

sociability (self-transcending)

fight

participating

tension

pleasure

pain

reward

punishment

relaxation

warding off

fight

self-asserting

fear

instability

actuality

LIMBIC
SYSTEM

MAP 23

The Mind-Splitters: The left and right hemispheres of the brain

Since the nineteenth century neurologists and brain surgeons have noted that tumours and excisions within the left hemisphere of the brain produce quite different effects on the patients' mental abilities than tumours or excisions made in the right hemisphere. Left hemisphere damage has long been associated with aphasia, the loss of language function, while right hemisphere damage so disturbs the patients' sense of body image that they cannot dress themselves, cannot orient themselves spatially and often cannot even recognize familiar faces.

More recently patients with lesions in particular parts of their two hemispheres have been tested for mental functioning and dexterity. Damage to parts of the left hemisphere impedes speech, language, verbal memory, mathematics and the sense of time; it also tends to be specific to certain organs and functions. Damage to the right hemisphere impedes performance in understanding visual and tactile mazes, perception of depth and movement, visuo-spatial organization, and tends to produce diffuse and general patterns of disturbance.

Even greater interest and excitement was aroused by the research of Roger Sperry, Joseph Bogen and Michael Gazzaniga on patients subject to severe epileptic seizures. These patients underwent radical surgery that severed the corpus callosum, a thick network of nerves joining the two halves of the brain. The purpose was to prevent the epileptic seizures dominating the entire brain, since with 'half a brain' patients could still take medication or summon help. What surprised the surgeons were the apparently small effects of so major an operation. It took a series of carefully constructed experiments to reveal that there are two separate minds within a single patient, a left hemisphere controlling the right-hand side of the body, a right hemisphere controlling the left-hand side of the body.

For instance, if a patient who has undergone the split-brain operation is given a pencil to hold in his right hand, where he cannot see it, he can immediately describe it as a pencil, since the right hand connects to the verbal left hemisphere. But if the pencil is placed in the left hand, the silent right hemisphere, unable to instruct the left, cannot describe the pencil. It is possible, using a tachistoscope, to beam messages exclusively to those parts of the left or right eye which are cross-connected to the right and left hemispheres. Thus the word HEART was flashed in such a way that HE was exposed to the right hemisphere and ART to the left. When asked to verbalize what they had seen, patients replied 'ART', but when asked to point with the left hand to a chart with several words, they pointed to 'HE'.

These experiments reveal not just the functional autonomy and highly developed division of labour between hemispheres, but also an extremely ténacious integrative tendency, which even major surgery only partially disturbs. The reason for using a tachistoscope in the HEART experiment is that given more than a second the eyes will scan the whole word. For the same reason the pencil-holding experiment will only work if the hands are extended through a screen, so that the eyes cannot 'help each other'. Even with eyes frustrated, the hands will try to help each other: the right hand, which is attached to clues processed verbally by the left hemisphere, will try to 'correct' the left hand!

After their operations patients can continue to write language with their right hands, as we would expect, but they can no longer draw properly, having lost the visuo-spatial capacity of the right hemisphere, which can no longer direct the right hand. In contrast, they can still draw with their left hands, after a fashion, although they are unable to write language. The researchers also found phenomena that suggested an unconscious mind split from the conscious one. For example, when a nude figure was unexpectedly beamed, via a tachistoscope, to those parts of the eyes connected to the right hemisphere, a female patient was likely to blush,

The human brain is divided into two hemispheres, the left and the right, joined in the centre by a large nerve track called the corpus callosum. When surgically sectioned, information received by one hemisphere is not known to the other, and patients have two uncoupled minds in a single skull. Most of the left eye, the left ear and the left-hand side of the body are connected to the right brain. Most of the right eye, the right ear and the right-hand side are connected to the left brain. The two hemispheres process information in quite contrasting modes. The left thinks analytically, discreetly and reductively. It is aware of temporal sequences and linearity and is involved in language and mathematics. The right hemisphere thinks holistically, synthetically, diffusely, processes inputs simultaneously and visuo-spatially and recognizes patterns and faces. The two modes follow the historic dispute in psychology between behaviourism and gestalt. Culturally the left hand has been associated with sinister, dark and illegitimate doings, while the right is straightforward. Neurologists have long called the right brain the 'minor hemisphere' and recent research supports left-hemisphere domination. Performance can be improved by giving the right brain an artificial advantage to restore 'equality'.

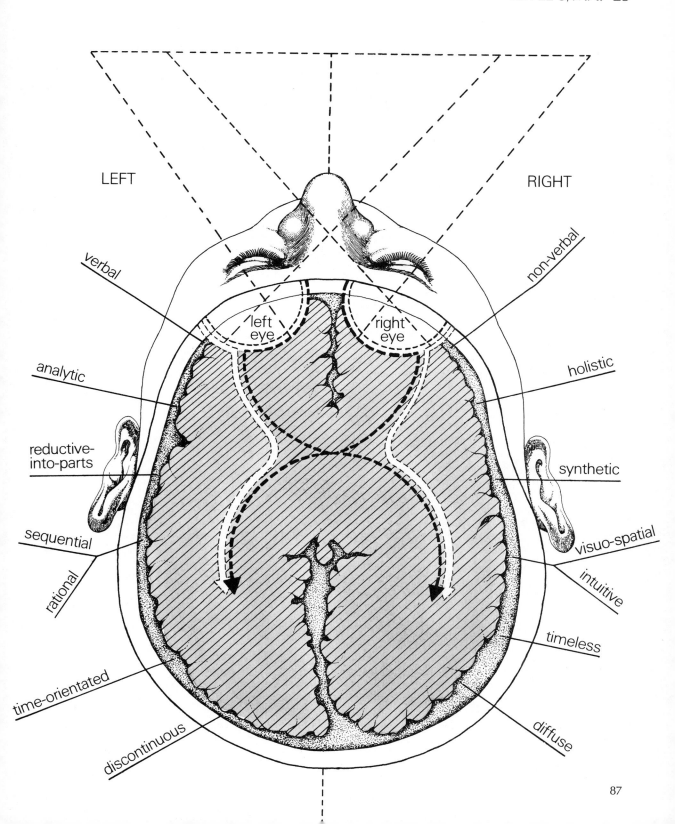

LEFT

RIGHT

verbal

non-verbal

left eye

right eye

analytic

holistic

reductive-into-parts

synthetic

sequential

visuo-spatial

rational

intuitive

timeless

time-orientated

diffuse

discontinuous

wriggle with embarrassment and say, 'What a funny machine you have there, Dr Sperry!' But the same patient cannot say what she has seen! The surgery has repressed conscious awareness, but not the feelings of impropriety that the image aroused. Similarly split-brain patients will declare 'I am not angry!' while their expression and body posture clearly indicate that they are.

Research has now gone far beyond these early experiments and has revealed hemisphere specialization in normal volunteers. Biofeedback instruments, which register the degree of electric discharge from the brain cells, show increased alpha rhythms in whichever hemisphere is resting, together with heightened electric discharge in the hemisphere that is working. Ask someone a verbal or mathematical problem and the left hemisphere begins to 'fire'. Present them a visuo-spatial problem and the right hemisphere 'fires'. Eye movements also correlate with hemisphere specialization. The eyes will typically move away from the more engaged hemisphere towards the side of the body controlled by that hemisphere, so that a lawyer rising to present his brief will glance to his right, a ballet dancer rising on her points will glance left.

Hemisphere specialization appears to be an endowment that is unique to human maturity. Neither other primates nor human infants are specialized. Indeed a small infant can lose an entire hemisphere and grow up normally – an extraordinary testimony to the organism's integrative capacities – but increasingly serious impairment results from losing either hemisphere after the age of about two or three. Most investigators have attributed hemispheric specialization to human language acquisition. There now appears to be an embryonic language capacity in the right hemisphere curiously similar to the Yin-Yang (see Map 3), with each half containing the seed of its opposite. By the same token it would be an error to conceive of the two hemispheres as containing homuncili, ie little musicians dancing in the right, mathematicisns wrangling in the left. Rather, both hemispheres show some activity almost all the time. They merely process information differently and in varying levels of relative intensity. There is some recent, but still sketchy, evidence concerning the effect of drugs. Generally speaking they seem to 'turn on' the right hemisphere, or in some cases, as with amphetamines, accelerate activity in the left. Yoga, Zen and other esoteric religious exercises seem to energize the right hemisphere by frustrating the left, or by narrowing it to extinction through meditative concentration. We can summarize the evidence by saying that in 95% of the population (who are right-handed, bilaterally specialized) the two hemispheres process information in the contrasting modes as follows:

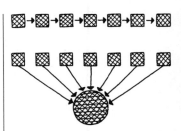

Simultaneous processing (bottom) is typical of the right hemisphere, linear processing (top) of the left hemisphere.

LEFT HEMISPHERE
Verbal, analytic, reductive-into-parts, sequential, rational, time-orientated and discontinuous.

RIGHT HEMISPHERE
Non-verbal, holistic, synthetic, visuo-spatial, intuitive, timeless and diffuse.

The discovery of the significance of the two hemispheres is clearly of momentous importance. The question as to whether introspection and insight into the nature of the human mind is worth while, or even possible, appears to have been emphatically affirmed. For the things that physiological investigation has now discovered, the minds of men have long intuited. From the Yin-Yang of Ancient China to the rock and whirlpool of Ancient Greece we have known, if darkly, that we are suspended between poles, meeting at cross-roads, hanging on crucifixes or meeting on narrow ridges. The table opposite summarizes some of the dual conceptions of the psyche in this book:

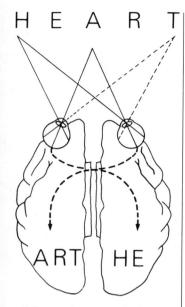

H E A R T

ART HE

If the word HEART is flashed momentarily to a split-brain patient, so that HE is exposed to the left eye (and hence to the right hemisphere) and ART to the right eye (and hence the left hemisphere), when the patient is asked what he has seen the verbal left hemisphere says ART while the silent right hemisphere selects, with the left hand, the word HE from several displayed on a board.

MAP NO	AUTHORITY	LEFT HEMISPHERE	RIGHT HEMISPHERE
1	Homer	Scylla	Charybdis
2	Greek Tragedy	*Hubris*	*Nemesis*
3	*I Ching*	Yang	Yin
		Time	Space
		Day	Night, etc
4	Genesis	Human Purpose	Unified Eden
6	Descartes	Mind	Body
8	Bakan	Agency	Community
9	Freud	Conscious	Unconscious
		Ego	Id
		Secondary process	Primary process
10	Jung	Thinking	Feeling
		Sensation	Intuition
		Persona	*Shadow*
12	Camus	Solitary	Solidary
13	May	Positivist	Existential
14	Laing	False self	True self
15	Becker	Denial of Death	Death
26	Blake	Natural Religion	Fourfold Vision
27	Koestler	*Sauter*	*Reculer*
		Commissar	Yogi
		Robot	Lotus
		Outlook	Insight
28	Getzels/ Jackson/ Hudson	Convergent thinking	Divergent thinking
29	de Bono	Vertical thinking	Lateral thinking
35	Buber	I-it	I-thou
39	Korzybski	Territory	Map
40	Russell	Object-level	Meta-level
41	Chomsky	Surface Structure	Deep Structure
46	Salk	Ego	Being
54	Kuhn	Normal Science	Paradigm Change
55	Varela	Tree	Net
57	Lévi-Strauss	Positive	Mythic

MAP REFERENCES
Binary concepts, hung between poles, see also moral dilemma, 5, 12–15, 22, 24–5, 28–31, 38, 43, 55–60; Optimizing brains, 1–3, 29, 40–42, 60; Split brain, 24, 28–9, 30, 55, 59, 60.

A whole additional theme concerns the pathology of splitting, that is, the incapacity of the two hemispheres to integrate their activities. This has been variously symbolized by the Fall of Man between the categories of good and evil (Map 4), the rending of the Veil of the Temple (Map 5), Mind–Body dualism (Map 6), denial and splitting mechanisms of the mind (Map 8), the split-off shadow (Map 9), the schizoid break (Map 11), the shutting out of death (Map 15), the division between the 'old brain' and the neocortex (Map 21), the Anomalous Monster (Map 40) and schismogenesis and 'double binding' (Maps 49, 50).

Finally we are vitally and ultimately concerned with hemispheric relationships (whether mental or geographical). The optimal manner in which these might relate is the concern of symmetry (Map 1), dialectic (Map 2), harmony (Map 3), archetypal unity and symbolization (Map 10), bisociation and holons (Map 27), creative synthesis (Map 24), congruence (Map 32), dialogue (Map 35), multi-levelled logical types (Map 40), synergy (Map 42), sigmoid curves (Map 47), Janus-facedness (Map 48), imbrication (Map 55), and so on.

MAP 24

Gods, Voices and the Bicameral Mind: The theories of Julian Jaynes

Julian Jaynes, a professor of psychology at Princeton, is responsible for the most intriguing and extensive thesis yet to emerge from brain research. Did our ancestors have god-directed minds? Is consciousness little more than 3,000 years old? He starts by asking what consciousness is — that irradicable difference between what others see and our own sense of self. Consciousness is not the same as being awake. To be knocked 'unconscious' is to lose many automatic functions. It is not continuity since even 'stream of consciousness' is full of gaps. The Cartesian notion of 'the helpless spectator' asks us to believe that the intensification of consciousness during decisions has nothing at all to do with outcomes. We know that we can learn, judge, think abstractly and even generalize without consciousness (see Map 9). Many skills like oratory, music and skiing fail us when consciousness interferes. Einstein had so many creative ideas while shaving that he would cut himself with surprise.

Jaynes' solution is that consciousness is a metaphor, a relationship between two or more unlike experiences joined by likenesses. The countryside 'blanketed by snow' is more than a superficial connection. It teems with associations, contours, warmth, protection, slumber, and an awakening in spring. Consciousness is a lexical field, whose terms are metaphors or analogues of behaviour in the physical world. We project syntheses of associations into an imagined screen within our heads. Consciousness has thus the relationship of a map to a territory, as when in the 'pith' and 'kernel' of Jaynes' thesis he mounts metaphors on metaphors in levels of abstraction (see Maps 39–40). The origins of even our most basic verbs are metaphorical. 'To be' is from Sanskrit *bhu* 'to grow'. 'Am' and 'is' derive from *amsi* 'to breathe'. Thus the metaphor of our being is literally stretched like a screen between brain hemispheres and between referents like growing, breathing and standing out (*ex-istere*). Conscious being is the relationship between these, a 'between'.

Jaynes sees consciousness as right–left brain synthesis with five characteristics: 1. *Spatialization*, when we stretch out dimensions of time and space. 2. *Excerption*, by which maps record only selected parts of the territory. 3. The *analogue 'I' and 'me'*, a projected personification of ourselves moving in space and time which anticipates doing and being done by. 4. *Narratization*, wherein events are selected for their congruence and sequential unfolding. 5. *Conciliation*, wherein experiences are consciously assimilated to each other.

With consciousness so defined we must recognize that in a book like the *Iliad* (shorn of its later accretions), human beings are not conscious at all! Words are not used metaphorically, but have only their original concrete referents from which consciousness later developed. Hence *psyche* in the *Iliad* means 'breath', not soul or conscious mind as it meant by the sixth century BC. *Thumus* means motion or agitation of limbs not emotional sensibility. *Nous* means simple perception not the imaginal mind, and so on. Jaynes believes that the world of the *Iliad*, indeed the whole known world of theocratic god–kings, prior to about 1500 BC was possessed of a *bicameral mind*, split in two, with a right hemisphere, executive part called a god, and a left hemisphere, follower part, called a man. Gods ordered men to act, directly or through priests and men obeyed. There was no argument, love or personal relationship with divine executors.

For the most part such minds would operate, learn, think, react and retain equilibrium as ours do, unconsciously. But when something unexpected happened and hence stressful, instead of a period of intense consciousness, with inner deliberation and argument, bicameral man would receive a god-like command from his right hemisphere instructing him to act, as Zeus ordered Agamemnon to attack before the walls of Troy. This is essentially similar to the reported auditory

Achilles directed by the goddess Athena, before the walls of Troy, to attack Hector. Throughout the 'Iliad' and in the surviving fragments of writing before the first millennia BC, there is little evidence that people were conscious. Jaynes argues that human brains from about 9000 to 1000 BC were bicameral, ie that the known halucinatory area in the right temporal lobe processed information intuitively and issued auditory, god-like commands through the anterior commissure to Wernicke's area in the left hemisphere, where the message was relayed or enacted.

In short, the brain was split in a manner similar to schizophrenic functioning, save that sociologically schizophrenics today are withdrawn, stigmatized and relapsed, while in bicameral ages collective cognitive imperatives sanctioned divine commands. Even contemporary schizophrenics have capacities reminiscent of archaic man. A majority of those not on Thorazine report matter-of-fact auditory hallucinations. Schizophrenics surpass normals on sensory perception, allowing themselves to be flooded. Many show the kind of endurance needed to build pyramids, with greater attentiveness in their right hemispheres than normals. Their somewhat thicker corpus callosi may produce greater reciprocal inhibition by one hemisphere of the other, in any event they switch between hemispheres less frequently, and when their left hemispheres become confused or deprived of stimulation, they switch more readily to the right. Theatrical hypnotism, with audiences reinforcing suggestions, is another modern echo of bicameral antiquity.

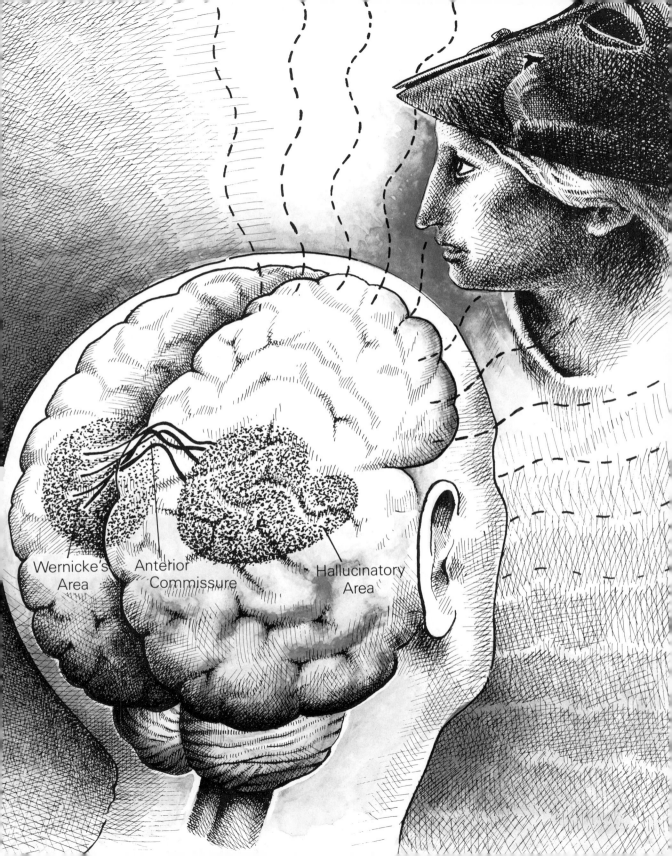

Wernicke's Area

Anterior Commissure

Hallucinatory Area

hallucinations in schizophrenia, which are frequently accurate comments on events, and which Jaynes regards as partial relapses to an earlier state of ancestral bicamerality. Just as contemporary psychotics have a low stress tolerance, combined with an existing schizoid form of personality organization, so that breaks occur readily, so bicameral civilizations heard stress-precipitated commands at almost every crisis point. The remarkable unanimity of such mass action is a consequence of pre-structured collective beliefs, just as the patients of phrenologists oblige with behaviour appropriate to the bump being magnetized and research has found that hypnotized subjects confine themselves to actions which they considered 'possible' and 'permissible' before hypnosis began.

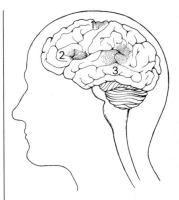

1. *Supplementary Motor Area*
2. *Broca's Area*
3. *Wernicke's Area*

Were whole peoples once organized by a mixture of hallucinated voices and hypnotic suggestions? Incredible? Jaynes has amassed considerable circumstantial evidence to which this precis cannot do justice. Recall from Map 23 that speech areas are almost entirely confined to the left hemisphere (that is for the 95% of the population which is right handed). This high degree of hemisphere specialization is peculiarly human, and is generally attributed to language acquisition. There are three major language areas (see diagram), the supplementary motor area, Broca's areas, low down on the left frontal lobe, and Wernicke's area, mostly in the posterior part of the left temporal lobe. The latter seems the most crucial, since extensive damage involves permanent loss of language function, while equivalent damage to the right temporal lobe produces deficit, despite the near-identity of neural structures. However, persons with left temporal lobe damage at birth utilize their right hemispheres to acquire language, so what is this vast under-utilized area for?

Jaynes believes that during a crucial period in our evolution, at the very time that language was being acquired by the left hemisphere, the right temporal lobe was pre-empted for the issuance of god-like commandments, across the thin anterior commissure that joins the two temporal lobes like a private corpus callosum. Auditory commands would have been the most economical code for getting elaborate information processing through so small a channel.

When this hallucinatory area was stimulated by an electric current in recent experiments by Wilder Penfield, subjects would hear voices (and sometimes have visions) addressing them. One typical subject exclaimed, 'That man's voice again! My father's . . . and it frightens me!' Others heard voices to the accompaniment of music, chanting or singing, which would criticize, advise, command, but they were consistently other than the hearer, often a dead relative or friend. We also know that while the right hemisphere cannot speak, or barely so, it can comprehend and interpret quite complicated instructions. Patients with strokes in their left hemisphere can obey their doctors or researchers in detail.

Recall also that when the corpus callosum between the hemispheres is severed or communication anaesthetized, one hemisphere can try and 'help' the other in the manner of two, independent persons. The left hemisphere feeling a frown on the face, produced by the right hemisphere, whose left hand knows the answer, will be prompted to change its verbal answer. It is like Athena taking Achilles in hand. For in many respects the right hemisphere acts in god-like ways. It is timeless, immediate, visionary, coherent, with recognizable forms and faces. It responds to over-arching purposes and grand designs and has an affinity for music, rhythm, cadence and patterns in general. It binds people together (religion is from *religare* 'to bind') and its intuitive style is given to inspiration and seeming miracle.

How could bicamerality have evolved? There was no one to cut the corpus callosum. Jaynes argues from studies that reveal the great plasticity of the brain to

'. . . all good poets, epic as well as lyric, composed their beautiful poems not by art, but because they are inspired and possessed. . . . There is no invention in him until he has been inspired and is out of his senses.'

'The Republic' Plato

'Why is it that when a person speaks to God it's prayer, but when God speaks to a person it's schizophrenia?'

Old joke

changes in environment. Persons with their brains damaged have developed additional areas to overcome injuries. The principle of natural selection could well have given an advantage over several millenia to persons bicamerally organized. They may have evolved from small groups of hunter-gatherers into whole communities remotely controlled by the internalized voices of god–kings, a form of social control far more sophisticated than the signs and calls of earlier primates, and one that allowed for the development of language.

Jaynes dates bicameral man from the Natufian settlement at Eynan just north of the Sea of Galilee, discovered in 1959. Those parts of it which date from 9000 BC show town settlements theocratically organized around the burial mounds of god–kings. Thenceforward theocratic organization spread rapidly with dead kings as living gods and their tombs as temples. We find them propped up on thrones of stone, surrounded by food and gifts. Later, some bicameral theocracies became literate, the Babylon of Mesopotamia, the Kings of Ur and Isin, the Memphite theology, and the Dead King's Voice of Osiris. These were not 'authoritarian' regimes, for there was no subjectivity or private ambition to crush, only an innocent obedience to voices reverberating in the brain.

The end of bicameral civilizations may have come from the strains produced by their initial success. Controlling more than a thousand people must have posed difficulties, but nothing compared with the conflicts resulting from collisions between god-programmed peoples each marching to a different drummer. The biblical story of the Tower of Babel may well refer to this. The spread of writing must also have weakened auditory commands. But the most proximate cause was surely the cataclysmic events in the second millenia BC, when volcanic eruptions on the island of Thera, estimated to have been 350 times greater than an H-bomb, turned half the world's known population into refugees and drowned the lost continent of Atlantis beneath a tidal wave 700 feet high. The once stable hierarchies crumbled in mass migrations, wiping out the great empires of the Hittites and Mycenae, as primal hordes turned on god–kings . . . Assyria having fallen into two centuries of anarchy emerged as a monster of sadistic ferocity, terror replacing the sudden loss of authority.

Yet there was no turning back to lost Edens. The languages, cities and foreigners were there and only consciousness could survive in the confusion. The *Odyssey*, which probably followed the *Iliad* by at least a century, is a myth marking the transformation. The heroes who battle before Troy 'were the will-less gigolos of divinities' whose Olympian rivalry was in bloody impasse. It took 'wily Odysseus' and his Trojan Horse to break free, conquer Troy, and defying gods wander homelessly abroad using the serpentine wits of an exiled Adam. In the *Odyssey* we suddenly encounter conscious actors, moral judgements and *psyche, nous* and *thumus* used as metaphors for consciousness. We find a similar transition between Amos and Ecclesiastes, from 'Thus Spake the Lord . . .' to 'For all things there is a season . . .' The Lord who walks in the Garden and closes the ark, yields to a Yaweh who appears only to Moses in disguise and condemns bicameral idolators.

Jaynes' thesis thus adds to Maps 1 to 5. The Greek epic poets in their tales of mythic heroes were surely celebrating a novel orchestration of hemispheric functions. Tragic drama stressed the price of consciousness, that the *hubris* of the analogue 'I' on the screen of consciousness could find itself in agonizing contradiction with real events. The psychic heroism of Orestes, Oedipus, Antigone, Socrates, and eventually Christ, was that all remained defiantly conscious in crucifying circumstances which threatened relapse into bicamerality and oblivion of mind.

MAP 25
The Holographic Mind: Karl Pribram

Two of the great puzzles of psychology are the apparent fusion within the mind of newly experienced events with earlier memories which we call learning and the amazing resistance of this learning to damage or elimination by even catastrophic injuries. Karl Pribram of Stanford University Medical School has recently proposed a far-reaching solution to both puzzles; each will be discussed in turn.

Firstly, we do not 'see' at all save by comparing outer images with inner remembered models. Newborn infants, for example, seem aware only of vague movements and intensities of light. Persons born blind but who have their sight restored in later years are visually incapacitated for many months by their lack of learned forms and must start from scratch to make the most elementary discriminations. Readers can test the mutual interference of perception and memory in pictures 1, 2, and 3 opposite. If 2 is covered up and you look at 1 first then 3, you will see the same 'young wife' in 3 as in 1; if you cover up 1 and look at 3 first then 2, you will see the same 'old mother-in-law' in 2 as in 3. Memory has altered your perception of 2. Or consider 'the impossible object' in picture 4. Your memory of normal, possible objects is struggling against your perception of this particular abnormal and impossible one. It takes conscious effort to realize the contradiction. Pribram contends that such contradictions form interference patterns in the optic tract.

Pribram has made extensive experiments in the visual and memory systems of nearly 2,000 monkeys. Recordings from electrodes implanted in the visual cortex produce waveforms that vary according to whether the monkey sees stripes or a circle. If the monkey is rewarded with a peanut for learning to push left or right panels, depending on whether stripes or circles are seen, then wave forms alter as he educates himself. This learned recognition and his 'intention-to-press' alter the wave forms *before* they register in the visual cortex and before the action is taken. Mutual interference between vision and memory has taken place. Where? In further experiments Pribram implanted multiple electrodes in: the visual or striate cortex, the inferior temporal cortex (responsible for visual recognition), the lateral geniculate nucleus (the 'relay station' on the main optic tract), and the visual colliculus (believed to guide movement of the eyes to objects of interest). He concluded that a 'feedback' system from the retinas of both eyes travel to the geniculate nucleus where they meet a 'feedforward' system, processed in parallel, which has been assembled in the visual colliculus. This assembly includes visual-recognition patterns, learned memories, as well as imputs from the association cortex and the emotionally volatile limbic system and brain stem (see Maps 19, 22). Wave forms from these converging systems merge in dialectical patterns of interference and we become conscious, perhaps painfully self-conscious, wherever memory and seeing conflict. Pribram has accumulated much evidence that many brain functions are analogous to holograms and such terms as 'wave form' and 'interference pattern' have special meanings in holography. The hologram is a kind of lensless photograph invented by Dennis Gabor who won a Nobel Prize for his work in 1971. While a normal photographic plate stores a two-dimensional image of an object seen from one perspective, a holographic plate (from *holos* 'whole') stores a three-dimensional code or representation. This code is created by a beam of light that has encountered an object crossing and so interfering with another beam of light that has not encountered that object. The hologram is explained in the margin but for this account a simpler illustration will suffice.

Suppose I drop two pebbles into a round pan of water and, even as they sink to the bottom, quick freeze the water's surface to produce a circular sheet of rippled ice (see margin). If I lift out the sheet, there, criss-crossing one another, will be two

Karl Pribram put a number of monkeys through tests in which they learned to distinguish circle patterns from line patterns and push the appropriate panel. During this exercise, recordings were made from various parts of the monkeys' brains by means of implanted electrodes, a method so sensitive that Pribram could tell what the monkeys were seeing and how learning affected that seeing. These experiments led him to revise the traditional model of how visual imputs are processed, in which subjects passively record, store and distribute imputs. Pribram found evidence that visual information is radically modified before it reaches the striate or visual cortex. Patterns of visual recognition feed forward from the inferior temporal cortex and the posterior association cortex, along with remembered forms from the striate cortex. These are assembled by the visual colliculus which guides the movement of the eyes towards objects of interest. Somewhere between the visual colliculus and the geniculate nucleus (the relay station on the optic track) seen images and imputs are compared with stored memories, interests and expectations and these appear to collide in an 'interference pattern'. This interference between visual input and expectation can be experienced by looking at box 1 then 2, and 3 then 2: remembering the 'young wife' (1) prepares you to see her again; remembering the 'mother-in-law' (3) prepares you to see her again. In box 4 the seen object has to struggle hard against the expectation that it is a normal object; in fact it is an impossible one but learning interferes with that recognition. Pribram believes that these interference patterns are similar to those in holograms.

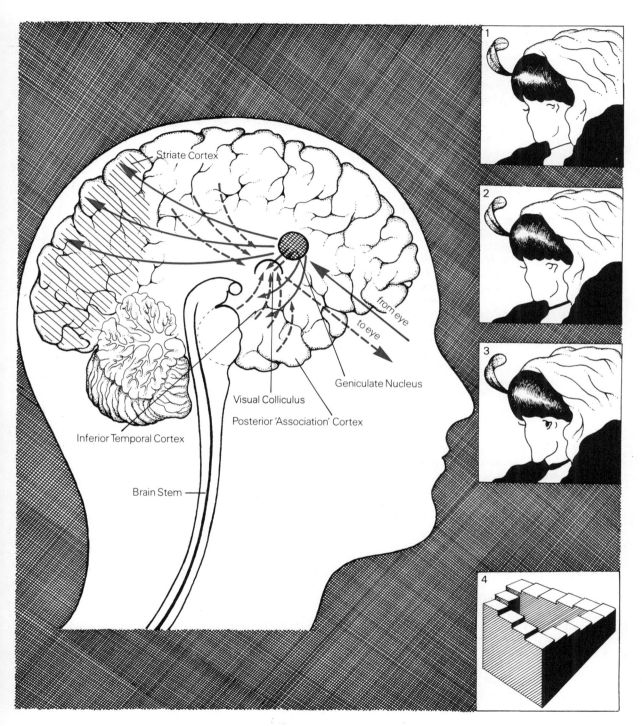

Striate Cortex

from eye

to eye

Geniculate Nucleus

Visual Colliculus

Posterior 'Association' Cortex

Inferior Temporal Cortex

Brain Stem

concentric patterns of frozen waves, whose spatial frequency (distance-between-waves) and mutual interference pattern are codes by which information can be stored. Were I to shine a coherent light source (ie a laser beam) through that sheet of ice, a spectral three-dimensional image of the two stones would be projected into space, a veritable ghost from the machine but joined by a single information code. Suppose now that I dropped the sheet of ice and it shattered into pieces. Its 'memory' of the two stones would not have been destroyed. Provided as little as a square centimetre remained that interference pattern of 'crossed ripples' would be distributed evenly and uniformally across its entire surface and the total memory could be reconstructed from its smallest part.

This is exceedingly important because it answers the second puzzle with which this account began, how human memory and learning prove so resistant to damage. Surgeons will tell you that extensive brain damage which will destroy selectively one or more functions does not selectively impair memories. These appear to move *en masse* like passengers on a ship, into the undamaged compartments. Over 90% of the optic track and/or visual cortex in cats and rats have been sectioned and still they remember what they learned. Mica strips, gold foil and hydroxide cream have been implanted there in attempts to segregate or to short-circuit memory areas, yet the memories themselves do not segregate. All remain or none since the coded ripples are everywhere.

Now, if ripples from two seen objects can have their mutual interference codified, so the ripple from a newly seen object could interfere with the ripple from a remembered object as the two meet in the vicinity of the geniculate nucleus; and interference would explain our problems of memory-impeded perception in boxes 1 and 4. Of course, we are not dealing here with water waves, nor do laser lights sear our brains, but the electrical discharges between the neural synapses (junctions) generate standing electromagnetic wave forms of which the alpha rhythm is the best-known example. The hypothesis is that waves of specific strengths, shapes and frequencies create permanent alterations in the molecular structures of our brain cells.

The process starts when a seen object throws its light on the mosaic of tiny receptor cells covering the retina of the eye. Some cells are sensitive to luminance, some to movement, some to lines, and they 'fire' in a pattern of variable excitation depending on what is seen. The layer of ganglion cells in the retina has millions of cross-coordinates so that each cell senses the excitement level of its neighbours. The third diagram in the margin shows the profile of smooth curvatures created. Analysis has shown that these waves are Fourier transforms of the firing patterns of the cells in the retina. A transform is a mathematical expression which mediates the change of energy from one form to another and which quantifies their equivalences. Thus the thousands of luminous dots on a television receiver are transforms of the electromagnetic radiation waves picked up by the aerial. Baron Fourier worked out the equations which are the basis of holography and of information transfer in the brain. Now if the brain encodes spatial frequencies in wave form a particular vision could evoke a memory by resonance if stored in the same frequency domain. A good analogy is the playing of say the G string on a violin while another tuned violin lies nearby. The sound from one will vibrate the G string on the second.

A holographic plate does not simply store one image-code. By altering the angle at which the light from the object strikes the plate and by altering the frequency of the laser beam, one cubic centimetre of plate can store ten billion codes in its finely layered texture. When a laser light of the same frequency and angle re-illumines the plate the original image is recreated, like a memory relived by reproducing its

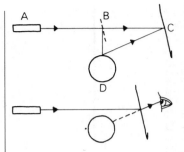

In holography a laser beam (A) is split by a prism (B) so that half the beam (known as the reference beam) travels onwards to the plate (C), while the other half (known as the control beam) illumines the object (D) which shines on the plate (C) in such a way that the latter encodes the interference pattern of the two beams, thus storing a three-dimensional impression of the object. When the human eye (lower diagram) looks through a plate reillumined by the same laser beam, a three-dimensional hologram of the object is seen.

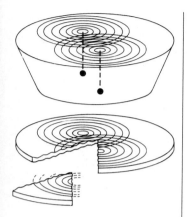

If two stones are dropped into a pan of water and the surface is quick frozen, the two sets of concentric ripples form an interference pattern. If a laser light is shone through the ice, a holographic image of the two stones is recreated. The images of the stones are encoded in every part of the rippled ice and can be recreated from as little as a square centimetre.

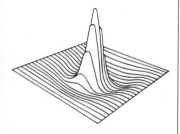

An idealized map of a visual receptive field representing the firing of a single ganglion cell in the retina of the eye when exposed to a source of light.

MAP REFERENCES
Consciousness of self, 2, 9, 13, 24, 28; Cybernetics, 30–1, 38, 45–51; Dualism, 2, 5–8, 12–15, 23–4, 28–30, 48, 53–5, 60; Hologram, see field, holism, holon, right hemisphere, 23, 28–9, 32, 47, 55; Interference pattern, see dialectics, 2–3, 35, 38, 42–3, 46, 51–60.

context. The same mathematical equation or spread function turns image into code and code back into image. Holographic storage is the most sophisticated, the most economic, and, from an evolutionary standpoint, the 'fittest-to-survive' of any method known to man. A computer in comparison is disabled by the malfunctioning of a single circuit. Holograms also characterize the principles of association. Where the light from two objects have their joint interference codified, the light from only one of them will re-illuminate the second like a linked memory.

However, if holography is to be more than an analogy what might produce an equivalent of the laser's coherent light? Light is 'coherent' when its waves are 'in step' and columnar like marching soldiers. Such coherence might be produced by the many thousands of parallel fibres in the optic track, by the 'hypercolumns' in the visual cortex or by rhythmic firing of cells. While many details of how the brain might resemble holography remain to be worked out, the experimental evidence for common operating principles, especially Fourier transforms, is overwhelming. Numerous experiments conducted by different research teams in recent years have showed that cells in the sensory cortex encode holographically. In one notable experiment subjects wore black leotards and performed skilled exercises against a black background. Small white circles were positioned over their major body joints and their motions filmed. The cinematograph record was of moving white wave forms and by subjecting these to Fourier analysis the researcher could tell exactly where each foot would land or hand descend. Was the code the researchers used the same as that in brains of their subjects? The results were identical.

The holographic hypothesis also provides the most plausible explanation for consciousness of self, that undeniable experience of standing out as personal projects who 'mind' what happens. If vibrators modelled on the human ear are placed on each forearm and their frequencies tuned, a point of sensation will at first jump periodically to and fro between them. But after habituation the sensation point moves midway between them. Here, then, is a 'feeling self' and embryo 'mindscape' created out of synchronized wave forms, with the individual able to project a self outward like the sound waves aimed by two stereo speakers.

Pribram's holographic model is potentially the stuff of scientific revolution, resolving at a stroke the sterile dualisms of mind and matter, humanities and sciences, existentialism and essentialism. If he is right, then 'immaterial' subjective experience alters brain structure, while that structure materially alters subjectivity and precise mathematical equations take the measure of both. He posits an open, intentional, cybernetic system of organism *plus* environment wherein consciousness is heightened by disparities between 'feedback' and 'feedforward' and mental breakdown is signalled by uncontrollable oscillations between the two with predictable delusions and hallucinations. In the next six maps 'feedbacks' and 'feedforwards' are synthesized by the creative mind (see Maps 26–31).

MAP 26

Cleansing the Doors of Perception: The vision of William Blake

Many believe Blake to have been mad, others call him mystical. Certainly his complex skeins of mixed metaphors defy distillation. So evocative are his analogies that the process of relating them to other maps would never end. I shall let them speak for themselves.

Milton is an autobiographical poem in which the soul of Milton, Blake's literary and spiritual mentor, returns from Paradise to the fallen state of Adam in a second attempt to justify God's ways to man. The Bard, the spirit of poetic genius binding Blake to Milton, has persuaded the latter that his Natural Religion (the world of Locke and Newton) was an error, which must be redeemed by a new pilgrimage. This is a projection of the conflict between Poet and Puritan in Blake himself.

On Milton's Track (see map) the poet first encounters Urizen (Reason) in guises including Moses bearing inscribed tablets of law, and a false priest of Natural Religion who baptizes Milton with the icy fluid of rationality. Milton is offered earthly dominions based on reasoning powers. He refuses, only to be tempted by Luvah (Passion), a virginal child.

Luvah and Urizen overlap with the two other spheres Tharmas (Instinct) and Urthona (Imagination) and together represent the Four Zoas, primordial human faculties who stood around the throne of Albion (archetypal man) before the Fall. They fell with Albion down into the flames and chaos which the map depicts. So now there 'lie in evil death the Four Immortals pale and cold'. The cause of their fall and their continued 'mournfulness of double form' resides in our selfhoods' original sin, that we refuse to merge the separateness of our identities in the love of Jesus and of fellow men. Rather we seek the purity and the apartness of Named Virtues and share Milton's morbid fascination for Passion controlled by Reason and his secret relish in the contrast between virginal innocence and pure guile.

So Milton is in the Satan space where Reason, Passion and Instinct contend in Corporeal War. Satan now offers his ultimate temptation, by inviting the poet to annihilate him and rid the world of evil for ever. But Milton perceives that Satan is not 'other', not separate like the physical world and physical body of Natural Religion. Satan is Milton's selfhood shut against the world which fosters external strife by refusing to open itself to inner conflict. To war against Satan is to decree an escalating power struggle between selfhoods increasingly shut in and incomplete. Nor can any teacher conquer Satan on another's behalf. Every potential creator carries within him an imprisoned self that can be redeemed only by union with others and by perception of the Infinite.

This brings Milton to the intersection of the spheres, 'the hallowed centre that holds the heavens of bright eternity', where Satan space touches Adam space. Those who come to this junction naked, vulnerable and alone and let their selfhoods become permeated by contending forces, those who argue angrily yet lovingly with their Bard in those 'Contraries that are Positives' will suddenly see the world not just from without like a black pebble, but from within. It is a world of concavities and chasms seen through the eye, both a world within the egg and egg within the world. Within the Mundane Egg is creation itself, where Reason, Passion and Instinct are reconciled by the powers of Imagination. Here are joined male and female, human and Divine, creator and emanation. The Adam space is the Eye with a vision of eternity, as intellectual spears radiate from the cleansed doors of our perception. Blake contrasts the struggling contraries of mental fight which lead to reconciliation and positive harmony with the mutually negating dualties of Puritan thinking. We have choice, he explains, to fight mentally within ourselves or fight physically between ourselves, a conception close to that of synergy discussed in Maps 42 and 43.

This map of the creative consciousness of man falling through fiery chaos is taken from Blake's own design. It depicts the spiritual pilgrimage of the poet Milton, the apostle of Natural Religion (ie Puritan Science), who returns to the consciousness of Albion (archetypal man) to discover and redeem Puritan error. Milton's Track enters the picture at bottom right.

He first encounters Urizen (Reason) the lowest of the Four Zoas, shown as hollow spheres, who is the false priest of Natural Religion. He is next tempted by Luvah (Passion) in the form of a twelve-year-old virgin. Blake contended that such hermaphroditic mixtures of reason/passion, experience/ innocence, male/female, pointed to the pathological repressions and severances of which Natural Religion was the chief exponent. Therefore the Satan space, the lower section of the Mundane Egg, represents Tharmas (Instinct), Urizen (Reason) and Luvah (Passion) in an unreconciled condition of enmity, imprisonment and impoverished vision within the opaque Egg.

It is only after Milton, and every would-be creator, journeys through conflict to the central intersection of the Four Zoas (or spheres), that these can be reconciled by the fourfold vision of Urthona (Imagination). Here the Satan space opens upon the Adam space, an analogue of the human eye. The Poet can then cleanse the doors of perception and look outwards and inwards upon a world that is infinite and is recreated new at every moment by the Mental Fight within.

MAP REFERENCES
Contraries as positives, 23, 30, 38, 42, 55, 57; Creativity, 27–31, 40, 55, 59; Fall, see also splitting, 4–8, 11, 48, 56; Natural religion, 5–8; Prison, 5; Satan, 8.

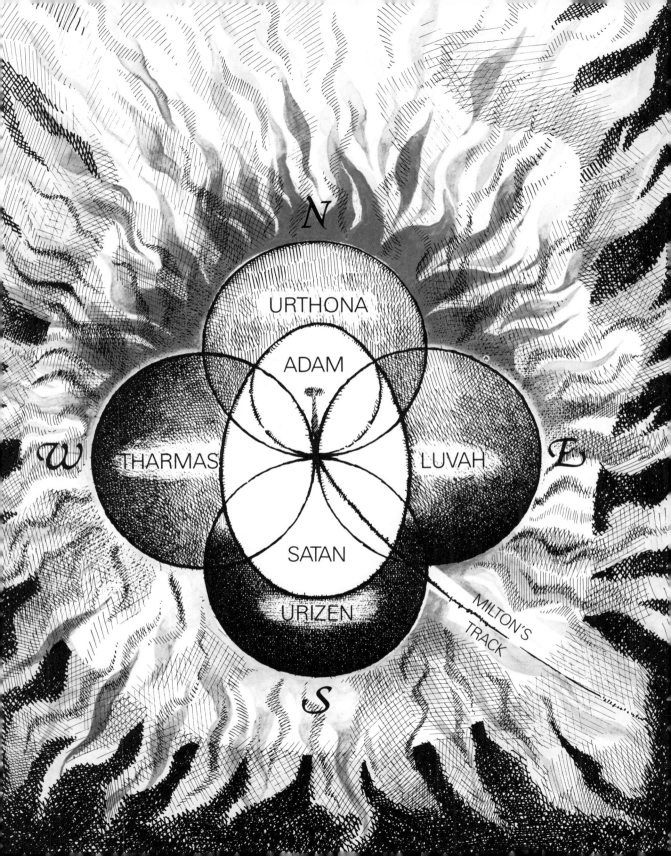

MAP 27
The Bisociating Mind of Arthur Koestler

A hitch-hiker was thumbing and bumming his way across the United States in the period just before a Presidential election. He had learned how to scrounge free drinks in local bars, by shouting aloud insults about whichever candidate he guessed was not supported in those parts. He came to a small, dusty town in Colorado and entered the first bar. 'Jimmy Carter is a horse's ass!' he shouted, but to his surprise the regulars manhandled him headlong onto the road outside. Believing he had miscalculated he entered the next bar and shouted, 'Ronald Reagan is a horse's ass!' but found himself once more sprawling in the dust. As he climbed bewildered to his feet, he saw a cowboy standing nearby, of whom he asked complainingly, 'If this ain't Carter country and it ain't Reagan country, what the hell is it?' 'Son,' replied the cowboy, 'this is *horse* country!'

To understand human creativity, says Arthur Koestler, it helps if we can first grasp the structure of wit (the word means both humour and inventiveness). In humorous stories like the one above, we witness a surprise collision between two self-consistent but mutually incompatible frames of reference. The first frame (the search for the free drink) is logically developed throughout the story, while the second frame, immanent but disguised within the story, pops up to deliver the 'punch line' to the first frame, so as to shatter it. The emotional tension accumulated by the story is suddenly deprived of its object and left hanging, causing an emotional discharge, an exhalation of breath, and the 'ha! ha!' reflex. Thus the hitch-hiker (and the story's audience) assume that Presidential candidates can be insulted by being compared to horses' asses. The townspeople assume that horses are thereby insulted. The story is funnier if the punch line is unexpected and its hostility is more apt if one takes a dim view of Presidential politics.

While in comedy frames of reference collide and shatter harmlessly, in tragedy the frames are juxtaposed in irreconcilable conflict. Hamlet soliloquizes on being and not being, on 'suffering slings and arrows' or 'taking arms against a sea of troubles'. The conflict leads to tragedy and the emotion of the audience is cathartically discharged, as the incompatible moral imperatives remain standing. In comedy, tragedy and creativity, then, two or more matrices, or frames of reference, are *bisociated*, as Koestler calls it. Yet in creativity a fusion or synthesis takes place. Instead of just colliding or contrasting, they become permanently joined in a new creation, wherein the whole is greater and qualitatively different from the sum of the parts. By this criterion the play, *Hamlet*, is creative, while the character, Hamlet, is not (in which lies his tragedy).

Consider the problem facing Archimedes. The King of Syracuse had been given a beautiful crown of gold, which he suspected of being adulterated with silver. He ordered Archimedes to find the answer. Archimedes knew the weight of gold per volume measure, the problem was to find the volume of a crown ornamented with filigree, without melting it down. For hours and days he thought in circles, but always returned to the same impasse. How do you estimate the volume of an irregular shape? One day he was taking a bath and idly watched the water rise around his body as he lowered himself in. At that moment the solution came to him in a flash: a solid object displaces water of a volume equal to its own. The crown could be immersed, the displaced volume of water measured.

It seems so obvious after the connection has been made, yet in great inventions the joined matrices of thought were initially far apart, belonging to different realms or disciplines, like electricity and magnetism before electromagnetism, like smallpox and the curious immunity of milk-maids, before cowpox was discovered and used to immunize populations. Few would think of connecting the serious business of measuring the volume of a crown with taking a bath. This helps to

Arthur Koestler has described 'the act of creation' as a bisociation of two (or more) thought-matrices (or frames of reference) which were previously unconnected with one another.

A good example is the story of Archimedes. He needed to discover whether a crown presented to his sovereign was really pure gold. He knew the weight of gold per volume measure, but how could he estimate the volume of an irregular, ornamented crown? For weeks he was frustrated, circulating around the problems, but reaching an impasse because he was trapped within the single 'crown matrix'. One day in a state of relaxed attention, he took a bath and saw the water rise round his body as he immersed himself. The solution came to him in a flash. The crown would displace a volume of water equal to its own: Eureka!

What had happened was that the 'crown matrix', A, had become bisociated with the 'bath matrix', B, and the synthesis came through the creative act of 'thinking on two planes'. Archimedes had at first thought that the answer could be found within the single frame, A, but repeated frustration led him to jump to B. Of course, finding the right 'second frame' is a major part of the problem, which is why creative solutions tend to come to us when our attention is wandering casually and subconsciously among alternative frames, rather than consciously focused on one.

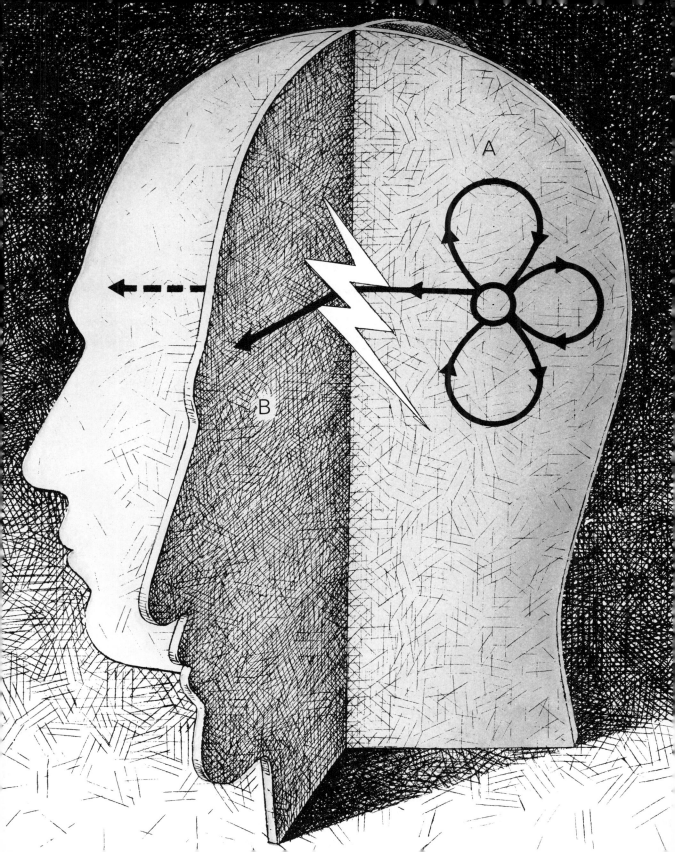

explain why creativity has so often been associated with dreams, leisure, free-association, spontaneity, feeling the unconscious mind and 'thinking on the side'. What blocks a solution is the overly narrow and single-minded concentration upon a single matrix or frame of reference. There is no solution so long as you think exclusively of altering the crown in some way in order to estimate its volume. Not until you step back from the problem to take another approach, or as the French say, *reculer pour mieux sauter*, can an additional frame be discovered that will qualify the question being asked. It is when we are relaxed, off-guard, and the ego is resting, that additional frames of reference bubble to the surface of consciousness.

Another famous example is Gutenberg's invention of the printing press. Again he faced a problem. Neighbours wanted to take copies of the Bible on a pilgrimage to Aix la Chapelle. He had seen playing cards being stamped on paper by inked wooden blocks, but to carve the Bible on blocks would take several life-times. He had watched grapes being pressed at harvest and had seen coins being minted by pouring metal into moulds . . . Eureka! 'A simple substitution which is a ray of light . . .' he wrote. 'To work then! God has revealed to me the secret . . . like a foot that multiplies its print, there is your Bible!' Gutenberg had taken the pressing function from the vineyard and had turned the minting of coins into the moulding of moveable type, which would leave its stamp on paper like playing cards. The fact that all three technologies were available to the people of that time illustrates the principle of ripeness. Someone else was bound to have put the three matrices together sooner or later. Indeed since Gutenberg spent much of his life in litigation with rivals, the 'sooner' or 'later' are moot points to this day. But note how qualitatively different the synthesis was from the sum of its parts. Cards, wine and money, surely the devil's work, but they combined to form a Bible, and less directly, a Renaissance and a Protestant Reformation, which sought the objective word of God in a printed book. Gutenberg's letters confirm that subconsciously the bisociation had already taken place. With a growing sense of excitement he knew it was coming. 'For a month my head has been working; a Minerva, fully armed must issue from my brain . . . '

The reference to Minerva illustrates that metaphors can 'stand in' for later connections; they are heuristic devices (ie devices that 'lead to discovery'). When Johannes Kepler observed that the earth was drawn around the sun by some invisible force he called it the Holy Ghost and likened earth to Christ and the sun to God. The metaphors, although later discarded, facilitated the discovery of the laws of gravity. Hence metaphors, which reveal 'the likeness of unlike categories', may serve as preliminary bisociations. Those who complained, for instance, that Freud's unconscious was but a metaphor, must now admit that the right hemisphere of the human brain, silent, non-rational and visionary in its processing of information, turns out to be curiously similar!

Koestler disputes the conventional piety that scientists search for data which only then reveals the necessary principles of its organization. Charles Darwin, as we know from his notebooks, was committed to his theory of evolution before the *Beagle* expedition. While the creative vision inherent in such a theory must be tested painstakingly against known facts, those facts do not alone explain the theory. We confuse what Abraham Kaplan calls the reconstructed logic of scientific discovery (ie its defence) with the logic of discovery. 'The bridge', says Koestler, 'is actually built before the pillars that hold it up, yet not all bridges are upheld!'

All this makes sense of what we know about highly creative people, their enjoyment of puzzles, paradoxes and anomalies, their scepticism about logical reasoning, their 'sleep-walking' propensities, their aesthetic and emotional feel for

'Satire is a verbal caricature which shows us a deliberately distorted image of a person, institution or society. The traditional method . . . is to exaggerate those features which he considers to be characteristic of his victim's personality and to simplify by leaving out everything that is not relevant. . . . The result is a juxtaposition in the reader's mind of his habitual image of the world, and its absurd reflection in the satirist's distorting mirror.'
'Janus' Arthur Koestler

'Let us face the fact: a large part of modern psychology is a sterile and pompous scholasticism which, with the blinkers of preconceived notion or superstitions, doesn't see the obvious; which covers the triviality of its results and ideas with a preposterous language bearing no resemblance to normal English or sound theory, and which provides modern society with the techniques for the progressive stultification of mankind.'
Ludwig von Bertalanffy quoted in 'The Ghost in the Machine' by Arthur Koestler

'The initials SPCDH stand for Society for the Prevention of Cruelty to Dead Horses. It is a secret society with international ramifications and with considerable influence on the intellectual climate of our time. . . . English insularism, class distinctions, social snobbery, trial-by-accent are all declared to be dead horses, and the innane neighings that fill the air must be emanating from ghosts. In the Sciences . . . we are constantly assured that the crudely mechanistic nineteenth-century conceptions in biology, medicine, psychology are dead, and yet one constantly comes up against them in columns of text books, technical journals and in lecture rooms . . . SPCDH is active. . . .'
'The Ghost in the Machine'
Arthur Koestler

the harmony of ideas, their seemingly tangential and discursive styles of thought, their intuitive leaps across boundaries, and the breadth of their knowledge. But creativity is not exclusively rare, historical or sublime. We all bisociate frames of thinking, thus constantly rediscovering personal solutions which are already well known culturally. Even the chimpanzee, Warshoe, who was taught sign language, bisociated his own sign for ducks out of the signs for 'water' and 'bird'. How many children do we hear saying 'gooses' instead of geese. It is unlikely that they have echoed the error. It is far more plausible that they have bisociated goose with the rule 'add s to make a plural'. They have put two and two together by laws of combination. Sensitive human relationships are another kind of bisociation.

Koestler conceives of human knowledge and biological evolution as processes of creative accretion. Bisociations are junctions which branch out like trees turned upside down. These holarchies, as he calls them, consist of holons. Holon is a synthesis of 'whole' and 'atom', so called because persons taking a stand at any junction and looking down will see parts below them, of which they are the whole or apex, while the same persons looking up, will see wholes above them, of which they are a part. Not just human knowledge, but the biological and psychological realms in general are organized holarchies. We are freest 'at the top' of these inverted trees and most determined 'at the bottom'. For example, we freely and consciously learn to drive a car, but the skill soon becomes a habit-hierarchy of automatic responses. The advantage is that we may soon be able to have creative thoughts while driving the same car that once occupied our full attention, but technologically and neurologically the automobile has become a fixed sub-assembly attached to us and we cannot let it go. Holarchies are therefore also subject to rigidity and inertia. Joining one to another may involve a radical undoing of habits and ways of thinking regarded as immutable. (See also Map 47.)

For all our capacities to make connections and so free ourselves creatively, some kinds of connections may be constitutionally harder for us to make than others, so that entire holarchies are split from each other in murderous animosity. Koestler believes we have a quasi-schizophrenic split between reason and emotion, between our two 'older brains' and the neocortex (see Map 21). The bisociations that could save us from mutual annihilation are therefore weak and faltering, while the purely cerebral ones that escalate weapon systems are strong, which makes mankind into the first (and perhaps last) genocidal species the world has known . . .

MAP REFERENCES
Bisociation, see: congruence, 32; creativity, 26–31; crucifixion–resurrection, 5, 59; dialectic, 52–5; dovetailing, 43; ecology, 48, 60; 'harmónia', 2, 58; holon, 47; imbrication, 55; 'sophrosýne' 2, 57; synergy, 42.

MAP 28

The Two Cultures Controversy:
Getzels, Jackson and Hudson

The process of creative thinking is here conceived as involving two sequential stages of processing information, divergent thinking followed by convergent thinking. The sequence may be repeated several times before a creative solution is achieved. The first, divergent stage, involves reformulating, elaborating and playing with the problem as presented. This may include an effusion of imaginative variations, akin to brainstorming, or the kind of free association favoured by psychoanalysis to unblock thinking. Divergence, when unappreciated as a thought process, may take place subconsciously as the individual is trying to sleep or rest. Hence Jules Poincaré reported 'that ideas rose in clouds' as he tried to sleep. When morning came he knew his problem was solved.

No sooner do creative persons sense that their divergent thoughts have produced sufficient materials to solve a particular problem, than the process of *converging* upon precisely the right answer will begin. Once the right question has been asked the answer may be a matter of logical, experimental, observational or mathematical skills. A good example of this is found in James D. Watson's book *The Double Helix*, where the process of casting about in search of the structure of the genetic code turned into a race as the researchers realized the information from which a correct deduction could be made was now available. It was a matter of who would converge first upon the correct answer.

It says much about the reification of experimental psychology that convergence and divergence have been 'discovered' as if they were separate objects floating in a miniature Newtonian universe of mind. Jacob Getzels and Philip Jackson conducted their research in the United States in the climate of the late fifties and early sixties. They were concerned that conventional tests of IQ and aptitude measured only the capacity to converge on answers to problems formulated by authorities. They attempted to design instruments to assess the capacity to originate questions, issues, possibilities and ideas. They called this divergence. They were clearly on the side of their 'divergers' against the heavy bias of post-Sputnik America with its policy of mass producing a technical meritocracy. At about this time, in Britain, Michael Young was writing *The Rise of the Meritocracy* to protest against the same bias. Such writings were to prove prophetic, as 'the silent generation' became noisy and a decade of divergence broke upon universities throughout the West.

By the use of open-ended tests which elicited from subjects imaginative stories to go with pictures, pictures to go with phrases, and multiple uses for such common objects as bricks and barrels, Jacob Getzels and Philip Jackson were able to establish that divergent thinking was an ability in many students, ignored and sometimes actively discouraged by educational authorities. Although some students combined both capacities, the two ways of processing information were not highly correlated, and the statistical techniques used presupposed their independence.

If, for example, an intelligent, convergent child with little divergent skill was shown a picture of a smiling man relaxing in an airliner, he or she would tell quite a stereotyped story. The man is returning from a successful sales convention. He plans to buy his wife a mink coat, and they will celebrate at the country club with martinis, steak and ice-cream. A highly divergent child told a quite different story. The man is returning from Reno after divorcing his wife. They broke up because she put on too much face-cream at night, which caused her head to slide across the pillow and smack into his. Luckily he's just invented an anti-skid face-cream and smiles at the prospect of making his fortune. While teachers applauded the first child's story, calling it positive and wholesome, they dismissed the second story as tasteless and anti-social. Students could not be expected to remain quiescent, the researchers warned, with their 'creativity' (as divergence was called) stifled. In Great

Divergence is the making in the mind of many from one. Convergence is the making of one from many. Mind is conceived as constantly branching out (on left) before narrowing to a point of decision (right), and so on in cyclical pattern. Creativity involves the entire cycle.

For example, creative persons will typically reformulate and elaborate the problem as presented, teasing out alternate strands and possibilities to generate an 'excess' of materials, symbolized by 'a branching tree'. At the mid-point between divergence and convergence, they intuit that the necessary ingredients of a new synthesis are now present. The diagram illustrates this by showing five strands originating from the branchings in the tree. It is these (and there could be fewer or more) which are used in a calculated convergence upon a solution to the problem.

Unfortunately our society is divided by crude stereotypes of the Two Cultures: the humanities are idealized as divergent, the sciences as convergent. The profusions of literati and artistic temperaments in general are dubbed 'creative', but this is an affliction of amateurs which confuses the twigs and branches of clever talk with major intellectual and scientific syntheses. The present gap between the Two Cultures robs both halves of significance.

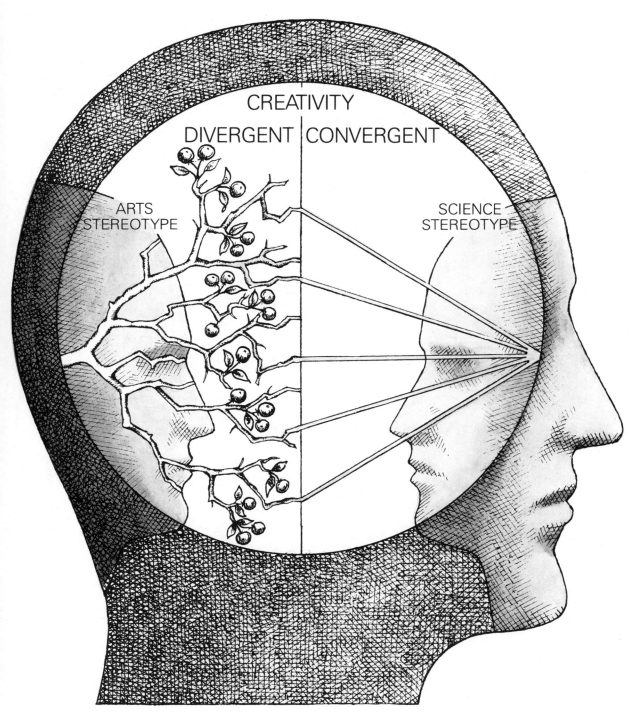

CREATIVITY

DIVERGENT | CONVERGENT

ARTS
STEREOTYPE

SCIENCE
STEREOTYPE

Britain Liam Hudson employed the open-ended tests of Getzels and Jackson in a major study of English schoolboys. He found that high divergers were mostly specialized in the arts and humanities while convergers were in the sciences.

What the open-ended tests versus the IQ tests were actually measuring was the gap between *The Two Cultures* to which C. P. Snow had drawn attention. Students scoring well on tests of divergence usually specialized in English, history, arts or modern languages. They tended to score significantly lower, if not low, on IQ tests, on which they were careless and inaccurate, but with greater strength on the verbal parts. Their general knowledge was high. Their interests were cultural, literary and dramatic. Students scoring well on tests of convergence usually specialized in mathematics, physics and chemistry, but also in classics where considerable discipline was required. They tended to score high in IQ tests, in which they were accurate and fast, but with weakness in the verbal sections (except the classicists). Their general knowledge was relatively low. Their interests were practical, mechanical and technical with some emphasis on the outdoors.

The personality characteristics of the two groups followed from their dominant styles of thinking. Convergers were more deferential to authority, less trusting of their feelings and impulses, less independent in their personal opinions, rather low in self-esteem and more mannered and self-controlled. All such traits are consistent with finding pre-existent technical solutions to problems set by authorities. In contrast, the divergers were more rebellious towards authorities, more trusting of their feelings, more independent of attitude, higher in self-esteem and more spontaneous in their self-expression. All such traits are consistent with the task of defining or redefining issues and problems, often in competition with authorities. We may note here that it was from the divergent disciplines, history, philosophy, languages, English and the softer social sciences that the impetus for student radicalism came in the United States, Britain, France and Germany. The sixties saw something akin to a 'divergers revolt' fed by affluence, modernism and mass communications, of which the philosophies of progressive education were one expression and the counter-culture another.

Hudson did not, in these later years, replicate the finding that divergers were an underprivileged minority. Indeed the higher status schools tended to favour the diverger 'born to rule' by defining moral and other issues, while the more middle-class schools tended to produce a converger class. Hudson also disagreed with the moral tenor of the American research, specifically that divergence was somehow nearer to growth, humanism and creativity. There was much wit and cleverness in the responses of divergers to open-ended tests. But scintillating conversation hardly adds up to creativity, save in a limited form. The high divergers were no more 'whole persons' than the high convergers, even if they were superficially more attractive as personalities. Indeed the closer Hudson looked at the divergent–convergent distinction the more superficial it began to appear. These disparate skills were closer to a public role than a private reality. Many convergers had very large vocabularies and when asked to imitate an arts graduate or instructor did so with torrents of scatalogical associations. Many divergers were quite capable of careful and detailed work, but were impatient of the time and effort required, especially when they could articulate so easily. Hudson also found that while many individual convergers could accept the 'science stereotype' when applied to their colleagues they would resist it as applying to themselves, and the same was true of divergers. Each claimed to be a secret converger or diverger.

An examination of the neurotic defences and personal limitations of those in each major category revealed that both divergers and convergers tended to over-

'Lettered gentility . . . is achieved at King's [College, Cambridge University], at the cost of a certain theatricality. It is hard, at times, to recall that the pictures are real, the port is real, that the candles in the candlesticks are real candles and not electric lights pretending to be candles; above all, that the people are creatures of flesh and bone. In my two years there as a Fellow, I found that a sense of illusion was rapidly becoming my standard experiental mode. The air of charade was all-pervasive: the sons of suburbia, like myself, parodied the lettered gentry; and the lettered gentry parodied the sons of suburbia parodying themselves. . . . Brilliant young scientists who knew nothing of life or art gave ham performances of the role, "brilliant young scientist who knows nothing of life or art". Vain art historians gave virtuoso performances of "art historians being distastefully vain". And the institution itself rose repeatedly to heights of dramatic absurdity.'

'The Cult of the Fact'
Liam Hudson

use their strong suits to escape being found out. Convergers learned to evade many issues by placing them 'outside science'. If a problem could not be formulated precisely enough to permit a technical solution it was no problem! They tended to take refuge from people in things. Divergers would often side-step unpleasant facts, by using their capacities for conceptual leaping to reach safer ground. By concentrating on problem presentation, the solution could be indefinitely postponed. They tended to take refuge from things in people.

In the last two decades the divergent–convergent distinction has become a crude and quarrelsome political stereotype used to symbolize contrasting forms of moral virtue. The Vietnam War, espoused by the Best and the Brightest, the veritable whizz-kids of scientism, showed us all the murderous consequences of 'crack-pot realism', the totally unimaginative and inhuman advance of technological 'convergence'. The electronic battlefields, the computerized body-counts, the professional detachment of bombardiers devastated South-east Asia as men locked their brains into different mental compartments from their emotions.

So much for the convergers, but what of the protest by divergers, the hawkers of conscience on street corners? Students claiming to personify 'compassion', 'humanism', 'peace' and 'progess' made of their university buildings an open-ended test. That the students had something real to protest about is undeniable, the problem is rather, that the demonstrators could *only* demonstrate. Highly skilled in the articulation of crucial issues, they were mostly without the interest, aptitude or patience to solve the problems they defined. Theirs was to wonder why, the doing and the dying were for convergers! Those who rallied at Woodstock, postured in Haight-Ashbury and shouted in the streets of Paris 'I am a Marxist of the Groucho variety!' made it clear that self-expression had become an end in itself, Protest was an art form. You diverged, to diverge, to diverge. The problem was essentially the split between the two modes. Powerless conscience lashed verbally at conscienceless power, doves and hawks furiously reproaching each other's incompleteness. Other consequences of splitting divergence from convergence are economic. It is not, then, surprising that a decade of protest seems to have yielded to one of threatened decline. 'What is a machine tool?' C. P. Snow asked at a literary cocktail party, 'and they looked shifty'. He was willing to bet that not 10% of those receiving first-class honours in humanities from Cambridge could say how a button was manufactured. For the pure arts and sciences are increasingly abstract; you diverge or converge in a 'free realm' above the industrial plasma of the country. Those professions which fall between these abstract purities: engineering, business management and the social sciences are increasingly despised as 'mongrel disciplines', which must carry on commerce (literally) between the two citadels of culture. This is mostly an Anglo-American malaise, although the French too have intellectuals largely ignorant of science. Germans and Scandinavians tend to contrast *Wissenshaft* ('knowledgemanship') with *Technic* (the making and running of things) and they treat the latter with great respect.

That genuine creativity, as opposed to clever repartee, needs divergence and convergence can be inferred from the research of Calvin Taylor. Creativity, he showed, was a reconciliation of 'opposite' endowments, as broadly diffused attention was brought to a sharp synthesis, remote things were associated, richness was pruned to parsimony, risking led to gaining, flexibility was joined to mastery and an insatiability for intellectual ordering rose phoenix-like from seeming chaos. Neither whole persons nor whole cultures can afford the present moral charades, which sever the totality of human endowments into posturing parts, cardboard cut-outs for instant recognition on television.

MAP 29
The Lateral Thinking of Edward De Bono

Long ago in the days of debtors' prisons· a merchant found himself sinking ever deeper in debt to a money-lender. Finally the money-lender revealed what he had really been after, the merchant's daughter. The debt would be forgiven, if . . . Realizing that father and daughter were aghast at the offer, the wily financier invited both to take a walk with him along a gravel path. Here he proposed that 'Providence shall decide'. 'I shall take two pebbles from this path', he said, stooping quickly as he spoke and gathering two stones. 'And I drop them', he did so . . . 'the white one and the dark one in this black bag. You will escape prison if your daughter agrees, without looking, to pick one stone from this bag. If it is the white one she goes free and your debt is forgiven. If it is the dark one, she is mine.' Reluctantly the merchant agreed, but his daughter's heart beat wildly. She was sure, well almost, that two dark stones had been put into the bag. It was a trial she could not win, and to unmask the money-lender's subterfuge would be equivalent to not choosing, and so sending her father to prison.

According to De Bono, the 'choice' which this young woman faced was an exercise in vertical thinking, a logical either/or with disaster at each end. While in this particular case the faulty premise underlying the 'choice' was contrived by a villain, we do not need villains to have inadequate premises. Errors of premises occur repeatedly in attempts to solve problems of every kind and vertical thinking which is uni-directional is completely at the mercy of its premises, right or wrong. Try for yourself to choose in the daughter's place! She is caught in a 'double bind' (see Map 49). What she did was an exercise in lateral thinking. She put her hand in the bag, withdrew a pebble, cried 'Oops!' and dropped it 'accidentally' amid the hundreds in the gravel at their feet. 'I'm so sorry', she exclaimed, 'clumsy of me. But you can tell the colour of the pebble I chose, by the colour of the one remaining in the bag.'

Consider a second example, and here vertical and lateral thinking work together in complementarity, like the left and right hemispheres of the brain, the second assisting the first when its premises prove faulty. On the map opposite we see the left and right hemispheres of a researcher – say a psychologist – trying to solve a problem. As we all must, he starts with a premise or paradigm. This word means an *a priori* mental pattern, which has been symbolized by the 'logic bubble' with a rectangle inside. The psychologist has assumed that the reality he seeks is 'rectangular' (which could stand for the stimulus–response model of behaviourism, the limited energy model of Freud, or many others). When he observes the pieces of behaviour 1 and 2, he immediately squares them. He then observes·3, and once again reality is rectangular! 4 and 5 would seem at first blush to pose difficulties, but not if he keeps faith with his cosmology. See 1, 2, 3, 4 and 5 are squared again! He gets a large research grant, and a tenured professorship. 'If I have been able to see further', he says modestly, 'it is because I have stood on the shoulders of giants'. And the Association for the Advancement of Square Behaviour rises as one to applaud him.

However, a year or so later he confronts the piece of datum numbered 6, and here is an impasse. Either the datum itself is erroneous, *or* psychological reality is not rectangular. For there appears to be no way in which 6 can be accounted for in the rectangular paradigm. Our psychologist may decide that 6, like the phenomenon of consciousness, does not exist, or does not lend itself to 'science'. His own rectangular paradigm will now become an ideology, a 'logic bubble' pushing away and repressing human endowments that do not fit (see bottom left), as the social sciences polarize. But if our psychologist is more than a hack he starts to think laterally using the right hemisphere. He runs several alternate patterns

An illustration of the manner in which vertical thinking (left brain hemisphere and left of map) works with lateral thinking (right hemisphere and right of map) to solve a problem. Suppose a psychological researcher conceives of the phenomena he is investigating as 'rectangular'. (This appears in the 'logic bubble' at top left.) 'Rectangular' is, of course, a symbol for any particular pattern conceived by Freudians, behaviourists, or cognitive psychologists as basic to their approach. It is called a paradigm.

He then examines the data 1 and 2, and discovers they form a rectangle. He adds 3, and still reality is rectangular, 4 and 5 seem irregular, but look a rectangle again! By now he is congratulating himself on his powerful paradigm which assimilates data like a snowball on a hill. But what about datum 6? Here is contradiction. Either the datum is wrong, or his paradigm, or both because they do not fit together. Typically the paradigm in his logic bubble will push away data that confounds prediction (bottom left).

But where mind advances the researcher reacts to frustration by thinking laterally with his right hemisphere, and back-tracking to reconsider the adequacy of the 'rectangular' paradigm. Several alternate paradigms, a 'star', 'pentagon', 'triangle' and 'parallelogram' flash through his mind. Would the six pieces fit any of these? Could any of them substitute for the rectangle in earlier experiments? Suddenly . . . Eureka! It's the parallelogram! Not only do all six data fit, everything organized by the rectangle can be organized by the parallelogram, and more.

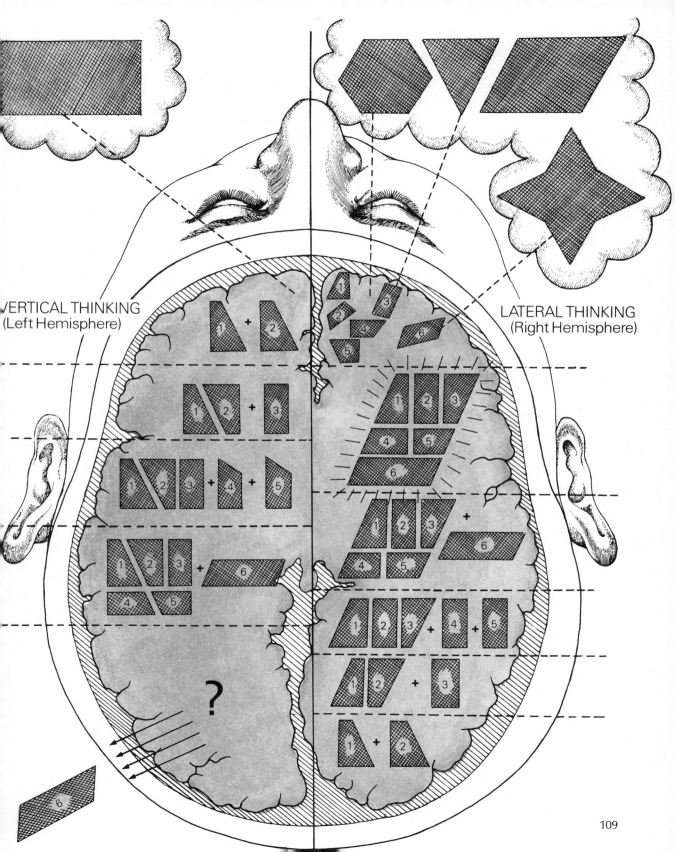

VERTICAL THINKING
(Left Hemisphere)

LATERAL THINKING
(Right Hemisphere)

109

through his mind, a star, pentagon, triangle and parallelogram which appear in the 'logic bubbles' (top right) and he plays divergently with the dissolved pieces of the rectangle paradigm (below) numbered 1 to 6. Note that the 'discrepant' sixth piece has been added rather than repressed, since he is trying to reconcile them all in one coherent, consistent, systematic and aesthetic schema. His task is complicated by the fact that this schema must also reconcile pieces 1 and 2, 1 and 2 with 3, and 1, 2, 3, with 4 and 5. In short, he needs to account for the earlier 'successes' of the rectangular paradigm, as well as its recent failure.

The first clue is a sense of inner excitement and expectancy, experienced while he is thinking about the parallelogram. And suddenly . . . Eureka! The parallelogram reconciles all six. But it does more. If he works backwards from his intuitive leap, it becomes clear that a parallelogram pattern will also reconcile elements 1 to 5, elements 1, 2 and 3 and elements 1 and 2. He has now accounted for the entire range of earlier investigation with the rectangular paradigm. At this stage he can hand the problem back to his left hemisphere for rigorous testing by the logic of vertical thinking and hypothetico-deductive methods. He can search for data 7, 8, 9, 10 and 11 in the confidence that his new parallelogram has a wide range of applicability. But frustration will occur sooner or later and once again lateral thinking will have to step in.

This, then, is how mind advances in the solution of problems and the creation of science, with vertical thinking grounded in a pattern which lateral thinking creates, qualifies and revises, allowing vertical thinking to re-orientate itself and once more plunge ahead. Note that De Bono's contrast between vertical and lateral thinking both underlines and elaborates distinctions made in earlier maps.

In Map 23, for example, we saw that the left hemisphere processes information in particular modes. It is analytic, reductive-into-parts, sequential, rational, propositional and time-orientated. Now we know better what these terms mean. They refer to vertical thinking which 'propositions' data with its own rational categories and persistently reduces and analyses information to make it fit. Note especially the arbitrary role played by time. If datum number 6 had been encountered before 1 and 2, the whole history of the 'science' would have been different, for 6 strongly suggests a parallelogram! The error of the rectangular paradigm was substantially influenced by the accidental sequence in which the data were examined, with every 'success' deepening the investigator's commitment to his faulty premise. As the philosopher Abraham Kaplan has observed, 'We are forever asking Nature whether it has stopped beating its wife'.

Lateral thinking also displays the characteristics attributed to the right hemisphere. It is timeless, diffuse, holistic, visuo-spatial, intuitive and simultaneous. Its aim is to synthesize new whole patternings and it scans intuitively over patterns and pieces searching for a simultaneous fit, regardless of their sequence of arrival. The distinction made by Arthur Koestler between 'thinking on one plane' and creative 'bisociation' is clearly compatable with vertical and lateral thinking (see Map 27). The parallelogram 'bisociates' all six elements of data plus the history of investigation in one 'Eureka!' Koestler's *reculer pour mieux sauter*, or 'pulling back to take a better running jump', is a good metaphor for the way lateral thinking reorientates vertical thinking to solve problems. The contrast between convergent and divergent thinking in Map 28 is also captured in this map. Vertical thinking converges on the data with its logical/methodological 'cookie cutter' and if its premises are adequate saves a tremendous amount of time. Lateral thinking diverges, looking at the problem from multiple perspectives—triangle, pentagon, star—until a better pattern (if available) is found.

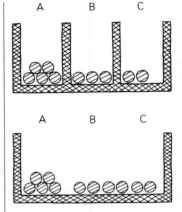

Vertical thinking retains classes, categories, labels and symbols arbitrarily assigned. Lateral thinking suspends these and plays with different arrangements.

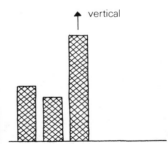

Vertical thinking develops the best alternative.

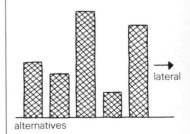

Lateral thinking generates other alternatives regardless of earlier success.

'When you return to your parked car on an icy day and the lock is frozen, the vertical thinker may try to heat the lock with his lighter in the wind. The lateral thinker may shelter and heat his key with the flame.'

'Mechanism of Mind'
Edward De Bono

'Our habits and style of thinking are largely derived from the disputations of mediaeval monks. Within the framework of the accepted idiom there is a great deal of skill and brilliance. But . . . a more positive future may need a more positive idiom.'

'Future Positive' Edward De Bono

However, De Bono's work is much more than a mere confirming and supplementing of earlier views. Both in his critique of the sacrosanct status of vertical thinking, and in his detailed descriptions of the lateral mode, he has done much to demystify creative thinking. He likens vertical thinkers to eunuchs employed in harems. They are strong, efficient and hardworking, yet incapable of generation, and one suspects that those who employ them want it that way. For while vertical thinking is superficially active, like knives, forks and spoons searching for materials to cut, poke and ladle, it is psychologically passive, a pattern highly resistant to change. To understand this passivity we must consider how memories are formed. De Bono asks us to imagine sequential spoonfuls of hot water dropped upon a block of mental gelatine. These should be compared to the pieces of data 1, 2 and 3 illustrated in this map. The early drops of water form hollows. Into these deepening hollows all the subsequent spoonfuls of hot water run. The pattern once set adapts the data to it, as the vertical thinker becomes the passive victim of an arbitrary sequence of sense impressions, and is increasingly unable to modify his paradigm as early impressions deepen. Only lateral thinking can bring us back to the realization that we are self-organizing systems, pattern-making creatures, not just pattern recognizers and imprinted followers.

Vertical thinking is always controlled by a dominant idea, whether dominant over young women, or just squaring everything it sees, it imposes a pre-fabricated technique upon reality. It is a self-maximizing, self-perpetuating system with, in social terms, much arrogance and rigidity of mind. An advanced industrial society with a pre-programmed, vertically thinking technostructure is potentially an ecological nightmare and a militaristic monster with its logical means of destruction firmly rooted in archaic value patterns. What intensifies this bias is that the achievements of lateral thinking can always be reconstructed by the philosophers and historians of science to look like vertical thinking. For thousands of years (see Map 24) we heard gods commanding us with injunctions equivalent to, 'Look for the parallelogram' or 'Think of the pebble still in the bag'. We would thank gods or daemons for the inspiration, and thank logic for moving us from premise to conclusion. When religion began to wane, the logical positivists and assorted Pope-bashers tried to persuade us that Logic had done it all, that Progress was a vertical line down which dispassionate scientists trod the stepping stones to truth . . . But this is a caricature of how the inquiring mind works, of the metaphors, the heuristic devices, the false steps to true conclusions, the conceptual leaps and lucky breaks.

Yet we must not fall into the trap of unlimited admiration for lateral thinking. De Bono lives in Britain, the land of aristocratic amateurs and armchair theorists, of brilliant inventions not exploited or developed into paying propositions. Those who refuse to switch over to lateral thinking, when vertical thinking founders, may be equalled by those who dabble laterally instead of harnessing technology. Oscar Wilde once remarked that an ever open mind was no better than an ever open mouth. We have to chew. Lateral and vertical, right hemisphere and left, must work together.

MAP REFERENCES

MAP 30

The Paradox of Creativity: Frank Barron and Jay Ogilvy

Frank Barron has undertaken nearly three decades of research into creative personalities in the arts, sciences and education. Creativity is notoriously difficult to measure or assess and to summarize his findings as 'seeming paradox and contradiction' is in no way to disparage them. Jay Ogilvy, a philosopher from Williams College, has suggested a model of 'multi-dimensional man' that reconciles such perplexities.

Barron found that, from the point of view of mental health, highly creative persons scored both lower and higher on such clinical tests as the Minnesota Multiphasic Personality Inventory. They appeared slightly 'neurotic' or 'psychotic' on measures of anxiety, depression, schizophrenia and deviance, yet were paragons of stability on measures of 'ego-strength', that is the power to rally from setback and generally cope with adversity. This apparent contradiction is resolved by the observation that the 'high creatives' deliberately challenge, shake, unstabilize, frustrate and disintegrate themselves in order to reassemble the parts better. To this end they are both masculine and feminine, logical and emotional, rational and idealistic, excitable and fairminded, moving continuously between such poles. Thus when confronted with a faked group consensus they will dissent boldly, although high scores on empathy suggest that they do this as much for the benefit of the group as for themselves. Creative personalities enjoy and prefer the unbalanced, the asymmetrical and the incomplete in art and symbolism, but they also enjoy completing these and making them balance! Perhaps for this reason they score high on flexibility, and equally so on intellectual ordering, as they reassemble what they take apart or break down. In religious beliefs they combine scepticism about fundamentalist dogmas with an often passionate search for symbolic meanings; they seem capable of greater doubt and greater certainty.

'It is just such persons who endure the bumpy ride of scientific progress with its crisis and coalescence, diffusion and integration, and revolution and consensus,' says Barron. 'Above all, creators remain drawn to the age-old paradoxes that philosophy grapples with [and] . . . that art occasionally resolves . . . the problem of the one and the many; unity and variety; determinism and freedom; mechanism and vitalism; good and evil; time and eternity; the plenum and the void; moral absolutism and relativism. . . These are the basic problems of human existence, and as far as we possibly can we arrange things to forget them.' But not so creative people: to them such issues are the warp and woof of consciousness itself, which draws the brain hemispheres into complementary functioning (see Map 23).

But must we impale ourselves on the horns of 'paradox'? Jay Ogilvy believes that we have taken from physics the rule that visuo-tactile senses cannot allow two different objects in one place at one time and have overgeneralized from this a principle of non-contradiction which is crippling to psychology. To claim that the creative person cannot precipitate disorder with new order in view, or cannot systematically doubt as a means to greater certainty is absurd. Order and disorder, doubt and certainty can surely be entertained simultaneously in one mind. They may have to be implemented sequentially, but that is different. Ogilvy suggests a cybernetic model of a multi-dimensional person in a polycentric equilibrium of unified Socratic virtues. Such a mind operates by a relational logic which signals greater or smaller differences in a quality . . . I have attempted to show this in Map 28 using Barron's research. No circuit is the master circuit, nor do the many derive from any one. It is not a hierarchy but a heterarchy of ever-shifting emphases, a Dionysian dance of information circuits. We must decentralize our personalities and societies to recreate a pantheon of human excellence (see Maps 1 and 2).

Uroborus, the self-devouring snake of paradox, provides a graphic symbol for the 'contradictions' of the creative mind. In this map the five concentric snakes represent the five seemingly contradictory traits which research has shown are present in creative personalities in unusually high quantities. If we take the paradox of disorder–order as an example, then it appears thus:

with maximum, but not pure, disorder on the left and maximum, but not pure, order on the right, while predominant disorder shades into predominant order at the top and predominant order into disorder at the bottom. We may say that creative minds disorder themselves to create new order from disorder; they doubt so as to become more certain and to doubt again . . . and so on. Indeed, the whole concept of 'paradox' may be nothing more than a failure to comprehend recursive systems which operate in patterns of mutual restraint and coordination. The creative individual flirts with doubt and disorder, enduring anxiety while intuiting the answer to his doubts. He then closes on an embryo solution and reorders the strongest and most certain structure that rational mind can apprehend. Creativity is an optimization of information circuits.

MAP REFERENCES
Cybernetics, 45–52; Dionysian, 2, 58; Mental health, 41–3, 51, 60; Paradox, see contradiction, 14, 40, 49–50, 52–7; Polycentrism, 2, 10, 26, 32, 48, 57, 59.

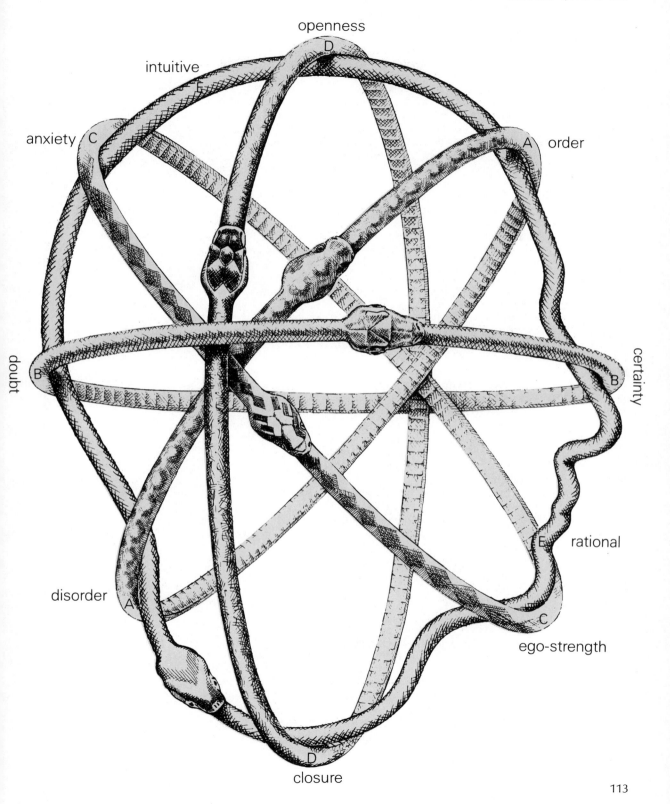

openness

intuitive

anxiety

order

doubt

certainty

disorder

rational

ego-strength

closure

MAP 31

The Structure of the Intellect:
J. P. Guilford's cubic factors

Creativity cannot exist in isolation. Those clichés of creativity, the Starving Artist or the Absent-minded Professor, or the penchant of progressive educators for finger-paints, all point to the dictum that 'the artistic temperament is an affliction of amateurs'. As a practical matter creative persons who lack the intelligence to appraise their own ideas, the discipline to check their hypotheses, or the fluency to communicate their results are unlikely to achieve recognition. Creativity is then a component in overall intellectual functioning, crucially dependent on other intellectual factors.

J. P. Guilford of the University of California began by looking at all-over creative performance, rather than potential, and at productive thinking with recognized outputs. Using factor analysis he has found a large number of components of intellectual functioning which he distinguishes because of their high levels of statistical independence. For example, if proficiency in tests of divergent thinking is largely independent of proficiency in convergent thinking (so that their correlation coefficients are low), while the presence of both skills in the same person makes high levels of creative performance more likely, then it makes sense to treat such capacities as separable, if not separate processes.

Guilford first distinguishes the *contents* of mental processes, from their *operation*, and from their *products* (see map). Four types of content, figural, symbolic, semantic and behavioural, are processed through five (roughly sequential) stages of mental operations. The content is cognized, compared to memory, divergently processed in spontaneous types of free association (see Map 28), subjected to disciplined and formal convergence and finally evaluated. There cannot, of course, be anything rigid about such a sequence and part processes would need to be repeated until the problem was solved. Such operations must have ends or products in view. These might consist of a unit of thought, classes of units, mathematical or other relationships, entire systems, information about changes, differences or transforms, or predicted implications, or quite possibly several products may be combined. (The laws of logic, for example, deal with classes, their relations and their implications.)

Guilford has found that certain mental operations are more crucial to creativity than others. Highly creative people have a kind of cognition that seeks out problems and anomalies and a kind of evaluation which remains unsatisfied while discrepancies remain (see Map 30). Factors measuring fluency, flexibility and orginality are found to operate most strongly at the most divergent stages of problem solving, while a 'redefinition factor' clearly distinguishes the convergent thinking of creative persons. Other factors affecting creativity are harder to assign to any particular stage. Insight can be taken to refer to the general richness of the associational matrix within the cube, a kind of porous membrane between compartments. To suggest this I have used dotted lines on some of the cubes on the map. However, it is notorious that while creative people must have enough intelligence for their resyntheses, highly intelligent people need not be creative. For this reason correlations between IQ and creativity fall to very low figures above the 130 IQ level. 'Associational fluencies' within the cube are clearly crucial, all the more so with our present information explosion, with its highly compartmentalized sources of knowledge. Creative persons are great generalizers, Guilford found.

Finally, intellectual capacity must have a behavioural outcome and a social connection or we could not be impressed by its achievements. The map shows a transform of mind extending beyond the skin and skull to make the productive thinker one with the environment. This vital relationship provides the theme of Level 5, Maps 32 to 38, which considers the psychosocial development of mind.

This map represents the cubic cross-matrix of factors J. P. Guilford found were inherent in intellectual performance. He divided these factors into Contents (bottom), Operations (top) and Products (right). The contents include figural materials (ie visual objects and auditory rhythms), semantic or conceptual meanings in verbalized form, symbolic materials (ie numbers, words etc) and behavioural materials. These contents are worked on in a series of mental operations: firstly there is the recognition that the problem exists and the manner in which it is visualized (ie cognition); secondly, it is compared to memory; then it is subjected alternately to divergent and convergent thinking (Map 28) and finally the results are evaluated. These operations create products in the form of units, classes, relationships, systems, changes and implications, all of which are the concerns of arts and sciences.

I have taken liberties with Guilford's original cube by bending it around to suggest the cybernetic nature of successive operations, and by adding an output arrow to link the thinking individual to his environment.

MAP REFERENCES
Associational matrix, 27, 29; Convergence–divergence, 28; Factor analysis, 20; Information processing, 48, 50; Intellectual functioning, 29, 38; Semantics, 39–41, 43–4, 60.

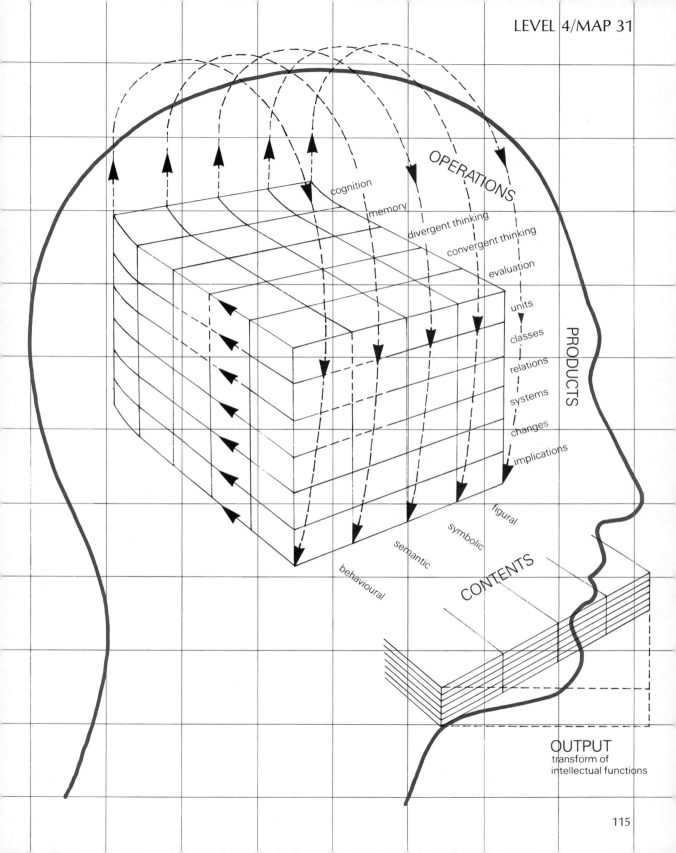

OPERATIONS

cognition
memory
divergent thinking
convergent thinking
evaluation

PRODUCTS

units
classes
relations
systems
changes
implications

figural
symbolic
semantic
behavioural

CONTENTS

OUTPUT
transform of
intellectual functions

MAP 32

The Positive Regard of Carl Rogers

Carl R. Rogers, the American psychotherapist, is the originator of 'client-centred therapy' and 'personal encounter groups'. Once an agricultural student turned student of religion, he still retains an earthy egalitarianism and mission to grass-roots psychology. In his work over the last three decades, he has proved a major force in the de-mystification of psychotherapy, and by returning to ordinary people some sovereignty over their own experience he has fought the colonizers of common sense. Those who complain that his conceptions are oversimple might pause to consider whether a psychology which seeks to emancipate lay persons can afford to intimidate them. He has broken with the first law of psychology-on-the-make, 'Demolish the comprehension of the non-professional'. The relationships Rogers describes are as fundamental for lovers, families, friends and co-workers as for professional psychotherapists.

Rogers conceives of the total personality as two overlapping circles, one of *self-structure* and one of *experience*: when self-structure includes experience, the person and what he or she says are *congruent*, when self-structure excludes experience, *incongruence* results. That part of self-structure which is outside experience (see area A on map) remains distorted and rigid, while experience that is denied and not incorporated by the self-structure (see C) remains alien and threatening. As a result, when highly incongruent persons communicate they are not 'present' in what they say; since their experience is unassimilated and unowned, they are unlikely to find understanding for a self that does not understand and a vicious circle results.

Rogerian counselling and communication aims to allow the personality at the bottom of the map to change itself to that at the top, from incongruent to congruent functioning. The person moves from feelings that are unowned, unrecognized and unexpressed, to feelings that are experienced with immediacy and spontaneously communicated. The self-structure moves from rigidly held judgements, nailed down by 'facts' and external evaluations, which ache with contradictions, owing to the segregation of self from experience, to a sense of integrity, wholeness, reconciliation, relief from tension, and a trust in one's own organism. As the point of evaluation shifts to within the self, a sense of positive worth, personal direction and a capacity to take risks develop. To foster this change and the growth of the congruent personality involves: an increasingly self-awareness of one's entire field of experience; the realization of one's ideals; a greater independence from social pressures to conform, combined with a capacity to understand other people's frames of reference; an increasing acceptance of one's self and others; and the expansion of consciousness into richer and more complex fields of meaning.

The 'simple' process of mutual understanding is, for Rogers, a vital but rare, near-heroic feat. 'Can I care', he asks, 'while still allowing the other to be separate? Can I leave the comfortable, familiar structures of my own self and enter the unfamiliar territory of another, knowing that I may never be the same, that from another viewpoint I could appear wholly deficient? Have I the strength not to be destroyed by his anger, frightened by his anguish, engulfed by his dependence, while accepting the integrity of both our points of view? Can I tread, sensitively and intelligently on the precious mental 'furniture' of another?'

Rogerian counselling insists that nothing is more doomed to frustration than assuming that we can change or direct a person from outside his own field of perception, by evaluations anchored exclusively in our own. If we could but accept the world he sees, then the barriers between him and the world we insist upon would crumble of their own accord, his congruence would grow, his personality mature.

Carl R. Rogers uses two overlapping circles to map the human personality, one of self-structure and one of experience. Personalities vary in terms of their congruence, the extent to which their self-structures are in touch with their experience; such congruence (or lack) is reflected in their communication with others. In this map the lower diagram shows low congruence and the upper high congruence. A change from the first condition to the second is the purpose of Rogerian counselling and represents growth in personality and communicative capacity.

Undeveloped, troubled and incongruent persons have large areas of self-structure (designated A) which remain untested and uncommited to contemporary experience. Where early influences have persuaded persons that they are incompetent, sinful, dirty or repellent, such painful evaluations will be kept out of conscious awareness and not communicated to others. Time further rigidifies and distorts these structures until such persons become loaded down with archaic, introjected attributions. At the same time a large body of new potential experience (area C) is either denied outright or not permitted to conflict with that narrowed structure of self (area B) of which incongruent persons remain aware. At the top of the map the principles of Rogerian communication have greatly reduced incongruence along with distortion (A) and denial (C). Congruence, integrity and the level of experience (B) have all risen.

MAP REFERENCES

The Congruent Personality

growth of personality

The Incongruent Personality

MAP 33
Abraham Maslow's Hierarchy of Needs

Abraham Maslow was one of the founders, in 1962, of what has become known as humanistic psychology. He conceived 'a positive theory of human motivations' organized hierarchically into a sequence of five salient needs, each of which rises in turn to dominate the organism and then falls away in proportion to its satisfaction. Thus the early and primitive human organism must first satisfy the needs for food, drink and exercise before any other concerns can become important. When physiological needs gain some measure of gratification, a second stage arises, a need for security, order and protection. One thinks of Eliza Doolittle's song in the musical *My Fair Lady*, 'Wouldn't it be Loverly', where she imagines a room, a fire, an armchair and plenty to eat. Later in the same song she imagines a third set of needs, for belongingness and love, of someone gentle who would 'take good care of me'. In the fourth stage, the need for self-esteem, prestige, status and acknowledgement arises – all of which are appealed to in the course of teaching Eliza to speak like a lady.

Finally, we seek self-actualization, the desire to be everything we are capable of becoming. Maslow made a special study of self-actualizing persons in history and contemporary society. He found them to be more efficient in perceiving reality, more accepting of themselves and others, more spontaneous in their relationships, with a tendency to centre on problems and their solution; to have a quality of privacy and detachment, an autonomy from cultural influences, a freshness of appreciation, a capacity for transcendence and oceanic feelings, a deep identification with humanity, more profound human attachments, a humorous and democratic character structure, and a rare capacity to resolve moral dichotomies and dilemmas.

Maslow's hierarchy of needs appears to reconcile Freud with his disciples: while Freud stressed physiology and security in the early years, Reich stressed love and attachment, Adler the need for self-esteem and Jung the search for self-fulfilment. Similarly, the schema also makes sense of many neurotic disturbances: compulsive overeating, bed-wetting, *anorexia nervosa* all appear as confusions of need levels, while complexes become buried 'lower needs' never sufficiently satisfied and impeding the need being consciously sought. Personality disturbance can be regarded as the maladjustment of needs. The authoritarian personality acts as if even more status and authority can assure his belongingness and security. Psychotherapy may be seen as a 'regression in the service of the hierarchy' as the patient's early concerns with security, belongingness and esteem are reconstructed and reaffirmed in an ascending relationship to the therapist.

The later Maslow was increasingly concerned with synergy, the process by which one need (or person) can combine optimally with another (see Map 42). The fundamental principle of the need hierarchy must therefore be synergistic. The self-actualizing person seeks fulfilment in a way that keeps other needs (and other persons) optimally satisfied. Developing persons do not, therefore, 'outgrow' or become 'superior' to lesser needs and less developed persons, rather, life is organized to satisfy all needs save the one which is insatiable, and which is given full head, that is the need to reach beyond oneself to the very frontiers of possibility and realize unknown potentials.

Unluckily for Maslow, his ideas became caught up in the counter-culture of the sixties in the United States and were interpreted in the tradition of 'positive thinking' and 'spiritual technology'. The man himself told the hippies who came to see him to find some challenging work to do. Self-actualization, he explained, was a description not a prescription. It could only come to those people concerned with something beyond themselves.

As part of the process of psychosocial development, Abraham Maslow envisages man as growing through a sequence of five stages each dominated by a particular set of needs. Firstly, by Physiological Needs such as those for food, drink or exercise; secondly by Safety Needs (security, order, protection); thirdly, by Belonging Needs (sociability, acceptance, need-love); fourthly by Esteem Needs (status, prestige, acknowledgement); and fifthly by Self-actualization Needs (personal fulfilment and growth). The peak of the earlier stage must be passed before the next and 'higher' need emerges to dominate the organism. This sequence characterizes not only growth from childhood to maturity, but the growth of cultures from subsistence to free self-expression. For this reason an individual's stage cannot be used as an automatic value judgement on personal worth, but is rather indicative of a benign social environment.

It is important to note that all needs are simultaneously present (or latent) in all persons at all times. The sequence refers to the strength of the need within the conscious purposes of the mind. Sudden emotional or physical deprivation will cause 'lower' needs to reawaken. Maslow's approach can include many psychologies, from behaviourism, which has anchored itself in physiological drives, to the more humanistic approaches concerned with creativity and self-fulfilment.

NUMBER, VARIETY AND RELATIVE SALIENCY OF WANTS

physiological needs

safety needs

social needs

esteem needs

self-actualization

PSYCHOLOGICAL DEVELOPMENT ⟶

MAP 34

The Etchings of Interpersonal Anxiety:
The dynamisms of Henry Stack Sullivan

The work of Henry Stack Sullivan represents a rare incursion of Irish–American influence into the vanguard of psychiatry, a field with many echoes of wandering refugee intellectuals of Jewish origins. As the founder–director of the Washington School of Psychiatry in 1936, Sullivan was the first major psychiatric authority to insist that 'personality' was purely hypothetical. All that we could observe of personality, and what clearly formed it initially, were the human relationships in which it took part. Even schizophrenics imagining trysts with Helen of Troy or embattled beside Joan of Arc were best diagnosed in terms of imagined relationships.

For Sullivan, personality was made up of the relationships in which it took part and the reciprocal patterns that these relationships formed. These patterns Sullivan called *dynamisms* and he defined them as the 'relatively enduring patterns of energy transformations which recurrently characterize the living organism'. Dynamisms are either biological or physiological. The first Sullivan did not elaborate on much but are concerned with satisfying basic needs such as hunger, thirst, sex and power. The second, which intrigued him more, guard the organism's need for emotional security; these he called *self-systems* or *self-dynamisms*. These first evolved through the child's relationship with his mother on whom he depends for emotional security. Through empathic feeling the child senses maternal disapproval and anxieties, these subtle punishments educate the child to behave in anxiety-inhibiting ways and his self-system becomes etched by fine gradations of anxiety. Sullivan likened the severe anxiety engendered by an angry or indifferent mother to a blow upon the child's head which cripples even the capacity to understand the reasons for disapproval. The control of anxiety is therefore vital to avoiding more anxiety, an issue of sanity itself. The tension which arises from unsatiated biological needs must contend with the tension (called anxiety) arising from anticipated disapproval of the manner in which biological satisfactions are sought. The human organism yearns for the 'tensionless euphoria' of secure satisfactions. (This is the most criticized of Sullivan's ideas, but is not vital to his larger thesis.)

Sullivan wrote few books and resisted refining his formulations, which resemble the loosely held constructs of a successful practitioner. Among his several interpreters, I believe the research model formulated by Timothy Leary and Hubert S. Coffey in the 1950s to be the most useful. Sadly this line of research was interrupted by Leary's conversion to LSD and the counter-culture, yet the map opposite remains remarkably fertile. It shows a number of common self-systems arranged in a circular pattern according to Sullivan's insistence that each self-system is reciprocal and interpersonal. Thus the managerial autocratic style (A, D) tends to evoke modest self-effacement (H, I) in the person addressed, while the latter style positively invites the former to take command; the blunt, aggressive style (E, D) so ruffles relationships that cooperative, overconventional persons (L, M) rush in to calm everyone down, and in turn invite the blunt aggressors to retaliate. And so on . . .

The reciprocities of self-systems can be loving, or pathological. The loving descriptions are contained in the inner circle of the map. The person who acts confidently and independently (B), is just as capable of listening respectfully and admiringly. His scepticism and dissent (F and G) in no way impair his willingness to give sympathetic help and support (N and O). Essentially such people are equal to the situation. They size up a social relationship and contribute the balancing element, leadership in a power vacuum, criticism in a smug consensus, or support where confidence is faltering. The pathological manifestations of self-systems are

Henry Stack Sullivan insisted that personality must be defined in terms of the human relationships of which it is part; these relationships encompass certain characteristic 'self-systems' or 'self-dynamisms', concerned with protecting the individual's need for emotional security and alleviating anxiety. An essential part of Sullivan's theory (and the map opposite) is the idea that self-systems evoke a reciprocal opposite response in another. The map is an illustration of Timothy Leary and Hubert S. Coffey's interpretation of Sullivan's theory.

Their circle consists of eight major segments which can be read anti-clockwise from A to P. The segment of dynamism most dominant in one person will typically evoke the segment on the other side of the circle: thus a predominantly managerial autocratic person (A, P) calls forth a modest self-effacing response (H, I) from one who seeks to comply, while the latter style invites the former to take command. These reciprocal responses can either be rigid and extreme (see outer circle) or adaptive and loving (see inner circle). In the former case the relationship is shaped by anxiety avoidance, as the individual goes to extremes to avoid threats to his emotional security; in the latter the individuals are free and capable of relating in all eight styles, depending upon interpersonal requirements, and the anxiety involved can be tolerated. The price paid in failure to develop 'all round' self-dynamisms is heavy.

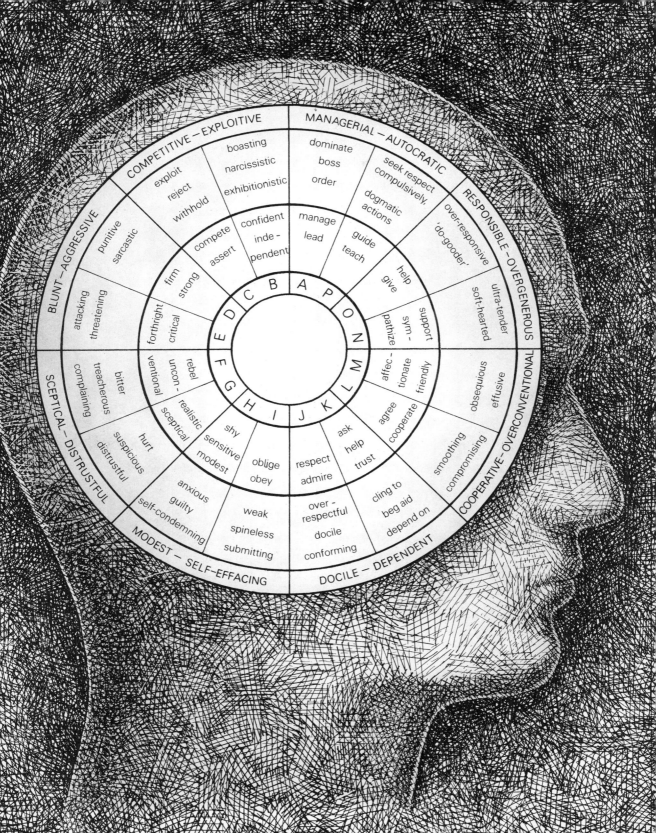

contained in the outer ring of the map. These dynamisms differ from the loving ones in two important respects. They are far more extreme, going beyond leadership to outright domination, or beyond scepticism to bitter distrust. They also tend to stick at one extreme. Thus: the exhibitionist will persist narcissistically to talk everyone down, no matter how great is the need for the listener; the punitive will attack even those desperate for friendship; the docile follower seems helpless to alter even a conformity which is leading to disaster. Rarely will such persons cross publicly to the opposite side of the continuum, and if they do the conversion is total, like a bully starting to cry, or a worm turning. Sullivan believed that such persons suffered from *parataxic distortion*, a process by which the growing individual distorts the meanings of words and symbols, ascribing to these private rather than consensual meanings. Hence such individuals will call their ruthless exploitation 'competition' (C), their dogmatism 'advice' (P) and their cringing submission 'duty' (I).

This distortion develops when the growing child splits his social world into 'good me' and 'bad me', with goodness coming to symbolize one direction in which security lies, and an opposite direction in which badness and insecurity lie. Rigid personifications of 'good' or 'bad mother' produce similar patterns, with the dominated child placating his 'good mother' (A to I), or a distrusting child fleeing to the farthest end of the continuum (O to G) to escape the suffocating overgenerosity of a 'bad mother' (see margin). In instances of the most severe anxiety the child may create a 'not me' category and dissociate whole segments of the circle of dynamisms, attributing disgusting extremities to someone else and depriving himself of even the moderate and loving versions of the dimensions involved. Hence a child may become unable to trust others or ask for their help because 'spineless' and 'sissy' behaviours have been so ferociously condemned in the past they continue to induce anxiety. Sullivan believed that such persons were often driven to take jobs in which they constantly bark out orders or constantly smooth out tempers.

The ingenuity of Leary and Coffey's model is that the profile of subjects can be plotted across the segments in this way. However, when a subject is assessed at different levels startling contrasts emerge. The combined ratings given a subject by staff, or by other patients in the same group or ward, may vary substantially from the subject's self-rating. Typically a mental patient will, for example, see himself as sympathetic and gentle on the inner circle, while others describe him as ludicrously soft-hearted and overgenerous on the outer circle, thereby confirming Sullivan's concept of parataxic distortion. A more extreme contrast is usually obtained by administering projective tests which tap not how the person relates but his fantasies. As we might expect fantasies are typically compensatory. The effusively cooperative and overconventional will dream of scourging their foes. The aggressively dominant, like the Marquis de Sade, dream of Justine in her delicious helplessness and similar *alter egos*. Such research supports R. D. Laing's contention in Map 14 that psychotic breakdown involves an uncontrollable and extreme oscillation between public dynamism (false self) and private fantasy (true self) brought about by the value absolutism of parents who prescribe total docility (J), self-effacement (H) and cooperativeness (I) in their children. Such expectations would almost certainly drive children into the 'outer ring' in search of security, while placing parents themselves at the opposite extremity of that ring. By administering the Minnesota Multiphasic Personality Inventory to large samples of patients, Leary and Coffey were also able to show that various dynamisms on the circle diagram correspond with known categories of psychiatric disorder (see margin).

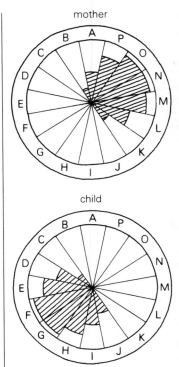

A typical reciprocal relationship between mother and child mapped on Leary and Coffey's circle. Here the mother's excess of responsible–overgenerosity (O, N) has evoked the child's scepticism–distrust (F, G). Note that segments P and M in the mother and E and H in the child are also excessive while complementary capacities within each person are lacking.

But how do these extreme self-dynamisms help to control anxiety and become identified with the individual's security? Let me illustrate this process by research I conducted at the Delancey Street Foundation, a half-way house for ex-convicts, ex-addicts and 'losers' generally. I was impressed with how repeatedly in their past lives offenders had colluded to control anxiety. A constant pattern was the 'Macho-and-the-Mama'. The delinquent sons had been typically dominating (A), braggardly (B), exploitative (C), punitive (D), assaultive (E), rebellious (F), and distrustful (G). Their mothers (and later wives or girlfriends were forced into similar patterns) responded with precisely opposite extremes. They were docile (J), begging (K), tearfully forgiving (L), ever-loving (M), soft-hearted (N) and trusting (O). The hardness, violence and bitterness of the sons were matched stride by stride with the weeping, wailing and prostration of mothers or their substitutes, as extremes escalated together. In self-justification the men were 'Shaft', 'Superfly', 'Cool-cat' and similar cardboard cut outs of ultra-masculinity, while mothers/partners clung to images of martyrdom, 'I-loved-him-all-the-more,' or 'the prostitute-with-heart-of-gold.' The men controlled their anxiety by coercing others into confirming their pretensions. The women tended to control anxiety by abject conformity and the total absence of any independent affirmations. All avoided the anxiety of making judgments about the appropriateness of behaviour by assuming that the harder the man, or the softer the woman, the better each was. As one armed robber put it, 'Why should *I* show tenderness or concern when *she* cries enough for both of us?'

The rehabilitation system had maintained these games instead of breaking them up. The idealistic social workers, psychiatrists and psychologists had tried 'to save a sickie' as the convicts contemptuously put it. The middle-class professionals guilty about being white, affluent and educated, and acutely anxious in their relationships with persons of different colour, race and class had been rigidly liberal and tender-minded in their ideologies, thereby fuelling the bitterness of their targets, who knew a performance when they saw one.

But readers who conclude that these criminals had been 'coddled' miss the point. The 'love' of someone trying to control his anxiety is not genuine affection and co-exists with appalling childhood neglect and/or professional cynicism. Try and 'love' a case-load of 80 persons! In addition these men had been brutalized in prison, at home and on the street. The reason they had long remained violent, suspicious, negative exploitive and harsh was because this single stance was simultaneously the best way of protecting themselves from brutality and the best way of extorting maximum indulgence from ideological 'do-gooders', whether mothers, substitutes or professionals. The conflict between the tough-minded conservatives of the prison business and the tender-minded liberals of 'rehabilitation' is just one more oscillation in a system manufacturing criminality (see Map 16). As the founder of the Delancey Street Foundation, John Maher, put it, 'We have the right-wing nuts who'd like to break into this place and beat everyone on the head, and then we have the weak-kneed, vicarious-thrill, radical-chic creepos who wanna kiss our ass . . . So you get schizo . . .'

MAP 35

Encounter on the Narrow Ridge: Martin Buber interpreted by Maurice Friedman

Martin Buber, the Hasidic philosopher, was a major spiritual antagonist of Nazism who emigrated from Austria to Palestine in 1938. His interpretation of dialogue has helped to bridge many of the world's great philosophical divides: the conservative and reform wings of Judaism, the Protestant and Catholic religions, and the concerns of humanists, psychotherapists, communitarians and the religious; it has also brought a missing social context to existentialism. When, in 1953, at the age of seventy-five, he accepted the Goethe Prize and the Peace Prize of the German Book Trade he delivered a typically paradoxical assurance: the sufferings of Jews could never be forgotten or forgiven, but this fact made his meeting Germans only the more important for his 'face' symbolized irradicable memories. In Maurice Friedman, Buber has found a tireless and dedicated translator and interpreter. Friedman sees Buber's importance in his challenge to Enlightenment, styles of thinking and the domination of the *I* of the investigator over the *it* of the investigated in modern scientism; an impersonal manipulation that is deeply implicated in the modern eclipse of God and the holocaust itself. 'According to the logical conception of truth, only one of two contraries can be true, but in the reality of life as one lives it, they are inseparable. . . The unity of contraries is the mystery at the innermost core of dialogue'.

In building an interpretation of dialogue that transcends the either/or of scientism, Buber begins, like other existentialists, with man 'vouching for his word with his life' and staking all on thought-in-action. But he is less admiring of existential fire in its own right, and puts most of his emphasis on the power of human commitment to evoke the other's response and build dialogue. The meaning of what is communicated cannot be defined by one party, it must be discovered through dialogue. A value is not something *I* invent, as Sartre would have it, but a quality *we* discover. Thus love, hope, anger, understanding must have meanings that are intersubjectively confirmed and discovered not unilaterally imposed. Above all, to achieve true dialogue, Buber stresses the importance of recognizing the uniqueness of the other person, for in this uniqueness we glimpse God in man. Thus one's response must be judged by *quantum satis* – has one brought to the human relationship enough of oneself and a sufficient quantity and quality of one's resources. Nothing less will do. 'In spite of all similarities every living situation has, like a new-born child, a new face, that has never been before and will never come again. It demands of you a reaction which cannot be prepared beforehand. It demands nothing of what is past. It demands presence, responsibility . . . you'.

It is through such a relationship that one can recognize that to be free is to accept at the hand of another: ought must not become duty but must be constantly re-evaluated in the context of living or 'swing in the empty air'. Abstract universal ideals must be realized in particular situations. Thus, for Buber, no one can have understood the Ten Commandments unless he has experienced a particular situation in which the force of each is appropriate. The purpose of dialogue is both to question and to reconcile – freedom and hate, decision and surrender, the abstract and the concrete, universalism and particularism, risk and security, distance and relation, similarity and uniqueness, the mysterious and the mundane, obedience and originality, ought and is, God and man.

Even good and evil are not exclusive choices. Rather, one must 'serve God with the evil impulse' until it encounters the grace of Thou and is made whole. In Buber's terminology, 'good' is therefore that decision which responds and reconciles; 'Evil' is non-response. 'If there were a devil it would not be one who decided against God, but one who, in eternity, came to no decision.' Evil 'comes to us as a whirlwind, the

Martin Buber's profound and complex interpretation of dialogue serves to bridge many of the world's philosophical divides. For Buber dialogue is something perilous. The path which leads to the security of the other's affection is itself insecure, a narrow ridge. We can only discover that we are acceptable, by taking the risk of discovering that we are unacceptable. In that moment of meeting each is infinitely vulnerable. Also, and more significantly, Buber is saying that social and psychological concepts need to be defined inclusively of one another, rather than, as at present, exclusively. If I is to include and share with Thou by a process in which risking makes each more secure, then whole sets of polarities must also be defined to include each other. The 'decision' of I includes an aspect of 'surrender' to the perspectives of Thou. Abstract ideas are realized in concrete encounters, joining not only the people but these categories themselves. When Buber says, 'You can only enter into a relationship with one set at a distance', he is defining cooperation as a dialogue between 'individuals' and so reconciling individualism and cooperatism. Unless people and their conceptions are thus joined the narrow ridge becomes a precipice.

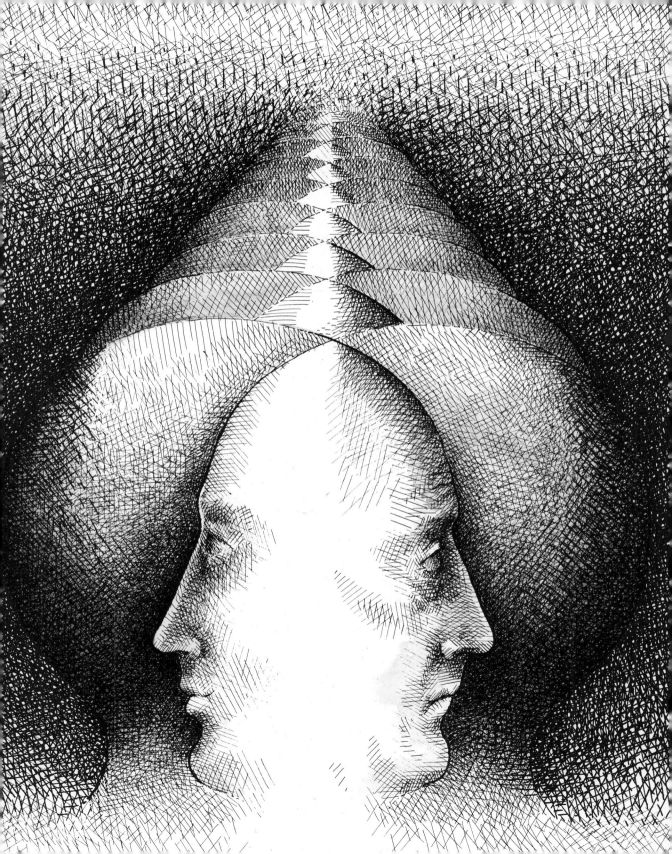

good has direction'. Evil is unreconciled divisive urges split from direction, action split from emotion, spirit from instinct, I from the other, and repression itself. 'It is a cruelly hazardous enterprise, this becoming a whole, becoming a form, of crystallization of the soul. Everything . . . which has been swashbuckling within us, must be overcome, and overcome not by elimination, by suppression, for genuine wholeness can never be achieved . . . where downtrodden appetites lurk in corners. Rather must all these mobile or static forces, seized by the soul's rapture, plunge of their own accord, as it were, into the mightiness of decision and dissolve within it'.

Such must be the decisive relationship between God and man. Buber's use of I and Thou to express this relationship translates poorly into English. The German *Du* is the familiar form of address suggesting intimacy. It is direct, mutual, present, and sharing, with none of the archaic overtones of the English 'Thou', as if one were addressing a dead Quaker. *Du* with its simultaneity, spontaneity, harmony, wholeness and guidance by facial recognition has all the characteristics of right-hemisphere brain functioning, while I–it is preponderantly left hemisphere (see Map 23). I–it connotes the world of cause and effect, our persistent itch to make some part of the process of dialogue into a master switch that controls it all. Fearful that the other will not confirm us, we pre-package our appeal to assure an impact. This robs meeting of its presentness, leaving us only with the past calculations and future ambitions of the technician who wants to know about people – 'what makes them tick' – but does not want to know them. However, no society can function without a great many I–it relationships. These are not wrong *per se*; it is only when they invade the personal realm to make intimacy instrumental, or when they eradicate all vestiges of the personal response in relationships between races, nations and classes that the danger becomes acute.

The creative energies of human dialogue must perpetually wrestle with the contradictions of our existence, rather than avoiding them from motives of scientific or religious purity. 'Good and evil, despair and hope, the power of destruction and the power of rebirth dwell side by side.' We need a divine force that 'penetrates the demonic in life' not one that 'hovers above it'. We cannot pretend, like weekend mystics, to achieve the unity of all by sacrificing the full seriousness of the everyday, and so 'flee from alone to the alone'. The origin of guilt is the failure to respond, to fail to become the person that one is called to become, and so never to experience two-fold feelings, the caress and the caressing, the gift and its receipt, the want and its satisfaction.

A delightful aspect of Buber's philosophy is its adroit commentary upon the endless list of human foibles, pretences, evasions and stratagems. He skewers every 'ism' remorselessly. Although he died in 1965, before he could react to the extravagance of the sixties, his writing appears to foresee it all as if he had been sadly shaking his head the while. 'Many years I have wandered through the land of . . . "erotic man". There a lover stamps around and is in love only with his passion. There one is wearing his differentiated feelings like medal ribbons. There one is enjoying the adventures of his own fascinating effect. There one is gazing enraptured at the spectacle of his own supposed surrender. There one is collecting excitement, there one is displaying his "power". There one is preening himself with borrowed vitality. . . There one is experimenting . . . all the manifold monologists with their mirrors, in the apartment of the most intimate dialogue!' Real love is not *in* anyone. It lies in the dialogue *between*.

Buber is especially harsh on the Hippie Heaven or what he termed 'the cry in twilight ages . . . for universal unreserve. He who can be unreserved with each passer-by has no substance to lose.' Though by the same token, one cannot

'In our age the I–it relation, gigantically swollen, has usurped practically uncontested, the mastery and the rule. The I of this relation, an I that possesses all, makes all, succeeds with all, this I that is unable to say Thou, unable to meet a being essentially, is the lord of the hour.'
'Eclipse of God' Martin Buber

'Man cannot approach the divine by reaching beyond the human: he can approach them through becoming human. To become human is what he, this individual man has been created for . . . This is the eternal core of Hasidic life and of Hasidic teaching.'
'Hasidism and Modern Man' Martin Buber

'Men do not find God if they stay in this world. They do not find him if they leave the world. He who goes out with his whole being to meet his Thou and carries to it all being that is in the world, finds him who cannot be sought.'
'I and Thou' Martin Buber

'To see a World in a Grain of
Sand
And a Heaven in a Wild Flower,
Hold Infinity in the palm of your
hand,
And Eternity in an hour'.
'Auguries of Innocence'
William Blake

'reserve oneself for God' like Kierkegaard rejecting the earthly presence of his fiancée Regina Olsen (see Map 12). You cannot renounce objects for God, as if he were one among objects. God was in Regina, not in some private audience that excluded her. However, it is for the quest for self-realization and personal fulfilment that Buber reserves his greatest scorn. He does not deny self-realization as an attainment, he decries it as a prescription because it leads us to aloneness. 'To begin with oneself, but not to end with oneself; to start from oneself, but not to aim at oneself. . . True, each is to know itself, purify itself, perfect itself, but not for its own sake − neither for the sake of temporal happiness nor for that of its eternal bliss − but for the sake of the work which it is destined to perform upon the world.'

Feelings, individuation, risk-taking, confiding, self-discovery are only parts of the process of relation, and their enhancement is its by-products. Each is gained only by aiming beyond. Hence security is found by hazarding the narrow ridge, freedom by accepting the other's confirming presence as one's destiny. The universal looks out at one from the particular face and the God of eternity stands in the presence of this moment. 'How lovely and how fitting . . . the *I* of Socrates! It is the I of endless dialogue and the air of dialogue is wafted around it in all its journeys, before the judges and in the last hour in prison. It never ceased to believe in the reality of men and went out to meet them . . . How powerful . . . and how legitimate, is the saying of *I* by Jesus! For it is the I of unconditioned relations in which the man calls his *Thou* Father in such a way that he is simply Son, and nothing else but Son.'

MAP REFERENCES
Contraries as true, 13, 16, 25, 26, 30, 34, 38−40, 42−3, 47, 53−5, 58−60; Dialogue, see also conversational domain, 12, 34, 39, 42, 51, 55, 59; Narrow ridge, see cusp, 56; Values defined inclusively, 12−13, 26, 30, 42−3, 51, 55.

MAP 36

The Force Fields of Kurt Lewin

Kurt Lewin (pronounced 'Leveen'), who brought his work from the University of Berlin to the United States in 1933, was psychology's first self-styled 'field theorist'; he died in 1947. Lewin's work is important because most psychology has followed Newtonian physics in assuming that theory should search first for basic units and only second considering how these might interact. Yet, in physics and chemistry in the nineteenth century, Michael Faraday and James Clerk Maxwell had caused a scientific revolution by their discovery that electromagnetic phenomena were first of all fields, currents and waves and only thus could the movement of any units or particles within these fields be explained. Hence the wave pattern of iron filings on a piece of paper above a magnet is explained by the overall magnetic field that creates the pattern. The answer is not discovered by asking what 'filing A' does to 'filing B'.

Lewin believed that the psychological fields joining the personality to its life-space (immediate environment) and the life-space to the larger environment beyond were strong enough to alter the meanings of 'facts'. Different people could vary totally in their response to identical facts, depending upon how these facts were organized and regarded. It has been found, for example, in a major survey of adolescents around New York, that the self-esteem of an adolescent correlates quite closely with the number of incidents of racial discrimination and abuse that he recalls. A major exception to this rule were Jewish adolescents, who remembered the abuse they received but had been taught by family and friends to expect it and defy it. In short, these children enjoyed a life-space organized and structured in a manner designed to defeat disparagement, and in the end their self-estimates were higher than those of Anglo-Saxon children.

The map opposite shows Lewin's conception of how the 'inner-personal system', consisting of groups of peripheral cells (p) and central cells (c), grows within a perceptual–motor system (P–M). This whole comprises the personality which exists within and organizes the (oval-shaped) life-space. Beyond the life-space is the environment. Some cells of the inner-personal system, and some divisions of the life-space, are cross-hatched to indicate rigidity of beliefs, while some are stippled to indicate flexibility. While no 'book of maps' can justify ignoring Lewin's keen map-making, I must confess that much of his mapping proved infertile and many of his lasting contributions are unmapped. Some agile leaps will be required to get from his earlier map-making to his later social activism!

Lewin conceived the process of development from child to adult in terms of the contrast between the bottom left oval on the map opposite and the top right oval. The following changes have been observed and tested experimentally by Lewin and his many students, such as Roger Barker, Tamara Dembo, Leon Festinger and Pauline Sears. Growth involves: 1. A strengthening of permeable boundaries around the life-space. (This is indicated by a thicker line around the adult's life-space, than the child's.) 2. Increased size and scope of the life-space. 3. Increased realism, ie systematic comparison of the inner-personal and psycho–motor systems with processes and forces in the life-space and environment. (The adult is less likely to confuse fantasy with reality.) 4. Increasing differentiation within all three systems, inner-personal, perceptual–motor, and life-space. The growing person develops more modes of behaviour, specific emotions, separable needs and branches of knowledge, as well as greater repertoires of social interaction. 5. Increased integration or organization of this variety. Clearly as sub-parts increase so must the complexity of their coordination. Lewin is not saying that adults are more unified, but only that increasing variety necessitates the concurrent growth of unifying capacities, so that differentiation and integration remain in balance or equilibrium.

Kurt Lewin was a brilliant psychologist but a curious map-maker, whose topography is little regarded today. The two ovals opposite represent the Life-Spaces (immediate environments) of a child (below) and adult (above) beyond which lies the world. The life-spaces are divided according to a subject's interests, with every space representing a 'fact', and contiguous facts joined with lines of varying thickness representing permeability. Cross-hatched areas are rigidly held, while stippled areas are flexible. The rings marked P–M stand for Perceptual–Motor Systems; these surround the Inner-Personal Systems and together comprise the Personality. The inner-personal system has peripheral cells (p) and inner cells (c) which usually contain needs. The personality impinges on and organizes the life-space and also includes areas of rigidity and flexibility which vary in permeability. The shaded areas in both inner-personal systems represent tension arising from a need triggered by an external factor (see arrows), such as thirst. In this condition the object in the life-space, drink, has a positive value (marked +) and induces a locomotion (dotted line) towards it. However, in his experiments, Lewin placed a barrier (B) across to block access (this was later employed as an analogy for racial discrimination and blocked opportunity). The effect of the barrier was to increase tension and promote disequilibrium in both personality and life-space. Unless a new equilibrium can be achieved the personality will regress.

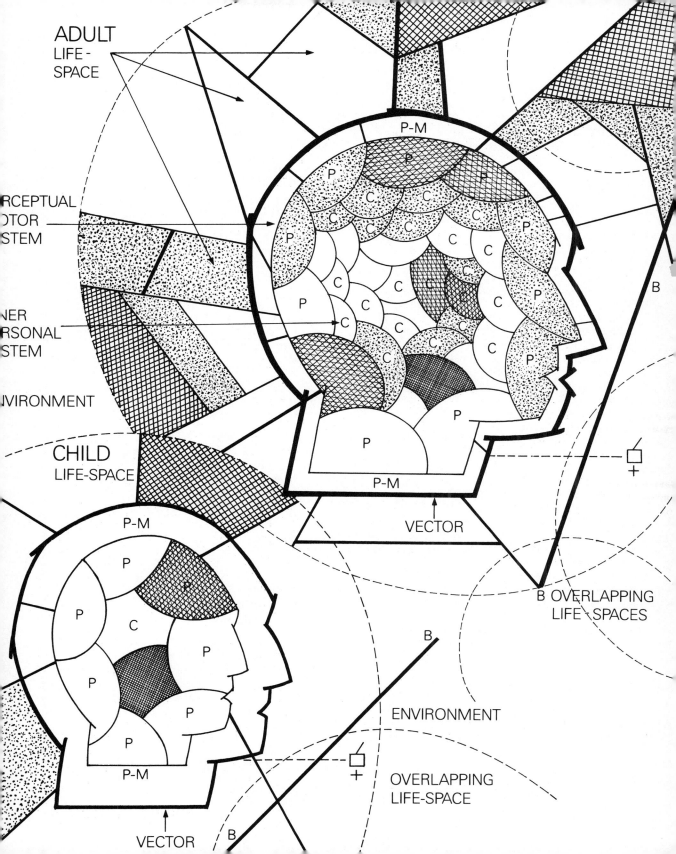

ADULT
LIFE-
SPACE

PERCEPTUAL
MOTOR
SYSTEM

INNER
PERSONAL
SYSTEM

ENVIRONMENT

CHILD
LIFE-SPACE

P-M

P

C

VECTOR

B

B OVERLAPPING
LIFE-SPACES

B

ENVIRONMENT

OVERLAPPING
LIFE-SPACE

P-M

VECTOR

6. A decrease in 'simple interdependence' and an increase in 'complex interdependence' occurs. This requires some explanation. When a child becomes hungry, for instance, the arousal in a single cell (see shaded area of the inner-personal system of the child) will tend to diffuse itself throughout the system as the tension rapidly spreads. Typically the whole child becomes agitated and agitates its life-space with its clamour. In the adult, hunger produces much more coordinated responses, resulting in a search for, and discovery of, food. In both cases, spreading tension activates the larger system, but with adults the inter-dependence and equilibrium-seeking is complex and organized. Different cells contain the tension in order to let it out through pathways that will solve the problem. A network of relatively rigid necessities, such as food, shelter, survival (cross-hatched on the map), are joined to flexible and alternate means of gaining these (stippled on the map).

With this theory, Lewin and his associates designed some ingenious experiments to investigate frustration, tension and regression. These demonstrate clearly that when children are frustrated by not being permitted to play with attractive toys placed in full view behind a partition, they will revert to more child-like modes of behaviour as measured by the criteria above. Blocked tension will diffuse through their systems as they become noticeably less organized in their play, less differentiated, less realistic and less coordinated. What Lewin showed was that a barrier erected within a child's life-space requires the reorganization of that child's personality in order to get round or through the barrier, and, failing this, that the personality will contract and regress in accordance with the reduction of opportunity in the life-space.

Lewin's critics accused him of laborious demonstrations of the obvious and of mapping commonplaces. His non-Freudian refugee status and 'exile' in the University of Iowa disadvantaged him academically. This must have influenced him to appeal beyond academia to the forces of social change, progressive politics, civil rights and planned change in institutions, and it was here that his theories found their fullest vindication.

One of his concepts was that of action-research. The researcher, he argued, has his own active life-space, as do those persons he investigates. So long as psychologists are content to observe with dispassion and passivity, what they discover will remain a worm's-eye view, insulated from the significance of dedicated lives and unusable by those who act boldly upon a priori convictions. The challenges of real life can rarely be simulated in contrived settings and, for a whole range of problems, the only suitable 'laboratory' must be at least a section of the real world. Lewin was himself a Zionist, who had seen his mother die in a concentration camp. He knew what he stood for and what he opposed. If values were declared 'up front', he argued, there would be less confusion between the values of the researcher and those of the researched. It was a fallacy to assume that detachment made one 'value free', because such an attitude is communicated to the subjects of research, and tends to make all concerned valueless.

Lewin was one of the first to insist that people were changed less by someone else appealing to their beliefs than by they themselves altering publicly, and being seen to alter, the operations of their life-space. Just before World War II the President of the American Jewish Committee, advised by Lewin, obtained a court order against Columbia University Medical School for maintaining a quota against Jews. In the glare of publicity the school was ordered to operate non-discriminatory enrolment procedures. Lewin later described such processes in the terms of unfreeze/change/refreeze, which correspond to the equilibrium/tension/re-

'There is nothing so practical as a good theory.'
'Field Theory in Social Science'
Kurt Lewin

'For too long social scientists have hung back from the fray, concerned with rituals of decontamination, with controlling their anxiety by rigorous method and defending their "dogma of Immaculate Perception". Any paradigm must be partly self-fulfilling. If nothing else we inflict our lassitude. The question, then, is not whether our values influence our research, but how?'
'Radical Man'
Charles Hampden-Turner

equilibrium formula that is central to his theory of personality growth. Yet he insisted that tension must be moderate, and the targets of change must have a clear way of reducing tension by means of legal compliance. He never forgot his experiments on the tension, frustration and resulting regression of children. This is why he insisted on refreezing at a higher level. People need rules and structures and unless these are built like banisters up a staircase the climbers will become tense and fall back again to the bottom, as had happened to black rights in the United States following Reconstruction. Societies, like persons, grow from 'quasi-stationary equilibrium' to ever new equilibria. Lewin warned that it was invariably more effective to use friendly persuasion to weaken the forces resisting change than to push and shove against them. And, indeed, for more than three decades Lewin's model of court-ordered public compliance has been the major instrument of social change in America. Among others, it greatly influenced the tactics of Martin Luther King (see Map 59).

Lewin also showed experimentally that people are more easily changed by being given the facts and allowed to decide for themselves than by unilateral persuasion. Alfred Marrow, a student of Lewin and owner of the Harwood Manufacturing Company, demonstrated experimentally that changes in production methods were much more effectively introduced by joint decision-making than by mere consultation, or managerial fiat. He measured morale and productivity under each condition. Control over shared life-space was the crucial variable. Consider how much more efficient it is to alter that single variable than intervene therapeutically in the inner-personal areas of a hundred workers! Two other students of Lewin's, Ronald Lippitt and Ralph White, conducted the famed experiments on autocratic, laissez-faire and democratic classrooms. The researchers found that the autocratic teacher and the one who merely let the children's 'natural goodness' bloom, both precipitated measured degrees of regression. It was the democratic teacher who produced more learning and all the evidence of mature behaviour in his class. Without, of course, abdicating his responsibility for the children, he asked for and received their assistance in making the classroom a better life-space for all concerned. (One wishes that the interminable debaters of traditional versus progressive education took account of this research so we would be spared their false dichotomies.)

The crowning achievement of Lewin's career came shortly before his death, when the Connecticut State Inter-racial Commission called for his assistance in their work. His solution was to take a small group of officials, civic leaders and organizers, who were responsible and willing to implement anti-discrimination policies, into retreat. Each member had imagined himself or herself to be struggling alone, and the mutual support, determination and enthusiasm engendered by that small group was an unforgettable experience. More important, they returned to their jobs able to coordinate their efforts against discrimination from more than a dozen directions. A method had been devised for giving lonely decision-makers the sustained support of intimate bonds with a group of like-minded people. In the small group's shared life-space the social map could be redrawn and all could pledge themselves to changed directions. From this small beginning grew the National Training Laboratories of Bethel, Maine. Much has since been said for and against 'T-Groups' but I doubt that Lewin ever conceived that people would wander into the woods to practise intimacy. For him, retreat was strategic, and its purpose was social advance; you gathered to incubate the will, the strength, and the social support to struggle effectively for a world where every man is sovereign of his own life-space.

MAP 37

Generativity and the Life-Cycle: Erik Erikson's concept of identity

In his classes at Harvard in the 1960s Erik Erikson, the psychiatrist, showed a French film called *Sundays and Cybèle*, directed by Serge Bourguignon and Antoine Tudal. It tells the story of an ex-airforce pilot, now a mental patient with amnesia, who befriends a little girl of twelve, abandoned by her father at a convent home for children. Posing as a relative, the man takes her out every Sunday and a deep friendship develops. She is discovering a fatherly affection she never knew. He is restoring to life a girl very similar to the one he caught in the sights of his machine-gun as he dived to strafe an Algerian village. (This trauma is the source of his amnesia.) At the film's climax the two are celebrating Christmas, but meanwhile the authorities have discovered their 'unhealthy' relationship. Having no gift to give him, the little girl writes 'Cybèle' on a piece of paper and puts it in a silver ball upon the Christmas tree. It is her true name, which the nuns refuse to recognize because it is 'pagan'. Beneath the tree she falls asleep, and the man finding her gift bends tenderly over her. At this moment, the police rush in and mistaking his intentions, shoot and kill him. They command the awakened child to give her name. 'I have no name', she cries forlornly, 'I have no name!'

Erikson's socialization of Freud's work has become justly famous, particularly his concept of *ego-identity*, 'The accrued confidence that one's ability to maintain inner sameness and continuity . . . is matched by the sameness and continuity of one's meaning for others'. Like Cybèle we must all gather up the important pieces of our experience, make a synthesis of them and ask significant others in our lives, 'Will you accept this configuration of what I am?' Upon such questions and the answers sanity itself depends.

Erikson's map of the human life-cycle is extraordinarily rich and subtle. On the left side of the grid, shown opposite, are 'the eight stages of man', the first five being elaborations of Freud's oral, anal, phallic, latency and genital stages (see Map 9), with three more stages taking the subject from adulthood to maturity; the challenges met at each stage are plotted diagonally from bottom left to top right; and the achievements or 'virtues' listed on the right (although Erikson added these much later and did not write much about them). Erikson based his theory on Heinz Hartmann's idea of an 'average expectable environment' of cradle, nursery, family, school, peer group, marriage, children and maturity. He is not saying, however, that this is how culture must or should be, but that these events trigger a sequence of responses; other environments might well alter the order or challenges, but a sequence of some kind will persist. First one newly-grown part of the ego-identity then another, is tested by the environment and surmounts (or fails to surmount) its vulnerability. Each step is an altered perspective with a different capacity using a different opportunity. 'Each comes to its ascendance, meets its crisis, and finds its lasting solution towards the end of the stage indicated.' Each new stage founds itself upon earlier stages, so that the manner in which initial crises have been met must affect the chances of resolving later ones. Cybèle suffered not merely from a blighted childhood, which drove her to find multiple solutions in a single friend, but from the failure of her culture to tolerate so improbable an attachment. Once a child is out of phase, its needs are seen as illegitimate and the odds against the deviant multiply.

But let us now go through the various stages of the life-cycle. Erikson sees the first crisis as *basic trust versus mistrust*. To acquire basic trust is 'the cornerstone of a healthy personality'. In this oral phase mouth meets breast and the child comes to trust in the sameness and continuity of providers. Unless the child feels that he can get a reliable someone to do something for him, there is a risk of acute infant depression, and, later in life, of regression into avaricious forms of oral sadism and,

Erik Erikson's map of the human life-cycle is presented in the form of a grid. On the left are the 'eight stages of man'; the challenges met at each stage are plotted diagonally from bottom left to top right; and the attainments or 'virtues' of each stage are shown on the right. The mental health and virtue (meaning 'inherent strength') of the individual depend upon how well the ego-identity has survived the preceding stages and their conflicts by incorporating (not rejecting) occasions for Mistrust within Basic Trust, moments of Isolation within Intimacy, and so on. The grid pattern may be filled in by particular individuals to show how previous crises tend to be present within the one that is temporarily ascendant. Hence a young couple struggling to cement Intimacy (stage 6) are likely to face issues of Trust, Initiative and Integrity within that struggle. The woman, for example, may ask herself, 'Can he hold a job? (stage 4). Does he respect my autonomy? (stage 2). Will he cherish our children? (stage 7). The couple may achieve Intimacy (or not) depending on how earlier crises have been met and on how well their current relationship can repair earlier failings. For in every individual both child and adult are present, and both meet in the other.

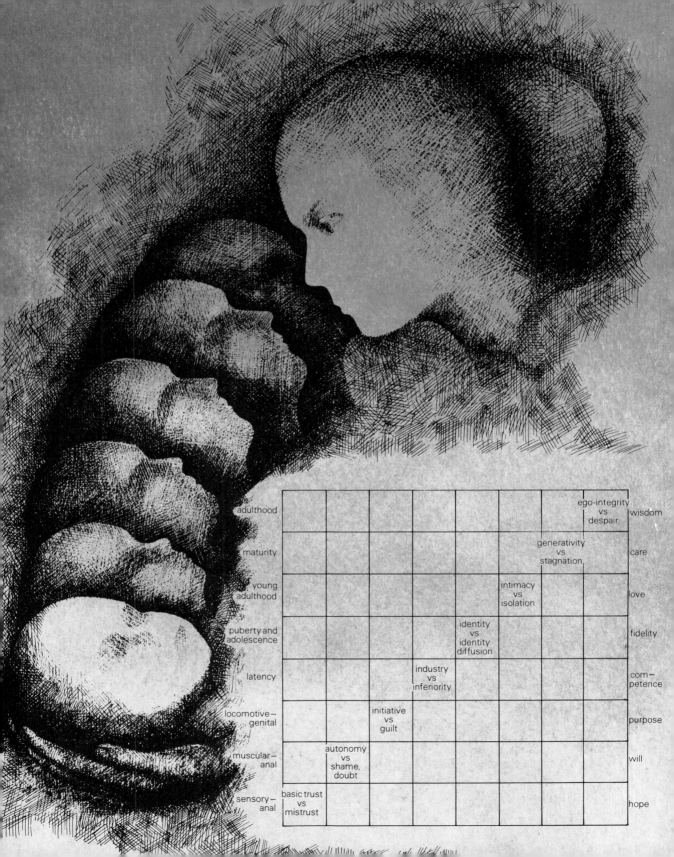

	1	2	3	4	5	6	7	8	
adulthood								ego-integrity vs despair	wisdom
maturity							generativity vs stagnation		care
young adulthood						intimacy vs isolation			love
puberty and adolescence					identity vs identity diffusion				fidelity
latency				industry vs inferiority					com-petence
locomotive-genital			initiative vs guilt						purpose
muscular-anal		autonomy vs shame, doubt							will
sensory-anal	basic trust vs mistrust								hope

in some psychotics, a chronic incapacity to respond to any kind of help or support. Basic trust imparts to us that faith in a responsive universe that underlies the realism born of later stages.

The next eliminative or anal stage develops between the ages of one and three as the child learns to keep the body system in rough balance: holding and letting go, rigidity and relaxation, flexion and extension. From this balance, or its lack, grows the crisis of *autonomy versus shame and doubt*. It is fatally easy at this stage to make a child ashamed and disgusted with bodily functions performed under the most public scrutiny. Adult judgements carry infallible weight. The consequence can be a life-long conviction that dirtiness and evil are associated with the body. We see such pathology in neurotic compulsions, their stinginess, their rituals of decontamination and obsessive orderliness, all disguising an underlying disgust at the human condition.

The child of four and five next enters upon the crisis of *initiative versus guilt*. This is the age of vastly improved locomotion (not just of walking *per se* but of searching, poking and intruding) and of precocious language acquisition with its concurrent explosion of imaginative powers. The child can visualize himself as grown up and such simple action roles as policeman or doctor are popular. The danger lies in the capacity for secret fantasies to arise where initiative is thwarted, as in the Oedipal attachment to the mother. The child is now capable of feeling intense guilt about illicit desires, and his embryonic conscience can be cruel towards himself or an inconsistent parent. At stake is the belief in a coherent system of universal goodness versus the terror of arbitrary and incomprehensible powers which can possess the mind. At this stage, Erikson sees the necessity for a clear boundary drawn by the family within which the child's sense of unbroken initiative has the freest feasible rein.

In the fourth stage of *industry versus inferiority* the child goes to school to discover the world of systematic instruction. Erikson gives short shrift to the perennial debate between 'formal' and 'progressive' educators. The child needs and enjoys an ecological mastery of the environment. To play is to gain imagined mastery of the things toys symbolize. Play, therefore, both refreshes the ego from struggles to learn in the schoolroom and visualizes the ends to which that learning can be put. Play is therefore complementary to work, but no substitute, any more than any fantasy can be a substitute for achievement. From school the child must develop a sense of industry stronger than occasional feelings of inadequacy. To fall seriously behind is to battle daily against humiliation, so that great energies are expended purely to defend against inferiority. Another pathology is the life of 'busyness' aimed entirely at warding-off feared deficiencies, a frantic running up the down escalator at the bottom of which live those beasts of the bourgeois imagination, the poor, the idle and the 'scroungers'.

At this point let me rescue Erikson's ideas from a common misinterpretation. He does not see trust, autonomy and initiative 'conquering' their opposites in some triumph of positive thinking. On the contrary every aware person needs to internalize experiences and occasions wherein mistrust, shame and guilt are entirely appropriate and inevitable. The positive learns from the negative without being overwhelmed. Erikson reserves special admiration for those like George Bernard Shaw (see margin) who can take the 'skeleton' of a drunken father and make it dance.

The ego-identity's greatest trial usually occurs in adolescence with the struggle of *identity versus identity diffusion*. Rapid bodily changes at puberty confront 'the autocracy of conscience' with the 'anarchy of drives'. The world suddenly opens to

'A boy who has seen "the governor" with an imperfectly wrapped-up goose under one arm and a ham in the same condition under the other (both purchased under heaven knows what delusion of festivity) butting at the garden wall in the belief that he was pushing open the gate, and transforming his tall hat to a concertina in the process, and who instead of being overwhelmed with shame and anxiety at the spectacle, has been so disabled by merriment . . . that he has been hardly able to rush to rescue of the hat and pilot its wearer to safety, is clearly not a boy who will make tragedies of trifles instead of making trifles of tragedies. If you cannot get rid of the family skeleton, you may as well make it dance.'

From the 'Selected Prose' of George Bernard Shaw quoted by Erik Erikson in 'Identity and the Life Cycle'

'Human evolution, for Erikson . . . has always the goal of finding ever-better patterns (or rituals) of mutual activation and regulation, [which] are the essence of culture. Culture is not simply a system of prohibitions and permissions. . . . The Eriksonian vision, which is more ecologically and theologically valid, sees self and society more as a system of complementary needs and activations.'

'Generative Man'
Don S. Browning

'For Erikson, the I–Thou relationship is not simply a duality. It is at least a quadrivium. It is not just adult meeting adult; it is the adult and child of one person meeting the adult and the child in another.'

'Generative Man'

many times its former size, with scores of potential carriers and the mass merchandizing of idols and ideals which deliberately bolster peer-group pressures towards mass conformity and transitory identifications. This is a time when whole-hearted and consistent recognition by parents and teachers of real accomplishment and meaningful achievements is quite essential, if a stable identity is to be preserved. Otherwise the young person faced with the diffusion of his identity into sparkling shreds may prefer a negative identity to none at all, one that will shock, violate and grab. Delinquency is fostered by labelling games. It is death by pat definition and pet diagnosis. Much current pathology, racism, sexism, classism, and juvenile gangs stem from a desperate attempt to purify identity within communities 'cleansed' of outsiders, (see especially Richard Sennett's work).

It is only when a firm identity has been fashioned that the self may be offered to another, risked in the closeness of intimacy where vulnerability is strength. Erikson describes this crisis as *intimacy and distantation versus self-absorption*. Implicit is Martin Buber's idea that distance is essential to true intimacy (see Map 35). The other has a separate space and allows you to enter. Only the self-absorbed cannot leave the safety of their fortress. This is Freud's genital phase, the mutuality of the fully adult. Out of personal intimacies children are conceived and there arises the challenge of *generativity versus stagnation*. Generativity is Erikson's most elegant and important conception, one that typifies his own intellectual life, which has been nourished by and nourishes the work of Freud with cross-generational devotion. Generativity is the care shown in establishing and guiding the next generation. It is loving creativity, for modern careless creativity is our grandest temptation and greatest fault. Generativity is a pattern and process that stretches from man's most archaic and unconscious biological tendencies to the highest cultural products of imagination. It is the generational complex which transcends the Oedipal complex to make us lovers and parents in the continuity of procreation. 'Evolution has made man a teaching as well as a learning animal, for dependency and maturity are reciprocal: mature man needs to be needed and maturity is guided by the nature of that which must be cared for.'

And so we come to the last crisis, that of *integrity versus disgust and despair*. Throughout the life-cycle the pieces have been assembled, structure built on structure around the ego's continuity. Now with death not too far away, can it all hold up or will it crumble? Are the links of love and meaning strong enough, so that we are ourselves content to fall away? 'Only he who in some way has taken care of things and people and has adapted himself to the triumphs and disappointments of being, by necessity, the originator of others and the generator of things and ideas – only he may gradually grow the fruit of the seven stages. I know no better word for it than integrity . . . It is a sense of comradeship with men and women of distant times and of different pursuits, who have created orders and objects and sayings conveying human dignity and love.' So in Erikson psychoanalysis becomes a positive ethical science, with the ego holding in synthesis the virtues of the eight stages, *hope, will, purpose, competence, fidelity, love, care* and *wisdom*, each caring and cared for by the other.

MAP REFERENCES

MAP 38

The Ascent from Plato's Cave: Moral development from Piaget to Kohlberg

In this map we encounter structuralism. This may be considered as a form of the field theory introduced in Map 36 but it is more indebted to biology and linguistics than to electromagnetism. Structuralism looks first to the principles by which an entire phenomenon is organized, and only then interprets the elements within that structure according to their relationships to the whole.

Jean Piaget is famous for having traced three broad stages in the development of the intelligence of children, in his studies from the thirties to the seventies. The first stage, from birth to seven, is the sensory–motor and pre-operational stage and is characterized by the child's intelligence being bounded by what he can physically perform or see performed. The second stage, from seven years to eleven, is the concrete operations stage when the child can symbolize concrete acts or operations without having to do them physically. In the third stage, from eleven years on – the child can think about thoughts, and 'operate on operations' and so conceive of general laws behind the array of particular instances. Transition from stage to stage is by *conflict* and *disequilibrium* followed by *equilibration*, as the child both assimilates the environment and adapts it to himself. Piaget also believed that moral conceptions went through such sequences, a notion which Lawrence Kohlberg at Harvard has taken much further to a widely researched theory of development of moral judgement. Kohlberg's six stages of moral development, tested over nearly two decades, are presented on the map opposite.

From about the age of two years to twenty-five (after which cognitive development usually ceases), a person will grow through at least the first few of the six stages opposite in a sequence which does not vary and is irreversible. The stage of moral reasoning which a particular subject has attained can be measured by presenting him with up to a dozen stories containing moral dilemmas and asking what the subject would do in such a situation. What is scored is not whether an answer is 'right' or 'wrong' but the structure and level of moral reasoning used to justify the solution. For example, he is asked to imagine that his wife is dying for lack of a locally manufactured drug. The sole supplier is demanding so exorbitant a price that he cannot find the money. Supplications are in vain. What does he do? Most subjects, although not all, say they would take the drug with or without some payment. Let us go through the stages of moral development to see what kind of reasoning accompanies each level.

Moral value in the first two preconventional stages is defined in terms of self-centred needs. At stage 1, the individual is primarily motivated by desire to avoid punishment by a superior power: 'God would punish me if I let my wife die. My father-in-law would make trouble for me.' At stage 2, concern has shifted to the satisfaction of quasi-physical needs. The individual develops an awareness of the relative value of each person's needs as his own drives are frustrated by demands for exchange and reciprocity: 'I have a right to my wife, and naturally this is more important than whatever rights the pharmacist may claim. No one is going to look out for my interest or my wife's unless I do.'

In the next two stages the subject is at the conventional level where moral values involve conformity to traditional role expectations and the maintenance of existing social and legal order. The stage 3 individual is motivated to avoid social disapproval for nonconformity and would like to be judged by his intentions: 'I'd do what any half-decent husband would do – save his family and carry out his protective function.' The stage 4 person understands how his role fits into the social institutions approved by others and he seeks to perform his duty – to meet the expectations of society: 'My wife and I submitted ourselves to a higher law, the institution of marriage. Society is held together by this institution. I know my duty.'

Lawrence Kohlberg has likened the six stages of moral development, opposite, to an ascent from the shadows of Plato's allegorical cave to the sunlight of True Justice. Between the ages of two and twenty-five, Kohlberg found that young people in many cultures develop from stage 1 onwards in an invariable, irreversible, step-wise sequence; the majority reach stages 3 and 4 but few reach stage 6. Each successive stage is a cognitive transformation of earlier ones with its own particular shape and pattern of response, and a new, intentional structure. Each level incorporates lower levels in a hierarchical system of increasing differentiation and integration. Change from one level to the next is precipitated by moral conflict involving expectations and reality, with thesis and antithesis giving way to higher synthesis. The developing person seeks an equilibrium between assimilating his social environment and accommodating it to him. This theory involves the interaction of the organism and the environment; it is not a purely biological sequence nor does it purport to estimate an individual's 'worth' apart from social opportunities. Unlike social learning theories, it is less concerned with learned contents which can be forgotten than with evolving moral values which are not.

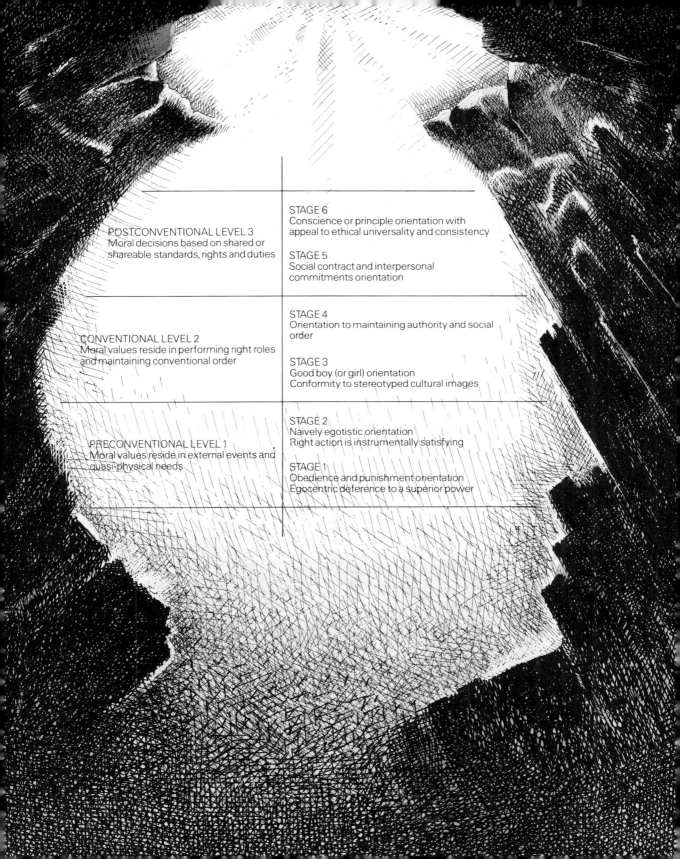

POSTCONVENTIONAL LEVEL 3
Moral decisions based on shared or
shareable standards, rights and duties

STAGE 6
Conscience or principle orientation with
appeal to ethical universality and consistency

STAGE 5
Social contract and interpersonal
commitments orientation

CONVENTIONAL LEVEL 2
Moral values reside in performing right roles
and maintaining conventional order

STAGE 4
Orientation to maintaining authority and social
order

STAGE 3
Good boy (or girl) orientation
Conformity to stereotyped cultural images

PRECONVENTIONAL LEVEL 1
Moral values reside in external events and
quasi-physical needs

STAGE 2
Naively egotistic orientation
Right action is instrumentally satisfying

STAGE 1
Obedience and punishment orientation
Egocentric deference to a superior power

The two postconventional stages represent the most advanced levels of moral development. Decisions are based on consideration of shared values rather than on self-centred interests or blind conformity to external standards. The stage 5 individual perceives his duty in terms of a social contract, recognizing the arbitrary nature of rules made for the sake of agreement. He avoids infringing the rights of others, or violating the welfare of the majority: 'My wife and I promised to love and help one another, whatever the circumstances. We chose to make that commitment and in our daily lives together it is constantly renewed, I am therefore committed to saving her.' The stage 6 person relies heavily on his own conscience and the mutual respect of others. He recognizes the universal principles that underlie social commitments and seeks to apply them as consistent principles of moral judgement: 'No contract, law, obligation, private gain or fear of punishment should impede any man from saving those he loves. I will take the drug and leave a fair price, and will subsequently try to persuade all concerned that the principle of justice was served by my act.'

In practice, of course, responses are not so neat or clear-cut, and elaborate scoring systems are necessary to estimate which stage of moral development is dominant in the subject's reasoning. Some interesting patterns have emerged from nearly twenty years of research. The vast majority of Americans and Europeans rarely develop beyond stages 3 and 4. Fewer than six per cent in most populations reach stage 6, and only about twenty per cent reach stage 5. The moral judgement level of mothers predicts the moral development of their children, but the father's level has little effect. Delinquents and criminals are preponderantly low, mostly 1, 2 and 3 with negative stereotypes – 'bad boy' as opposed to good. The level of moral judgement attained predicts behaviour not just in theory but in practice. Hence in a notorious experiment in which subjects are ordered in the name of psychological research, to inflict dangerous levels of electric shock upon a 'volunteer' (the pain and shocks are faked) seventy-five per cent of those at stage 6 but only twenty per cent of the rest refuse the brutal obedience. Moral development, it seems, tends to correlate with Piaget's intellectual stages, especially the transition from concrete to formal operations, as does high IQ, college education, privileged social opportunities, youthfulness and the affluence of a culture. Sons and daughters at college tend to outstrip their parents.

Before the reader starts to get indignant, let us rid ourselves of some popular misconceptions. 'Superior moral judgement' in no way estimates a person's intrinsic 'goodness' or 'worth', which remains safely in the divine province. Kohlberg is measuring an interaction of person and environment, and this cannot possibly estimate the value of the person apart from his social advantages. Those in high social positions in wealthy countries are obviously better enabled to propose sweeping solutions to 'impossible' dilemmas. Hence Kohlberg's positive correlations between higher moral judgement and greater social power are to be expected, and in no way discredit a blue-collar worker who cannot easily conceive of himself instructing his corporation on moral issues.

It is important to note that the lower moral stages suffice for most people, places and problems. If a car nearly runs me down, my 'fear of punishment' (stage 1) and my cursing a drunken fool (stage 3) who won't let me walk in peace (stage 2) are adequate responses to the occasion. Only a prig would begin a moral disquisition on alcohol and it is for the judge and the driver's psychiatrist to make more complex judgements. Although such judgements are on different levels they would probably all share the conclusion that the driver is a menace. Moral dilemma only occurs when the routine system of social judgements is for one reason or another

'There is a type of constructive non-violent tension which is necessary for growth. Just as Socrates felt it was necessary to create a tension in the mind so that individuals could rise from the bondage of half-truths, so must we see the need for non-violent gadflies to create the kind of tension in society that will help men rise from the dark depths of prejudice and racism.'
'Letter from a Birmingham Jail' by Martin Luther King quoted by Lawrence Kohlberg

'One may well ask "How can you advocate breaking some laws and obeying others?" There are two types of laws, just and unjust. One has not only a legal but moral responsibility to obey just laws. One has a moral responsibility to disobey unjust laws. An unjust law is a human law not rooted in eternal and natural law. Any law that uplifts human personality is just, any law that degrades human personality is unjust.'

Martin Luther King quoted by Lawrence Kohlberg

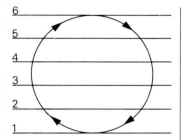

In this revision of Kohlberg's conception, moral development is seen not just as going up the hierarchy to define a pure form of the Platonic Good, but coming down again, to manifest specific, concrete Aristotelean instances of that good at all stages of the hierarchy.

incompetent to deal with a particular case. Kohlberg's means of measuring moral judgement (ie the fictional situations with which he tests his subjects) all involve the breakdown of the system. The 'bad system' gives 'good persons', or more precisely 'caring persons of sufficient social power', an opportunity to consider reform.

Kohlberg's research has shown that 'consciousness can be raised' and the level of moral judgement increased by classroom arguments and Socratic-type discussions. Consider the example of the dying wife: if students are invited to come to terms with the conflict between two stages, they are likely to transcend the opposition and move up a stage in moral awareness. Hence, 'I will be punished for stealing' (stage 1) versus 'I should have the continued service of my wife' (stage 2) tends to be reconciled by the stereotype of 'the half-decent husband saves his wife' (stage 3). Research has shown that students will tend to prefer the highest stage that they are capable of comprehending and will later start to use it regularly. Similarly the dilemma of, 'It's illegal to steal' (stage 4) versus 'We promised to love and help each other' (stage 5) is reconciled by stage 6. 'Let my wife have her life and the pharmacist a reasonable profit, according to the principle of justice.'

In recent years Kohlberg's theory and research has run into increasing criticism, even abuse, for being blatantly pro-Western, culturally biased in Platonic and Lockean directions, and for emphasizing the cerebral moralities of privileged academic talkers and symbolizers to the neglect of genuine social achievements. With a brief, if fundamental, addition to Kohlberg's position, I believe his critics can be mollified and the value of his work conserved. His 'bias' lies in the need to assault the coherent value hierarchy in order to measure it. His higher level judgements are responses to simulated chaos. The 'good' he seeks to measure is the capacity to abstract a principle of justice or conscience from social contradictions, precisely what Plato did when faced by the decline of Athenian society. But why is this 'virtue'? Surely the discovery of the form, 'Justice', is but the first step in the process of implementing that ideal and this involves a repairing of the social-moral hierarchy torn by contradictions (or by Kohlberg's methodology).

If we appreciate a man like Martin Luther King, whom Kohlberg quotes as inspiration, we see a man who did not withdraw to the contemplation of Good within an academy of rich young men as the social system collapsed. He climbed the moral hierarchy, the better to come down and repair its levels. King certainly spoke of conscience but Kohlberg's own research would show that this was insufficient as people rarely understand moral statements more than one level above their own habitual stage. For this reason King forged a social movement (stage 5) which saw that civil rights laws were passed and implemented by the courts (stage 4). He set up brilliant, televized, moral pageants in which black people were conventionally good and peaceful (stage 3) and white racists were stereotypically brutal, even as he publicly claimed the rights of his race to ordinary human satisfactions (stage 2).

But the theme over all was harmony and integration, not merely between the races, but between levels of moral awareness. Where the principle of justice infuses relationships, laws and images, social virtue is restored. King fragmented in order to better reconcile. It is within the entire cycle of healing divisions that virtue and development lie. This 'virtuous circle' is both Platonic and Aristotelean, abstract and concrete, cerebral and loving, Western and Eastern, individual and social. In his eagerness to measure, Kohlberg fragments the hierarchy and 'finds' 'good' persons in 'bad' systems, and measures only a small cerebral arc of the virtuous circle. If we allow for that, his work remains an important and impressive approach to an issue that has long been ignored.

MAP 39

Words and Things, Maps and Territories: The semantics of Alfred Korzybski

In this map and the five that follow (Maps 39–44) I consider how the mind uses and misuses language in pursuit of expression and communication.

Alfred Korzybski was a Polish–American scientist, linguist and philosopher who founded The Institute for General Semantics in Connecticut, USA in 1929. His avowed mission was the creation of 'an empirical general theory of values' and a non-Aristotelean framework for understanding the relationship between language and the objects to which language refers. This would be a 'new general discipline'. Korzybski regarded language, with its 'time-binding' qualities allowing us to hand down increasing information from generation to generation, as both a blessing and a danger, since defects of that language structure would be handed on as well. Language fails entirely to make one crucial distinction. It assumes that words and the things they describe are identical and, so, fails to distinguish between 'maps' in our minds and the territory such maps refer to. In fact the word and thing, map and territory relationship is one of similar structure but not identity, and words may have a structure all their own which falsifies the territory to which they refer.

For example, the subject–predicate, or subject–verb–object structure of a typical sentence, seriously muddles the distinction of map and territory. Take an ideological dispute in which A says, 'As an Individualist I must fight collectivism', B replies, 'As a Cooperatist I must fight selfishness'. Each speaks as if minor embodiments of Individualism and Cooperation were tripping off their tongues to strike the other. But, of course, there is neither substance nor essence to the 'Individuality' within and 'Cooperation' is no sacred object inhabiting the soul. There is only the pattern of generally acknowledged differences which we have identified with codes. The word 'cooperative', and a living cooperative community have a structural relationship similar to one inch to one mile on a road map, save that ideological maps are rarely as reliable!

What happens is that we confuse the language, thrusting from subject to object, and its exclusive Aristotelean classifications of A or not A, with the less antagonistic form of the territory. We find ourselves verbally fencing and conflicting as depicted on the map. Much political rhetoric consists of rubbing together the intentional meanings of group words: 'Love, brotherhood, equality, cooperation!' Too rarely do we ask how the 'thing' we describe differs from the word used. To do so might lead to the discovery that Individualists can docilely cooperate, while Cooperators ferociously compete! For, while Aristotelean logic can usefully classify objects, it is vitally important to question the logic that so classifies and to see that the other classifications are possible. When mind itself is cut into exclusive fragments, we once again confuse the word with the thing, the mapper with the mapped, and believe the mind must contain no 'contradiction'.

Korzybski urges upon us the image of language as a self-correcting cybernetic system, with verbal-visual maps that are tentative and hypothetical and always open to revision and amalgamation. These can never represent more than a part of the territory and are best seen as informed relationships between mind and environment. Maps, in other words, are contexts we can share with each other to judge differences. So far from individualism and cooperation being a 'contradiction', these are poles on a map coordinate, enabling us to understand that human beings separate in order to unify in order to separate, in an endless cybernetic loop. When we distinguish the map from the territory the spectre of contradiction vanishes. A and non-A may have to exclude one another from a single piece of territory, but both can be plotted on the same map. Moreover action-A can be taken within a context (or map) that aims at non-A. Hence individualism can further cooperation, or vice versa. To this issue of contexts we now turn.

Our habitual way of speaking is structured in a straight line, a one-way purposive motion in which a subject employs a verb to affect some object. But herein lies a danger since the words passing our lips are in no way identical to the objects they refer to; the first are codes or 'maps', the second are the actual territory. Hence, when A says, 'As an Individualist I fight collectivism', and B replies, 'As a Cooperatist I fight selfishness', each tries to make an object of the other, and each pretends that his words are that object. The laws of Aristotelian logic tend to pit Cooperation against Individuality as exclusive classifications, so that they clash like crossed swords when structured as rhetoric (top), ignoring the fact that in the social territory individuality and cooperation entwine.

To counter this tendency in language, Alfred Korzybski urges us to act as self-correcting systems with verbal scimitars joined into cybernetic loops (bottom). Thus a sentence does not end when it 'hits' its object but returns reflexively to the map that made it, so that A and B can each check map against territory. So if A and B are both subject and object, both map and territory, with information (not things) going around, then surely this reconciles their silly dispute? So the 'arc of individualism' joins the 'cooperation arc' to make a circle, as each becomes more of an individual by being confirmed in a cooperative relationship.

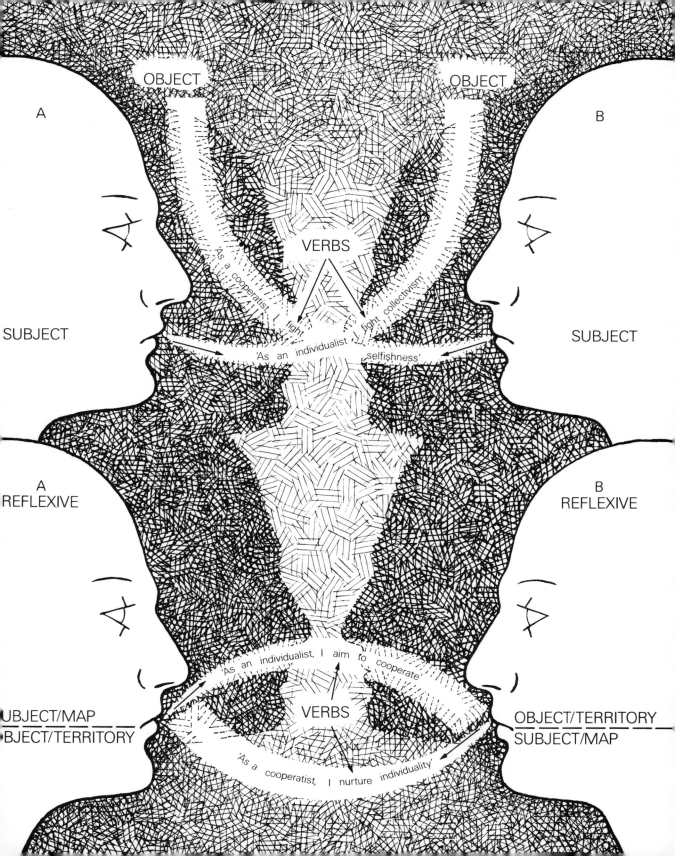

MAP 40

Solving the Monstrous Riddle:
Russell, Whitehead and logical types

When Oedipus approached the city of Thebes he found it besieged by a monster called the Sphinx ('she who binds'), with the face and breasts of a beautiful woman, the body and claws of a lion and eagle's wings. Crouching at the only mountain pass that allowed access to Thebes, she asked all wayfarers a riddle seemingly as monstrous as herself: 'What creature is it that walks on four legs in the morning, two legs at noon-time and three legs in the evening?' Those confounded by the riddle she devoured, and the city grew hungry and desperate. Then Oedipus came to the pass, confronted the Sphinx and answered, 'Man. He crawls on all fours in infancy, stands upright in maturity, and leans upon a stick in old age.' The Sphinx sprang to her death over the precipice. The Thebans acclaimed Oedipus and crowned him their king.

What had Oedipus grasped about human nature and communication that had escaped those whom the Sphinx devoured? He understood, albeit intuitively, that human language has a hierarchical structure, with more than one level of meaning. Bertrand Russell and Alfred North Whitehead were the first to note that objects within a class – say, several different kinds of chair – and the class itself – 'all chairs' – are at different levels of logical type. A class cannot be a member of itself, so that 'all chairs' is at a level above 'chairs 1, 2, 3 and 4. Benjamin Whorf extended this idea of levels to communication. There is communication and there is meta-communication, that is words, postures or gestures that are about other words. Hence, if you know a policeman well, you may be free to give him a jovial punch in the ribs. The punch is communicated within the context of play and friendship. Your smile says, in effect, 'this punch is not a real punch'. If by any chance the policeman does not see it in this context, you may find yourself in jail, charged with assaulting an officer. We know from observing their play that animals also have meta-communicative signals, such as, 'this fight is a mock-fight'. In these circumstances kittens beyond a few weeks old retract their claws and puppies let their lips overhang their teeth. They learn to fight in ways that do not harm each other.

Gregory Bateson's description of the training of dolphins at the Oceanic Institute in Hawaii provides another fruitful avenue. Let us recall that dolphins are among the most playful of all animals and masters of mock-attack. At first the trainer rewards the dolphin for specific (object level) behaviour, such as flipping its tail or doing a back-roll. Then, suddenly, this pattern of reinforcement ceases and the dolphin is rewarded only for new behaviour, that is tricks not performed with the trainer before. The investigators were asking in effect, since the dolphin recognizes a whole class of behaviours called 'play' can he also recognize the class of behaviours called 'new'? The short answer is yes. The dolphin may be bewildered for as much as half an hour as the repetition of each old trick goes unrewarded, but then it appears to understand what is required, and goes into an amazingly rich repertoire of elaborations, constantly producing new variations of behaviour. The significance of this for the human mind is profound. It breaks the prison cells into which Aristotelean logic has locked our various faculties so that every characteristic must be A or not-A. Human integrity has the structure of paradox, as each successive trick the dolphin performs is both like and unlike its predecessor. The dolphin is determined by its trainer yet free of him. It acts lawfully yet randomly, with conformity yet originality. How can I say this? It sounds as monstrously illogical as the Sphinx herself. The answer lies in the fact that one side of each paradox is at a different level of language from the other. When we speak of the dolphin being lawfully determined and conforming to its trainer's command this refers to a class of behaviours called 'new'. When we speak of the dolphin being free and acting

The structure of language is hierarchical and resembles a staircase, from an object level that describes the world, to a meta-level that describes the words which describe the world, to a meta-meta-level that describes words about words about worlds, and so on. . . . When the Sphinx asked Oedipus her dreadful riddle, 'What creature is it that "walks" on "four legs" in the "morning", two legs at "noon-time" and three "legs" in the "evening"?' Oedipus was able to see that the words in inverted commas were metaphors, ie words about words and not words about the creature. He therefore answered 'man' and the evil Sphinx committed suicide.

Oedipus confronted irrationality and horror and saw within it only a human confusion, an externalization of the conflicts in our being. It was a confusion between logical types or language levels. Many horrors in our society – madness, criminality, violence, war – seem connected with an incapacity to distinguish symbols from reality, or to hold our values within a context of 'higher' values. Persons reduce themselves to 'evil contradictions', which then drive others to madness or oppression. This episode in mythology tells of one triumph of mind over the irrational. But Oedipus was to fail in his answer to a large riddle – that of the meaning of his own existence . . .

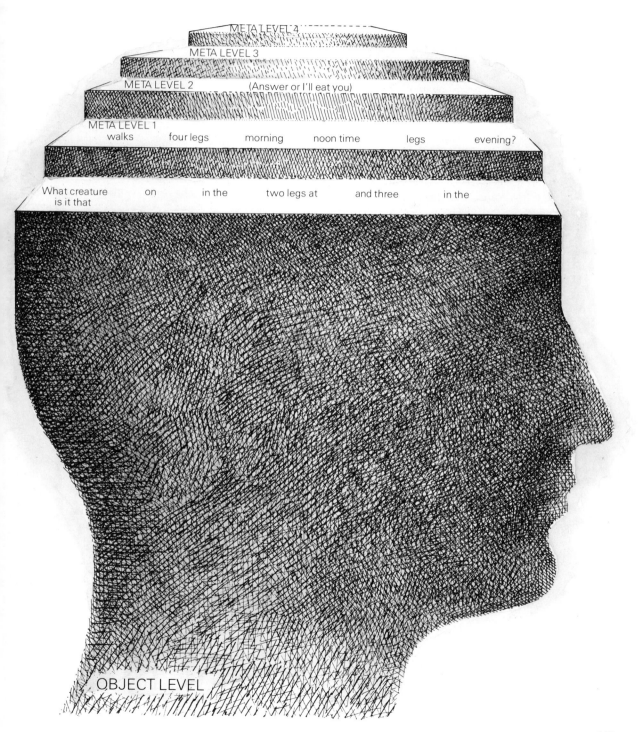

META LEVEL 4

META LEVEL 3

META LEVEL 2   (Answer or I'll eat you)

META LEVEL 1

walks   four legs   morning   noon time   legs   evening?

What creature   on   in the   two legs at   and three   in the
is it that

OBJECT LEVEL

with randomness and originality this refers to specific behaviours within a class.

Just as there are levels for communication and behaviour so, as Rudolf Carnap pointed out, there are levels for language: the *object level* of language (that is a language as nearly as possible descriptive of physical objects) and secondly a *meta-level* of language which is about language itself. One of the more usual forms of meta-language is the metaphor, literally 'the transfer' of words or objects. The 'Swan Lake' ballet shows not a dancer who is a swan, but a dancer like a swan. Her art temporarily fuses swan/not swan. We are now in a position to understand how Oedipus unlocked the riddle of the Sphinx. At first glance this she-monster appears to be describing another monster, one that sheds and grows legs in a single day. She binds us, alike by her contradictory aspects and her words. Yet these contradictions may be overcome and evil destroyed by treating parts of the communication as an object-level description and other parts as metaphors, expressed at a higher meta-level of language:

META LEVEL		walks	four legs	morning
OBJECT LEVEL	What creature is it that	on	in the	two legs at
META LEVEL	noon-time	legs	evening?	
OBJECT LEVEL	and three	in the		

Thus separated into levels, we can readily see that words descriptive of objects are below the horizontal line, while words about words are above. The monstrous appearance of the creature described in the riddle is the result of the confusion between different levels of logical typing. Once we see that 'walks', 'four legs', 'morning', 'noon-time', 'legs' and 'evening' are all metaphors referring to other words, and not directly to the animal, the riddle is solved.

In this book we have already encountered several theories about the conflicts symbolized by the Sphinx. The ancient Chinese would probably have warned that Yin and Yang had split apart (see Map 3). For the Judaeo-Christian tradition the Sphinx resembles the Tree of Knowledge (see Map 4): you choose, but fall between the divisions of good (mother) and evil (lion). For Freud the desire for maternal incest provokes the castrating claws of the father (see Map 9). Jung saw the Sphinx as the archetype Good Mother–Destroying Mother, a contrast deeply etched into the collective unconscious of all who must depend on parental care (see Map 10). Erich Fromm has likened the Sphinx to our relationship with the state. We can form a symbiotic relationship with totalitarianism, nurtured to the point of narcissism and delusions of omnipotence within its 'womb', and yet we remain in terror of its disciplines and cravenly obedient to its monstrous commands. Hence Nazis could be at one second on their knees before authority and the next at the throats of their enemies; they could behave as moral sucklings ferocious in the service of the state (see Map 11). For Rollo May the Sphinx stands for the tension between power and innocence, love and will. Oedipus found the monster outside the gates of Thebes, a projection outwards of the conflict in men's souls, and he took it back within himself. Only within us, in moral struggle and responsibility, can conflict be reconciled (see Map 13). Otto Rank and Ernest Becker would have seen the monster as the Life (mother) and Death (lion) paradox; we can remain bounded, small, impotent, dependent, meek and profane close to the mother's body, or be unbounded, great, powerful, free, proud and celestial on wings that defy gravity and death (see Map 15).

'One may say broadly that all animals that have been carefully observed have behaved so as to confirm the philosophy in which the observer believed before his observation began. Nay, more, they have all displayed the national characteristics of the observer. Animals studied by Americans rush about frantically, with an incredible display of bustle and pep, and at last achieve the desired result by chance. Animals observed by Germans sit still and think, and at last evolve the solution out of their inner consciousness . . .'
'Unpopular Essays', Bertrand Russell

'That the person is unfree is an essential assumption for a scientific view of human behaviour . . . When we say that he is autonomous – as far as a science of behaviour is concerned, that means miraculous.'
'Beyond Freedom and Dignity' B. F. Skinner

'We assume that the thief who is caught and imprisoned understands that he is being punished for stealing. Yet if no attempt is made to change his premises, it is likely that he sees himself as being punished for not stealing well. This explains why punishments based on behavioural learning theory have so consistently failed. They do not touch the higher levels of logical typing.'

Gregory Bateson in conversation with the author

'Learning occurs at different levels . . . Zero learning is characterized by specificity of response, which – right or wrong – is not subject to correction. Learning I is change in specificity of response by correction of errors by choice within a set of alternatives. Learning II is change in the process of Learning I, eg a corrective change in the set of alternatives from which choice is made. Learning III is change in the process of Learning II, eg corrective change in the system of sets of alternatives from which choice is made.'

'Steps to an ecology of mind' Gregory Bateson

I would submit that the Sphinx means all these inner conflicts and more. The contents of moral dilemmas and psychic conflicts are likely to keep changing. For Freud's Vienna, it was sex versus respectability, for Jung's Zürich it was religion and the new science of psychoanalysis. Athens at the time of Sophocles had troubles enough: the scientific atomists were vying with religious holists, freedom was struggling with fate. What is constant in the legend of the Sphinx, and what speaks to us over the more than two thousand intervening years, is the structure of the story and the creature. Evil triumphs when an irreconcilable contradiction confounds us at the object level of communication. We find ourselves simultaneously attracted and repelled, soothed and terrified, rooted and aroused. This juxtaposition of opposites alerts both hemispheres of the brain (see Map 23), precipitating conflict between them. The right brain sees in the Sphinx a relationship to a mother, the left brain sees combat with a lion. The normal responses collide, paralysing consciousness and splitting the mind. This is what happens in schizophrenia (literally 'split soul') and the psychic break is accompanied by the incapacity to go up and down the hierarchy of logical types or to distinguish metaphor from description.

If the structure of evil is a contradictory juxtaposition, the structure of growth, creativity and integrity consists of complementary characteristics 'nesting' within the contexts of each other. For the ancient Chinese either Yin or Yang contains and constrains its opposite. For Christians, the crucifixion becomes a creative resurrection. For Freud, the child learns to love his mother within the context of paternal prohibition against incest, and learns to challenge his father within the context of maternal prohibition against murder. For Erich Fromm, the sane society means one in which the citizens are weaned from dependence so that, like Socrates, they show their loyalty through dissent, and insist on acting freely within the law. For Otto Rank and Ernest Becker, the artist must express Eros in his work yet receive the verdict of God or posterity with Agape. For Rollo May there must be an interweaving of dilemmas, for Gregory Bateson an ecology of mind. Both would applaud Blake:

'Joy and Woe are woven fine
A Clothing for the Soul divine.'

Perhaps the greatest visible triumph of 'laminating' complementary values at different levels of logical typing is our system of parliamentary democracy (see Map 58), which has evolved in the teeth of rationalism. We have a 'loyal opposition', persons opposed to specific acts of government, but loyal to the institution. We debate openly but vote secretly, electing public representatives who exercise private conscience. A law, coercive upon us, upholds a freedom of action within that law. The values at each end of these continua are alternatively manifest and latent, behavioural and contextual, object level and meta-level. Each is restrained in its exercise by the frame imposed by its complement, for the purpose of enhancing the whole . . .

MAP REFERENCES
Context, 42–3, 46–50, 55, 58–60; Contradiction, 2, 5, 11–14, 42–3, 49–50; Dovetailing, see imbrication, nesting, 42–3, 48–51, 55, 58–60; Logical types, 42–3, 53, 55, 58–60; Play, 2, 57–8; Riddle, 54, 57–8.

MAP 41

The Linguistics of Therapy: Noam Chomsky, Richard Bandler and John Grinder

Richard Bandler and John Grinder's new application (1978) of the linguistics of Noam Chomsky to psychotherapy has won the assent of some famous therapists for this illumination of the healing arts. According to Chomsky's conception of generative grammar and syntactical structures, the mind is free to generate an infinite number of lawfully structured sentences. The language acquisition of a child between the ages of two and five is so prodigious that an innate and intuitive linguistic competence must be assumed, ie an *a priori* rational faculty. Children know grammatical rules before even hearing the constituent words. They will typically say 'gooses', not geese, thereby improving the consistency of language.

The map opposite is derived from Bandler and Grinder's examples of a person forming a 'linguistic map' from his general experience. This much-reduced model of vast memory stores is essential to avoid inundation by trivia. Yet, in forming this map, generalization, deletion and distortion occur. All of us generalize, from leaning on the back of a rocking chair to rocking chairs in general for instance, but some overgeneralize to 'all chairs'. Similarly we all have to make deletions, but in this process live options may be sacrificed. Distortion in fantasies, ideals and ambitions can affect our perception of reality and cripple our model for living.

In therapy, the client seeking help may state, for example, 'I became angry and hit him'. In Chomsky's terminology this is called the *surface structure* of a statement, the origin of which lies in a more complete linguistic representation called a *deep structure*. Suppose the latter reads, 'I became angry and hit my boss with the dictaphone'. This might be rendered by several alternate surface structures, seven of which are shown. A native speaker hearing only two or more of these could intuit (ie perceive directly without reasoning) their common derivation from the deep structure. His inability to state the transformational rules involved in no way lessens his innate, unconscious capacity to follow the transformation. However, when the client transforms from deep to surface structures the generalizations, deletions and distortions may be clues to his distress. For example: the *passive* transformation on the map weakens the hitter's responsibility; the *permutated* transformation blames his feelings; the *deleted* structure omits mention of the boss and the employment implications; the *nominalized* structure turns anger from a process to a 'thing' that commands; the *ambiguous* structure (common in schizophrenia) confuses hitter with hit; the *missing reference* structure omits the victim and so overgeneralizes; the *presupposition* transformation includes a hint of provocation.

As Bandler and Grinder have pointed out the therapist's intuitive task is to uncover the deep structure beyond surface statements and then probe this depth for the generalizations, deletions and distortions involved in forming the linguistic representation itself. This map therefore makes considerable sense of earlier maps. For example, it vindicates Freud's notion of pre-verbal, primary processes which unconsciously shape awareness and a variety of defences and repressions. It also supports Jung's work on word-association and his advocacy of progressively deeper descent into a collective unconscious, linguistically structured with archetypes, and discoverable by intuitions and feelings (see Map 10). And it substantiates Laing's idea of a truer, deeper self, betrayed by false surface manifestations and driven mad by oscillations between levels (see Map 14). Linguistic structures are also clearly involved in the stages of moral development evolved by Piaget and Kohlberg (see Map 38). Finally modern therapeutic techniques of enactment, relaxation, psychodrama and guided fantasy can be seen as ways of comparing the client's often impoverished map with the more vivid realities experienced in action.

This map is derived from Bandler and Grinder's analysis of a person's linguistic map in the context of psychotherapy. Although all linguistic maps represent and reduce experience, persons with problems in living can be said to suffer from impoverished and inadequate maps. Thus a client's statements about a problem are likely to consist of several Surface Structures or variations of a Deep Structure, in this case, 'I became angry and hit my boss with the dictaphone'; each surface structure suffers in some way from generalization, deletion or distortion (see map). By using his intuition as a native speaker of the form of syntactical structures, the therapist can recognize the various surface structures and the deep structure from which they derive. However, the deep structure statement is not itself the whole truth; it is only part of the client's linguistic map and is itself a generalized, deleted or distorted linguistic transformation of the client's general experience. It is the therapist's task to probe the generalizations, deletions and distortions involved in forming the linguistic map itself.

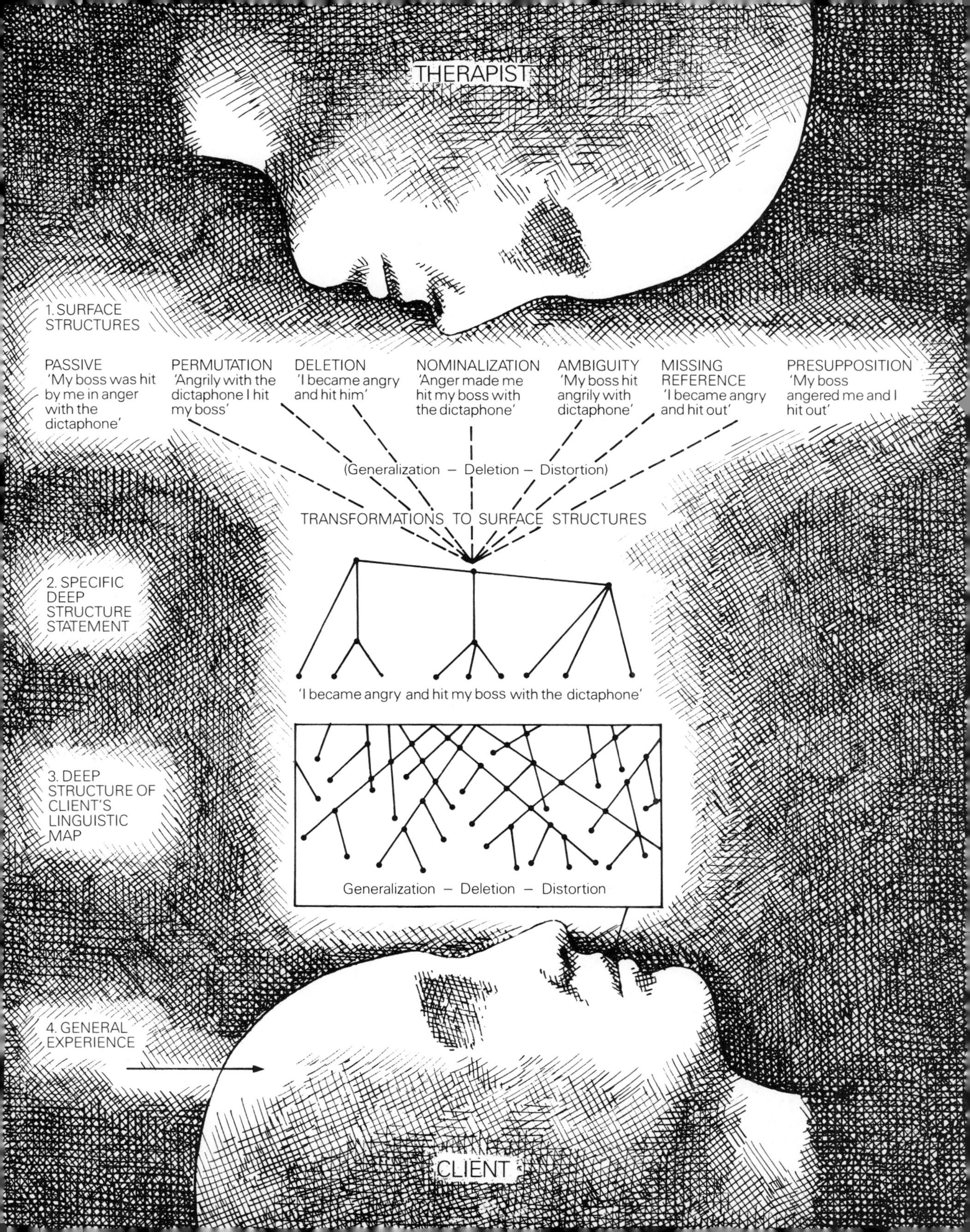

THERAPIST

1. SURFACE
STRUCTURES

PASSIVE
'My boss was hit
by me in anger
with the
dictaphone'

PERMUTATION
'Angrily with the
dictaphone I hit
my boss'

DELETION
'I became angry
and hit him'

NOMINALIZATION
'Anger made me
hit my boss with
the dictaphone'

AMBIGUITY
'My boss hit
angrily with
dictaphone'

MISSING
REFERENCE
'I became angry
and hit out'

PRESUPPOSITION
'My boss
angered me and I
hit out'

(Generalization — Deletion — Distortion)

TRANSFORMATIONS TO SURFACE STRUCTURES

2. SPECIFIC
DEEP
STRUCTURE
STATEMENT

'I became angry and hit my boss with the dictaphone'

3. DEEP
STRUCTURE OF
CLIENT'S
LINGUISTIC
MAP

Generalization — Deletion — Distortion

4. GENERAL
EXPERIENCE

CLIENT

MAP 42

The Synergistic Mind: Buckminster Fuller, Ruth Benedict and Abraham Maslow

In this section on communication, language has emerged as a rather flawed gift, leading us too often into contradictions, conflict and the 'digitizing' of Nature's continuous sweeps. How serious is this situation? Is there no way of thinking by which emotive expressions might be reconciled? The theme of this map is that human values *per se* are reconcilable by a process known as *synergy*. The theme of the following is that far more commonly we conceive of value judgements in a quarrelsome and lethal manner.

Synergy comes from the Greek *synergia* 'a working with', and describes the capacity of two forces, persons, or structures of information to optimize one another and achieve mutual enhancement. We shall now trace the definitions and implications of synergy in the physical sciences (Buckminster Fuller), in anthropology (Ruth Benedict) and in psychology (Abraham Maslow), before seeing how value judgements might also be harmonized.

Buckminster Fuller defines synergy as the behaviour of whole systems unpredicted by the behaviour of their parts. This is a general principle in science drawn from numerous special cases wherein the whole is more than the sum of its parts in strength, cohesion, attraction, meaning or complexity. For example, the metal alloy of chrome, nickel and steel is immensely stronger than any one of these metals and than all of these together. Their synergy in the jet engine prevents the whole from melting. Fuller asks us to consider the two triangles opposite. They cannot usually be structured into planes, and in conventional arithmetic one triangle plus one triangle equals two. But if we break the triangle, at the point where one end must anyway be superimposed on the other, we have a helix, and two helixes can be combined into a tetrahedron which is a stable structure. We have made four triangular faces out of two, three dimensions out of two, and a system with an inside and an outside out of pieces that had neither. This is no trick, it is the way atoms are structured. It explains why, when chemists try to isolate atoms and molecules out of compounds, they can never explain their associated activities. The synergy is destroyed by separation. In this illustration, $1 + 1 = 4$. Let us now combine two tetrahedrons to form a cube. This cube has more strength, resilience, mutually gravitational attraction, complexity, stability and facets than the mere four triangles of which it is comprised. I suggest this as a metaphor for the integrity and synergy of mind.

Ruth Benedict, the anthropologist and poet, is credited with introducing the idea of synergy into social science. She had made an exhaustive comparative study of American Indian communities and felt intuitively that at least three, the Zuni, the Arapesh and the Dakota, had something vital, secure and likeable about them, while the Chuckchee, the Ojibwa, the Dobu and the Kwakiutl gave her the shivers. She poured over her variables and classifications, the geography, climate, size, whether they were matrilineal or patrilineal and their attitudes to suicide, but nothing worked, either singly or in combination. Perhaps because she trusted the poet in her, she looked for the pattern that was in none of the pieces and called it 'synergy'. 'From all comparative material', she wrote, 'the conclusion emerges that societies where non-aggression is conspicuous have social orders in which the individual by the same act and at the same time serves his own advantage and that of the group . . . not because people are unselfish and put social obligations above personal desires, but when social arrangements make these identical.'

At about this time Abraham Maslow was studying 'self-actualizing persons', his term for a group of historical and contemporary persons of outstanding creativity, character and achievement (see also Map 33). He found after Ruth Benedict's death in 1948, that fragments of her manuscript on synergy which she had lent him were

Take two triangles, light and dark, break each at one corner to form two helices; join these to form a tetrahedron. Repeat the entire sequence until there are two tetrahedrons and combine these. The resulting structure is, unlike the separate parts, three-dimensional not two, has eight faces not four, has an inside and an outside, and is stronger, more stable, resilient, cohesive and complex. Buckminster Fuller's cube demonstrates vividly the principle of synergy, the process by which formerly separate or opposed forces work together; it represents a whole which is unpredictable from any of the parts, a synthesis that creates new forms at higher levels of complexity. Fuller points out that in our cultural mania for specializations, we are blind to synergistic principles but we would do well to bear in mind that the chief reason for the evolutionary extinction of biological species is over-specialization. Buckminster Fuller's cube is for me a symbol of the way in which human values and mind combine to form integrity; it remains to be seen if it is more than a metaphor. Synergy can also be visualized as the third side or product of two values plotted on dual axis diagrams (see following page). In this event the 'synergy of synergies', represented by the assembly of triangles, is a symbolic model of the interpenetration of 'opposite' human capacities, whose potential conflict is transformed in optimal relationships.

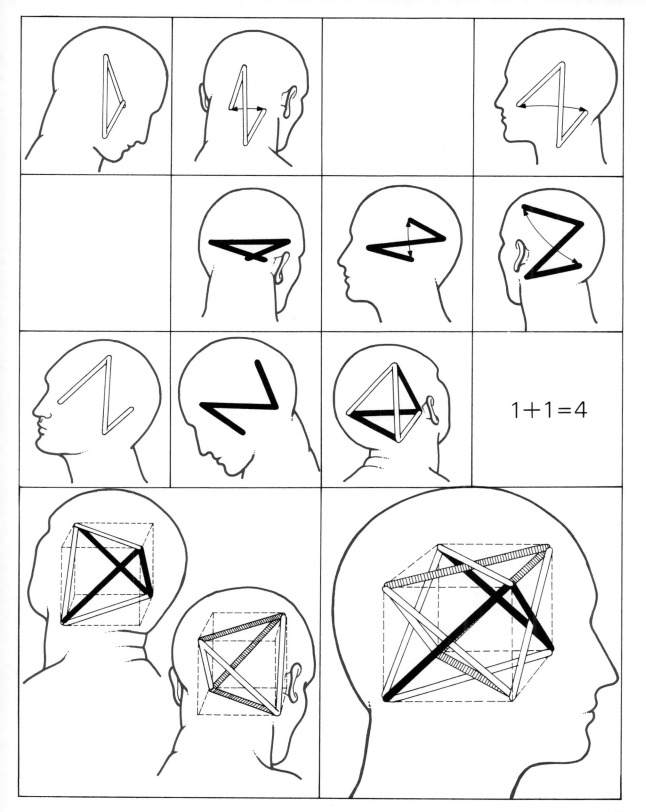

1+1=4

the only surviving record of her work, and he tirelessly expounded the theme. For he had found 'a rare capacity to resolve value dichotomies' in his own sample of self-actualizers, of which he wrote in *Motivation and Personality*. 'The age-old opposition between heart and head . . . was seen to disappear where they became synergic rather than antagonistic . . . the dichotomy between selfishness and unselfishness disappears . . . Our subjects are simultaneously very spiritual, and very pagan and sensual. Duty cannot be contrasted with pleasure nor work with play when duty *is* pleasure . . . Similar findings have been reached for kindness–ruthlessness, concreteness–abstractness, acceptance–rebellion, self–society, adjustment–maladjustment . . . serious–humourous, Dionysian–Appollonian, introverted–extraverted, intense–casual . . . mystic–realistic, active–passive, masculine–feminine, lust–love, and Eros–Agape . . . [all] coalesce into an organismic unity and into a non-Aristolean interpenetration . . . and a thousand serious philosophical dilemmas are discovered to have more than two horns, or paradoxically, no horns at all'.

My only caveat to Maslow's beatific vision is that synergy must *itself* acknowledge an opposite which is 'conflict'. To look back at famous people accustomed to applause is different from seeing their earlier struggles to reconcile real dichotomies. There is no 'resurrection' surely without crucifixion. On this hard-headed note, let us consider some practical and thoroughly researched applications of interpersonal synergy. Robert Blake and Jane Mouton train managers and their organizations to optimize a technological 'Concern for Production' with the humanitarian 'Concern with People', approximately the Two Cultures controversy discussed in Map 28. Managers form groups and are invited to rate one another, themselves, their group, their 'at work' colleagues and their organizational climate on a dual-axis grid (see margin). People, groups and organizations may be 9/1 Top Heavy, 1/9 Lop-sided, 5/5 Stand-off, or 9/9 Integrated (or synergistic). The 9/1 boss is a 'task-master', the organization a 'sweat-shop'. The 1/9 boss is a 'nice guy', the organization a 'country club'. The 5/5 boss is a 'compromiser' in a 'cold war'. The 9/9 boss inspires and helps subordinates to do an exellent job in a creative climate. When Louis Barnes and Larry Greiner of the Harvard Business School evaluated this management training, they found not only that employees and companies had moved towards a 9/9 synergy back at their jobs after training, but that many other dichotomous values had been reconciled. There were reported increases in self-confidence and respectful attention, in decisiveness and flexibility, in strong arguments in committee and their reconciliation, in self and other awareness, in profitability and implementing the Civil Rights act. Synergy is indivisible.

If we look carefully at values implicit in, for example, the process of learning, can we doubt that these are synergistic too? Much is made, for example, of the scholar's capacity for doubt, questioning, tentativeness, yet personal convictions and commitment and passionate searches for truth are admired too. The capacity for an abstract intellectuality is axiomatic, as is the necessity of dealing with the concrete, the practical and the real. It is obvious, surely, that the scholar must embrace all these values, going up the abstraction ladder the better to come down, and systematically doubting his convictions. We can avoid the problem of contradiction by stating that doubt and conviction, abstract and concrete are at different levels of logical typing (see Map 40). You doubt the data while being convinced of your method or context. You later commit yourself to the data but question the context or method that gave rise to it. One is always the 'map', the other the 'territory' (see Map 39).

'I spoke of societies with high social synergy where their institutions insure mutual advantage from the undertakings, and societies with low social synergy where the advantage of one individual becomes a victory over another, and the majority who are not victorious must shift as they can.'

Ruth Benedict quoted by Abraham Maslow in the 'Journal of Individual Psychology'

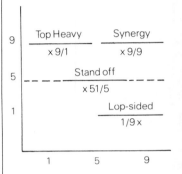

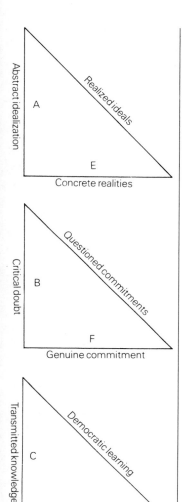

A similar reconciliation can be made between analysis into parts (or in human terms individualism) versus synthesis into wholes (or cooperatism). Finally that hoary old controversy between 'traditional' educators with authorities transmitting knowledge versus 'progressive' educators who encourage the natural initiative and noble savagery of students is falsifiable dichotomy also. We analyse in the context of synthesis, or vice versa, and transmit knowledge the better to elicit initiatives from students who in turn transmit to us. All these potentially conflicting values must be first polarized and then reconciled synergistically. But if either polarization or synergy fails we have vice rather than virtue. The whole may be expressed as a feedback loop thus:

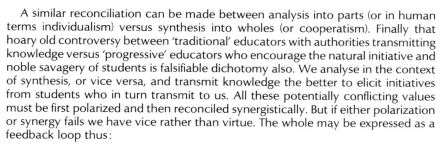

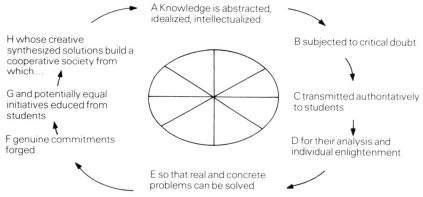

A Knowledge is abstracted, idealized, intellectualized

B subjected to critical doubt

C transmitted authoritatively to students

D for their analysis and individual enlightenment

E so that real and concrete problems can be solved

F genuine commitments forged

G and potentially equal initiatives educed from students

H whose creative synthesized solutions build a cooperative society from which...

Several reservations should be noted. The order of values in this cybernetic sentence is arbitrary, and unavoidable bias is introduced by using the structure of an English sentence (see Map 39). In this case abstracted knowledge has been made the subject of a sentence that does something to students. To restore ecological balance to this loop we could create a cycle of present participles without beginning or end: abstracting → doubting → transmitting → analysing → realizing → committing → educing → synthesizing → abstracting → ... Next we should give disputants the right to start at any point, ie make any of the participles into the subject of their sentence, and provided all disputants aim at the synergy of values involved it is possible to move from argument to reconciliation.

If we take all four of the continua from the cybernetic loop, ie A–E, B–F, C–G and D–H and bend each continuum to form two sides of a triangle, then we can add a third side which is the synergistic product of the first two. For example A–E Abstract ideals–Concrete Realities combine synergistically to produce 'an accumulation of realized ideals'. Similarly B–F Critical Doubt–Genuine Commitments create a body of 'tested and questioned commitments'. The same goes for all four continua (see margin). These trinities of dimensions grow in a sequence of extension, unbalancing, corresponding extension, rebalancing. We are now in a position to return to the four triangles in the original map which synergized to make two tetrahedrons and thence a cube. Here each aspect of learning is optimally integrated with the others, creating a stability, coherence and strength that begins to do justice to the brilliance of some minds. Yet this kind of values integrity is rarely achieved ... a problem to which we now turn ...

MAP 43

The Lethal Structure of Morality:
Charles Osgood to Charles Hampden-Turner

We saw in Map 42, that values can be synergistic and moral disputations reconciled. Yet more commonly, it seems, our moralisms betray us into win or lose conflict. If an instrument similar to a geiger-counter could be invented that counted moral judgements instead, we would learn to duck as people became increasingly 'moral', since lethal force is usually imminent. So far from moral fervour being an alternative to force, it is frequently the overture, the accompaniment and the memorial to it. We have the curious capacity of verbally goading one another to ferocity.

No wonder, then, that many academics have regarded value judgements as some manner of intellectual swamp into which no self-respecting scholar ventures. The naturalistic fallacy, 'you cannot get an "ought" from an "is"', and the consigning of values to some vortex of subjectivity have been the commonest defences. But if we accept that human beings are motivated to develop and to learn, then the claim that moral outlooks have no bearing on these processes strains credulity. Moral abdication is no answer to the moral failings of conventional judgements.

I contend that moral judgements as most commonly utilized have a pathological structure. In relationships of greater intimacy these judgements are usually modulated and tamed by affection. It is in broader political and international relationships that moralism tends to run amok. In nearly three decades of research, Charles Osgood has shown that people think evaluatively in linear, bi-polar terms in a manner similar to a crucifix. Nearly all evaluative words plotted on Osgood's semantic differential can be placed upon a two-axis diagram, Bad–Good, Active–Passive, and there is considerable agreement among respondents on the placements shown in the small map opposite. What this implies is that nearly everyone thinks of values as things possessed in quantity or at least exhibited in some degree, and that in times of danger a strong and forceful good should be exhibited without any ideal limits, although there may be practical limits to the strength and goodness that one person can muster. As in Orwell's *1984*, there is 'double good', 'double ungood' and 'double–double good' to our strictly linear moralities.

I try to show what this leads to in the main map opposite. Here we have a St Andrew's cross of two yardsticks split at the centre. The high ends are 'good', the low ends are 'bad' and the dispute is between Dissent/Equality/Rebellion common on the political Left (in Western cultures), and Patriotism/Authority/Loyalty, common on the political Right. (I am thinking here especially of the socio-political atmosphere in the United States during the Vietnam War, to which I was witness.) When political partisans speak they use language into which goodness and badness have already been injected, and they state a 'choice' in terms which indicate that they have already chosen the only 'moral' alternative. 'Are we going to fight patriotically, and give our loyalty to duly elected authorities in this hour of national peril, or will we treacherously subvert our national leaders?' This sentiment was fairly typical of 'hawks', to whom the 'doves' replied. 'Are we going to rebel against imperialism and elitism of all kinds, for a world that respects one another's equality?' Every extra degree of good for doves is an extra degree of bad in the eyes of hawks and vice versa. The 'downwards' of one is the 'upwards' of the other as if the signposts to heaven and hell had been switched. Consider several other characteristics of this quarrel.

First the argument is totally 'non-rational' in the sense that there is no agreement on premises, and it is severely threatening for either to see himself, even for a moment, as the other sees him, sunk in evil, utterly inferior. Second, each has a

The map above shows that many years' research with Charles Osgood's Semantic Differential technique (a method of rating words to discover their evaluative dimensions) has led to two major variables which pattern responses, Active–Passive, Bad–Good: hence 'elation' is an active good, 'guilt' a passive bad. This has led me to distinguish two structures of morality, the One-Dimensional Morality of the map opposite with linear yardstick running downwards from conceptions of good and evil and the Synergized Conception of Morality in the map overleaf. One-dimensional moralities have dogmatic rhetorics infused with pseudo-choices between say: (good) Patriotism versus (evil) Dissent. They refuse to face the dilemma of opposite virtues. This evasion of internal struggles leads to external wars. Synergized ethics recognize virtues at either end of a values continuum. Where the individual dissents this is expressed in the context of his patriotism. Where the individual decides that patriotic duty comes first he explains that the country he loves permits people to dissent, and is therefore worth supporting. Such 'patriots' and 'dissenters' would respect each other, disagreeing only about which values should be manifest.

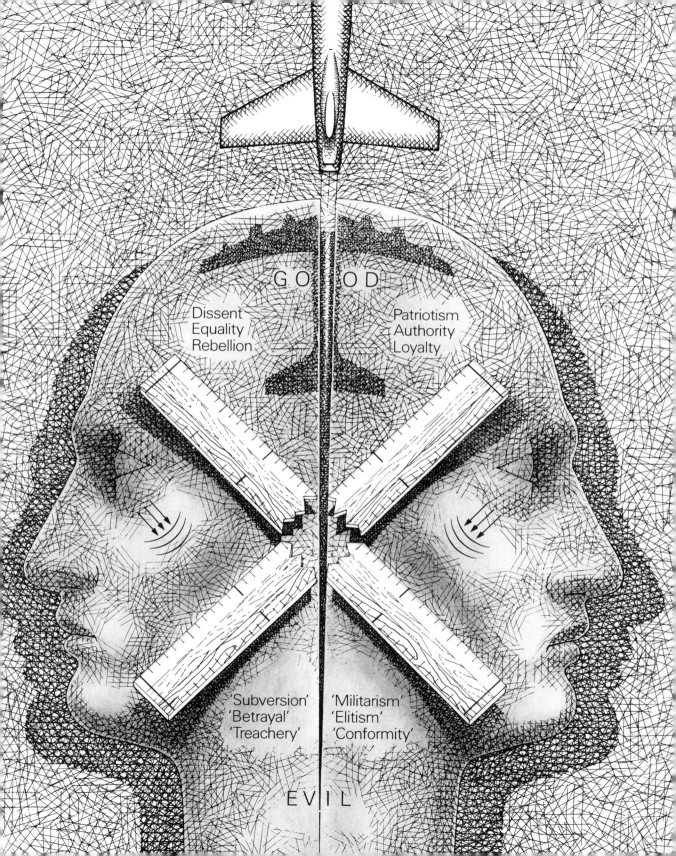

mirror image of the other. Goodness slopes from Left to Right for doves, but in the picture of themselves insultingly reflected by hawks Goodness slopes from Right to Left and they are ludicrously demoted. The same applies to hawks reflected in the eyes of doves only vice versa. Both remain blind to the other's view-point, yardsticks passing in the night. Third the 'map' which each side is using becomes increasingly discrepant with what is clearly happening in the 'territory' (see Map 39), so that both camps are personally threatened by the failure of their moral maps to predict realities. Instead of questioning their one-dimensional values each blames the other for frustration of a glorious vision. Peace (or victory) could have been achieved by now, but for them.

Fourth, in a condition where mapped values are consistently frustrated, there arises the temptation to worship and celebrate the map itself, idolize ideas and turn inwards in incestuous self-acclamation. 'Never mind whether our demonstration prolonged the war, we are Beautiful People.' The moral gesture falls in love with itself, as frustration feeds the dream which mystifies reality. Similarly, death and disaster in the territory become dedicated to the exalted ideals of Patriotism and Rebellion, idols hungry for human sacrifice. Fifth, and exceedingly important, the moral yardsticks split at the point of passing from Good into Evil. Any 'elitism' or 'conformity' in the dissenter is 'not me' and so long as he sticks evil labels on such words they remain 'not me'. The hawk similarly regards all his very natural doubts about the war as 'subversive' and 'treacherous' ideas within him and splits them off. And where integrity should be there are jagged breaks. Sixth and consequently, the process of escalating moral indignation is paced by escalating inner repressions (see downward arrows on Map 43). At some level the Patriot hawk must realize that his values are at least capable of an interpretation horribly dissonant with his own heroic version. Could his loyalty and love of country be nothing more than 'the last refuge of the scoundrel', a knee-jerk conformity? Unthinkable! and yet those 'pinkos' keep saying it. To smash those demonstrators is to smash his inner doubts. The dove may similarly resent the charge of cowardice and so 'bravely' violate the peace at home.

America's history is especially prone to 'Red Scares' and what Richard Hofstadter called the 'paranoid streak', yet the United States has fewer real communists in its 'territory' than virtually any other developed country. The explanation, I suggest, lies in a desperate need to preserve the Puritanism of a 'linear morality', for which the presence of a devil at the base of one's yardstick is essential. In the absence of war, the Reds must be beneath the beds, and their invisibility only testifies to the extent of the conspiracy. But, of course, the real enemy is inside, the 'upright' moral yardstick haunted by its submerged and evil rear end, an analogue on the human body itself.

As war intensifies, the 'glorious' values on the map, pushed to ever greater extremity, wreak havoc in the territory. As bombs flatten hamlets a renewed intimation of the evil buried deep in mind and ideology grows among the witnesses. Such disaster could not befall mankind if we were not at some fundamental level 'rotten at the core', steeped in original sin. The Patriot pushes down on his dissent, splits it off and hates the fragments called 'subversive thoughts' (see Map 13). The Egalitarian pushes down and splits off the idea that he too acts with authority, and keeps finding bits of 'elitism' in himself and brothers. Why is it that at the very pinnacle of virtue, we find that we have reached by some mysterious path an abyss of horror? Even the Gettysburgh Address was muttered hastily with handkerchief to mouth, immortal words amid the stench of mortality.

And finally let us note, that the one-dimensional absolutes of pure moralities are

In Mark Twain's 'The War Prayer' the country was in 'great and exalting excitement'. War was declared, 'in every breast burned the holy fire of patriotism'. In one church the minister was praying fervently for glorious victory, when an aged stranger 'pale even to ghastliness' stalked up the aisle and ascended the pulpit. He explained that he was the messenger of Almighty God who had heard the prayer. But like most of the prayers of men 'it is not one, but two, one spoken, one unspoken'. God would grant the prayer but only if the congregation was prepared to hear and to approve the unspoken part. And so the stranger prayed. 'O Lord our Father, our young patriots, idols of our hearts, go forth to battle – be thou near them . . .' help us to tear their soldiers to bloody shreds with our shells; help us to drown the thunder of their guns with the shrieks of their wounded, writhing in pain; help us to lay waste their humble homes with a hurricane of fire; help us to wring the hearts of their unoffending widows with unavailing grief, help us to turn them out roofless with their little children to wander unfriended the wastes of their desolate land . . . We ask it in the spirit of love, of Him who is the Source of Love . . .'

'Morality is simply the attitude we adopt to people we personally dislike.'
'The Ideal Husband' Oscar Wilde

'Demonstrators should not burn the American flag, they should wash it.'
Norman Thomas
quoted on CBS news

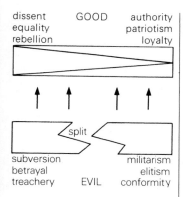

dissent   GOOD   authority
equality   patriotism
rebellion   loyalty

subversion   militarism
betrayal   elitism
treachery   EVIL   conformity

The Synergized Conception of Morality: here 'dovetailed' values lead to growth and development and hence to good, while split-off and repressed values lead to regression, violence and mental breakdown. The person thinking synergistically will know both kinds of value, but understands the need to incorporate the fragments below.

never tested and so never falsified. The hawks remain convinced that we never tried to win in Vietnam. The dove denies that peace was ever tried. Since ultimate patriotism and perfect equality are but map-references, idealizations of a territory that never was, the moralists end in hating imperfect man as a mere shadow of the eternal form.

What can be done about our murderous moralities? There are clues in the psychotheology of Harry Williams (Map 5), the anxiety studies of Rollo May (Map 13) and the dilemmas of Laurence Kohlberg (Map 38). We have to face the anxiety or the 'crucifixion' of moral dilemmas and do so at the outset before guilt makes them too agonizing to bear and we are forced to externalize inner conflict. This conflict is not the pseudo-choice and rhetorical affirmation of positive versus negative values, such as Equality versus Elitism, but the far more difficult reconciliation of positives that conflict, Dissent versus Patriotism, or Rebellion versus Loyalty. Painful although it is, we must use Tillich's 'encompassing reason' to build an ecology of values, and so fashion unique combinations of universal values to fit particular situations.

The way of doing this is suggested in the map in the margin. Here there is still good and evil but their structure is radically different: hawk values (used without initial capitals, since they are neither idols nor things) have been dovetailed with the dove values of dissent, equality and rebellion. By this I mean that one set of values contains the other within it. Dissent and rebellion occur in the context of loyalty and patriotism, as they did for Socrates (Map 2). He rebelled against the Athens he loved, and attempted by a dialogue of equals to improve the legitimacy of the authority he finally obeyed.

It is not easy to synthesize value contraries in the teeth of existential anxiety, but it is the only way. Why, after all, should we heed the political dissent of a person unless we believe that in the wider context he is a patriot passionately concerned for us? The rebel is convincing only if we appreciate his loyalty to our larger good. Here, then, is the crucial distinction between those value systems which help personalities and groups to develop and those value systems which spell regression, disintegration and death. The distinction is not *in* the separate values at all. There is no 'essence' of just authority as opposed to oppressive elitism. The distinction is found *between* the values in their structure and pattern. Values that promote development interpenetrate synergistically. Values that destroy are split, contradictory, and conflicting, with the one dominating its opposite, and the opposite lashing back in wild oscillations of conformity/treachery, militarism/subversion, only dignified by terms such as 'Patriotism' and 'Rebellion'. This is the meaning of the split continuum at the bottom of the map, in contrast to the 'dovetailed', integrated and synergized values continuum above it.

Finally, and on a personal note, I cannot pretend to be impartial on hawks versus doves in the Vietnam War. I believe the war to have been a terrible mistake and wrote as much at that time. I also believe that at least some doves, although not enough, realized that their rebellion must be loyal and their dissent patriotic, and that they must, as Camus put it, 'respect the limits in which minds meet'. That was for me a new morality which we cannot live without.

MAP REFERENCES
Body–mind, 6, 14–15, 18, 21, 55, 59–60; Idolatory, 7, 11, 15–16, 26, 35, 39, 50; Linear thought, see also catastrophe, one-dimensional thought, 4–5, 14–15, 22, 28–9, 34, 53, 56, 60; Split, 6, 12, 23–4, 28, 34, 40, 49–51.

MAP 44

Freud's French Revolution:
Jacques Lacan interpreted by Sherry Turkle

Jacques Lacan, the French 'Protestant' Freudian, has said that it takes ten years to comprehend him. Most of his public statements seem designed less to inform people than to beguile them into lengthy personal exploration under Lacanian auspices. Space limits me to sketching just a few beguilements. Finding Lacan in the original unreadable, I have leant heavily on *Psychoanalytic Politics* by Sherry Turkle, an American professor of sociology. Freudianism, Turkle argues, was not popular in France until the May student uprisings of 1968. The French faith in human reason, their dislike of German ideas, the neurological slant of French psychiatry, the hostility of the Catholic church to sexual topics and of Marxists to 'bourgeois' privatism, and the intellectual fashion of criticizing America, where Freudianism is medically established, all combined to limit Freudian influence. Then Jacques Lacan, along with 'the national psychodrama of 1968', changed everything. Lacan made Freud fit for France by reinterpreting the master in symbolic and linguistic terms using the structuralist and rationalist traditions of Ferdinand de Saussure, Jean Piaget (see Map 38) and Lévi-Strauss (see Map 57). By substituting an interpretative science of listening and understanding for 'therapy' or 'adjustment', by advocating a thoroughly anti-medical, intellectualist approach that denied American hegemony, Lacan rebelled against the 'popes' and 'bishops' who had institutionalized psychoanalysis, and, like Luther and Calvin appealed directly to the 'objective word' of Freud's 'scripture' (see Map 7).

If we regard the revolts of the sixties as a crisis of the 'arts and communications culture', infuriated by the limits of rhetoric to change reality (see Map 28), then it is not difficult to understand Lacan's appeal. He gave rational substance to those who live by symbolizing and offered them an opportunity to reappraise their revolt. But Lacan's lasting accomplishment has been the raising of our interpretation of Freud by one or more levels of language, or logical type (see Map 40). Incestuous desire, castration fear, penis envy, etc are no longer to be seen as signs, ie words standing in direct relation to things, but as symbols, maps, metaphors, ie words about words, but not the thing (see Map 39). To say that a woman has 'penis envy' is not to claim that anatomy is destiny or that biology dooms her to jealous rage, but that the phallus has come to signify power in our society and that women resent their social subordination. Culture imposes meanings upon anatomical parts.

Lacan believes that the unconscious is structured like language but through associations, not causal links, which are discoverable through the poetry, the puns, and the word plays with which his ideas abound. For example, we are *parlêtres* 'talking beings [who] go by the letter'; or *çaparle*, 'the Id speaks'. He cites Freud's case of the Rat Man, who feared rats (*ratten* in German), conflicts over his father's unpaid instalments (*raten*), the loss of his sister, Rita, and impending marriage (*heiraten*). Most influential has been Lacan's recasting of the Oedipal conflict, now seen as the child's progression from an imaginary order of significantion to a symbolic order. The *imaginaire* order, or mirror phase, witnesses the child's *désir de la mère* again a pun, meaning 'desire for mother' and 'mother's desire'. The child wishes to complete the mother, to be, symbolically, her phallus and is mirrored in his mother's gaze. This phase ends when the child takes the father's name (*nom*) in an act of identification, which is also his 'no' (*non*), ie the prohibition of 'incest' with her. At this moment society and the symbolic order claim the child and emesh him. The *nom* thus comes to signify 'mother's desire', which in turn signifies the phallus, in a chain of signification leading from consciousness to the unconscious. Repression is thereby redefined as the relegation of one symbolic level by the next and higher level. Analysis retraces this 'chain' back and downwards to the 'real' (*réal*). The 'real' is beyond language, an aching need.

These knots are based on those drawn by Lacan himself; when one (the symptom) is cut all come apart. The circles represent the symbolic order (the language by which our society structures our thought and communication) and the imaginary order (the state in which the child is 'mirrored' in his mother). The symptom (which is examined in Lacanian psychoanalysis) joins both to the real (an unappeasable desire for a missing element in life). The symptom is the key to analysing, ie taking apart, the separate circles. The symbolic order may have many additional links since living languages mount symbols upon symbols, metaphors on metaphors. Analysis therefore proceeds via a 'chain of signification' down through links of symbolism, to the imaginary and thence to the real, using the symptom as a trail.

Lacan is especially scornful of the American ego psychologists and their 'autonomous ego' (see Maps 11, 13, 15, 33, 37). For him the ego is the source of alienation, the bearer of neurosis, the centre of all resistance to help and seeks endlessly mere substitutes for 'the object of lost desire' buried in the unconscious. Above all the ego and its vanity block our realization that the symbolic order has shaped us and lives through us.

MAP REFERENCES
Freudianism, 8–10, 15, 37, 53; Logical types, 40, 42–3, 49, 55, 58–60; Metaphors, 40, 46, 59; Protestantism, 6–9, 12–13, 26, 52–3; Repression, 5, 9, 11, 13–16, 43, 48, 50; Student revolt, 28, 43, 60.

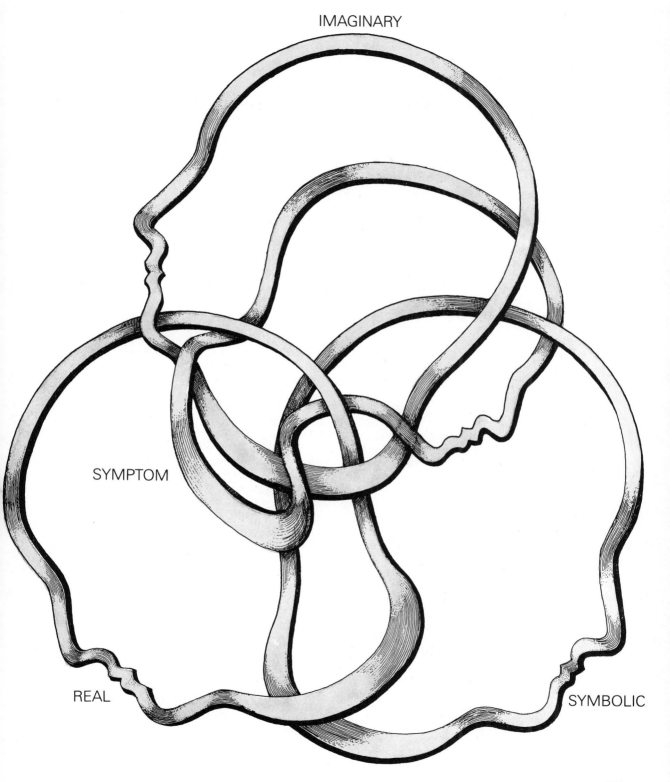

IMAGINARY

SYMPTOM

REAL

SYMBOLIC

MAP 45

The Problems of Life:
Bertalanffy and General Systems Theory

Ludwig von Bertalanffy was a Viennese professor of biology who emigrated to Canada in 1949. Soon afterwards he founded the Society for the Advancement of General Systems Theory and remains its acknowledged inspiration; he had been nominated for a Nobel Prize when he died in 1971. His book, *Problems of Life*, is a classic treatise on the failure of 'robotic' and reductive explanations of living organisms. Why, he asked, does a live sponge reduced to mush by being forced through a fine sieve spontaneously reorganize itself? Why when certain 'organizer' cells are transplanted from the leg to the tail of an embryo newt does the creature grow two tails? How do you explain 'equifinality', that when an organism's usual path to its end state of development is blocked it will take path after path, repeatedly, to achieve that end? Where organs usually employed in this process are damaged, as in injury to sections of the brain, other parts will come into play to replace them.

Bertalanffy's answer to these observations, given thirty years before such models gained acceptance, was that life is first and foremost a system of self-organization, a developmental unfolding at progressively higher levels of differentiation and organized complexity. These wholes are not reducible to their parts and their developed forms are qualitatively different from earlier forms. The organism, moreover, is dynamic rather than static, open not closed and searches spontaneously and actively for stimulation, rather than waiting passively to respond. However, Bertalanffy was not content to remain with biology. If the organism was an open system interacting with its environment, could biology as a discipline do anything less? He joked about psychologists who claimed that their discipline was at a crossroads. Psychology *is* a crossroads and the mind of man a meeting-point for symbolic systems. From this conviction general systems theory was founded, aided by the converging efforts of such persons as Norman Weiner in cybernetics, Anatol Rapoport in game theory, Heinz Werner in psychology and Claude Shannon in communications.

General systems theory is thus a 'discipline of disciplines' with especial emphases on psychobiology and ecology. It is a study of those wholes whose principles are comparable whatever the nature of their particular components. For example, the cybernetic feedback model came originally from the technology of thermostats and governors on steam engines, but it has, as we shall see in Maps 48 to 50 considerable validity for social, personality and value systems generally. But to take the simplest example first, the map shows the minimum necessary components of a cybernetic system. Stimuli register upon a receptor, R, which scans specifically for them. From R, information codes (not the thing itself) travel to the direction centre, A1, which by amplifying, inhibiting or otherwise steering the system triggers action in the effector, E. From here two kinds of messages flow: one sends a response which may effect the stimuli, the other is a feedback loop to the receptor which informs it of the action taken by the effector. This completes the self-correcting system. In the case of a heat-seeking guided missile, the effector would inform the receptor that direction changes had been made to track a shifting target.

To convert this system to the condition of a live organism it is necessary to add a self-organizing capacity (SO). This would include the genetic code which instructs the organism to develop; in humans it would also involve the various capacities of mind – the purposive feedforward devices of the holographic memory store (see Map 25), varieties of creative bisociation (see Maps 26–31), sequentially unfolding stages of moral judgement (see Map 38) and a grammar of linguistically generated values (see Map 41). It is such characteristics of the human mind that turn targets into values and mere responses into ethical aims.

According to Ludwig von Bertalanffy, one of mankind's tragedies is that we have more values for complex organizations and systems than for personal conduct. This imbalance dooms the individual's morality because we are inescapably systems-within-systems and our values are increasingly dependent on context. It is this failure to comprehend systems that has made our society disordered and antagonistic.

The minimum necessary components of a cybernetic system are illustrated in the map. Stimuli from the target (right) travel to the receptor (R), then to the direction-finding centre which amplifies or inhibits information (AI) and changes the behaviour of the effector (E). E now responds in two ways: it both implements the orders it receives and feeds back a signal to the receptor that a change has been made. What makes a human being more than a guided missile is his capacity for self-organization both in terms of the genetic code which instructs the organism to develop and in terms of mind. This is what turns targets into values and mere responses into ethical aims. Thus to transcend hostile academic disciplines and warring international systems, we must develop self-organizing general systems of symbolic relationships which reconcile empiricism with dialectics (Maps 52–5), classes and races (Maps 58–9) and the human species with its environments (Maps 46–60).

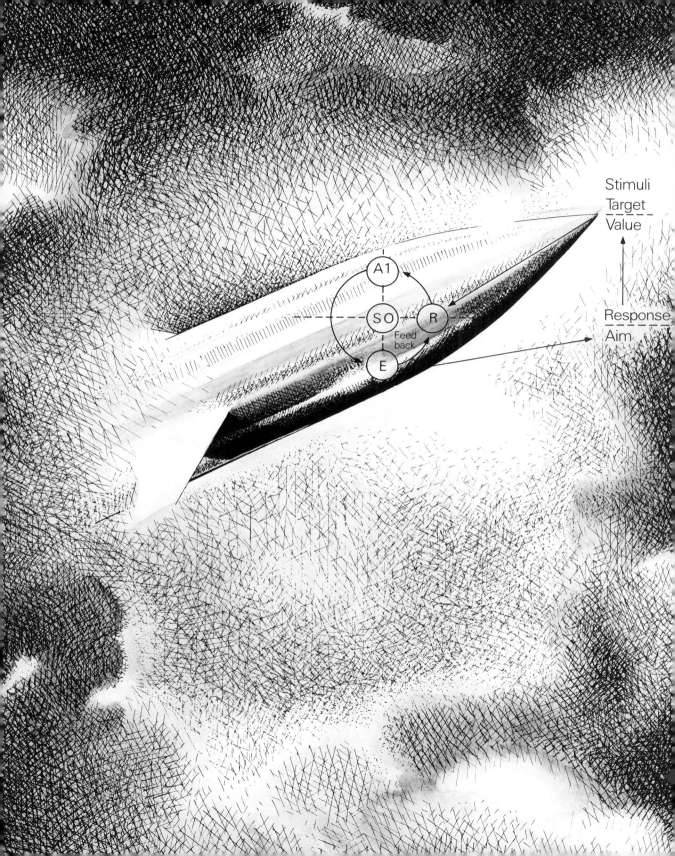

Stimuli
Target
Value

Response
Aim

A1

SO   R

Feed
back

E

MAP 46

The Wisdom of the Finest Fit:
The sigmoid curves of Jonas Salk

Jonas Salk, the biologist, insists that we must transcend our group or nation to show an urgent concern for the survival of our species. Biological evolution exemplifies the processes by which opposing tendencies are reconciled, a lesson which human groups in conflict over values might do well to emulate. A recurrent example of the self-regulation and genetic control of natural systems is the sigmoid curve which represents in number the growth of population in a closed system. However, whether we are dealing with the population increase of fruit-flies, or of sheep introduced into a new area or whatever, such curves have an inherent tendency to level off. Note that this levelling off is a genetically programmed feedback effect in response to a signal from the environment. There are grim exceptions to this levelling-off tendency. Cancer cells multiply exponentially defying systemic restraint and ultimately destroying the host. The Brown Lemming population explodes then re-accommodates by mass suicides every few years.

If we look at graphs of human population (estimated to reach 6.1 billion by the year 2000), or the level of natural resource utilization, or industrial pollution, or the extinction of species with which we 'share' this planet and of oxygen producing vegetation, then we find exponential increases in these trends with only local levelling-off. Salk places our human species at the intersection point of the curve opposite. Our near-vertical ascent either levels off in a transition from Epoch A to Epoch B, or we doom ourselves to a catastrophic plunge on the graph, whether triggered by genetic or environmental limitations; we shall have failed to survive upon a degraded planet.

The problem is that our programmed genetic restraints and potentials are overlayed by levels of 'rational' calculations which ignore the biological 'wisdom' of evolution. We are organized in a hierarchy of physical, chemical, biological, socio-biological and metabiological systems. Each level expresses the potentials of the lower levels but must also abide by its constraints. For example at the biological level: the somatic systems of our bodies express some portion of our genetic endowments; the individual expresses some portion of the capacities inherent in the species at the sociobiological level; finally at the metabiological level the ego expresses some portion of the capacities inherent in what Salk calls its *being*, that is the combination of physical, chemical, biological and sociobiological systems which make up its human endowment. The ego both actualizes that endowment and exercises restraint according to the limits of that being.

Now we know that these limits exist in all realms of biological life and must find some expression in the human, and we know enough of biological structure to recognize its message. Those value systems concerned with dynamic equilibrium, aesthetics, complementarity, reciprocity, justice, interdependence, reconciliation, creative optimal syntheses, and intuitions of truth and beauty are the 'language' biology speaks. Myths with their transformations and metaphors with their structure of integrated differences are, Salk believes, modes conveying an evolutionary wisdom, less concerned with the survival of the fittest than the survival value of the finest possible fit between the dualisms of life.

We urgently need a philosophy of 'both . . . and' to qualify the present 'either/or'. Once it was either our survival, or that of other species and natural elements, so we conquered, multiplied and subdued. Now we face an ego whose intellect, reason, objectivity, morality, differences, competitive nature, power and 'win or lose' psychology desperately needs a being whose intuition, feeling, subjectivity, realism, ability to differentiate, cooperate, and influence and reconciling powers can contain it. Not self-expression or self-restraint, not exponential growth or plateau, not inner or outer nature but all of these in the finest fit we can devise.

The sigmoid curve mapped opposite represents a programmed genetic predisposition towards regulation in the populations of numerous species. Whether we are concerned with fruit-flies or grazing herds their populations first rise and then flatten out in two arcs, identified here as Epochs A and B. The first is an epoch of ascent and mastery; the second of balanced coalescence. Jonas Salk believes that we have now reached a point midway on the sigmoid curve, where our exploding population and self-aggrandizement must yield to a process of progressive deceleration in which Epoch B's Being Values largely reverse Epoch A's Ego Values. This will cause shifts such as those from intellect to intuition, reason to feeling, objectivity to subjectivity, group differences to differentiated structures and power to influence, as the pressures change. Where once men died for lack of sufficient assertion, we now perish from excess. Epoch A was anti-death, anti-disease, self-repressing and externally constrained; Epoch B will be pro-life, pro-health, self-expressing and self-restraining.

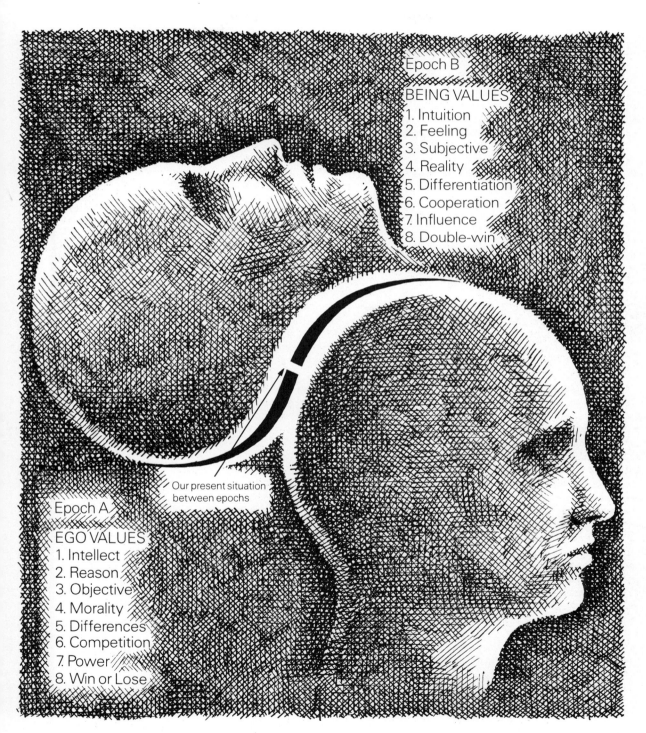

Epoch B

BEING VALUES
1. Intuition
2. Feeling
3. Subjective
4. Reality
5. Differentiation
6. Cooperation
7. Influence
8. Double-win

Our present situation
between epochs

Epoch A

EGO VALUES
1. Intellect
2. Reason
3. Objective
4. Morality
5. Differences
6. Competition
7. Power
8. Win or Lose

MAP 47

The Holarchy of Living Nature:
The passionate pessimism of Arthur Koestler

Koestler does not give us much time. Human beings have always had to live with the 'mind-splitting fear of their own deaths', with a consciousness emerging from 'a prenatal void and drowning in a post-mortem darkness'. But since Hiroshima we have had to live with the prospect of the death of our species. Had Hitler been born twenty years later how 'final' indeed, might have been his 'solution' and space-ship earth would have been transformed to a 'Flying Dutchman drifting among the stars with its dead crew'. For who looking dispassionately at the human race from Cro-Magnon to Auschwitz to the Gulag Archipelago can doubt that we are technological giants yet ethical pygmies, who day by day increase our power to terrify each other and so overburden our all-too-frail capacities for social understanding?

At the centre of our problems Koestler sees a confusion of parts versus wholes, and hence of self-assertion versus integration, egoism versus altruism, competition versus cooperation, autonomy versus dependence, and aggression versus sexuality. We attempt to seize upon the virtue of one or the other, only to discover that they transform themselves into their opposites at a higher level. For example, the 'organization men' who work cooperatively for big corporations allow the latter to compete, sometimes with ferocity.

Koestler begins with biology where both holism and atomism have proved to be culs-de-sac. The constant affirmation that the whole is more than the sum of its parts, 'a rose is a rose is a rose', tends to evade the task of detailed description. The 'nothing but' reductionism of neo-Darwinian evolutionary theory or of stimulis–response theory in psychology has become sterile and tends to dismantle the very organization and relationships that distinguish living material. The concept of the *holon* transcends parts and wholes in favour of a Janus-faced whole which is also a part, depending on whether it looks down the organic hierarchy (mapped opposite) to the parts of which it is the whole, or whether it looks up the hierarchy to the whole of which it is a part. Since hierarchy has connotations of bureaucracy and militarism, and since Koestler's model can have permeable, reorganizable divisions with countless feedback loops and flexible strategies, he suggests the word *holarchy*.

The particular holarchy illustrated here reaches from organisms at the highest level to entities which are smaller than the sub-atomic. Each nodal point is a holon, which cannot be reduced to, nor predicted by, the parts beneath it. These 'sub-wholes' not only help to organize those parts beneath them, but have high degrees of autonomy from the wholes above them. The human heart, for example, has back-up pacemakers which will take over from each other in cases of strain or difficulty. Each level has its own built-in codes of rules, the mitochondria, for example, are tiny power-plants which extract energy from nutrients by a chain of chemical reactions involving fifty steps. A single cell may have up to five thousand such power plants. This tree diagram could equally well represent a locomotor holarchy of 'limbs, joints, individual muscles, and so on down to fibres, fibrils and contractile proteins'. We are all familiar with the autonomous nature of our own body parts. The way our hearts thump in emergencies, the 'cold sweat' anxiety and the sexual organs that rise (or not) to the occasion. Often these give a more accurate account of our feelings than do our words.

Koestler does not intend to restrict his holarchy to biology or anatomy. The 'three brains' in Map 24 are organized as a holarchy, as is the need hierarchy in Map 33, the life-stages in Map 37, the moral judgement levels in Map 38, the logical types in Map 39, and the Chomskyan linguistics in Map 41. 'All complex structures and processes of a relatively stable character display hierarchic organization regardless of whether we consider galactic systems, living organisms and their activities, or

This map represents a 'holarchy', Koestler's term for a hierarchically organized, self-regulating, open system of 'holons' represented by junctions A to J. Holon is coined from the Greek 'holos' meaning whole, and 'on' meaning entity, as in proton or neutron; hence a holon is a whole to those parts beneath it in the hierarchy but a part to those wholes above it. Like Janus, the Roman god of doorways, a holon looks both ways: towards wholes and parts, cooperation and competition, altruism and egoism, integration and self-assertion. In turn the holarchy itself may be part of a larger holarchy, for example the organism illustrated here is part of a larger social system (indicated by dotted lines).

The holarchy mapped here is not solely applicable to biology, it could as easily represent social organization, anatomy, linguistics, technology or the branching of knowledge. For the holarchy is best regarded as a conceptual tool, not as an end in itself but as a key capable of opening some of nature's combination locks which stubbornly resist other methods.

social organizations.' Knowledge branches out from disciplines, in technology or in library catalogues. Evolution is itself a climb to ever higher levels of complexity.

A familiar example of holarchic function is everyday speech. We have a non-verbal idea of what we want to convey and must try, sometimes struggle, to express it. The idea triggers, stepwise, a series of functional holons, which transforms our meaning into strings of sentences with well-formed grammatical and syntactical structures, furnished with words, spaces and sounds, which in turn trigger coordinated muscular contractions of tongue and vocal cords. The potential autonomy of lower levels is illustrated by exceedingly fluent speakers, who, with seeming ease, trigger whole sub-assemblies of ideas. Others like Billy Bud may struggle to find words and lash out physically instead. We can be prisoners alike of over-facile phrases or desperate inhibition.

Speech also enables us to distinguish fixed codes or canons of rules, from flexible strategies allowing choice. All comprehensible speech must obey rules of syntax and grammar, yet within such rules an infinite number of lawful sentences can be created (see Map 41). Such freedom has nothing to do with randomness or resistance to 'science'. Freedom versus determinism is itself Janus-faced, involving at one and the same time the autonomy of the holon and its integration with lawful relationships. Hence the pianist gives personal interpretation to music written for him, and the poet evokes our admiration by a freedom of expression which seems unforced by the real constraints of metre, rhythm and rhyme. In short, that venerable dividing line between freedom and determinism, mind and body, whole and part, autonomy and cooperation has dissolved into a plurality of degrees. As one moves to the top of the human holarchy higher degrees of freedom are experienced, but we are necessarily constrained by our own needs for personal and social integrity, 'No man is an island. He is a holon'.

The holarchic human condition is full of psychological insight. A large number of mental disturbances consist of subordinate parts of the human hierarchy splitting themselves off from the whole and exercising a kind of 'backlash' or tyranny. For example, trembling, compulsions, phobias, paranoid delusions, hysterical reactions, rage, panic and manic activities, can all be seen as the breakaway of a particular holon from control by and integration with the larger holarchy of the individual, as well as the individual's integration within the social holarchy. But Koestler is chiefly concerned with even wider sociocultural manifestations of malaise, what he calls the 'infernal dialectics' of self-assertion versus integration (or self-transcendence). Cultural harmony requires that these two tendencies remain in equilibrium, but there are three major forces that endanger and periodically upset this equilibrium. First, we tend to see the two inseparable aspects of the Janus-face in absolute moral terms and to isolate one from another, so that we split the human endowment between cooperation and competition, pitting 'heroic' self-interest against state-subsidized 'altruism' in holy wars. Koestler sees this as a defect of language made worse by the plurality of tongues. Second, we confuse integration and the chronic child-like yearning learned in the many years of infant dependency for fusion and symbiosis with figures of authority. Our growth from compulsory dependence to as compulsory an alienation precipitates mass stampedes back towards submission, identification and uncritical acceptance of paternal creeds. Thirdly, and for Koestler most importantly, there is the 'evolutionary design error' discussed in Map 21, wherein the neocortex is poorly coordinated with the two older brains, which are crucially involved in emotional reactions. This makes us overassertive cerebrally and technically, while remaining poorly and uncertainly integrated with our highly volatile limbic systems which are ever liable to runaway (see Map 24).

'Perhaps it is we, the screamers, who react in a sound and healthy way to the reality which surrounds us, whereas you are the neurotics who totter around in a screened fantasy world because you lack the capacity to face the facts. Were it not so this war would have been avoided, and those murdered within sight of your day-dreaming eyes would still be alive.'
'The Yogi and the Commissar'
Arthur Koestler

'On my first day at school, aged five, in Budapest, Hungary, I was asked by my future class-mates a crucial question. "Are you MTK or an FTC?" These were the initials of Hungary's two leading soccer teams, perpetual rivals for the team championship, as every schoolboy knew – except little me, who had never been taken to a football match. However, to confess such abysmal ignorance was unthinkable so I replied with haughty assurance "MTK of course!" And thus the die was cast; for the rest of my childhood in Hungary, and even when my family moved to Vienna, I remained an ardent and loyal supporter of MTK; and my heart still goes out to them, all the way across the Iron Curtain . . .'
'Janus: A Summing Up'
Arthur Koestler

'One may say broadly that all the animals that have been carefully observed have behaved so as to confirm the philosophy in which the observer believed before his observations began. Nay, more, they have all displayed the national characteristics of the observer. Animals studied by Americans rush about frantically with an incredible display of bustle and pep, and at last achieve the desired result by chance. Animals observed by Germans sit still and think, and at last evolve the solution out of their inner consciousness . . .'
'Unpopular Essays'
Bertrand Russell

'Dialogue with Death', 'Darkness at Noon', 'Arrival and Departure', 'The Yogi and the Commissar', 'Twilight Bar', 'Insight and Outlook', 'The Invisible Writing', 'The Sleepwalkers', 'The Lotus and the Robot', 'The Act of Creation', 'The Ghost in the Machine', 'Beyond Reductionism', 'The Challenge of Chance', 'The Heel of Achilles', and 'Janus' are all 'holonomic', paradoxical and 'bisociated' titles of books by Arthur Koestler.

'Chairman Mao's swim across the Yangtze river was a great encouragement to the Chinese people and revolutionaries throughout the world, and a heavy blow to imperialism, modern revisionism and the monsters and freaks who are opposed to socialism and Mao Tse-tung's thought.'
New China News Agency
quoted in 'Janus'.

MAP REFERENCES
Freedom versus determinism, 6, 40, 50, 52; Hierarchi view, 21, 33, 38, 41, 55; 'Infernal dialectics', see also bifurcation, oscillation, schismogenesis, 22, 34, 43, 48–51, 56–60; Symbiosis, 11, 40.

Koestler insists that it is our excesses of devotion and self-transcendence, far more than selfishness or anger, that are responsible for mass annihilations and genocidal wars. Groups rather than individuals are the major killers. The individual soldier is typically socialized into respecting authority and peer-group influence, so he kills for his leader and his friends like the well brought-up boy he is. Because we have codes for human relations but few, if any, for group relations, we repeatedly fail to grasp that if you make individuals more devoted and selfless this allows their group to be more destructive and selfish. Anything in the holarchy that binds parts unconditionally to a holon, permits that holon to tear itself unconditionally from the larger holarchy, so that loyal nationalism makes for treacherous internationalism or, as Koestler puts it, 'The egotism of the group feeds upon the altruism of its members'.

Koestler makes much of Stanley Milgram's laboratory experiment in obedience where 'assistants' to the psychological experimenter are ordered to inflict electric shocks of escalating intensity to a seemingly agonized 'volunteer' in order to discover 'the effect of pain on learning.' Over 60% of the 'assistants' (who are the real subjects being tested for their degree of compliance to cruel commands) inflict maximum voltages, labelled as 'extreme', to a victim who feigns passing out from the pain after clamouring to be released from the experiment. Signs of sadism, aggression or satisfaction were rare among the many subjects tested who were generally very upset by their orders. The chief influences pushing them to comply were a socialized deference towards authority and their identification with a 'scientific project' (ie personal devotion to an egotistic group). We have taught individuals to sublimate their aggression but not their devotion.

Koestler's holarchy is easily reconcilable with his theory of creativity (see Map 27). The bisociation between two or more matrices of thought, expression or behaviour synethesizes two previously separate holarchies, as the theory of electromagnetism bisociated two previously discrepant fields of knowledge, the space–time continuum joined 'absolute' space to 'absolute' time and the principle of complementarity bisociates waves and particles by a Janus-principle of alternate perspectives. It follows that freedom and consciousness increase as one approaches the apex of the holarchy but that the holons are held in place by numerous branches which, having become habitual, are pushed down below the threshold of consciousness. It is for this reason that great creators must grapple with unconscious roots, unearthing a tangle of buried assumptions and *reculer pour mieux sauter*, 'pull back the better to leap'.

MAP 48

Alcoholism, Cybernetics and Unconquerable Souls: The 'self' and Gregory Bateson

If there is one social scientist whose mind humbles me and whose courage and example in defying social science orthodoxies spurred me to write this book, it is Gregory Bateson. Yet he remains stubbornly high on the abstraction ladder most of the time, dealing largely with errors of scientific conception, although his critiques suggest devastating consequences. At the risk of misinterpreting the extraordinary subtlety of Bateson's thought, I shall try to make the practical implications of his work clear. My flawed renderings should at least encourage greater public attention. Time could be running out.

I begin with Bateson's views on alcoholism, perhaps the most down-to-earth of his writings. I will warn readers when I start to interpret. For Bateson the alcoholic is afflicted less by drunkenness than by sobriety from which drinking is a temporary release, the escape from an insane premise – the belief that he must be stronger than his condition, that he possesses an 'unconquerable soul' embattled with the Bottle. It is the error of Descartes (see Map 6) that the mind must control the body.

To understand this error, we need first to study Bateson's cybernetic conception of mind. An old-fashioned steam locomotive makes a useful analogy. At the top of the map opposite, the governor (B) consists of two balls attached to a rotating centre shaft. The faster the train goes the faster the shaft turns the higher the balls spin in a centrifugal pattern. The height of the balls progressively reduces the fuel (C) intake, which slows the cylinder (D), which slows the flywheel (A) moving the engine, which slows the turning shaft (B), which causes the balls to descend, which *increases* the fuel (C). What we have, in short, is a self-correcting system of mutual restraints which keeps the train at constant speed; if any one part of the circuit increases, a decrease in the corresponding part will modulate it, and vice versa. But suppose someone tampers with the governor. Now instead of the high speed of the rotating balls decreasing the fuel supply, it increases it, which increases the speed of the cylinder shaft, the flywheel and soon the train goes into uncontrolled 'runaway' or 'oscillation'. The driver is helpless. In fact, the word governor is a misnomer. No single part of the circuit governs any other part. Its 'intelligence' is in the entire circuit of (normally) self-correcting, homeostatic elements. The error of believing that the governor governs is analogous to the alcoholics belief that his 'will power' should be in charge. He has reified the concept of self and is attempting to regulate an entire cybernetic system by increasing the 'strength' and the 'power' of that one part. But, of course, as you increase the 'strength' of the governor's rotation you increase 'the fuel supply', in this case alcohol. The two run away together!

So far I have followed Bateson exactly, but the locomotive analogy is limited and I would like to convert it into the semantic elements of a value system. Bateson provides a lot of help here but stops short of actually giving us one. He stresses that values have a binary structure, power–surrender, exhibitionism–spectatorship are his examples. What these words transmit is information and this is 'news of differences'. The sentence, 'My aunt is angry with me because of the letter she did *not* receive', illustrates the fact that 'nothing', because it is different from a letter, can constitute a trigger for anger. There is no billiard ball striking another and transmitting energy in the mind, only differences which can be as insubstantial in their mass or force as zero correspondence.

What then are the values held by the alcoholic that lead to runaway? Bateson suggests a pride in the self and its will power, not a pride of accomplishment, not 'I succeeded' but 'I can', 'I can risk a drink, stay sober', and like any other boast it needs its challenge, the constant presence of drinks and drinking, an alcoholic polarization. 'Let me now interpret Bateson by attempting to make a circuit of these valuing processes:

Gregory Bateson sees the mind in terms of a cybernetic system, including the body and the environment, similar in some respects to that of an old-fashioned steam locomotive. The flywheel (A), which carries the engine's load at a particular speed, turns the shaft of the governor (B) making the two balls spin upwards and outwards centrifugally. The higher these balls spin the less fuel (C) is released, which slows the action of the cylinder (D), which slows the flywheel (A), which by lowering the spinning governor releases more fuel, which, of course, quickens the entire circuit. In short, this is a self-correcting system in which the increase (or decrease) in the speed of any one part causes another part to restrain (or enhance) it. However, if these mutual restraints break down the system goes into oscillation or runaway.

This analogy provides a useful illustration for alcoholism. The problem with many alcoholics is that they see themselves in terms of a Beleaguered Self doing battle with the Bottle, of Will Power fighting against Weakness (which they locate outside their conscious purposes). But just as you cannot control a steam engine by merely increasing the speed of the governor, so you cannot balance your mind by maximizing will power. The notion that governor and fuel are opposed triggers the escalation of both so that the entire circuit breaks out of mutual restraints. To stabilize the situation the cybernetic system must be re-established, all parts of the loop must be accepted, and an ecology of mind established.

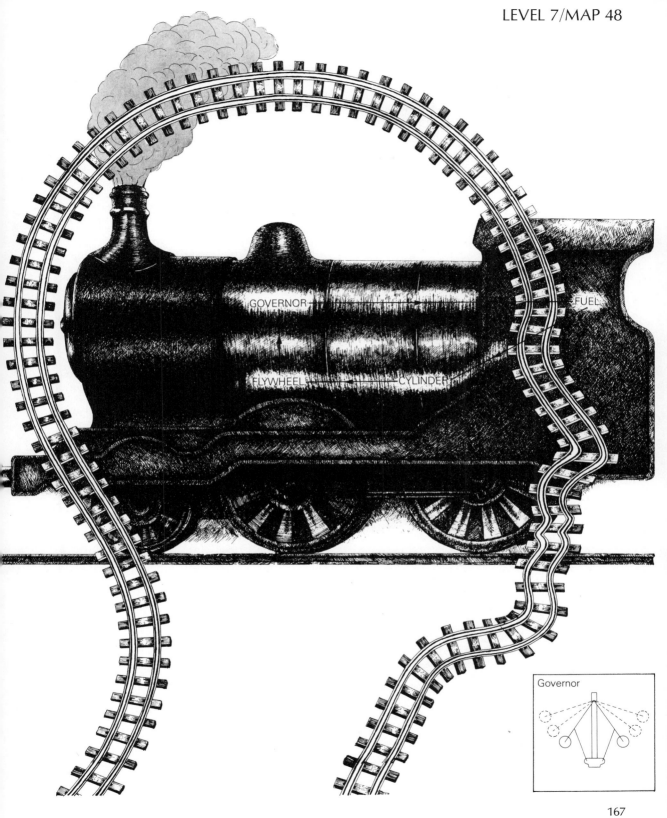

GOVERNOR

FUEL

FLYWHEEL CYLINDER

Governor

The binary values and 'alcoholic polorization' involved are: 1–I exhibitionism – spectatorship, 2–II strength – weakness, 3–III sober independence – drink dependence, 4–IV will power–surrender, 5–V risk–security. The individual has given positive evaluation and included within his concept of a conscious, willing self: exhibition, strength, sobriety, independence, will power and risk. He has given negative evaluation and excluded from the concept of his own mind and self: spectatorship, weakness, dependence, surrender and security. Indeed, so unconscious and ego-alien are values I to V, that I have drawn a 'short-circuit' arrow that severs them from the conscious values 1 to 5. The alcoholic treats these cut-offs of repressed values as something happening *to* him, visitations by the Bottle, or betrayal by his own emotions of his 'strength of mind'. Typically we attribute to our bodies all ideas peripheral to consciousness, so that 'the spirit is willing but the flesh is weak'. If, to quote Pascal, 'the heart has its own reasons', this is because 'heart' is a part of the cybernetics of mind which we have displaced beyond the narrow confines of conscious purpose. It is perilous to try to control the circle I to V by manipulating just the conscious arc 1 to 5. The unit of survival is the organism plus the environment; and mind is as much in the environment, in the surrender produced by drinking and in the security provided by the police, as it is within the skull or skin. When a blind man taps his way down the path where is his 'mind'? It is in the tip of his cane and in the differences discovered between curb and path in addition to his brain.

The fallacy of 'encapsulated man', as Joseph Royce has called it, is responsible for more pathologies than just alcoholism. At bottom is a total misapprehension of where the trouble lies. Our materialist society and science tries to locate the problem *in* a thing, in a 'bad value', in 'drink', in 'weakness', or in 'dependence'. As in Map 43, we use linear yardsticks of virtue that make strength 'good' and weakness 'bad' and we split-off this badness from us. But suppose 'weakness' or 'security', are not in themselves pathological but that the pathology lies in the severance of their relationships with their complementary values, 'strength' exclusive of 'weakness' or 'risk' exclusive of 'security'. Once such continua become split they continue to feed around in excitation while ceasing to contain or constrain one another (see margin).

Bateson calls this process of splitting *schismogenesis*, literally 'a growing split in the structure of ideas'. He identifies two varieties, symmetrical and complementary. Symmetrical schismogenesis starts with the matching of drink for drink, 'strength' for 'strength', 'risk' for 'risk' between two or more persons. The game escalates until the drinkers come full circle into the complementary phase in which exaggerated 'strength' is matched by total weakness and collapse, and 'will power' by abject surrender to drunkenness. The consequence of this is that the alcoholic redoubles his conscious determination to remain sober. There, he fell off the wagon again! Could

Out of the night that covers me
Black as the Pit from pole to pole
I thank whatever gods may be
For my unconquerable soul . . .
Under the bludgeonings of
                              chance
My head is bloody, but unbowed
                              . . .
It matters not how strait the gate,
How charged with punishments
                              the scroll,
I am the master of my fate;
I am the captain of my soul.
    'Invictus' William Ernest Henley

'Consider a man felling a tree with an axe. Each stroke of the axe is modified or corrected, according to the shape of cut face of the tree left by the previous stroke. This self-corrective (ie mental) process is brought about by a total system, tree–eyes–brain–muscles–axe–stroke–tree that has the characteristics of immanent mind.'
    'Steps to an Ecology of Mind'
                    Gregory Bateson

'God grant us the serenity to accept the things we cannot change, courage to change the things we can, and wisdom to know the difference.'
    The Serenity Prayer of Alcoholics
                    Anonymous

strength

curity ———————— risk

weakness

there be a stranger argument for 'will power' and 'strength of character'? And so the governor waves its balls and the fuel intake increases as the system goes into mounting oscillation between extremes and runs away. Most attempts to help the alcoholic at this stage will founder on his dualism. Sympathize and succour him and he suffers revulsion at his 'weakness'. Attack, abuse or challenge him and he postures the more.

Most professional psychologists agree, and it is a humbling admission, that the best hope for many alcoholics is the amateur self-help organization Alcoholics Anonymous. Its first prescription is in its title, anonymity for the overmighty self. This is not chiefly for self-protection but to put the overall principles of ecology above personality. AA prescribes an 'embrace' of the intoxicated values but without intoxication. It says, 'You are powerless against alcohol and must come to believe in a power greater than yourself'. This power is God, but a very personal God 'as *you* understand him to be'. The individual is a part of that power and must learn to live in harmony with it.

It may be impossible to help the alcoholic until he 'hits bottom' and unstabilizes his system so that the symmetrical pattern is broken, along with the conception of a singular selfhood subduing the earth. The surrender of the self, in which 'obsessions of the mind' heal their split with 'allergies of the body', is a spiritual experience. To those not yet ready to surrender AA says, 'Go and do some controlled drinking.' This helps the subject to prove to himself, that one drink is usually enough to make the disowned side of the cybernetic loop lash back and reclaim him. 'Once an alcoholic always an alcoholic', says AA. Not because this is literally true, it isn't, but because the conception of the self must expand permanently to incorporate alcoholic experience. The relationship between the individual and his God acknowledges a ground of being extending beyond the known self (see Map 5). This is paralleled by the 'buddy system', wherein each member may call upon and be called by a friend in need, so a new bond with the community is established. Much as wine symbolizes communion, the alcoholic has taken the symbol for the reality and uses drinking as a substitute for the relaxation, fusion, surrender and security of deep personal relationships.

Finally, we should note that splitting and oscillation can polarize many different kinds of value system and is by no means confined to the *machismo* syndromes detailed here. The 'serenity prayer' of AA is a hymn to the ecology of mind, to constant movement between fused values – risk and security, power and surrender, dependence and independence – to heal the splits between them and develop all synergistically.

MAP REFERENCES
Alcoholism, 50, 56; Cartesian dualism, 6–8; Conscious purpose, 50, 55–6, 60; Ecology of mind, 3, 47, 50, 55, 58–60; Oscillation, 14, 16; Runaway, 22; Schismogenesis, 47, 49–51, 56–60.

MAP 49

The Double Bind and Schizophrenia: Bateson, Don D. Jackson, Jay Haley, John H. Weakland

The 'double-bind' theory of schizophrenia has always suffered from one particular handicap. In a world so full of dilemma and domination it has proved difficult to state what is *not* a double bind. Once one is alerted to psychological situations wherein persons are 'damned if they do and damned if they don't', then one tends to wonder why millions of people are not as psychotic as hooty owls. I must therefore preface this discussion with my own interpretation of 'normal conflict' between people and their values. Everyone who brings up children is obliged at times to correct them. The cornerstone of socialization is 'I love you but . . .', whether tacitly or overtly stated. Where 'I love you' is not believed or believable, little else will work. Most parents manage to hold their children's basic identities as persons in the context of an overall, mutually affirmed affection and *within* that context explain how specific behaviours could be improved upon. When a small child runs into a busy road and is snatched back and shaken by an irate mother then no contradiction is implicit. 'Mother is furious because she loves you', is an entirely comprehensible statement, despite the fact that the love needs to be inferred and is hardly manifest at that moment.

During the course of this book I have been evolving cybernetic loops of binary values; let us now consider a typical 'socialization circle' of mother and son.

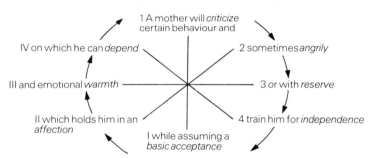

1 A mother will *criticize* certain behaviour and
2 sometimes *angrily*
3 or with *reserve*
4 train him for *independence*
I while assuming a basic *acceptance*
II which holds him in an *affection*
III and emotional *warmth*
IV on which he can *depend*

The potential 'contradictions' between criticism and acceptance, anger and affection, reserve and warmth, independence and dependence, are resolved by ensuring that when one in each pair is 'message', the other will be 'context' so that opposite ends are always at a different level of logical typing (see Map 40). His mother's criticism, anger, reserve and stress upon his independence are expressed in the context of acceptance, love, warmth and dependability. Her effectiveness as a communicator will depend on this contrast between 'figure' and 'ground'. Only if she loves well can she criticize effectively. She might, of course, reverse the order above, and praise him warmly and affectionately, but even here the weight and significance of her words lie in their contrast with her known capacity for reserve and criticism. Without this context her praise lacks 'the difference that makes a difference'. A mother perpetually babbling blessings is best ignored! What then is the conflict in the double bind, bearing in mind that all values 'conflict' within a cybernetic system of mutual restraints? My suggestion is illustrated in the main map. A double bind is a confusion as to which of two contrasting values or ideas should be regarded as 'message' and which as 'context', or which as 'figure' and which as 'ground'. Does mother hate certain things I do in the context of love or does she just pretend to love me in the context of real hatred? This is so important a difference, so terrifying an uncertainty that the inability to decide is ample grounds for insanity.

The 'double bind' is a statement made at at least two levels of logical typing in which the context, or meta-message, which comments on that statement appears to invalidate the statement made. For example, a mother saying to her small daughter, 'Go to bed you're tired and I want to get more sleep!' is ostensibly expressing solicitude for the child although the mother's tone and expression may say, 'I'm sick to death of you!' However, from the child's point of view it may not be clear whether the mother is speaking in tired irritation out of a background of genuine love and concern (left of map) or whether the mother is feigning her love out of a background of genuine hatred and resentment for a child she never wanted (right of map). There is a vital difference here which means survival itself to the child. If the child is unsure of her mother's love, she may need to falsify her own experience and decide she is tired after all; distortion may be preferred to a realization of abandonment. In addition, as her mother will typically become even more hostile if the child shows she recognizes her mother's underlying resentment, the child is forced to collude in the concealment of the mother's dislike. This split between levels of logical typing may be so confusing to the child that it may be visited on her mind as schizophrenia, literally 'split soul'.

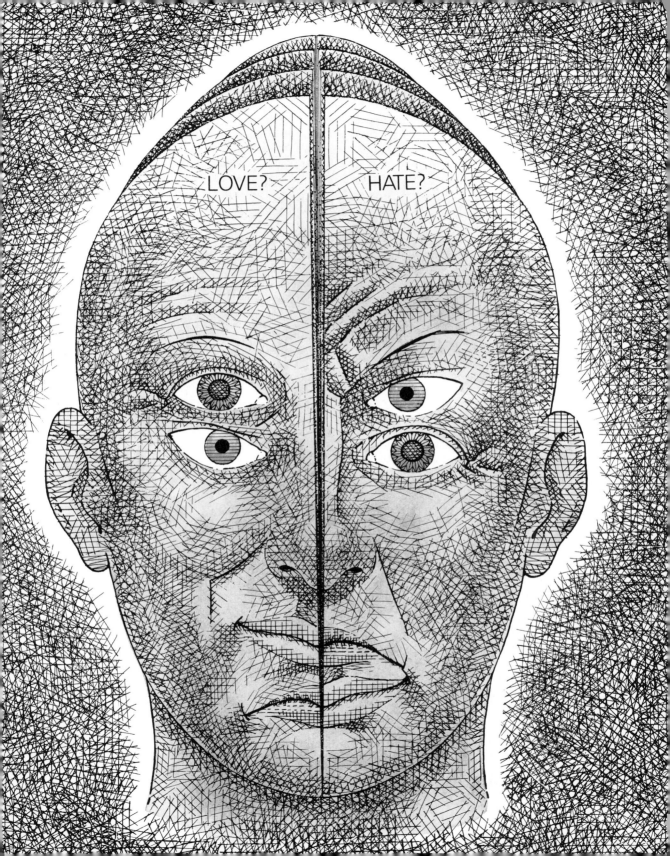

Let us consider the clinical case history which Gregory Bateson and his co-workers have provided. A mother visited her schizophrenic son in hospital. He was glad to see her and impulsively put his arm around her shoulders whereupon she stiffened. He withdrew his arm and she asked, 'Don't you love me any more?' He then blushed, and she said, 'Dear, you must not be so easily embarrassed and afraid of your feeling'. Moments later she was shown out as the son became agitated and suffered a violent relapse. Consider the construction placed by the researchers upon this incident. There is a primary injunction from mother to son, 'Express your feelings and continue to love me.' There is a secondary, conflicting injunction disguised at a higher level of abstraction or logical type and communicated by the mother stiffening with revulsion. This says, in effect, 'But if you do express loving feelings I will punish you.' There is also a tertiary injunction which orders the son to continue trying to express his loving feelings which she insists he has for her. Hence he is forbidden to withdraw. Finally she is denying that her disgust is disgust, 'Do not see this withdrawl as withdrawal', and she punishes him for correctly identifying it. In this double bind the son is punished whatever he does and is forbidden to comment upon the trap in which he finds himself. I would therefore characterize the double bind as an ever-reversible figure–ground relationship and an ever-ambiguous oscillation between message and context, with conflict not only between levels but within them. In order to believe in his mother's love the son needs to falsify his own experience, to pretend what he noticed did not occur.

Why should the mother behave like this? Generally because she feels deep, sometimes unconscious, resentment towards the child, who may not have been wanted and whose very existence constitutes a burden. Yet she must conceal this fact from herself and from the child and so trains him to deny every sign of her own underlying resentment. Her simulated affection must be confirmed so she too can believe in it, and her frequent withdrawals of affection must be accounted for by her child's unpardonable errors and stupidities. She accomplishes this elaborate, if unconscious, deception by learning to achieve total control over the social contexts in which she and her son interact. Whoever controls the definition of a social situation can say whether any piece of behaviour within that context is good or bad. So he uses her control to switch the context back and forth in a way which justifies her, and, where necessary, unjustifies him.

Let me illustrate this with a semantic analysis of the incident in the hospital, using two values continua from the 'socialization circle' on the previous page. The dimensions warmth–reserve and independence–dependence (or dependability) have virtues at each end, and typically one is exhibited in the context of the other. So that my warmth has reserve in the background (I will not slobber over you), and my reserve warmth. But when values are inappropriately or clumsily expressed we give them negative terms, hence overemotional versus cold suggests an excess of warmth or reserve. Selfish versus clinging suggests an excess of independence or dependence which fails to meet the requirements of the particular human relationship. So when the mother stiffens and withdraws, she is saying in effect, 'I the reserved and independent one find you to be overemotional and clinging. It offends me.' When the son withdraws blushing, she at once switches contexts. 'I, the warm and dependable one, find you cold and selfish. It offends me.' She is always right. He is always wrong. Her incapacity to love him in the 'territory' is compensated for by artful manipulations of a moral 'map' in which she monopolizes virtue and leaves him with all the vice. Essentially she is crippling his capacity to move to and fro on values continua, fitting either end within the context of the other, a social skill basic to all relationships.

'How do you know you are God!'
'When I pray to him I find I'm talking to myself.'
'The Ruling Class' Peter Barnes

Mr Barrett (The father of Elizabeth Barrett Browning): 'But you must [obey me] . . . out of love, not fear . . . I said just now that you had displeased me. I take it back! You will never know through any deed or word of mine, how grievously you have hurt your poor father.'
'The Barretts of Wimpole Street' Rudolph Besier

'In a psychiatric hospital, failure to be an easily manageable patient – failure, for example, to work or to be polite to the staff – tends to be taken as evidence that one is not yet "ready" for liberty and that one has need of further treatment. The point is not that the hospital is a hateful place for patients, but that for the patient to express hatred of it is to give evidence that his place in it is justified and that he is not yet ready to leave it.'
'Asylum' Erving Goffman

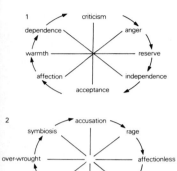

What is remarkable about the double-bind theory is its capacity to make comprehensible, from the schizophrenic's point of view, a very large number of otherwise bewildering symptoms. It has been found, for example, in research reported by Don Bannister and Fay Fransella, that schizophrenic symptomology increases markedly in all areas touching on personal relationships while moderating substantially in purely intellectual or technical areas. Symptomology increases sharply with 'serial invalidation', George Kelly's term for repeated disconformation. The schizophrenic's hallucinated voices issuing contradictory injunctions could hardly be a concidence. The inability to go up the abstraction ladder and use logical types properly is marked, as is the incapacity to label metaphors correctly or assign the correct mode to messages sent or received. Patients jump from context to context as if afraid of being trapped, and make statements which eliminate reference to who is speaking to whom. They carefully eliminate all premises, distort or omit references to time and place, and make glancing references designed to provoke but not engage.

The theory is also able to account for different kinds of schizophrenia in terms of different escape strategies from approaching binds. The authors state: 'He might, for example, assume that behind every statement there was a concealed meaning which was detrimental to his welfare. He would then be exclusively concerned with hidden meanings and determined to demonstrate that he could not be deceived . . . and will be characteristically suspicious and defiant. . . He might choose another alternative and . . . accept literally everything people say to him; when their tone or gesture contradicted what they said, he might establish a pattern of laughing off all these meta-communicative signals . . . or he might choose to try and ignore them . . . and hear less and less of what went on around him, and do his utmost to avoid . . . a response from his environment . . . and concentrate on his own internal processes . . . by being withdrawn perhaps mute.' These are portraits of paranoid, hebephrenic and catatonic schizophrenia respectively. If the logical types that discriminate between context and behaviour collapse then the cybernetic cycle of socialization will go into runaway, oscillation and extremism. In normal behaviour, we may recall, criticism 'nests' within basic acceptance, anger within affection, reserve within warmth and independence within dependence or vice versa (see margin diagram 1). Such behaviours are mutually containing and constraining like the self-correcting system of a locomotive (see Map 48). But once the values continua split, behaviour breaks from the constraint of context and the self-exciting system spirals out of control (see margin diagram 2). Schizophrenia means 'split soul', while paranoia comes from *para-nous* 'a mind beside a mind'. Each end of each continua in the socialization cycle escalates to an extreme. Hence criticism-within-basic-acceptance becomes wild paranoid accusations split from an inner plasticity. Anger-within-affection becomes violent rage or erotic precocity, reserve-within-warmth becomes affectionlessness or 'inappropriate affection', while independence-within-dependence escalates into autistic delusions or chronic, foetal symbiosis. Scores of schizophrenic symptoms can be created simply by splitting normal reciprocities assunder, and exaggerating each one.

MAP REFERENCES

MAP 50

Authoritarianism, Schismogenesis and the Self-exciting System: Bateson and Nevitt Sanford

An account of the human mind must sooner or later confront its genocidal capacities. The systematic, drawn-out, gloating destruction of nearly seven million people in Nazi concentration camps dashed at one stroke all conceptions of ethical progress in human culture. Nor, as the files of Amnesty International will attest, is this an isolated or German peculiarity. Something is dreadfully wrong with mind and society; no one who pretends to social science can afford to look away.

A brave attempt to explain the authoritarian personality was made by a group of researchers headed by Nevitt Sanford in the late forties. They used attitude measures such as the F (fascism) scale made up of neo-Freudian insights. From this emerged a mass of characteristics typifying American-style authoritarianism. I believe, however, that Gregory Bateson's concept of *schismogenesis* (a growing split in the structure of human interaction and in the ideas communicated), in conjunction with Sir Geoffrey Vickers notion of *a self-exciting system*, organize the data on authoritarianism much better. The following arguments are my own as are all errors of interpretation. No implication is intended that the theorists have collaborated or endorsed my account.

Maps 40, 42, 45, 48 and 49 have familiarized us with cybernetic systems. There are those in a steady state with their binary values, such as: desire–resilience, or courage–security, in mutual balance and restraint, and there are others which get trapped in a vicious circle of excitation. Suppose I desire a fair maiden and am prepared to show increasing degrees of courage in an attempt to win her favour. If I also have the resilience to survive discouragement, I may gain the security of her arms and our mutual desires can be satiated. Even if I did not win her, I would be wise in the interest of my security to moderate my desire. In both instances my value system is self-correcting and mutually modulating. But suppose, instead, that frustration and resilience excite my desire so that I fix on one part of the cybernetic loop and magnify it into an obsession? Fresh from the *Ring of the Nibelung*, with its thunderous point and counterpoint and Wagnerian crescendoes, the vision of my beauteous maid becomes ever more enthralling as my frustration mounts. Like Siegfried it may be that every assault on my security only redoubles my courage as my resilience and desire blaze. Once caught in this system it becomes hard to extricate myself. Were the maid suddenly to fall into my arms, the chances of her living up to my ethereal visions of mountain nymphs wreathed in mist would be too much for both of us. Being too repressed sexually to allow love-making to climax my saga, I am left with the 'clean' collision of Love and Death, in which ideals live for ever and only people die. My self-exciting system has become a way of death. Its heady romanticism is a 'map' celebrating itself. The real maiden in the 'territory' is soon forgotten as my red rose, my sword, lyre and glorious passion serenade themselves.

The Nazi swastika provides an apt symbol for both this dislocation of the cybernetic loop and the self-exciting centrifuge. The hooks in the cross can be seen as breaks or splits upon the two continua of binary values, so that 1. Desire (top left) has broken away from I Resilience (bottom right), while 2. Courage (middle right) has split from II Security (middle left). The arrows circling the swastica show that its 'broken arms' continue to excite each other, while the splits in each continuum destroy the mutual modulations and restraints, as the system auto-stimulates, oscillates and runs away. This runaway extremism calls into question whether such terms as 'courage' and 'security' are appropriate. I argued in Map 43 that we can distinguish empirically split values continua from synthesized values continua and it makes sense therefore to use positive evaluations, courage–security, for synthesized values, and negative evaluations, recklessness–cowardice for the split

The swastika provides an apt symbol for schismogenesis – 'a growing split in the structure of human interaction and the ideas communicated'. The words used here are simply illustrative since schismogenesis splits all moral interaction and discourse by going into runaway and oscillation on the principle of: the more of 1 (Desire) the more of 2 (Courage), the more of I (Resilience) the more of II (Security). Hence the typical rhetoric: 'Our desire and courage must be resilient in the pursuit of security.' Readers may similarly trace: 'By the power of our rebellion each becomes more subject in obedience to the Führer', and 'Triumph and love of Fatherland demand the sacrifice of fighting.' The 'magic' of such rhetoric is that it appears to unite such value oppositions as 7 Triumph – VII Sacrifice and 8 Love – VIII Fighting, and the vision of more and more of every imaginable virtue heralds a Second Coming. In truth, however, one value in every pair is being postponed: fight now, love later; sacrifice now, triumph later. The tension splits apart values continua 1 from I, 2 from II and so on (symbolized by the cracking hooks in the swastika) and destroys the mutual modulation of the self-correcting system. Since such splits can be empirically confirmed, is one not justified philosophically in labelling the severed ends as vices not virtues? Thus, Desire–Resilience become frenzy–reaction, Power–Subjection become brutality–submission, and so on round the swastika where the vices lie like concealed poisons in the crooks of the cross.

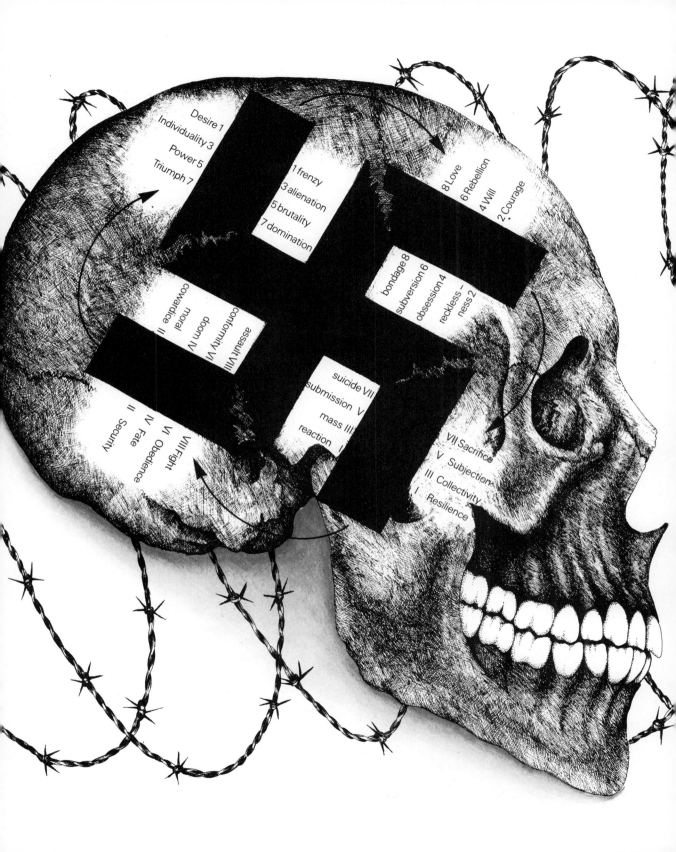

values of schismogenetic systems. Thus while the Nazi regime celebrated those 'good' value absolutes on the outside of the arms of the swastika, the real and negative implications were carried within the crooks (see map) in an organized system of self-delusion. Their vaunted collectivity was crass conformity, their will the narrowest obsession, their power brutality. (It says much for the poverty of our ethical senses that even today language analysts inform us there is no meaningful distinction between such terms.)

We can now appreciate better the ecstasies greeting Hitler's accession to power. The exhilarating experience of a schismogenetic society in its early stages of runaway is that oppositions are magically unified. Dauntless courage will bring us total security, as the fighting stormtrooper wins the love of the aryan mother and her blue-eyed tots. The smashing of laws and codes brings the rebel into greater obedience to the führer and super-loyalty makes the conservative radical and the radical conservative. The self-exciting system has an ersatz 'creativity' and a pseudo synergy. It is as if the eternal verities had been put in a centrifuge and spun round, more love and more aggression, more nationalism and more socialism, more classicism, (symbolized by neo-Roman monuments) and more romanticism (symbolized by flaming torches and galumphing pig-tailed peasants). The serried ranks personify order, the dammed up emotions disorder, war now for everlasting peace! Like the alcoholic's (see Map 48) it is an intoxicating vision in which he both indulges and is 'stronger' than indulgence.

The difference, a crucial one, between pseudo and genuine creativity and between schismogenesis and synergy lies in the mere juxtaposition of contrasting values compared with their meaningful synthesis. Unfortunately an aestheticism that intuits the creative is not very widely distributed and we are easily hooked on crude contrasts: the pornography of 'pure' womanhood in the toils of Jewish seducers; the little ones mixing with the great ones at children's parties at the Berghof; men from every German province declaring their unity at Nuremburg.

Our materialism has taught us to look at values like things and to seek ever more of them. So we are blind to cracks that appear between them and we do not see the monster hatching. Yet with training, the splits are not difficult to see and occur simultaneously at psychological and sociological levels. Sanford *et al* found that two principle traits of authoritarianism were *anti-intraception*, the refusal to look within oneself, and *projectivity* the casting of the inner outside. These characteristics help to insulate the values proclaimed from the force of its opposite gathering within. The 'courageous' fanatic will not see his unwillingness to survive defeat for the moral cowardice it is, the incapacity to live with error. He believes he can segregate courage from fear but cannot. A highly predictive item on the F-scale was the most split one. 'There is hardly anything lower than the person who does not show a great love, gratitude and respect for his parents.' It is split between levels of logical typing (see Map 40), since the message is love and respect while the tone is disgust and hatred. (What if his parents do not respect their parents?) Note also that love is for insiders, one's parents, while denunciation is for a whole universe of undutiful offspring.

Splitting repeats itself sociologically in ethnocentrism and the progressive disparagement of persons as they deviate from one's own condition, Jews, blacks, communists and homosexuals being favourite targets. Ethnocentrism is essential to self-exciting systems. Love can only be reconciled with aggressiveness where insiders have agreed on the outside targets of attack and praise the predators. Likewise obedient rebels need outsiders against whom to rebel, a gang to solidify obedience and sacred womanhood to protect. Splitting is greatly exacerbated by

'All of German history is nothing but a continuous chain of battles against its enemies . . . The German soul is Faustian! In it lies the instinctive bent towards work and the longing for redemption from the mind.'
'Michael' Joseph Goebbels

'The mission of woman is to be beautiful and to bring children into the world . . . The female bird pretties herself for her mate and hatches eggs for him. In exchange . . . the mate stands guard and wards off the enemy.'
'Michael'

'The cell into which generation after generation of German romantics have finally fled from liberty's weight is a word-cell, their fanatic faith in some rigid authoritarian dogma.'
'Meta-Politics' Peter Viereck

*Turning and turning in the
          widening gyre
The falcon cannot hear the
          falconer;
Things fall apart; the centre
          cannot hold;
Mere anarchy is loosed upon the
          world,
The blood-dimmed tide is
          loosed, and everywhere
The ceremony of innocence is
          drowned;
The best lack all conviction, while
          the worst
Are full of passionate intensity.*

*Surely some revelation is at hand;
Surely the Second Coming is at
          hand.
The Second Coming! Hardly are
          those words out
When a vast image out of Spiritus
          Mundi
Troubles my sight: somewhere in
          sands of the desert
A shape with lion body and the
          head of a man,
A gaze blank and pitiless as the
          sun,
Is moving its slow thighs, while all
          about it
Reel shadows of the indignant
          desert birds.
The darkness drops again; but
          now I know
That twenty centuries of stony
          sleep
Were vexed to nightmare by a
          rocking cradle,
And what rough beast, its hour
          come round at last,
Slouches towards Bethlehem to
          be born?*
'The Second Coming' W. B. Yeats

official lies, but it is a serious question whether such officials could recognize a lie as such. In a country where war assures peace and Hitler's 'patience is nearly exhausted' what difference is there between such categories? They swell up side by side in a fearful ambiguity that paralyses the decision of European statesmen, with every new demand a 'last' demand, and every 'concession' fuel for combustible indignation.

The image of a centrifuge, which draws values into definitions exclusive of their contraries, would help to account for the extreme conventionality and stereotyped thinking found in authoritarian samples. Women are 'pure' or 'whores', worshipped and/or exploited. People in general are strong or weak, 'decent, sane and normal' or 'low, feeble-minded and crooked'. But perhaps nothing makes more surely for schismogenesis, then or today, than 'the dehumanizing concept of conscious purpose' as Bateson calls it. The Nazis, like 'cultural alcoholics' preached the Triumph of the Will and *Mein Kampf*, taking one part of a cybernetic loop and magnifying this into a national obsession. What happened is exactly what a cyberneticist would predict, not will but fate and doom, in that curious fascist admixture of advanced technology and mysticism. 'I go the way that Providence dictates with all the assurance of a sleepwalker', Hitler said. Will power fed around the circuit to seal his fate. We have freedom, Geoffrey Vickers insists, but it is 'freedom in a rocking boat'. You push and the next moment nearly capsize.

But if a schismogenetic system is 'turning and turning in the widening gyre' (see margin) and if 'things fall apart, the centre cannot hold', how did the Thousand Year Reich cohere for even twelve years? The answer lay in its ever greater propensity for domination and submission. This domination is not just of people by people but of ideas by ideas. The capacity for mutual excitation is produced in a manner similar to the charcoal burner who damps down his furnace to create a white heat of repression within; 'strength' bearing down on weakness, 'courage' upon security, creates insatiable fears and needs for security which no victory can assuage. 'The Nazi', said Churchill, 'is either at your knees or at your throat'. The traits of domination and submission and loneliness 'chase' each other around the vicious circle.

Finally these systems auto-destruct from sheer frenzy. The more people they murder, the more the glazed eyes of the dead appear to reproach their killers, the worse therefore the victims must have been to deserve it, the more all *kammaraden* must affirm this and the more dissenters must be persecuted. Such immeasurable suffering needs an immeasurable good to sanctify it, a Final Solution that solves all social problems for ever, and shuts the mouth of every last detractor. The end is the *Götterdämmerung*, the Twilight of the Gods, the opera Hitler had seen a hundred times. Courage, Will, Desire, Fate, Sacrifice, Obedience, with all other false reifications come crashing down upon Brünhilde, who, taking upon herself the sins of the gods, rides into the flames to innaugurate an era of Love. When the dust settles and we examine the burnt fragments, what are they but heaps of kitsch and cliché comprising 'the soul-defying banality of evil'.

MAP 51

The Cybernetics of Mental Health: Charles Hampden-Turner

In 1958 Marie Jahoda published her *Current Concepts of Positive Mental Health*. I updated these in 1970 in my book *Radical Man* adding to her list some more and recent conceptions. An abbreviated list along with my summation is below.

CRITERIA OF MENTAL HEALTH	THEORISTS	MAP NO.	SUMMATION
1. Productive	Erich Fromm	11	The person
Creative	Frank Barron	30	*exists*
Existential	Rollo May	13	freely
Conscious decision	Martin Buber	35	↓
2. Respect	Erich Fromm	11	through the quality
Social awareness	H. S. Sullivan	34	of his/her
Moral cognition	Lawrence Kohlberg	38	*perception*
Cleansing	William Blake	26	
Perception			↓
3. Individuation	Carl Jung	10	the strength of
Ego-identity	Erik Erikson	37	his/her *identity*
4. Competence	R. W. White	—	and their synthesis
Self-love	Erich Fromm	11	Into an experienced
Ego-strength	Frank Barron	30	*competence*
			↓
5. Decision	Martin Buber	35	He/she *commits*
Generativity	Erik Erikson	37	this
Will	Rollo May	13	↓
Ego participation	Gordon Allport	—	with intensity
Congruence	Carl Rogers	32	and authenticity
Authenticity	J. F. Bugental	—	in the human
			environment
			↓
6. Holy-insecurity	Martin Buber	35	by periodically
Existential dread	Søren Kierkegaard	12	*suspending* and *risking*
Courage to be	Paul Tillich	13	experienced meanings
			↓
7. Relation over distance	Martin Buber	35	in trying to *bridge the distance* to
Overcoming aloneness	Erich Fromm	11	others
Leap of faith	Søren Kierkegaard	12	↓
8. Consensual validation	H. S. Sullivan	34	and make a *self-confirming* and *self-transcending* impact
Self-confirmation	Martin Buber	35	
Self-actualization	Abraham Maslow	33	↓
9. Resolving dichotomies	Abraham Maslow	42	and through a dialectic achieve
Dialectical resolution	F. J. Varela	55	*synergy*.
Synergy	Ruth Benedict	42	↓
10. Integrity	Erik Erikson	37	Each will try to *order*

This model of psychosocial development is presented as a self-correcting cybernetic system which joins with others in a double-helix pattern through relationships. (The analogy of the double-helix is from the DNA molecule which contains and, via RNA, transmits coded instructions for the unfolding organism.) In the double helix in the illustration the segments are joined by ten rungs, not five as in DNA, linking identity to identity, confirmation to confirmation and so on, so that each segment of each helix is enhanced and developed. In this way it is possible for existence to be enhanced, perceptions improved, committed competences to be confirmed and increasingly complex learning to result. Helices can join, separate and rejoin, learning from persons they have encountered and deriving lasting benefits or deficits from the experience. Both emotional and informational aspects of such relationships are ideally synergistics (Map 42) so that deep feelings are intensified by mutual sensitivities and creative syntheses arise from combinations of experience.

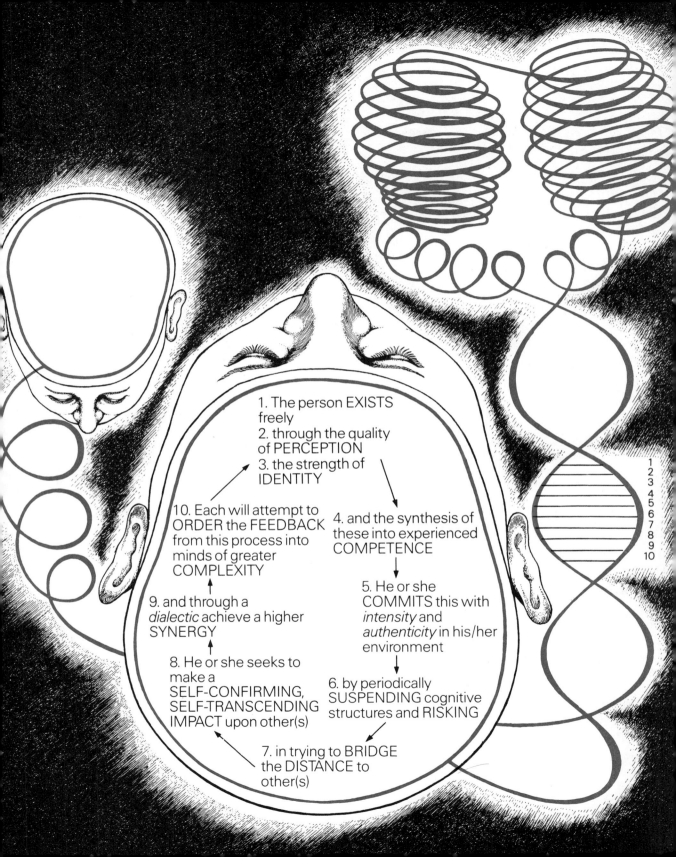

1. The person EXISTS freely
2. through the quality of PERCEPTION
3. the strength of IDENTITY
4. and the synthesis of these into experienced COMPETENCE
5. He or she COMMITS this with *intensity* and *authenticity* in his/her environment
6. by periodically SUSPENDING cognitive structures and RISKING
7. in trying to BRIDGE the DISTANCE to other(s)
8. He or she seeks to make a SELF-CONFIRMING, SELF-TRANSCENDING IMPACT upon other(s)
9. and through a *dialectic* achieve a higher SYNERGY
10. Each will attempt to ORDER the FEEDBACK from this process into minds of greater COMPLEXITY

1
2
3
4
5
6
7
8
9
10

Expanded	Kurt Lewin	36	the *feedback* into
Life-space			minds of greater
Moral Complexity	Lawrence Kohlberg	38	*complexity*

If we take the ten summations above we can create from these the cybernetic loop described in the map on page 179. This model of psychosocial development has the following characteristics: it is a field theory and an open self-correcting system transacting with its environment; all its parts are *both* interdependent, being mutually defining according to their functions within the whole, *and* they have the local autonomy of the holons described by Koestler in Map 47, so that perception and identity, for example, are 'sub-wholes' of a larger system; elimination of, or defects to, any one segment of the cycle can crucially alter the meaning of other segments. For example, a sense of *competence* that has not been *risked* and *suspended* becomes oppressive and coerces *confirmation*.

Since a cyclic process of this kind can develop all of its capacities, so as to learn better *perception*, stronger *commitment*, across wider *distances*, and higher *synergy*, it makes sense to regard it as a development helix. Because there are always at least two persons involved this becomes a double helix. For example, my *perception* is almost never independent of the fact that I, too, am seen; my *identity* will shift from father, husband, man, writer depending on whom I address; my *competence* will be much reduced if menaced by a black-belt judo champion; and were I suddenly transported to a Chinese village the sense of social *distance* would greatly inhibit my interactive capacities. It therefore makes sense in illustrating the double helix to join identity to identity, confirmation to confirmation and so on by a series of cross-linkages, like the spiral ladder formed by the molecular structure of DNA, save that here we have ten linkages per spiral convolution instead of five.

Thus persons develop by mutual enhancement between helical processes which can join, separate, rejoin and transmit their codes one to the other like messenger RNA. Crucial to this entire process is the concept of synergy (see Map 42) which operates at more than one level of logical typing (see Map 40). There is synergy in the sense of an optimal relationship between the helices of both parties and in the additional sense of an optimal combination of their individual personality resources, so that I do not commit myself beyond my range of perception and to someone not prepared to confirm me. Finally synergy reconciles apparent contraries, the integration of personality and its risk and suspension, confirming and being confirmed, distance and bridging it.

I have developed several reservations since proposing this model ten years ago. First the sentence structure biases the entire dynamic towards those processes which are the subjects of the sentence. Second, this turns a recursive, ever-circling system into an arc, leading to the potential idolization of conscious purpose (see Maps 48, 50). The objection is, however, quickly repaired and the equality between the many concepts of positive mental health is restored, by treating the cycle as a loop of present participles: existing – perceiving – identifying – mastering – committing – risking – suspending – distancing – bridging – confirming – transcending – negotiating – synergizing – integrating and existing again. Any person or group must have the right to begin at any point on the cycle and provided the entire cycle of resources is thereby enhanced that choice is vindicated and growth is fostered. It makes sense to start with the least developed segments so that any emphasis thereon is equilibrating. We could say to a particular patient for example, 'Your life is too narrow; until you learn to *bridge the distance* to a larger circle of acquaintances you will not achieve the breadth of

'Life spirals laboriously upward to higher and higher levels paying for every step . . . It passes into levels of higher differentiation and centralization and pays for this by loss of regulability after disturbances. It invents a highly developed nervous system and therewith pain. It adds to the primeval parts of the nervous system a brain which allows consciousness that by means of a world of symbols grants foresight and control of the future . . .'
'Problems of Life'
Ludwig von Bertalanffy

'No human being can develop save through the prolonged connection with other beings. The circuit of polarized vision precedes all mind and all knowing. It is anterior to and ascendant over human will. And yet the mind and the will can both interfere with the dynamic circuit an idea, like a stone wedged in a delicate machine, can arrest one's whole process of psychic interaction and spontaneous growth.'
'Psychoanalysis and the Unconscious'
D. H. Lawrence

integration and wide *perceptions* you seek'. We could say to another, 'You are too rigid. Not until you have *risked* and *suspended* the concept of yourself in the face of someone with the power to *confirm you*, will you find the interpersonal *competence* you seek.' Every individual has a different pattern of strengths and weaknesses, so that a different cybernetic sentence is appropriate in each different case. Synergistic balance, as Karl Menninger would say, is the vital and ethical issue, We can create vices out of all the segments of the cycle by inflating them, and more vices by deteriorating them:

PRINCIPLE OF DEVELOPMENT	INFLATION	BALANCE	DETERIORATION
1. Existence	Anarchical	Creative	Sterile
	Laissez-faire	Original	Conventional
2. Perception	Hyper-vigilant	Respectful	Callous
	Inquisitorial	Perceptive	Insensitive
3. Identity	Egotistic	Self-aware	Anonymous
	Self-centred	Distinctive	Self-effacing
4. Competence	Dominant	Virile	Weak
	Brutal	Potent	Impotent
5. Commitment	Fanatical	Dedicated	Passive
	Carried away	Involved	Indecisive
Intensity	Over-emotional	Caring	Apathetic
Authenticity	Ingenuous	Sincere	Tricky
6. Risk and	Reckless	Morally courageous	Failure of nerve
Suspension	Vascillating	Flexible	Rigid
	Abdicating	Adaptable	Bigoted
7. Bridging the	Subverted	Cosmopolitan	Ethnocentric
Distance	Traitorous	Tolerant	Factionalized
8. Self-confirmation	Manipulative	Impressive	Ingratiating
and	Self-gratifying	Self-actualizing	Frustrated
Self-trans-	Otherworldly	Immortal	Mundane
cendence	Religiose	Seminal	Limited
9. Dialectic	Winning	Optimizing	Losing
leading to	Assimilated	Mutual	Authoritarian
Synergy	Coalescent	Cooperative	Separatist
10. Ordered feed-	Lofty idealism	Expanded	Simplified
back and	Elaborately	consciousness	black/white
complexity	rationalized	Cultured	Dichotomized

From this it becomes clear that any runaway or oscillation of the cycle which causes disintegration or splitting of mutual restraints will cause a large variety of inflations/deterioration with the first always paid for by the second. It is possible, for example, to derive most of the symptoms of schizophrenia by simply splitting inflations from deteriorations in an oscillating pattern; the paranoid schizophrenic, will be anarchical in his thinking with bizarre pseudo-creative neologisms and extravagantly mixed metaphors, hypervigilant, self-centred and so on; the catatonic will be sterile, insensitive and passive, adopting rigid postures and so on.

So profound are the implications of thinking in recursive systems (ie cybernetically), as opposed to cause–effect and subject–object, that paradigms or patterns of thought, become crucial aspects of mental functioning – to these we turn in Level 8, Maps 52 to 56.

MAP REFERENCES
Criminals, 34, 38; Cybernetics, see also self-correcting systems, 22, 25, 30, 38–9, 46–50, 58–60; Oscillation, 14, 16, 22, 48; Schizophrenia, 14, 34, 49, 56; Values, 5, 13, 42–3, 58–60.

MAP 52

Mind as Relationships of Production: From Hegel to Marx and Engels

Little has proved so sterile academically as the post-war animosities which divide German philosophy from Anglo-Saxon empiricism. The Nazi and then Stalinist legacies have blinded much of contemporary social science to the immense wealth of psychosocial insight in the writings of G. W. F. Hegel, Friederich Engels and especially Karl Marx. As no conception of human mind can afford to ignore Marx's ideas, I will attempt to counter the many distortions of his position, sketch his powerful critique of our society and, finally, try to account for the marked tendency of the system he envisaged to run away with tragic consequences.

A common mistake is to confuse Marx's 'materialism' with our own variety which attempts to reduce social and human phenomena to physical and corporeal atoms. His materialism was an upending of Hegel's idealism: while Hegel believed that our minds were shaped by the abstract categories and ideals of Reason (a doctrine of forms derived from Plato), Marx contended that the relationships by which men worked together to produce their livings (ie their concrete daily labours) formed their consciousness. Strictly speaking materials, as such are not involved. It is 'the sensuous human activity . . . and practice' of working *on* materials in networks of relationships. The crucible is sociological.

Marx was only stating what research has since repeatedly confirmed, that habitual action and role-playing are far more potent influences on attitude formation than the exchange of ideas. This does not mean, as some critics have asserted, that we are helpless captives of institutions and doomed to 'false consciousness'. It does mean that we need more than sheer imagination to change ourselves, that the belief we can easily transcend our working conditions is an illusion, like the upside-down image in the camera. In fact we are rooted to the manner in which our work is performed. Marx was not objecting to ideas, only to ideas disconnected from daily living. Nor did he deny human freedom but rather drew attention to those working relationships which provide the leverage to free us. 'The life process of society does not strip off its mystical veil until it is treated as production by freely associated men and is consciously regulated.' This humanist–naturalist synthesis was for Marx a 'unifying truth', joining subject to object, man to nature and potential to realization. This organic vision of mutual interconnectedness gave Marx and Engels an almost ecological vision, and an understanding that the antagonism between human beings and their environment must be reconciled (see margin).

Dialectics are another issue on which empiricists are at daggers drawn with Marxists. Yet I believe the use of dialectics must be distinguished from abuse. In map after map we have found that categories of mind have their complements, or as dialecticians say their negations, yin and yang (see Map 3), superego and id (see Map 9), thinking and feeling, (see Map 10), and the whole list of bimodal attributes of the split-brain (see Map 23), culminating in cybernetic loops of mutual restraints (see Maps 45–50). Now Hegel contended that when we see the isolated appearance of something we know by reason that it is contained within its negation. We know, for example, that life ends in death, however vivacious someone appears. Our bodies' cells are continuously dying and renewing, moving towards the realization of a genetic ideal in a freedom within the law (see Map 45). Brain structure, information theory and linguistics all go far in supporting a binary, rule-bound, generative rationalism. Those who dismissed Hegel may have to reinvent him. Nor can anyone with an awareness of the condition of contemporary psychology fail to recognize Engel's warning about human science without dialectics. It becomes 'one-sided, limited, abstract and loses its way in insoluble contradictions' (see margin). How ironic it is to see Engels charge positivists with 'metaphysics' when that

Marx contended that the relationships of production cut and shaped the human mind. The capitalist system and the mechanics of production (see inside of head) made work meaningless and monotonous, mutilating the mind which does not seek purely economic rewards but to realize its creative potential. The division of labour in plants and factories reduced men to things, denied relationships and disintegrated consciousness. Commodities became effigies of one's alienated powers and substitutes for relationships (see outside of head). However, those most oppressed by contradiction and alienated in their work are those in whom revolutionary struggle creates a new consciousness of human solidarity and a reunified existence which is destined to demolish the old order.

In his 'Economic and Philosophic Manuscripts' Marx wrote that the faculties of mind could only be awoken and developed by a corresponding element in the working environment so that aestheticism needed beauty, service to people a living community, and love a subject of devotion. Sadly these manuscripts were not published until the thirties and not translated into English until 1959. The 'revisionist' Marx with his humanist credo was in fact the original Marx.

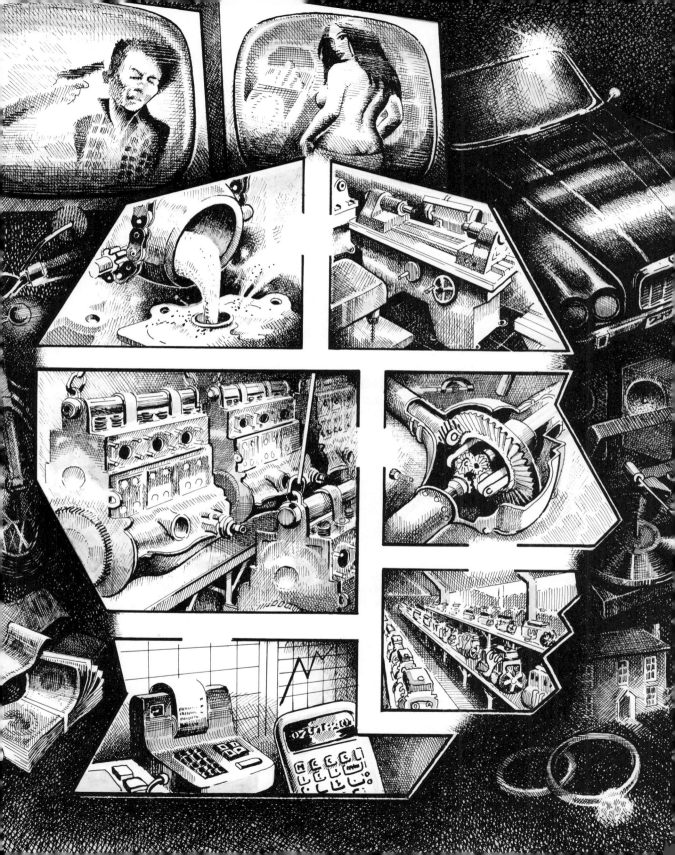

is precisely the label they would stick on him! To positivists a world divided into atomic facts and pieces is one as devoid as possible of a *a priori* metaphysical constructs. To a dialectician, however, assumed disconnectedness is the metaphysic, while the world of growing, living patterns and interconnections is a self-evident reality.

How, then, do Marxist dialectics function? Do they constitute a likely growth dynamic? Curiously Marx never discussed the issue of dialectics as such and we are left to infer the process. So let us first consider how the contradictions of capitalism are said to come about, and how they reach a state of such tension that the organized working class emerges to overthrow the disintegrating fabric of society and unify its contradictions. The capitalist mode of production assembles increasing numbers of workers around technologies of increasing power and output. This process sharpens the contradictions between the human potential of the work force and the reality of their condition. Potentially the workers are organizable, unifiable, able to make or break the system, with a capacity to produce enough surplus for much fairer and wider distribution. In reality, the workers are kept disorganized, divided, weakened, dominated and impoverished. Here are all the necessary components of a just society, yet their relationships remain pathological, a situation maintained by the atomism of capitalist science. The mechanics of factories make work meaningless, monotonous, with the divisions of labour that descend like steel dicers upon minds and relationships. This leads to the severance of organic bonds between subject and object, man and nature, work and self-realization. The tool now uses the man who, 'physically exhausted and mentally debased', is estranged from his own creative powers and falls into subservience to the very thing he created. Like some ghost in a machine he moves amid 'dead objectifications which cannot recognize his life behind the fixed form of things'.

Even where reforms create 'well-remunerated slaves', workers can only *have* by increasing failure to *be*, since, 'The less you *are*, the less you express your life, the more you *have* and the greater is your alienated life.' This 'thing' is purchasable. Such 'commodity fetishism' precipitates excesses of 'useful' things, as 'all passions are submerged in avarice' and their insatiable needs grow to buy back effigies of lost connections. So men prostitute women, buying their bodies and now even their photographed and simulated body parts. For the contradiction, as even Daniel Bell has recently confirmed, is that ascetic capitalism, with its gospel of thrift, repression and self-denial, now requires for its own continuance orgies of indulgence and escalating appetite, an ethos that undermines its own foundations. Surely a crunch must come?

I maintain that there are two distinct kinds of dialectic in the writing of Marx and Engels, a benign synthesized variety of micro-dialectics, mixed in with a dangerously oscillating variety of macro-dialectics, ever liable to run away (see Maps 22, 48–51). In the first they are seeking a synthesis of opposites in which the integrity of both values are respected, so that abstract deals are vindicated by grounding them in concrete experience, freedom discovers the networks of necessity, self-expression is united with social utility, wealth is seen as a capacity to give not just receive, creation is joined to the creator, and the individual finds a connection to his species and all species in a vision of social ecology.

In the second, contradictions are stated as if a 'good' end were about to smash a 'bad' end; opposite ends of the same continuum are in a win–lose, zero–sum contest and mind is at war with itself. The rhetoric is that alienation, domination, licence and selfishness will be righteously crushed by brotherhood, equality,

'Within the capitalist system all methods for raising the social productiveness of labour are brought about at the cost of the individual labourer; all means for the development of production transform themselves into means of domination over and exploitation of the producers; they mutilate the labourer into a fragment of a man, degrade him to the level of an appendage to the machine, destroy every remnant of charm in his work and turn it into hated toil; they estrange from him the intellectual potentialities of the labour process in the same proportion as science is incorporated in it as an independent power.'
'Das Kapital' Karl Marx

'Let us not flatter ourselves overmuch on account of our human conquest of nature. For each such conquest nature takes its revenge on us. Each of them, it is true, has in the first place consequences on which we counted, but in the second and third places it has quite different unforeseen effects which only too often cancel out the first . . . it is still more difficult in regard to the more remote social consequences of these actions.'
'The Dialectics of Nature' Friederich Engels

'To the metaphysician things and their mental images, ideas, are isolated to be considered one after the other apart from each other, rigid, fixed objects of investigation, given once and for all . . . For him a thing either exists or it does not exist; it is equally impossible for a thing to be itself and at the same time something else . . . cause and effect stand in equally rigid antithesis one to the other . . .'
'The Dialectics of Nature'

'Roberts (a leader addressing strikers): "You've forgotten what this fight 'as been . . . I'll tell you now this once again. The fight of the country's body and blood against the blood-sucker. The fight of those who spend themselves with every blow they strike and every breath they draw, against a thing that fattens on them and grows and grows . . . That thing is Capital! . . . A white faced stony-hearted monster . . . 'Tis not for this little moment of time we're fighting – not for ourselves our own little bodies, and their wants, 'tis for all those who come after throughout all time. . . . for the love of them don't roll up another stone upon their heads, don't help to blacken the sky, and let the bitter sea in over them . . . They're welcome to the worst that can happen to me . . . to us all, aren't they? If we can shake [passionately] that white-faced monster with the lips, that has sucked the life out of ourselves our wives and children, since the world began. If we have not the hearts of men to stand against it breast to breast, and eye to eye, and force it backward till it cry for mercy, it will go on sucking life; and we shall remain for ever what we are [in almost a whisper] less than the very dogs." '

'Strife' John Galsworthy

historical necessity and socialism. The fallacy is that such negative evaluations as 'alienation' and 'domination' are distorted forms of dissent and authority, which become vices by being split-off. You cannot therefore smash the vices without also killing the virtues. If the problem is disconnection, then the very act of smashing disconnects! What Socrates died for was the whole dialectical continuum of dissent *and* authority. Similarly, you cannot smash selfishness without killing independence which is 'self-concerned-with-others'. You cannot smash licence and leave responsible freedoms unimpaired. The problem with macro-dialectics is that the swings from one extreme to another may take a generation or more. Necessity is for now, while freedom will allegedly arrive later. The dictatorship of the proletariat and centralized bureaucracy is now, while the classless society and withering away of the state come later. The whole subtlety of a dialectical ecology of mind is debased by the indefinite postponent of one end of the dialectic. If psychosocial development is a process of learning, what will twenty years of 'crushing reaction' teach you – to live as brothers?

The real tragedy of Marxism is the failure to understand the disabling anxiety produced by contradictions. This grows inexorably sucking all involved into the cusp of catastrophe (see Map 55), with its purges plots and revolutionary terror. What *hubris* to imagine that contradictions, the very structure of social evil, cripple capitalists alone! How could Marx, who yearly read the plays of Aeschylus, have thought that his revolutionary heroes were immune from *peripéteia* (see Map 2)? For, of course, the crushing of domination and the smashing of alienation only represses and intensifies these hated values until they rise again: the leader's face atop ten thousand poles; the cult of personality supposedly buried with the bourgeoisie is born again and 'history is repeated . . . the second time as [grim] farce'. Communism becomes caught in the same kind of self-exciting system as fascism (see Map 50), as collectivism represses and so excites domination which in turn excites collectivism, and so around in a vicious circle of splitting values mounted on a centrifuge.

The failure to comprehend levels of logical types (see Map 40) is a basic error. Equality, fraternity and relationship are genuine values in desperately short supply but they must be active at the meta-levels of language not just in concrete behaviours. What this means is that the concrete manifestations of brotherhood must, at higher levels of abstraction, be 'brother' also to its negation (or complement) which is individuality. The failure to see this will split the dialectical continuum and turn 'brotherhood' into the bludgeon of individuals, hence the 'contradictions' of communism.

MAP REFERENCES

MAP 53

One-Dimensionality, Dialectics and the Marx–Freud synthesis: Herbert Marcuse

As a young man Herbert Marcuse was a member of the German Spartacist Movement, a left-wing revolutionary splinter group crushed by the Berlin government in 1919. He later became an Hegelean philosopher and joined the Institute for Social Research in Frankfurt in the early thirties. The school fled to Geneva and thence to New York in 1934, bringing such luminaries as Erich Fromm, T. W. Adorno, Max Horkheimer and Marcuse himself to the United States.

In *Reason and Revolution* published in 1941, Marcuse established Hegel's credentials as a revolutionary philosopher and fired the opening shots in what was to be a life-long campaign against the 'one-dimensional' viewpoint of empiricism and positivism. He saw Hegel as the exponent of the historical force of critical reason in society that dissolves the *status quo*. As an enthusiastic supporter of the French Revolution, Hegel saw in reason the power to change society using the dialectical tension between the real and the ideal. As Marcuse put it: 'To know what a thing really is we have to get beyond its immediate given state (S is S) and follow out the process in which it turns itself into something other than itself (P). In the process of becoming P, however, S still remains S. Its reality is the entire dynamic of its turning into something else and unifying itself with its 'other'. The dialectical pattern represents a world permeated with negativity, a world in which everything is other than it really is, and in which contradiction and opposition constitute the laws of progress.' Marcuse later suggested that the process was cybernetic, 'A state where being attains fulfilment, where the tension between "is" and "right" is resolved in a cycle of eternal return'. In contrast, positivism recognizes a single immediate identity, like a still photograph of a runner on a circular track which loses the vital tensions between 'start' and 'finish'. 'In a world where facts do not present what reality can and ought to be, positivism amounts to giving-up the real possibility of mankind for a false and alien world.'

Equally repellent to Marcuse was the relativism and dualism in Western philosophy which contrasted a private world of culture, freedom and beauty with a workaday ugliness and misery. Jean-Paul Sartre's notion that he was 'free' of the Nazis by dint of rebellious thoughts and disguised satires especially offended Marcuse. The free spirit in the enslaved body only perpetuated the established economic order. In fighting against the latter, Marcuse was able to show the extent to which Hegel had anticipated Marx. Apart from the dialectical methods they shared, Hegel had been the first to write of the alienation of workers, the objectification of their labour 'governed by uncontrolled forces and laws in which man no longer recognizes his own self'.

The rise of German fascism, Stalin and the Moscow trials, and the belated discovery of Marx's early philosophic manuscripts, all combined to give members of the Frankfurt School deep misgivings about the health and strength of the Communist Revolution. Capitalism was visibly recovering from the Depression, while the Soviet Union was exhibiting gross insensitivity to ethical and psychological issues. Perhaps the theories of Freud could correct the mis-applications of Marx and throw light on the Nazis' mania. While Erich Fromm reinterpreted Marx as a humanist (see Map 52), Marcuse concentrated on the concepts of alienation, consciousness and the abolition of labour.

He argued that Soviet Russia had so little ameliorated the human condition because it had taken over the factory system *in toto*, making a fetish of the abolition of private ownership as the cure-all of worker alienation and ignoring Marx's insistance that the entire industrial structure must be redesigned and labouring, as presently constituted, abolished in favour of a new individualism. The Soviets had installed precisely the 'crude communism' that Marx had warned against, with an

If we rotate the two-dimensional image opposite ninety degrees we can create Marcuse's 'One-Dimensional Man'. In the two-dimensional mode, persons recognize facts but in the context of critical reason; in the one-dimensional mode facts dominate. Herbert Marcuse argued that positivism and the dominant view of Anglo-American empiricism had shrunk our social and political consciousness to single linear dimensions in which the positive side (+) masks the negative side (−), so that everything tends to be viewed from the perspective of technological rationalism, operational control and self-propelling productivity which dominates nature and which systematically orders our lives in a manner designed to obscure alternatives. Our predigested language labels Western institutions and allies as 'free' and describes as 'democratic' the current manner in which elections are organized, thereby eliminating all tension between the actual and the ideal. Even poverty is reduced to a 'fact', instead of being regarded in the context of affluence or in the context of revolt by poor people against a condition that affronts critical reason and which negates their potential development.

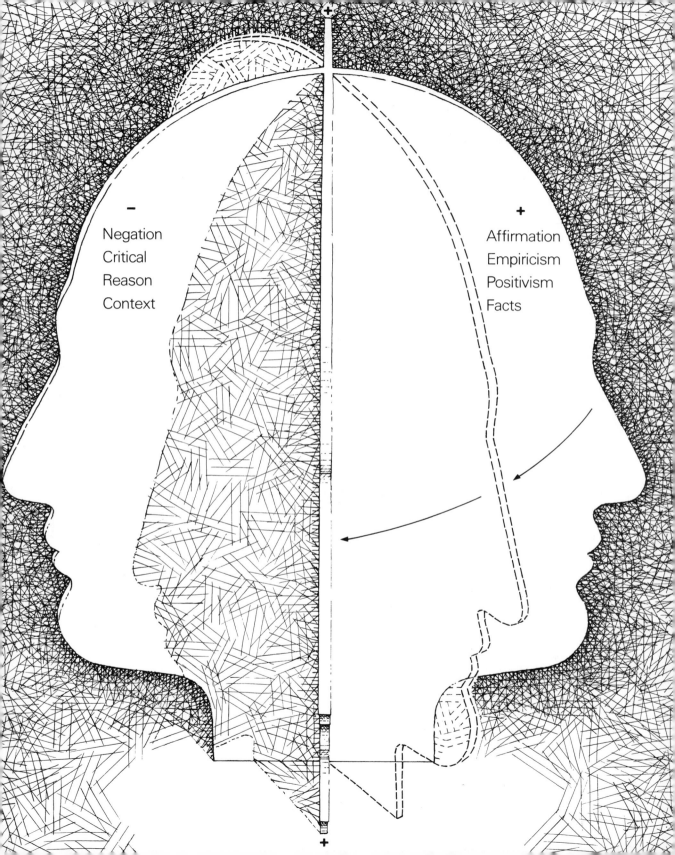

abstract state capitalism that negated human personality. The Soviets had also misinterpreted Marx on freedom and human consciousness. Only the opportunities for revolutionary praxis were historically determined. These must be seized and consciously implemented by the critical reason of individuals. Eschewing the approach of Erich Fromm, who softened some of the harsher and more pessimistic ideas of Marx and Freud, Marcuse now embarked upon a radical synthesis of their views, one which would take him to the unconscious roots of the betrayed revolution and make him equally unpopular to authorities in both Russia and the United States.

In 1956 he published *Eros and Civilization* which claimed to discover a latent radicalism in Freud similar to that which he had earlier discovered in Hegel, even though the manifest attitudes of both men had been conservative. Marcuse began by denouncing the revisionists of both Marx and Freud who in deference to 'common sense', a word as hateful to Marcuse as positivism, had muted the revolutionary ire of Marx and the darker side of Freud's vision, especially the death instinct, the unconscious, the cauldron of sexual repression, and the hydraulics of dialectical energy (see Map 9). To Marcuse the primal crime in which brothers band together to slay their chief patriarch and divide his women amongst them was the central metaphor of political civilization. The father's prohibition is the origin of guilt and the incest taboo.

Marcuse proceeded to fit Freudian ideas into Marxist categories while managing to avoid any mention of Marx, a most curious subterfuge. Starting with Freud's contention that all civilization is based on the repression of sexual libido and the pleasure principle, Marcuse coined the notion of *surplus* repression, clearly intended to accord with the accumulation of surplus value, ie economic value over and above the needs of subsistance. Hence, while all civilizations are necessarily repressed, the specific capitalist order of our historic period exacts a repression surplus to necessity, corresponding to Marx's concept of alienation. This surplus could therefore be thrown off or rechannelled without endangering social order.

Marcuse rechristened Freud's reality principle the performance principle, again suggesting its historically specific and exaggerated form under capitalism, aided and abetted by protestant compulsions to work for the sake of work. With body and mind thus reduced to instruments of alienated labour, individuals must attenuate libidinal ties with one another. The sexual zones of development – oral, anal and phallic – become desexualized along with much of the rest of the body and sexual instinct becomes overlocalized in the genital area. This creates our world of pressures to public performance in which Eros is privately off-loaded, lest it interfere with industrial routines.

In Marcuse's scheme the primal crime becomes a capitalist allegory with proletarian brothers slaying the entrepreneur. This turns out to be a failed revolt against authority, since guilt over slaying the father and over mismanaging the revolution leads the brothers to reinstate paternal tyranny. In addition, they continue to repress Eros in deference to a performance now dedicated to a corporate state instead of a private corporation but employing the same alienated relationships of production in competing with the West. The change in economic ownership has not altered the deeper psychological reality of surplus repression as industrial oppression perpetuates sexual repression.

By retaining Freud's hydraulic model, Marcuse could argue that the energy devoted to performance, repression and Thanatos must be withdrawn from pleasure, libido, and Eros and that the United States was in danger of self-destruction through displaced sexual aggression. Just as its steady improvement of

Karl Marx used to live in Dean Street in London's Soho. It has changed totally since his time. Yet I wonder if he might not recognize the 'commodity fetishism' and 'one-dimensional sexuality' – the rows of inflatable 'adult' dolls, the shiny plastic loneliness, the obsession with flagellation, domination–submission, disconnected rubber genitals and mechanical aids' to potency. Marx always stressed that these fantasies were latent in capitalism; the only difference now, he would say, is that they are manifest.

'Religious distress is at the same time the expression of real distress and the protest against real distress. Religion is the sigh of the oppressed creature, the heart of a heartless world, just as it is the spirit of a spiritless situation. It is the opium of the people . . . Criticism [of religion] has plucked the imaginary flowers from the chain, not so that man will wear the chain without any fantasy or consolation but so that he will shake off the chain and cull the living flower.'

'On Religion'
Karl Marx and Frederich Engels

'Je participe
Tu participes
Il participe
Nous participons
Vous participez
Ils profitent'
Poster in student–worker revolt,
Paris 1968.

output created the conditions for the overthrow of the capitalist order in the view of Marx, so the 'success' of the performance principle had made its surplus repression no longer essential. While the neo-Freudian 'revisionists', particularly Fromm, had been condemned for their optimism and eclectic, atheoretical values, *Eros and Civilization* outdoes all optimists by using the dialectic of Thanatos and Eros as a kind of catapult that hurls civilization from a military industrial hell to a 'polymorphous perversity' of love-making and eroticized work.

By the time he wrote *One-Dimensional Man* in the sixties the sexual revolution had arrived and narcissism was threatening. But Marcuse, a theorist to the last, did not like his sex to be 'empirical'. He now abandoned the idea that advancing science and technology would undermine the repression necessary for their continuance. So completely predicated were they upon one-dimensional thinking, that they enlisted the forces opposed to them, turning even sexuality into joyless compulsory performance. He now returned to elaborate the themes of *Reason and Revolution* and attacked the 'happy consciousness' that surrendered its critical reason before 'facts'. When science treats nature as an object of control, then human nature also becomes controlled and scientific domination necessitates our submission. The 'Happy Consciousness' which tolerates this state of affairs is a repressive tolerance, neutral as between the manipulators and manipulated. The very categories in which we think blind us to realization that we can negate oppressive realities, placing them in the context of a 'Great Refusal'.

What are we to make of Marcuse? He is a trenchant critic of the social sciences but his proposed alternatives generally fail to convince. Is even the most skilfull blending of the less plausible hypothesis of Freud and Marx more than intellectual gymnastics? Empiricism is no longer one-dimensional as cybernetics show, and the attempt to put reason above 'mere' facts is likely to unleash 'other-dimensional men' violently certain of their reasons. While every fact exists within a context, that context too can be observed and verified. To regard the context as necessarily superior can lead us to excuse revolutionary terror by it 'historical context'. Another problem is the use of the term 'contradiction' to contrast stages in the life process. It is not a contradiction in the usual sense of the term to say that a living person is now dying. It *is* a contradiction to see a ghost since this implies 'living death' in a single moment of time, as in Map 13. The idea that people and cultures 'grow by resolving contradictions' is a dangerous half truth. Contradictions also drive them to states of unimaginable cruelty and ferocity. The next three maps explore this issue.

MAP REFERENCES
Capitalism, 7–8, 52; Cartesian dualism, 6–8, 48, 52; Freud, 9; Marx, 52; One-dimensional, see also linear thought, 4–5, 14–16, 22, 28–9, 34, 43, 60; Repression, 8–9, 14–16, 34, 43.

MAP 54

The Structure of Scientific Revolutions:
Thomas S. Kuhn and Allan Buss

The conflict between empiricists and dialecticians has rumbled through much of this book and especially the last two maps. A possible resolution is suggested by the work of Thomas Kuhn, the historian of science. He suggests that science has at least two levels or modes of operation: normal science proceeds empirically and incrementally by fitting observations and facts into an agreed body of theories and assumptions (on this level empiricism and positivism however one-dimensional work well); however, periodically sciences undergo revolutions in their underlying paradigms, and these move dialectically so that the new paradigm struggles with and supercedes the old.

By paradigm Kuhn means the patterns of assumption, methods and theories to which scientists make a prior commitment upon joining their professional colleagues. Paradigms give answers to the following kinds of question. 'What are the fundamental entities of which the universe is composed? How do these interact with each other and with the senses? What questions may legitimately be asked about such entities and what techniques employed in seeking solutions.' The answers supplied by professional education 'are both rigorous and rigid' and 'exert a deep hold on the scientific mind'. It is necessary when scientists say that they have 'discovered' something or 'tested' a certain proposition to remember that they are not speaking about their paradigms. Tests, discoveries, measurements, and observations all take place within the paradigm or context. As Kuhn observes, 'Normal science and research are strenuous and devoted attempts to force nature into the conceptual boxes provided by professional education.'

It is no part of the aim of normal science to call forth new sorts of phenomena. Essentially work within an accepted paradigm consists of puzzle-solving, in a manner reminiscent of jig-saws and crossword puzzles, wherein the rules of solution are given and a combination of high intelligence and convergent thinking (see Map 28) is necessary to demonstrate the paradigm's range and applicability. To laymen the experiments may seem esoteric and miniscule. Scientists rarely ask such fundamental questions as whether peace can be assured, cancer cured or crime controlled, for such issues are rarely within their paradigm's scope, which accordingly 'insulates a (scientific) community from the socially important problems that are not reducible to puzzle form'. So habitual becomes the paradigm that the word 'metaphysical' is generally reserved for a priori assumptions which are not one's own, while questions one does not wish to answer are consigned to other disciplines with punishments administered to those straying from the conceptual box.

Kuhn argues from historical evidence that paradigms, unlike hypotheses, are not abandoned when they are falsified, since this would involve relinquishing whole structures of organized knowledge. Typically, more and more anomalies accumulate until there are a distressing number of phenomena unaccounted for by the paradigm. It is at this point that rival paradigms arise and the conflicts between them are bitter, ideological, rhetorical and political in style. Several scientists may resign from their studies in anguish, while many more realize that the whole significance of their life's work and commitment are at stake. Even so the new paradigm is unlikely to find acceptance unless, in the style of Map 29, it can make sense of the discoveries organized by the old paradigm in addition to the multiplying anomalies. Once established, however, the new paradigm proceeds by increments as did the old. Allan Buss, a dialectical psychologist at the University of Calgary, has argued that historically psychology had been subject to cyclic revolutions, from 'reality constructs the person' to 'person constructs reality'. It is time, surely, to close the loop.

According to Thomas Khun, scientific paradigms (patterns of basic assumptions about nature) undergo periodic revolutions. A paradigm will typically only collect data which fit its pattern though anomalous findings also accumulate. In applying Kuhn to psychology, Allan Buss argues that both behaviourist and Freudian paradigms assumed that 'reality constructs the person'. For behaviourists, stimuli in the environment and rewards shape the person's response (see arrow from 1 to 2); for Freudians irrational and unconscious forces determine a limited energy mechanism (see arrow from I to II). In contrast, cognitive and humanistic psychologists have stressed that 'the person constructs reality' (see arrow from 3 to 4); while ego psychologists have also stressed mastery (see arrow from III to IV). Historically psychology has oscillated between these four paradigms although all four distort reality. Buss argues that we need a dialectical psychology that takes in the whole cybernetic circle: we must remake our environment and social relationships in the knowledge that these help to remake us; we must be two-dimensional, reciprocal and interactive, balancing the psychology of the individual with the sociology of the system.

MAP REFERENCES
Anomalies, see also catastrophe, contradiction, 14, 40, 49–50, 53, 55–7; Normal Science, see also convergence, left brain, 23, 28–9, 55; Paradigm, see also a priorism, 6–8, 52–3, 55, 60; Positivism, 6–8, 47, 53.

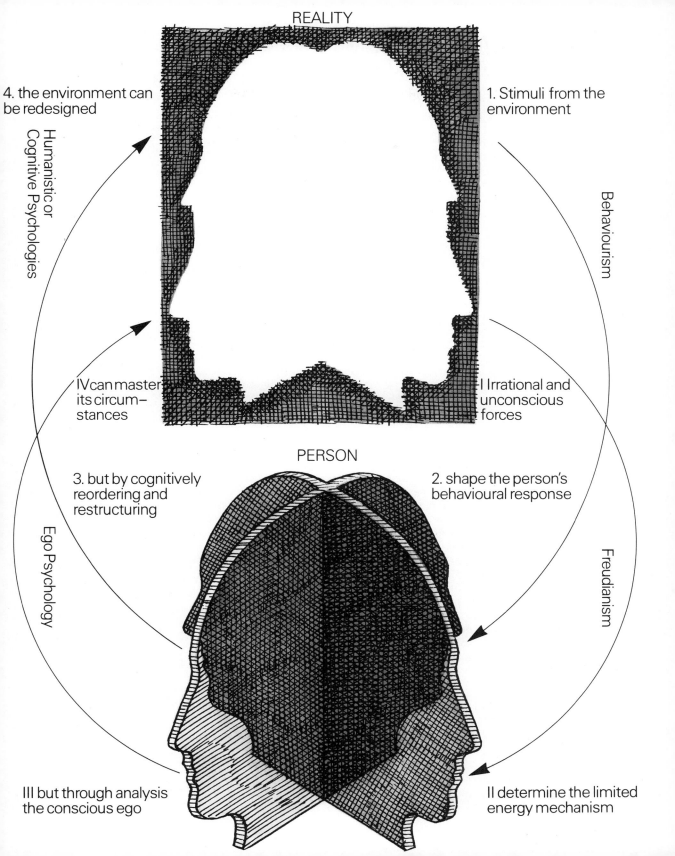

MAP 55

Dualities, Dialectics and Stars:
The view of Francisco Varela

We have considered the Marxist and Hegelean objections to 'one-dimensional' empiricism in Maps 52 and 53. We have seen that the surface empiricism of 'normal sciences' can disguise a history of dialectical movements among their underlying paradigms (see Map 54) so that positivism and dialectics could operate simultaneously at different levels of language (see Map 40). Francisco Varela, a Chilean emigré to the United States, recently evolved a fascinating synthesis between dialectical and cybernetic viewpoints. Varela proposes that dualisms or dialectical 'contradictions' such as mind/body, whole/part, context/text, territory/map, being/becoming, intuition (right brain)/logic (left brain) or environment/system should be conceived of as 'stars'. All stars consist of 'the it'/'the process of becoming it' where the slash or oblique stroke means 'consider both sides of'. Hence, we must 'consider both it and the processes leading to it'.

In approaching social phenomena, therefore, we must take into account: the whole and the organization of parts constituting that whole (see Map 47) the context and the particular texts or behaviours which occur within it (see Map 40); the territory and the maps that have more or less revealed that territory (see Map 39); the identity of our being and the life-crises by which we became that being (see Map 37); the intuitive right brain and the logical, propositional left brain which tests those intuitions (see Maps 23, 29); the environment of the Garden and the systemic human activity that cultivates or wrecks its ecology (see Map 4). In this way two of the major themes running through this book can be reconciled: the cybernetic or network image of mind in Maps 1, 2, 10, 22, 26, 30, 31, 37, 39, 45, 48 to 51 and the hierarchic or tree image of mind in Maps 4, 5, 7, 9, 18, 21, 24, 27, 28, 33, 40, 41, 47, 49.

The map opposite represents both of these themes and their resolution. The network on the left, including the loop A, B, C, D, represents the mind as a whole, of which the brain's right hemisphere has an intuition; it represents context, territory, being and the ecology of environment. The tree image on the right represents one of the many programmes that comprise mind: conscious purpose has made A its subject, so that B, C, and D are the parts, maps, logics and sequential systems by which A seeks to realize itself. Note that such hierarchies are temporary, could have been otherwise ordered and that pruning the net at point A is an arbitrary choice, one that could potentially wreck the Garden as an ecological network in favour of the Tree of Knowledge with the poisoned fruit.

Varela's resolution, the star, differs from both the philosophical dualism which shatters the image of man segregating mind from body (see Map 6) and from Hegel's dialectical philosophy. Hegel referred to his pairs as contradictions (see Maps 52, 53), a term applicable only to contraries of the same logical type (see Map 40), and their affirmation and negations were often, although not always, treated like win or lose clashes between symmetrical objectives, hence their revolutionary and violent implications. By using the image of two triangular shingles or roof-tiles joined or imbricated in the shape of a star, with the one emerging from beneath the other, conflicting ideas are presented as being at different levels of logical type – they become non-contradictory, mutually specifying and restrain each other in their complementarity. The network is unbalanced by the purposively striving tree, and the tree rebalanced by the constraints of the network.

We urgently need such a paradigm shift if the predatory nature of human purposes is not to wreck our ecological balance. Varela borrows from Gregory Bateson the concept of a conversational domain in which minds are jointly defined as a conversational pattern (left) and bodies as participants in that pattern (right). We must accept responsibility for the paradigm we adopt for now our very survival depends on the ecology of the human species and its environment.

Two opposing conceptions of mind have run through much of this book: the idea of a 'net' or cybernetic feedback loop, a kind of Garden of Eden where harmony reigns but consciousness is lost; and the idea of a 'tree', which persons create whenever they make parts of their mind, eg their bodies, behaviours and techniques, the servants of their conscious purpose or self. The net is intuitively perceived as a whole by the brain's right hemisphere; the tree is logically perceived as a sequence of actions by the brain's left hemisphere. While the tree gives direction to the net, it constantly endangers the balance of the latter. Francisco Varela has suggested that such Hegelean pairs as mind/body, whole/part, context/text, territory/map, being/becoming, environment/system, can be identified with the net and tree respectively. Consider the first in each pair as 'it', and the second as 'the process of becoming it'. Then the behaviours of our body will ultimately form our mind, the exercisings of our parts will make the whole, the reconciliation of many maps will eventually approximate the territory and the many systems will constitute a total environment. 'It' and the 'processes of becoming' are like two triangular tiles or shingles joined or imbricated to form a star. By looking at the star from one side or the other, 'it' or 'the processes of becoming' are seen as emerging from the context of its opposite.

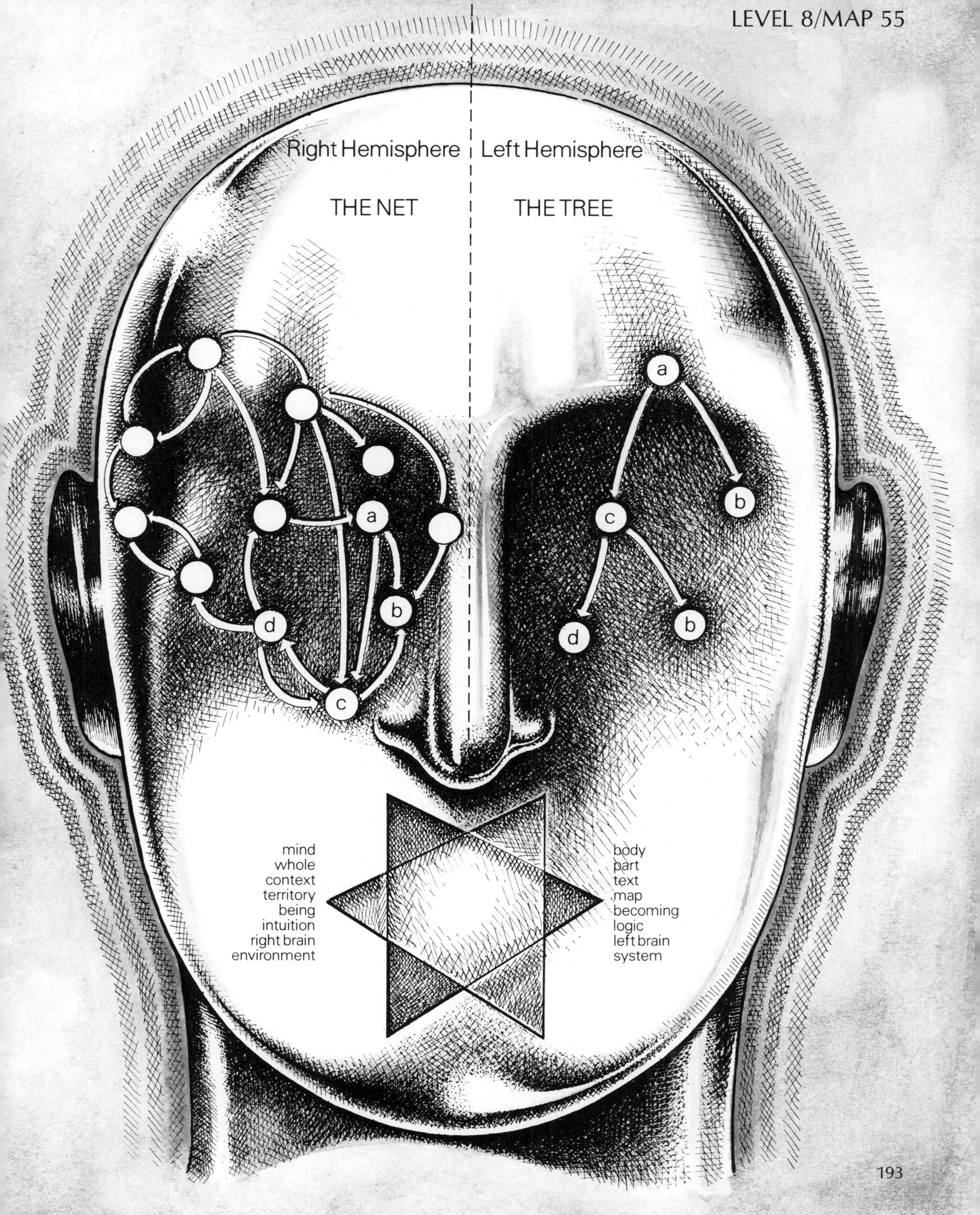

Right Hemisphere | Left Hemisphere

THE NET | THE TREE

a

b

a

c

b

d

c

d

b

mind
whole
context
territory
being
intuition
right brain
environment

body
part
text
map
becoming
logic
left brain
system

MAP 56

The Cusp of Catastrophe: René Thom, Christopher Zeeman and Denis Postle

The word catastrophe comes from Greek tragic drama (see Map 2) and refers to the sudden twist of dénouement in the plot, as when Oedipus changes from authoritative investigator to disgraced criminal, from insider to outsider, originator to originated. Catastrophe theory is the invention of René Thom, the French mathematician; Christopher Zeeman, a professor of mathematics at Warwick University, has made considerable progress in creating analogues of catastrophic social events and developing topologies of multi-dimensional surfaces; and Denis Postle, a British television producer and science writer, has made extensive applications of the theory to the dynamics of mind and behaviour. Catastrophe theory can be useful wherever there is a spectrum of interaction between two or more independent influences, forces or variables which combine to influence some mood or behaviour in a manner leading to discontinuous jumps, oscillations and changes, often of a sudden and catastrophic nature.

Take, for example, the combined influence of the superego and the id in Freud's psychoanalytic theory (see Map 9). The id, we may recall, consists of clamourous libidinal energies and drives. The superego consists of internalized moral prohibitions and aspirations derived from parents and authorities of childhood. The map opposite consists of a three-dimensional graph with a flat lower surface and folded upper behaviour surface. The lower surface includes the two independent forces: the superego, which increases in strength from point A to point B and all across the surface from point C to point D; and the id, which increases in strength form point A to C and all across the surface from point B to D. These two forces combine to influence the behaviour surface above, in a manner that depends entirely upon their relative strengths. In the vicinity of a on the behaviour surface both forces are so weak that their conflict is minimal. In the vicinities of points c and b first the superego is so weak, and then the id is so weak that conflict is still minimal and behaviour smooth. But in the vicinity of point d an immensely powerful superego is struggling to hold in check a raging id. The map shows the cusp by which a surface range of behaviour labelled moralism has folded itself above another range of behaviour labelled lust; degrees of moral fervour are measured by the increasing distance between the lower and behaviour surfaces, reaching a maximum at d–D. We can immediately see what will happen if the superego slackens or the id force increases. Behaviour will shift away from d towards c with a catastrophic descent from moralism to lust, the Reverend Arthur Dimmesdale of *The Scarlet Letter* caught with his trousers down. His ego helpless to mediate between a fierce sexuality and a puritanical inhibition. The shape of the cusp has been projected upon the lower surface in the area within the dotted lines. This is called a bifurcation set and maps the precise points at which moralism jumps to lust and back again. The behaviour within the bifurcation set is not available to the individual caught in this conflict between id and superego. He teeters between extremes.

Note the extraordinary vindication of Freud's theory which the cusp catastrophe represents. There is the unconscious folded beneath the conscious mind, the latter repressing the former which is ever likely to erupt. The danger of a catastrophic regression, the intellectual defence against impulse, the denial of mounting feelings, the reaction-formation in which moralism escalates, the desperate inner anxiety of going 'over the edge', and the ego desperately straddling a growing fissure, a split in the centre of the personality.

Our 'first' catastrophe is told in the myth of the Fall (see Map 4) and can be mapped in a style similar to Freudian theory, but using degrees of obedience and freedom instead. Hence in diagram 1 the lower surface A–D, B–C measures

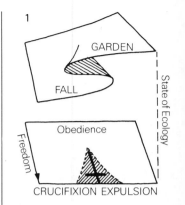

The map opposite is a cusp catastrophe and models the effect of two independent variables, known as 'control dimensions', upon a third range of behavioural outcomes. In this example the cusp has been used to model a situation familiar in Freudian theory. On the lower surface of the graph degrees in the strength of the patient's superego are measured from left to right across the surface A–B, C–D; while the strength of the id forces are measured on the surface A–C, B–C to give a hypothetical coordinate X. Hence this client has a very strong superego barely containing an almost as strong id. The effect of this is shown on the upper behaviour surface where a conscious moralism represses underlying lust. Should the superego weaken and the superego–id coordinate move from X to Y, a catastrophic descent occurs from moralism to lust as behaviour jumps discontinuously across the bifurcation set. Within this cusp moderate eroticism is totally unavailable to the patient who teeters to and fro between inhibition and lechery.

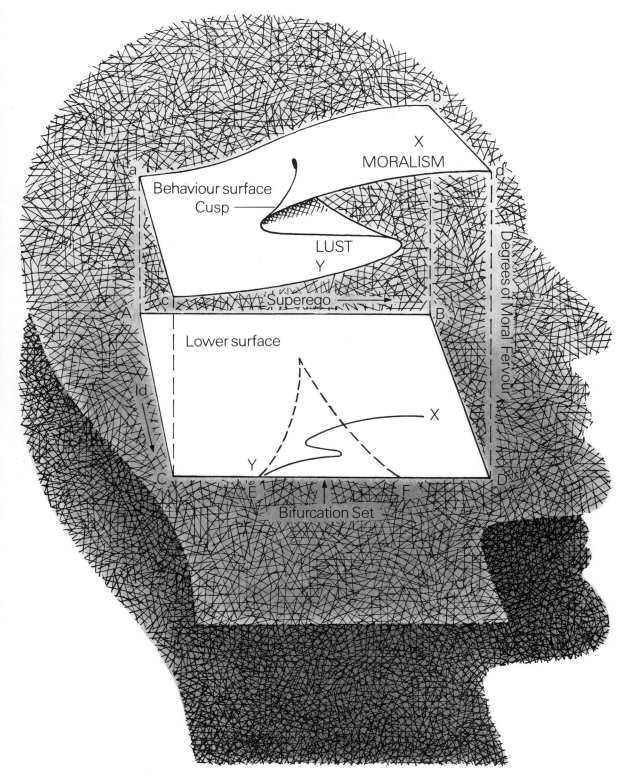

X
MORALISM

Behaviour surface
Cusp

LUST
Y

Superego

Lower surface

X

Y

C   D
E   Bifurcation Set   F

Degrees of Moral Fervour

increasing degrees of freedom. Mankind could remain free within the law of God (or the ecology of the Garden) by remaining close to point c on the behaviour surface, but no sooner did Adam's freedom involve disobedience to the ecology of the Garden, than the move towards d precipitated his Fall, the very shape of which move is serpentine. Adam's deployment of a tree of conscious purpose upset the network of cybernetic restraints (see Maps 48, 50, 55).

The cusp also represents a kind of crucifix between the 'known self' and the 'unknown self' in Harry William's psychotheology (see Map 5) as the individual suffers crucifying tensions between mind and body or faith and doubt. If the integrity of personality is literally 'buried within the cusp', then crucifixion between the extremes and a 'descent into hell' where the buried values lie, is a necessary prelude to 'resurrection' where the prisoner arises from his tomb and the Fall is redeemed.

The S shape of the cusp also bears a remarkable resemblance to Carl Jung's concept of The Way, the winding path from thinking to sensation to intuition to feeling by which those in analysis find their way from the conscious surface to the unconscious depth (see Map 10). There they discover archetypes, self-portraits of the instincts, with axes which criss-cross in a manner extraordinarily similar to those of multi-dimensional catastrophe models, where three, four, six or more variables create fold-within-fold. And who looking at the persona (mask) on the behaviour surface can doubt that its shadow lurks behind, a dark brother hiding in the cusp? And beyond the shadow lies the soul-image, for which the persona yearns because it has shut itself away from its 'lost opposite'. Straighten out the folds in the behaviour surface and we see that soul-image is indeed at the other end (see diagram 2).

There is a theme to the catastrophic events running through this book. The subject attempts to maximize one dimension or value of behaviour but discovers that there is always another end. The way to become more certain, for example, is to entertain doubt, not to evade every issue that threatens you with uncertainty or to think 'positively' or practise positivism. Professor Parkins in Map 13 tried to maximize certainty, detachment, fact, and empiricism, but instead was haunted by their opposites, doubt, horrid intimacy, anomaly and fantasy. There arose from the bed in cusps and folds 'an intensely horrible face of crumpled linen'. The creature appeared dead yet alive, random yet ordered, intimate yet alien. Now such contradictions terrify precisely because the centre of integrity of behaviour has disappeared into the fold or cusp. Under normal circumstances life *becomes* death, order *becomes* random, the alien *becomes* intimate and so on, but where 'becomes' falls within the bifurcation set and the opposites lie outside it, these oppositions are juxtaposed in sinister contradiction.

The doomed attempt to maximize but one dimension was implicated in R. D. Laing's theory about the onset of schizophrenia (in Map 14). As a child, Julie was, according to her parents, 'sweet, obedient and clean', by which they meant that she was exactly and only as *they* defined her, a being-in-itself, of refined 'goodness'. In an attempt to live in this unlivable situation, Julie developed a schizoid personality organization which split her experience into a false self upon the behaviour surface and a true self hidden within the fold. Behind the 'sweet, obedient and clean' surfaces which her parents commanded, her 'true self' was 'angry, rebellious and dirty'. No sooner did she reveal this hideously discrepant aspect, than her parents had her certified insane, 'Better mad than bad.' In diagram 3, we see the schizoid personality originating at the point of the cusp and gradually widening as the two selves part company. This increasing discontinuity of

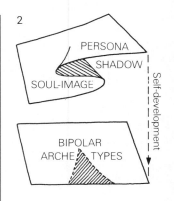

2

PERSONA
SHADOW
SOUL-IMAGE

Self-development

BIPOLAR
ARCHE TYPES

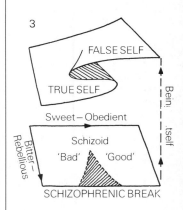

3

FALSE SELF

TRUE SELF

Bein. .tself

Sweet — Obedient

Bitter — Rebellious

Schizoid
'Bad'   'Good'

SCHIZOPHRENIC BREAK

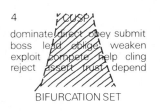

4

CUSP

dominate direct obey submit
boss lead oblige weaken
exploit compete help cling
reject assert trust depend

BIFURCATION SET

MAP REFERENCES
Bifurcation, see also schismogenesis, 47–51, 57–60; Catastrophe, see also tragedy, 2, 4, 24, 35, 54, 57–60; Contradiction, 14, 40, 49–50; 53–5; Maximization, see linear thought, 4–5, 14–16, 22, 28–9, 34, 43.

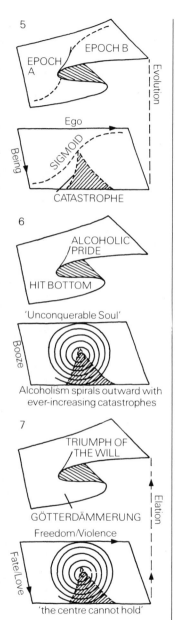

5

EPOCH A

EPOCH B

Evolution

Ego

SIGMOID

Being

CATASTROPHE

6

ALCOHOLIC PRIDE

HIT BOTTOM

'Unconquerable Soul'

Booze

Alcoholism spirals outward with ever-increasing catastrophes

7

TRIUMPH OF THE WILL

GÖTTERDÄMMERUNG

Elation

Freedom/Violence

Fate/Love

'the centre cannot hold'

behaviour causes a psychotic break, as Julie oscillates uncontrollably between true and false selves, utterly obedient then shrieking recriminations.

These catastrophe surfaces also make good sense of Henry Stack Sullivan's reciprocal self-systems in Map 34. In their pathological forms the dynamisms lose their centre and only the outer extremes remain, leading to psychotic, neurotic and criminal behaviours. For example, one person becomes stuck in the dominating and exploitative mode pushing the other into the reciprocal extremity of submission and weakness. The extremity of one excites the extremity of the other and they oscillate, with the middle range of behaviours falling into the cusp or bifurcation set (see diagram 4).

How do we begin to repair catastrophes? Clues come from Level 4 on creativity. Koestler, in Map 27, defines creativity as the discovery of connectedness or bisociation between a conscious surface and a submerged surface. Creative ideas bubble up through the cusp during moments when the mind is resting enabling the creator to 'think on two planes'. In divergent thinking (see Map 28) or lateral thinking (see Map 29) the mind jumps from level to level turning tables on exploiters. A major prophylactic against catastrophe is to question the proposition that the two or more values, or forces, influencing behaviour *are* necessarily independent of one another. Both the tradition of Anglo-Saxon empiricism and the Marxist–Hegelean doctrine of contradictions see conflict between independent forces where this might not be so. The act of creation discovers connections. Similarly Martin Buber in Map 35 redefined such ideas as distance and relationship, abstract and concrete, in terms of an indivisible I–Thou connectedness which also relates categories. Note that the point where the cusp begins on the behaviour surface is very like Buber's narrow ridge, with a precipice that soon yawns if this divide is not negotiated.

The sigmoid curve, introduced by Jonas Salk in Map 46, is the gentle curve by which genetic evolution takes corrective action just as the cusp begins to fold. Salk is saying that unless we develop the evolutionary values of 'both . . . and', nature's dialectical pattern, an evolutionary catastrophe will enfold us trapping us between ego and being values (see diagram 5).

Catastrophe theory gives perhaps its most dramatic support to Gregory Bateson's concept of schismogenesis, 'the growing split in the structure of ideas', precipitated by mutual interaction and clearly evidenced by the widening bifucation set. We can now appreciate the path of the alcoholic in Map 48 who cycles from alcoholic pride to falling off the wagon, to sobering up, to pride and falling again (see diagram 6). Finally we see that fascism caught in such self-exciting contradictions as Freedom–Fate, Domination–Submission, Loyalty–Rebellion, Violence–Love, fulfills Yeat's prophecy, 'turning and turning in its widening gyre the falcon cannot hear the falconer . . . things come apart the centre cannot hold . . .' As the cycle widens the catastrophic jumps from freedom to fate, violence to love, gather in frenzy and intensity and half of Europe is sucked into the vortex (see diagram 7).

One thing is certain we cannot entertain lightly the theories of contradiction propounded by Hegel and Marx (see Maps 52, 53); we could be talking of the end of the world. The Greeks knew better (see Maps 2, 57, 58): they enacted on stage, at a meta-level above reality, the process by which value absolutes buckle beneath *peripéteia* into their antithesis. Such scenes shocked the entire civic culture into looking, suffering and learning to survive (see Maps 2, 57, 58).

MAP 57

The Binary Code of Myth: Claude Lévi-Strauss

Throughout Level 8, Maps 52 to 56, we have been dealing with paradigms. One name for a paradigm unashamed of its *a priori* structure is myth. A myth is not something which is untrue but a shared cultural context for communication. As Claude Lévi-Strauss, the anthropologist, has shown myths may vary in fanciful details while sharing a common structure or pattern which is one with the pattern of mind itself. Lévi-Strauss holds that, 'What man says, language says and what language says is said by society.' It follows that the categories in terms of which primitive societies classify, mythologize and organize are also the basic categories of the minds that formed those societies. Therefore social categories can be read back into the structures of the mind. Lévi-Strauss is much influenced by Marx, Freud, existentialism, linguistics, geology and music. From these he has deduced that mind has a rhythm of opposites in which every conscious point has an unconscious counterpoint. Just as the sounds we utter when speaking language originate in the musculature of the mouth, which makes vowel sounds of varying pitch contrasted with consonants, sharp or diffuse, so myths have rhythms of contrast. Although infinitely variable in details, myths are held to contain a universal, primitive, non-rational logic which in contemporary societies has been buried beneath technical reason. The endless branching out of technical reason alienates us so that 'hell is other people', while for primitive societies 'hell is oneself', and logic is sociable.

Myths are ways of teaching unobservable realities by way of observable symbols. The contradictory nature of social life is conveyed by the bearers of tradition to novices, so that they comprehend the frustrations of the ideal by the real. Since myths are orally transmitted, there will be gaps and distortions but a reiterated 'musical score' conveys the structure despite missing parts. The Theban legends in Greek mythology provide one example. Lévi-Strauss suggests that the code running through these stories concerns the overvaluation of kinship as compared to social obligations on the one hand and the undervaluation of kinship on the other. Also in evidence, somewhat less plausibly, is the theme that man has sprung form one earth as opposed to being born from two parents. In the story of Oedipus and Antigone, for example, King Laius, warned by the oracle that his infant son Oedipus will murder him, tries to kill the baby (undervaluation of kinship). But Oedipus is saved when a shepherd gives him to the Queen of Corinth, who treats him as her natural son (overvaluation). Warned again by the oracle, Oedipus leaves Corinth, only to kill a stranger, his real father, on the road (undervaluation). He then outwits the Sphinx, is acclaimed as King of Thebes and marries his own mother, Jocasta (overvaluation). The twin sons of Oedipus by Jocasta quarrel. One marches on Thebes, which the other defends. They kill each other, as the Spartoi did before them (undervaluation). Creon, now king, buries the one but orders the other to rot unburied. Antigone disobeys by burying her brother (overvaluation) and is entombed by Creon (undervaluation).

It is difficult to see why these polarities should be more significant than others. Are not the stories just as much about the clashes of fate verses freedom, scientific atomism versus religious holism, external facts versus internal relations, *hubris* versus piety or outlook versus insight? 'Nothing to excess' the Greeks taught, and what better way to impart the lesson than by a long series of dramas in which the characters founder on Scylla or Charybdis leaving the audience free to steer its way between? The name of Laius means 'left-sided'; the name of his father, Labdacus, means 'lame'; Oedipus means 'swollen foot'; is it mankind's curse to limp one-sidedly in continual ethical imbalance? The final play in each trilogy usually demonstrates reconciliation: to this we now turn.

Logic is both positive and mythic. Mythic logic is a reiterated dialectical code that runs through stories like a musical score and contains the universal structures of mind itself. The Oedipus myths, for example, alternately affirm and deny that kinship is of greater importance than conflicting social obligations and follow Freud in contrasting sexual with aggressive instincts. The sexual affirmation, or overvaluation of kinship, is found in such dramatic extremes as the incest of Oedipus and Antigone's burial of her brother. The aggressive affirmation, or undervaluation of kinship, is found in the murder of his father by Oedipus and the fratricide of the latter's two sons. The resulting juxtapositions mother/wife and brother/combatants are augured throughout mythology by such anomalous monsters as the Sphinx, half-mother (so nurturant of kinship), half-monster (so devouring of kinship).

MAP REFERENCES
Logical types, 42–3, 53, 55, 58–60; Myth, 1–4, 10, 13, 24, 40, 58–60; Pattern, 58–60; Reconciliation, see synergy, 43, 51, 55, 58–60; Riddle of Sphinx, 12, 40, 48, 58.

AFFIRMATION	DENIAL
OVER-VALUED BLOOD RELATIONS	UNDER-VALUED BLOOD RELATIONS
	Because of a prophecy Laius tries to kill his infant son…
Oedipus, who is rescued and raised in Corinth by the King and Queen, who deceive him into believing he is theirs…	
	Grown to manhood, he kills a stranger on the road. This man is Laius, his real father…
Oedipus goes on to kill the Sphinx and for this, he is crowned King of Thebes. He marries his own mother, Jocasta, who conceives…	
	Twin sons and a daughter. One son raises a foreign army against Thebes and his brother. The invasion is defeated but the brothers slay each other…
Their sister, Antigone, disobeys her uncle, the new King, by burying her invading brother's body…	
	and as a penalty, is herself entombed
The King is over - whelmed by remorse	

MAP 58
The 'Oresteia' and the Myth of Democracy

Initially performed in 458 BC, the *Oresteia* of Aeschylus won first prize at the Athenian drama festival. The *harmónia* and *symphrónasis* on the stage presaged the Golden Age of Athens herself, that was to last until the death of Pericles nearly thirty years later. The myth was the reality. Democracy is one of those phenomena which the social sciences have never adequately explained. The affinity of democratic procedures to drama, their paradoxical mock-conflicts or agreements-to-disagree, their vaguely defined yet powerful norms and the *a priori* allegiance demanded of all participants, combine to make democracy 'unscientific'. Despite this, it is no exaggeration to say that only democratic institutions appear to stand between the human race and periodic plunges into barbarism. The contrast in the quality of life of those covered by democratic procedures and those not covered is no less startling today than it was in the Greece of the fifth century.

Ironically it was the French Revolution and later Marxism that took pride in a science of society constructed upon ground cleared by revolution and founded on first principles. But as Raymond Ruyer remarked, 'While most lasting empires and constitutions have been built without preconceived ideas and overall plans, structures which have been too consciously designed have lasted just long enough to fall heavily on builders and spectators alike.' Let us see, then, what the *Oresteia* can teach us about democracy. Its background has a barbarism worthy of the twentieth century, for the Greeks used the hell of inhumanity to motivate men to reconcile themselves. I am much indebted in the argument that follows to George Thomson's *Aeschylus and Athens* and to discussions with Rollo May.

The background to the *Oresteia* is the curse on the House of Pelops. Atreus and Thyestes, the two sons of Pelops, disputed the succession. Atreus drove Thyestes out of the state, secretly murdered his children and, at a feast of pretended reconciliation, served Thyestes the flesh of his own children bringing down his curse upon the House of Pelops and Atreus's sons Agamemnon and Menelaus. Paris, a son of the King of Troy, falls in love with Menelaus's·wife Helen and they elope to Troy, precipitating the Trojan Wars. Agamemnon assembles a fleet of ships but the goddess Artemis witholds the fair wind needed to set sail for Troy. She can be propitiated only if Agamemnon agrees to sacrifice his beloved daughter Iphigenia. He summons his daughter ostensibly to a marriage with Achilles but slaughters her instead, arousing the murderous hatred of his wife and her mother, Clytemnestra.

The trilogy opens immediately before the victorious Agamemnon is about to return to Argos (Menelaus has been lost in a storm). Clytemnestra is intriguing with a surviving son of Thyestes to be revenged on her husband for the death of their daughter and has sent her young son Orestes out of the country. On Agamemnon's return with his captive princess, Cassandra, the conspirators murder them both. In the second play, Orestes, grown to manhood, is ordered by Apollo to avenge his father's murder. He returns secretly to Argos, and, helped by his sister Electra, murders Cytemnestra and her paramour in a ritual re-enactment of the earlier killing of Agamemnon. Up to this stage the dialectic of point and counterpoint is that of Greek tragedy in general, every rejoicing at 'victory' gives way to deepening apprehension as the trough follows the wave of catastrophe (see Map 56). The final play, The *Eumenides*, expresses the structure of harmony and reconciliation. Since the *Oresteia* is the only trilogy written and performed as one drama which has survived, and, since Aeschylus and his contemporaries represent the acme of Greek civilization, the structure of this play is crucial.

Orestes has hardly slain his mother, than he finds himself beset by the Furies, 'gorgon-like, all clad in sable and entwined with coils of writhing snakes'. Driven near to madness, Orestes wanders like a soul in search of salvation until he

Democracy is a form of theatrical human play in which talking about physical disagreements and discussing potential disasters can prevent them occurring; it is a process that substitutes verbal conflict for more dangerous kinds. It is not surprising, therefore, that Greek democracy grew from a corpus of myths and tragic dramas. The 'Oresteia' of Aeschylus enacted the myth of democractic processes even as its institutions were being established. We cannot comprehend democratic values without the conception of language levels (Map 40) in which each value is expressed within the context of its complement. Hence in this map dissent occurs within the context of, and surrounded by, loyalty, as in the idea of a 'loyal parliamentary opposition'. Paradoxically, when loyalty is directly expressed it too is contained within a system embodying the right to dissent. Similarly freedom is expressed within the context of law that both protects and limits it . . . and so on. As the cybernetic loop revolves, democratic values shift dialectically between figure and ground. There is no real contradiction because one in each pair is always at a meta-level above the other and contains and constrains the activity of its opposite, so that democratic systems avoid the 'runaway' and catastrophes we discussed in other maps. Indeed the system often seems wiser that its participants who orate as if freedom or law, dissent or loyalty could know no bounds!

collapses with exhaustion at the shrine of Apollo, his protector. Apollo directs him to appeal to Athena, prophesying that she will deliver him from his tormentors. So he journeys yet again to Athens, the Furies still pursuing. More is involved than the predicament of Orestes. This is a dispute among the gods themselves representing not merely different sets of values but different organizations of society. On the one side are the Moira, representing the older tribal divinities, who give to each soul its *moira* or just portion. The Furies are agents of the Moira, angels of torment, ministers to the supreme judge of dead in the underworld and bearers of the ancestral curse upon the House of Pelops that originated in the killing of kin. On the other side is Zeus representing the newer gods and the Olympian family. His interpreter is Apollo, god of truth and intellect, who publicly scorns the Furies for their primitive blood-lust and upholds the right of contractual marriage and property inherited through the male line. While the Furies are uninterested in the murder of Agamemnon, who was not the kin of Clytemnestra, they are outraged by the killing of Iphigenia and Clytemnestra. At stake is the reason of Apollo versus the visceral emotions of the Furies, the aristocratic tradition of private expiation for sins versus the tribal tradition of public retribution (roughly the difference between 'guilt' and 'shame' cultures) and the claims of the upper and lower classes.

In making Athena the judge between the disputants, Aeschylus was portraying Athenian culture as the harmony of the ancient world, with the new middle classes as the mediators between aristocrats and the common people. Athena was seen as greater than Apollo because she fused male and female values being brave in battle and skilled in the arts of peace. Above all she was the goddess of *sophrosýne*, moderation, restraint and the arts of persuasion. Athena immediately announces that this case is too important to be decided by her alone. Since the gods are themselves in dispute no direct appeal to their authority can suffice, so ten mortal men of Athens must act as a jury of peers. While Orestes is to be judged by his peers, the authority of that judgement will be supreme. While gods inspire mortal men it is for men to weigh those inspirations upon the Pythagorean 'beam in balance'. The Furies proceed to argue that fear consequent on wrongdoing is the basis of law, humility and respect, that without loyalty to kin there is chaos or despotism. Apollo then appeals to duty and to honour, Agamemnon fought heroically for his country preferring public duty above private sorrow and was cut down while resting in hearth and home.

So the jury casts its lots. They come out equal, five to five, symbolizing the mean. Athena then casts her deciding vote for Orestes, and, as the Furies rise to a new crescendo of recrimination threatening to blight the whole state of Athens, Athena serene and measured in her tones, works the art of her persuasion. The Furies have not lost, she tells them, the vote was even. What she proposes is a new order in which they will share power with her and with men, as they will share sovereignty in the mind of Orestes. Justice must reign now in the heart of each person. Because no person or state can live without respect or fear for authority she asks them to visit their punishments on those who offend against the due processes of law and democracy, especially perjurers. For while all crimes will now be judged according to their absolute, prohibitions against the corruption of justice are still necessary. She begs the Furies stay within the land of Athens but to moderate their emotion and win an honoured place in every home, to help the land grow fruitful with vines but not let the wine drive men to madness. The Furies are transformed by this acceptance, as reason and emotion find a new integrity. They are turned into the *Eumenides*, the 'Kindly Ones', and, throwing off their black robes, dress themselves in the crimson of the harvest festival. Now the eagle is reconciled with the snake,

'I bid my people honour and
uphold
The mean between the despot
and the slave
And not to banish terror utterly
For what man shall be upright
without fear?
And if you honour this high
ordinand
Then shall you have for land
and commonweal
A stronghold of salvation . . .'
Athena in the 'Oresteia'

'The function of the myth-dramas is to bring the audience to a new level of experience which embraces both Apollo and the Furies, both freedom and responsibility, both love and hate, both the daemonic and the rational . . .'
'Myth and Culture' by Rollo May in 'ARC Directions'

'In 1961 I lectured on the 'Oresteia' in the largest modern theatre in Athens . . . to an audience of two thousand . . . It was illustrated with extracts . . . The tumultuous applause that greeted the finale and the light that shone in so many tear-stained faces showed that Athenians respond to the contemporary appeal of their greatest poet as deeply today as they did twenty-four centuries ago. Let them be his judges, now as then.'
'Aeschylus and Athens' George Thomson

the symbolism of sky and earth, freedom and necessity, the new order and the old, vision and viscera. I agree with Rollo May's therapeutic interpretation of Greek tragedy, that it preformed the 'working through' of personal conflicts, a role which in our mythless contemporary culture has to be performed privately by psychotherapy. The separation from mother, the severance of bonds, the call to duty and the pursuit of truth are all elements of growing to maturity, as well as being milestones for human cultures at crucial periods of development.

How are we, in an age when myths have been dishonoured, to recapture their paradoxical structures? Map 58 shows a cybernetic system of figure and ground reversals. Although these look like 'impossible objects' visually, their language structure is one of complementary values, integrated at different levels of logical type (see Map 40). Just as Oedipus answered the riddle of the Sphinx by distinguishing descriptive from metaphorical language, so we can comprehend democracy by seeing that one half of the 'contradiction' is at a different language level. In democracy we are loyal and we dissent, but the dissent occurs in the context of a greater loyalty to the system and conversely the loyalty when exhibited is one dedicated *to* a system embodying dissent. As the cybernetic system revolves, dissent and loyalty, freedom and law, private conscience and public representation 'change places', with one always the context in which the other occurs. Hence freedom is enjoyed within the law: so when the law is enjoined upon the individual and the state exercises its monopoly of force this is done in the contexts of the rights of the accused and in deference to the freedom of others. Similarly the legislator exercises a private conscience within the context of a public representation; when elections come the roles are reversed – now the electorate judges their representative in the context of his public record.

Within the cybernetic loop each 'background' value contains and constrains the value figuring in the 'foreground'. Hence no value is absolute, causing the system to run away and go into a catastrophic revolution. Nor is this a 'golden mean' with every value compromised and moderated. There is no ideal limit to the passion of dissent or the tenacity of private conscience provided, like Socrates, that these remain attached to their complements, that private conscience is for the State of Athens, freedom is for the improvement of its laws. More values are involved than this map shows. In a democracy we openly persuade each other to vote secretly – the secrecy prevents untoward public pressures. We compete for office or economic rewards within the wider system of cooperation, or cooperate within corporations or political parties for a wider system of competition. We treat each other with equality because that is the best facilitator of different kinds of excellence. Open and secret, cooperation and competition, equality and excellence, all move alternately between language levels in a symphony of manifest and latent, point and counterpoint, a structure which those raised on mythology intuitively understood.

MAP 59

'I have a Dream!'
Martin Luther King and the myth of America

The man who in living memory most clearly and mostly successfully used mythology in a massive programme of social change was Martin Luther King. Today, a host of mock-revolutionary detractors have trampled on his memory in a frenzy of black or white *machismo*. Yet the passage of time and the trough of the seventies allow us to appreciate just how far he towers above them. I hope to show that King understood, albeit intuitively, that: the 'cross' of psychosocial tensions is the only escape from the prison of racism (see Map 5); that mind–body dualism cripples us (see Map 6); that racist anxieties can only be resolved by 'encompassing reason' (see Map 13), and the synthesis of Left and Right in culture and personality (see Map 16). He also showed brilliant understanding of the levels of moral judgement (see Map 38) and his use of biblical and other metaphors (see Map 40) was an inspired exercise in 'dovetailing' or 'imbricating' both ends of the dialectic (see Map 55), in overcoming the pathology of our moral discourse (see Map 43) and in creating human synergy (see Map 42).

King's background as a preacher made him familiar with the metaphors of imprisonment and crucifixion. He often likened black Americans to Israelites in Egypt, and preached that 'redemptive suffering', the crucifying psychic tension between poles, was the way to freedom. If we adapt the 'prison bars' and 'crucifixes' from Williams in Map 5 to the situation of Southern blacks, we get these relationships:

The 'bars' do not merely segregate blacks from whites, they split the value systems of both. Whites employ an extremist, Bible-belt fundamentalism to extol a mind that represses the body, a souless power that brutalizes powerless souls and a coercive discipline of blind loyalty to the white race. At the same time, they project upon blacks the repressed and rejected halves of their own values, so that blacks are alleged to possess animal bodies, smouldering with passion for Pure Southern Womanhood, other-worldly 'souls' of escapist religions and dangerously dissentient appetites. The domination used to make blacks submit 'blackens' half the value system creating the violent dynamisms of Map 34.

King's first and crucial insight was that simple 'revolution', even were it possible with a 10% black American population, would only revolve the prison. The seizure of local power by disciplined and race-loyal blacks would mean disaster. His answer was 'self-purification', a process taught in special schools for non-violence where pupils were taught to endure the social tensions of standing between value polarities. Thus:

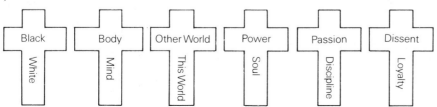

King understood that racism is a product of mind–body dualism. Neither whites nor blacks can just order themselves to be unprejudiced. To do so causes the body

Segregation, Martin Luther King explained, is not merely the dividing of person from person but the splitting of value from value within personality. The 'white thesis' becomes estranged from the 'black antithesis' and humanity as a whole is crippled. The three 'white dimensions' are represented on the three superimposed crucifixes in this map by: White–Mind, Power–(in) This World and Discipline–Loyalty (to white supremacy). The three 'black dimensions' are represented by: Black–Body, Soul–(in the) Other World, and Passion–Dissent (as in blues idiom).

King taught his followers a 'spiritual purification' and 'redemptive suffering' by which he meant a taking of the centre ground between the arms of the three crucifixes. By integrated demonstrations, black and white bodies were placed together on the line with black and white mental convictions. In the same way, the passionate dissent of black Americans learnt the hard discipline and tenacious loyalty of a non-violent faith in the American Dream. Realizing that racism puts blacks in a perpetual 'double bind', where they are pushed into cringing or revolting then punished for either extreme, King taught his followers to tilt in neither direction but, comporting themselves as equals, civilly yet emphatically refuse to be bound.

to revolt, so that even (or especially) those whites determined to be brothers discover that their intimacy is cursed. The problem is the unbearable level of visceral anxiety. You may *want* to like black people but the tension in your muscles takes its toll. This gnawing anxiety *is* controllable but at a fearful price: when white approaches black they collude in playing highly stereotyped reciprocal roles of domination and submission. To break this habit is very difficult. It is necessary if you are black to 'teach your body' not to panic in the presence of white authority figures. Civil rights tactics were brilliantly designed to include 'a relaxation therapy' which overcame the kind of conditioned phobia to white commands illustrated by Poussaint's experience in the margin. When marchers prayed, knelt, sang, or sat down together in the face of sherrifs' deputies, they were relaxing their bodies in the presence of a threat, which earlier had knotted their stomachs with terror until a cringing submission had eased the pain. Moreover, because whites and blacks among the marchers shared their physical danger and tightened and relaxed their nervous systems as one, they experienced the genuine integration which comes from putting integrated bodies on the line with integrated beliefs.

Not just mind and body, black and white were joined, King brought social purpose to cloistered religion and the fresh breeze of idealism to smoke-filled rooms of politicians. He persistently used religious language to refer to political and secular objectives: 'I've been to the Mountain Top, I've seen the Promised Land!' Such phrases reconciled the other-worldly 'escapist' black religion of tin-shack revivalism with unmistakable political aims in *this* world. It is not possible to 'grow' people unless you nurture their roots. You cannot lead them into the future without treasuring the past and if you try they will panic, like revolutionaries caught in the Terror.

Essentially similar was King's conception of 'soul power'. Blacks must take the soul which oppression had driven deep inside and assert it publicly. He taught his followers to stand upright, look oppression in the face and demand their rights with civility and dignity. The more open and flexible you were in making this request, the more convinced and tenacious would you subsequently become if that request was officiously refused. His followers needed confidence. They had to learn their moral conviction step by step and King understood those dynamics better than anyone. Every degree of passion had to be matched with the iron discipline of non-violence. He asked of them not repression but supression of the impulse to retaliate. They would dissent vehemently against the abuse and oppression heaped upon them but always in the context of an equal and opposite loyalty, a loyalty to the humanity of the other, to the land that had freed its slaves and had implanted in the protesters the very idea that they were created equal. Even King's voice with its rising and falling rhythm and cadence suggested the ecology of his values. No matter how strident his anger, and the night in 1956 when his own house and family was bombed tested his non-violent faith in America to the hilt, he always spoke from within the American Dream, in a furious, crucifying tension of faith and protest, a lovers quarrel to the end.

In 1963, in a great march on Washington, he spoke in the very shadow of the Lincoln Mermorial. Only King could have spoken to Movement people in the language of bankers with that uncanny feel for an entire nations' pulse. 'So we've come here to the nations' capital to cash a cheque . . . when the architects of our Republic wrote the magnificent words of our Constitution and the Declaration of Independence, they were signing a promissary note . . . It is obvious today that America has defaulted on this promissary note. Instead of honouring this sacred obligation, America has given her Negro people a bad check – a check that has

'The policeman shouted:
"Hey, boy! Come here!"
"My name is Alvin Poussaint. I'm a physician"
"Alvin, the next time I call you, you come right away, you hear?"
I hesitated. "You hear me, boy?"
My voice trembling with helplessness, but following my instincts of self-preservation I murmured, "Yes, sir." '
'Rapping in the Ghetto' from 'Transaction' February 1969

'If you will protest courageously and yet with dignity and Christian love, when the history books are written in future generations, the historians will have to pause and say, "There lived a great people – black people – who injected new meaning and dignity into the veins of civilization." '
Martin Luther King in Montgomery

' "Why don't you use your charisma, your brilliance, to help us live not die?" Malcolm X spoke almost in a whisper, "Because they hurt us too much. Because there is no way of living with them. Because they will deceive and hurt us in the end." King stared at him, "The final truth isn't that you hate the white man. It's that you hate being black. You can't see beyond your personal rejection." '
'King' by William Johnston

'An unjust law is a law not rooted in eternal and natural law . . . that uplifts the personality. Any law that degrades human personality is unjust . . . An unjust law is a code that a . . . majority group compels a minority group to obey but does not make binding on itself. This is difference made legal . . . A just law is sameness made legal . . . One who breaks an unjust law must do so openly, lovingly and with willingness to accept the penalty . . . the individual who breaks the law that conscience tells him is unjust and willingly accepts the penalty . . . is in reality expressing the highest respect for law.'

'Letter from a Birmingham Jail'
Martin Luther King

'There's talk about what might happen to me from some of our sick white brothers . . . But it doesn't matter to me now, because I've been to the mountain top! . . . Like anybody I'd like to live a long life. Longevity has its place. But I'm not concerned about that now . . . He's allowed me to go up the mountain! and I've looked over, and I've seen the promised land! I may not get there with you, but I want you to know tonight . . . that we, as a people, will get to the promised land! And I'm happy tonight. I'm not worried about anything. I'm not fearing any man! Mine eyes have seen the glory of the coming of the Lord!'

King's Memphis sermon, the night before his assassination

MAP REFERENCES
Anxiety, 9, 12–15, 34, 49–50, 56;
Crucifixion, 2, 4–5, 10, 12, 15, 27,
30, 42, 56; Mind–body dualism,
6, 14–15, 18, 21, 43, 55, 60;
Rebellion, 12, 14; Relaxation, 20;
Synergistic versus maximal
values, 2, 13–16, 28, 51, 55–8, 60.

come back marked 'insufficient funds'. But we refuse to believe there are insufficient funds in the great vaults of opportunity of this nation . . .'

The skill with which the Left- and Right-wing dimensions of personality are reconciled in this passage is extraordinary (see Map 16). King attached the cohesion and discipline of black Southern churches to a Supreme Court which had long since ordered desegregation, to an unusually liberal Congress (after the 1964 Goldwater debacle), to a Kennedy legacy, to a television media that portrayed demonstration in the manner of tragic drama (see Maps 2, 58). This potent combination of forces did more for black rights in five years than had been accomplished in the previous century.

Night after night the television news showed black people conducting themselves with firmness, yet restraint, while white Southern segregationists spat and sneered, bombed and murdered, their faces so distorted with hatred that one believed oneself witnessing the nervous breakdown of an entire life-style. I suggest that two kinds of value system were confronting one another: the traditional 'maximizing' structure wherein loyalty, power, discipline, patriotism and mind are pushed to their logical extremities, while their complements are both repressed within and projected outward upon an 'inferior' 'bodily' race; and an optimal synergized value system (see Maps 42, 43) in which each value is balanced and reconciled with its complement. I believe that for those with a maximal, absolutist and fundamentalist system of valuing, King and his followers appeared as the devil incarnate. In a value system of patriots and traitors, pure (white) women, and dirty (black) whores, of red-blooded Americans and perverted pinkos, what is one to make of those who stand ambiguously in the centre, who *gently* assert themselves? King fell on his knees like submissive Tom preachers had always done, but then he rose up and marched. He sounded humble in the very act of defiance, orderly while creating disorder. Not only did he refuse to be pushed to the 'weak' ends of value constructs, he also refused to 'fight like a man' for the strong ends. To a believer in the stereotyped and polarized role-relationships of racism the man was a hideous hybrid; like 'the face of crumpled linen' in Map 13, he was the nemesis of one-dimensional man, of the need to control anxiety by the manipulations of either–or and I–it.

The motives of those who murdered King were basically those of the people who poisoned Socrates, crucified Christ, beheaded Thomas More and shot Gandhi. We are tortured by the ambiguity of those who employ encompassing reason (see Map 13), who embrace not just the value we prefer but its negation, and, maddened by anxiety, we kill those who stretch themselves between our fanaticisms to heal us. This explains why the Movement could not sustain its progress. Only a small proportion of the nation really understood King. Even his supporters included many who sought to refight the Civil War, who naively believed that radicalism was the new yardstick of absolute virtue. King was not radical enough! The flagburners proved that one-dimensional morality and the either/or of technical reason were winning after all, as encompassing reason died between police and rioters and the ambiguous morality of love-in-anger yielded to pure hatred. Long before Kohlberg conceptualized the growth of moral judgement (see Map 38), King had explained it from his Birmingham Jail (see margin). Three 'extremists' had died on Calvary, he wrote. Still we cannot tell the one in the centre from the other two.

MAP 60
Ecology or Catastrophe?

This final map does not pretend to be an ultimate distillation but an attempt to integrate some major themes of the book, for the variety of patterns is irreducible, and the dreams of rival disciplines to become The Great Phallus originating all other inquiries is a part of our problem. First social science is inevitably moral science. If there is no attention without intention, then the selective focus of our paradigms (see Maps 52–6) have moral consequences and it behoves us to be aware of them. This is not a signal to start trumpeting our moral commitments to freedom and love, since values too strenuously proclaimed fulfill themselves in unanticipated and catastrophic forms. I believe the advocates of value freedom to have been right, at least in their portent of disaster inherent in ideologies. The problem is this: human beings perceive, speak, symbolize and process information in bimodal patterns while moral judgements tend to fasten obsessively on *one* of two modes. In Map 23, for example, I listed 33 ways in which rival theorists had conceived of the bilateral specialization of the left and right brain hemispheres. Yet few of these divisions have not been subject to murderous factionalism – Puritans versus Catholics, Mind versus Body, Freedom versus Deteminism, Arts versus Sciences, Communism versus Individualism. The war of geographical hemispheres is that of brain hemispheres, half-truths duelling to the death.

The kind of moral science I advocate is one discoverable only in the crucible of anxiety (see Map 13), in the 'incessant movement of contradiction' (see Map 12) and in the painful awareness that there are always at least two positive values in conflict, so that growth is the resolution of dilemma (see Map• 38). Such conflicts as individualism versus cooperation, or in the realm of data atomism versus holism, are the results of our verbal and numerical habits of encoding those differences which constitute information. Nature does not consist of sawn-off segments and extremities, only the language and measurements we use to describe nature has this digital structure. Our delusion that words are things (see Map 39), our continuing incapacity to read the Sphinx's riddle (see Map 40), threaten us all with destruction. If we break the continuum joining individuality to cooperation, we split the human endowment and turns its broken halves into idols, (Maps 43, 47, 49, 50).

It is necessary, therefore, to reject both the behaviourists insistance on strict, causal determinism (see Maps 6–8) and those humanists, who, heedless of Icarus, treat human freedom as a flight onward and upward (see Map 33). There is no freedom in seeking to conquer the larger life-patterns of ecological connectedness, only self-destruction. Every time we make a 'tree' of our conscious purpose (see Maps 4, 55) we must deal with the ecological 'garden' or 'net' of which that tree is a part. We can push nature but she recoils catastrophically upon us (see Map 56). The answer is not to denigrate freedom but to discover that it lies within the laws of recursive systems (see Maps 45–51). Attempted 'triumphs of the will' turn into their opposites, addiction and mania, see (Maps 48, 50) as the tragedies of Oedipus and Agamemnon are endlessly repeated (see Maps 2, 57, 58).

In Map 42, we saw that catastrophe can be avoided by creating an ecological synergy among values. If we take the rival positions espoused by progressive versus formal educators, we can create a cybernetic loop of their polarizations as shown on page 210. The conflicts can be seen by contrasting the words at the opposite ends of the axes. The resolution is achieved by optimizing all elements.

In Map 42, we saw that complementary values taken from both poles of a values continuum can be top-heavy, lop-sided or synergistic, and we can plot these conditions by bending the continua into dual-axis diagrams (see page 211). A glance at these should be enough to remind readers that higher education is balanced precariously between catastrophes. In the early sixties the indictment of

The human organism has either an ecological, co-evolutionary relationship with its environment or a catastrophic one of attempted conquest and backlash. The ecological relationship (top) shows the person's profile (left) within the context of his environment (right); he can only succeed in increasing his own personal values A–D by simultaneously nurturing his environment, social and natural, to render it more responsive A–B. Point C represents an optimal ecology of organism–environment which could in particular situations stand for such values as individualism–cooperation, part–wholes, rebellion–loyalty. That complementary values here go up or down a step reminds us that they must be expressed at different levels of logical type to avoid contradiction (Map 40); be dovetailed (Map 43) or imbricated (Map 55), and be cybernetically constraining and containing.

But our situation is potentially catastrophic (bottom). For centuries Puritan science embarked on a conquest of the environment, even repressing personal satisfactions to the end of moving from A to E. However, accumulating wealth led inevitably to the consumer society and extended indulgence in personal appetites, as the graph swung from E to F, and people cashed in on environmental manipulation. Soon, however, the pillaged environment and tortured social system may give way beneath the predators and a catastrophic fall in environmental quality occur as society falls into the cusp at point G (Map 56) and a rapid decrease in personal satisfaction and environmental response takes the human race backwards . . .

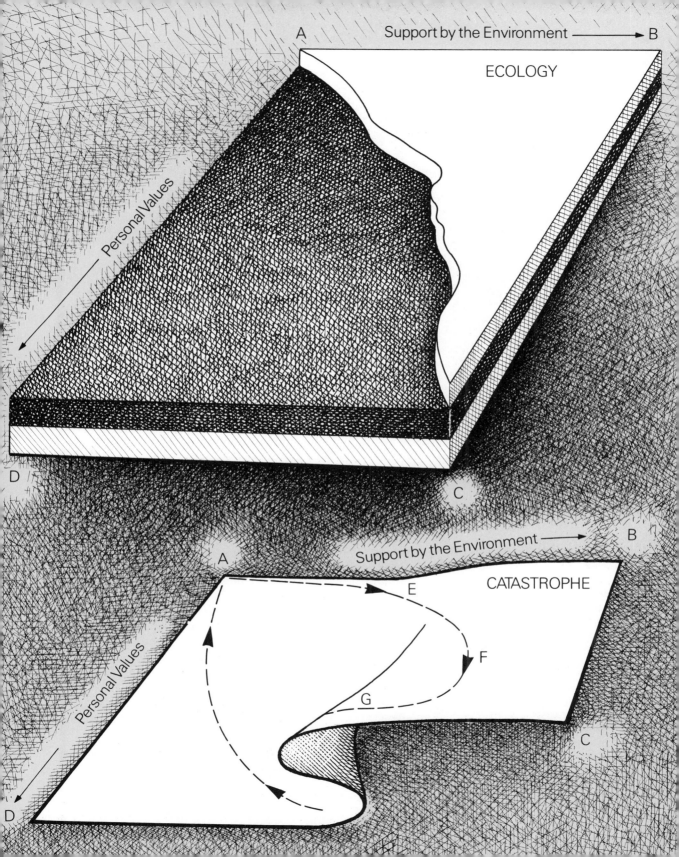

MAP 60

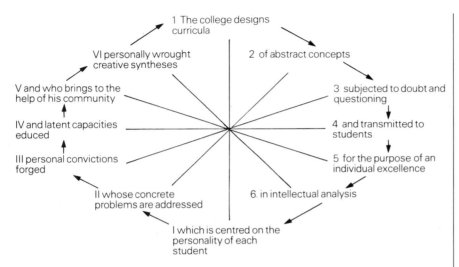

1 The college designs curricula

2 of abstract concepts

3 subjected to doubt and questioning

4 and transmitted to students

5 for the purpose of an individual excellence

6. in intellectual analysis

I which is centred on the personality of each student

II whose concrete problems are addressed

III personal convictions forged

IV and latent capacities educed

V and who brings to the help of his community

VI personally wrought creative syntheses

'Warren [Warren S. McCulloch, 1898–1969] was speaking very slowly. "I am by nature a warrior and wars don't make sense any more. I am a king, but I'm an anarchist, and in my country there are simply no laws . . . Now the difficulty is that we, who are not single-celled organisms, cannot simply divide and pass on our programs. We have to couple and there is behind this a second requirement." Warren began to weep. "We learn . . . that there's a utility in death because . . . the world goes on changing and we can't keep up with it. If I have any disciples, you can say this of every one of them, they think for themselves.

Very softly Gregory said, "Sure Warren."

"Freedom from and freedom for". We sat in silence for a long pause. "Coffee?" said Warren.'

From the 'Conference on the Effects of Conscious Purpose on Human Adaptation' July, 1969, convened by Gregory Bateson, quoted by Catherine Bateson in 'Our Own Metaphor'.

traditional college education, especially in the social sciences, was a familiar litany. The system had disappeared up the abstraction ladder and dared not come down, evading real people and their problems, it busily qualified trivia and qualified its qualifyers. By an exaggerated scepticism, it managed to dismiss as meaningless most of the world in which people lived and to define the human conscience as 'unverifiable'; while 'brilliant' lecturers played verbal games, a Silent Generation of students eschewed social responsibilities for grades and personal advancement.

So came the revolt of the sixties, spearheaded in most cases by social science students frustrated by the failures of their disciplines. There were brief moments of creative ferment but when the tear-gas cleared the top-heavy had become the lop-sided. Every swear word was now a search for existential validation. Cults of touchy-feely and instant enlightenment popped up to peddle positive thoughts. It became 'authoritarian' to give a lecture, and academics became 'resource persons' waiting around to be utilized in democratic class-rooms. Many students affected a contrived inarticulateness, 'Like . . . y'know . . . I mean . . .', a style intended to convey feelings too profound for words but which increasingly resembled sheer density.

However the choice is not between the poles at all but between an ecology of 'both . . . and' or the catastrophe of either/or in which the top-heavy are ever subverted by the lop-sided. The map at the beginning of this section compares ecology (top) with catastrophe (bottom). In ecological relationships the values describing the processes are defined inclusively of one another (see Map 35). For example, free individuals find fulfillment in lawful cooperation, while the laws of that cooperative relationship free and individualize the persons involved (see Map 42). Such an ecological pattern can also connect many other complementary endowments. These valued processes 'nest', the one in the context of its complement always at different levels of language or logical type (see Map 40). Another way of conceiving this is as dovetailing values (see Map 43), as imbricating affirmation–negation (see Map 55), or as shifting democratically between figure and ground (see Map 58). In catastrophic relationships values are defined exclusively and independently (see Map 56). Hence ideological disputes arise that pit

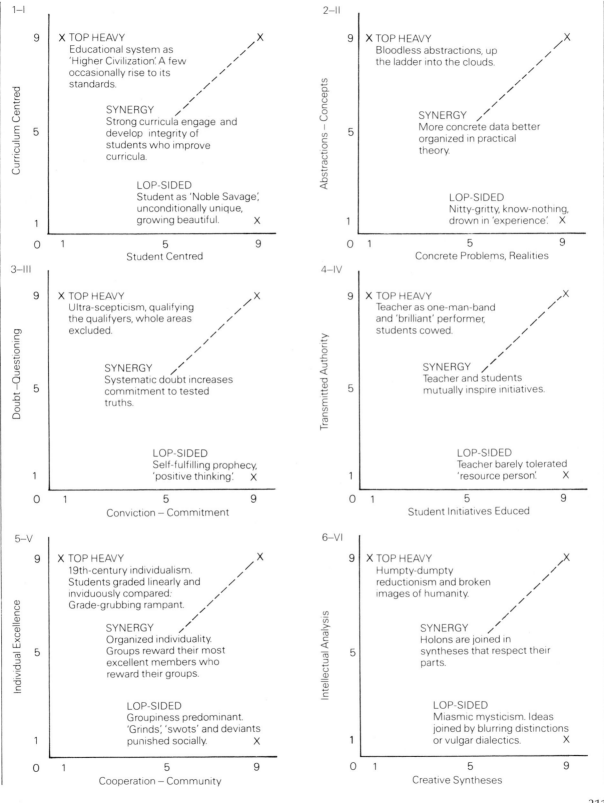

1–I

9 X TOP HEAVY
Educational system as
'Higher Civilization'. A few
occasionally rise to its
standards.

SYNERGY
Strong curricula engage and
develop integrity of
students who improve
curricula.

LOP-SIDED
Student as 'Noble Savage',
unconditionally unique,
growing beautiful. X

Curriculum Centred

0 1 5 9
Student Centred

2–II

9 X TOP HEAVY
Bloodless abstractions, up
the ladder into the clouds.

SYNERGY
More concrete data better
organized in practical
theory.

LOP-SIDED
Nitty-gritty, know-nothing,
drown in 'experience'. X

Abstractions – Concepts

0 1 5 9
Concrete Problems, Realities

3–III

9 X TOP HEAVY
Ultra-scepticism, qualifying
the qualifyers, whole areas
excluded.

SYNERGY
Systematic doubt increases
commitment to tested
truths.

LOP-SIDED
Self-fulfilling prophecy,
'positive thinking'. X

Doubt – Questioning

0 1 5 9
Conviction – Commitment

4–IV

9 X TOP HEAVY
Teacher as one-man-band
and 'brilliant' performer,
students cowed.

SYNERGY
Teacher and students
mutually inspire initiatives.

LOP-SIDED
Teacher barely tolerated
'resource person'. X

Transmitted Authority

0 1 5 9
Student Initiatives Educed

5–V

9 X TOP HEAVY
19th-century individualism.
Students graded linearly and
inviduously compared:
Grade-grubbing rampant.

SYNERGY
Organized individuality.
Groups reward their most
excellent members who
reward their groups.

LOP-SIDED
Groupiness predominant.
'Grinds', 'swots' and deviants
punished socially. X

Individual Excellence

0 1 5 9
Cooperation – Community

6–VI

9 X TOP HEAVY
Humpty-dumpty
reductionism and broken
images of humanity.

SYNERGY
Holons are joined in
syntheses that respect their
parts.

LOP-SIDED
Miasmic mysticism. Ideas
joined by blurring distinctions
or vulgar dialectics. X

Intellectual Analysis

0 1 5 9
Creative Syntheses

MAP 60

'individualism' and 'the Free World' (including Chile) against 'collectivism' and 'coercion'. Each polarized bloc attempts to purify its values, of which Puritanism (see Maps 6–8) is an historical example. This ends in contradiction when the repressed pole erupts (see Map 13). Instead of nesting within their complements catastrophic systems oscillate (see Maps 14, 49) go into runaway (see Maps 22, 48) and suffer schismogenesis (see Maps 48–50) with ever widening bifurcations (see Map 56), as the tragic heroes suffer *peripéteia*, or the opposites of their intentions (see Maps 2, 56–8).

Implicit in these arguments has been a method of reconstituting the meaning the coherence and the psycho-logic of value judgments. For most of this century the heirs of logical atomism first analyzed value systems into verbal pieces and then pronounced each fragmented judgements as without testable meaning. They failed, however, to ask whether their analysis had not destroyed the meaning inherent in the whole, ie in the unbroken continua and patterns *between* the judgements. Consider the hawk–dove moralizing in the Vietnam War, where 'patriotism' and 'loyalty' were pitted against 'treachery' and 'subversion'. Here is how the positivists would have analysed this unseemly clamour:

EVALUATION	DESCRIPTION	PRESCRIPTION
'Loyal, patriot'	= supports the war	(a good thing)
'Conforming militarist'	= supports the war	(a bad thing)
'Dissenting rebel'	= condemns the war	(a good thing)
'Subversive traitor'	= condemns the war	(a bad thing)

Social science, the philosopher concludes, should throw out the exclamations of preference about good or bad things and *describe*.

Admittedly value judgements *are* used in this unprofitable manner but is there no other way? These maps have shown that judgements of virtue are justifiable if they enhance the patterns joining that value to its complement. For example, loyalty or dissent are correctly evaluated as positive (a good thing) if either act succeeds in enhancing or protecting the *entire continuum* of loyalty–dissent, as well as the larger cybernetic value-system of linked continua. Similarly acts of patriotism or rebellion are correctly judged as virtues where they succeed in protecting or enhancing the capacity of patriots to rebel and rebels to remain patriotic. Judgements of vice, such as militarism or treachery are correctly used where either act leads to *splitting the value continuum* and so breaking the system which joins love of country to the capacity to rebel against it. Subversion or conformity are correctly designated as vices if they destroy the patterns joining loyalty to dissent. Note that the test of vice or virtue is empirical and pragmatic. When value judgements are enacted, they either increase the salience and synergy of the elements in the value system or they split and diminish those elements. We can measure, observe or otherwise estimate such growth or regression.

'No man is an Island, entire of itself; every man is a peace of the Continent, a part of the maine . . . Any man's death diminishes me, because I am involved in Mankinde: and therefore never send to know for whom the bell tolls; It tolls for thee.'
'Devotions' John Donne

MAP REFERENCES
Both . . . and, 2, 5, 10, 12–14, 16, 23, 28–30, 35, 47; Continua, 1–3, 10, 22, 26, 30, 34, 43, 51, 58–9; Ecology of mind, 48–50, 55; Moral Science, 5, 11–13, 37–40, 42–3, 46–7, 51; Semantic loops, 38–9, 42–3, 48–9, 51.

Bibliography and Acknowledgements

INTRODUCTION

I am indebted to Viktor E. Frankl's book *Psychotherapy and Existentialism* (Harmondsworth, Penguin, 1973) for the idea for the shadows map. I am also indebted to *Models of Man* by James G. Dagenais (The Hague, Nijhoff, 1972).

MAP 1

Here and throughout the Greek maps I was first inspired by Rollo May's *Symbolism in Religion and Literature* (New York, Braziller, 1970). Good fortune sent me for review Jay Ogilvy's *Many Dimensional Man: Decentralizing Self, Society and the Sacred* (New York and Oxford, Oxford University Press, 1977) from which I discovered James Hillman's *Revisioning Psychology* (New York, Harper & Row, 1975). *The Nature of Greek Myths* by G. S. Kirk (New York and Harmondsworth, Penguin, 1976) made good background reading, as did *The Greeks* by Anthony Andrewes (New York, Knopf, 1967). Edith Hamilton's *Mythology* (New York, Mentor, 1959) is a delightful summary of the Greek myths.

MAP 2

All the volumes cited under Map 1 helped me here but in addition and most importantly *Aeschylus and Athens* by George Thomson (New York, Haskell, 1940; London, Lawrence & Wishart, 1973). The *Theban Plays* of Sophocles (New York and Harmondsworth, Penguin, 1979) never fail to move me, as does the *Oresteia* by Aeschylus (New York and Harmondsworth, Penguin, 1979).

MAP 3

My interest in the *Tao* was first aroused by Alan Watts in *The Way of Zen* (New York, Vintage, 1959; Harmondsworth, Penguin, 1970) and reawakened by *The Tao of Physics* by Fritjof Capra (Boulder, Colo, Shambhala, 1975; London, Wildwood House, 1975). The *I Ching or Book of Changes* by R. Wilhelm (Princeton, NJ, Princeton University Press, 1967) is a most impressive volume.

MAP 4

The Garden of Eden myth is discussed by every psychologist with 'ultimate concern'. I'm grateful to Don S. Browning's *Generative Man* (New York, Delta, 1975) for the idea of comparing interpretations.

MAP 5

Harry Williams was my dean at Trinity College, Cambridge. His essay 'Theology and Self-awareness' in *Soundings* edited by A. R. Vidler (New York and Cambridge, Cambridge University Press, 1962 and 1966) first aroused my interest. For this map I consulted several of his books: *The True Wilderness* (New York and Harmondsworth, Penguin, 1968); *True Resurrection* (New York, Harper & Row, 1972; Mitchell Beazley, London, 1972); *Tensions* and *The Joy of God* (both New York, Penguin, 1979; London, Mitchell Beazley, 1979). Williams, incidentally, acknowledges a debt to Rollo May.

MAP 6

Almost the entire map is taken from Floyd Matson's *The Broken Image* (New York, Braziller, 1964), a marvellous book and a monument to graceful prose; it is, sadly, out of print. See, however, *The Idea of Man* (New York, Delta, 1974) also by Floyd Matson. Gilbert Ryle's *The Concept of Mind* (New York, Barnes & Noble, 1949; London, Hutchinson, 1949) was also useful.

MAP 7

Max Weber's *The Protestant Ethic and the Spirit of Capitalism* (New York, Scribner's, 1930; London, Allen & Unwin, 1977) is essential and goes well with R. H. Tawney's *Religion and the Rise of Capitalism* (New York, New American Library, 1977; Harmondsworth, Penguin, 1977). Actually the idea for this map came from Michael Walzer's *The Revolution of the Saints* (Cambridge, Mass, 1965) in which he discusses 'the doctrine of the objective word'. David C. McClelland's *The Achieving Society* (New York, Free Press, 1961; Chichester, Halstead Publishers, 1976) showed just how strong the grip of 'achievement motivation' is on industrial societies. *The Religious Factor* by Gerhard Lenski (New York, Anchor, 1963) was also consulted.

MAP 8

Henry Murray's famous address 'The Personality and Career of Satan' was reproduced in *The Journal of Social Issues*, October 1962, and subsequently taken up in David Bakan's brilliant book *The Duality of Human Existence* (Boston, Beacon Press, 1966).

MAP 9

My summary draws heavily on one by Hans Herma in *A Handbook of Psychoanalysis* (Cleveland, World Publishing, 1950); the map illustration is also adapted from this book. For beginners I recommend *Sigmund Freud: A general introduction*, John Rickman (ed.), (London, Hogarth Press, 1954). Of Freud's published work I would recommend: *New Introductory Lectures* on *Psychoanalysis*, James Strachey (ed.), (New York, Norton, 1965; London, Hogarth Press, 1958); *The Interpretation of Dreams* (New York, Avon, 1955; Harmondsworth, Penguin, 1976); *The Psychopathology of Everyday Life* (New York, New American Library, 1952; Harmondsworth, Penguin, 1975); and *Totem and Taboo* (New York, Norton, 1952; London, Routledge, 1950). The unconscious generalization of anxiety reported at the beginning of this map is from K. Diven's 'Certain determinants in the conditioning of anxiety reactions' in *Journal of Psychology* III, 1931.

MAP 10
I am almost totally indebted here, especially for the maps, to *The Psychology of C. G. Jung* by Jolande Jacobi (New Haven, Yale University Press, 1973; London, Routledge & Kegan Paul, 1969). For those who prefer the original source, *The Portable Jung*, Joseph Campbell (ed.), (New York, Viking, 1971) is well selected. Jung's *Collected Works* (Princeton, NJ, Princeton University Press, 1970; London, Routledge and Kegan Paul, 1971) is for those who are serious. A good introduction is Anthony Storr's *Jung* (New York, Viking, 1973; London, Fontana, 1973).

MAP 11
This map is adapted from Erich Fromm's *The Heart of Man* (New York, Harper & Row, 1964). Other essential reading includes *The Sane Society* (New York, Holt Rinehart & Winston, 1955; London, Routledge, 1949); *Fear of Freedom* (New York, Holt, Rinehart & Winston, 1941, under title *Escape from Freedom*; London, Routledge & Kegan Paul, 1960); *The Art of Loving* (New York, Harper & Row, 1956; London, Allen & Unwin, 1957); *Man for Himself* (New York, Fawcett, 1965); and *The Anatomy of Human Destructiveness* (New York, Fawcett, 1973; London, Routledge, 1949). There are almost no good criticisms of Fromm but see *Generative Man* by Don S. Browning, op. cit. Map 4.

MAP 12
Søren Kierkegaard is recommended for an instant depression especially *Fear and Trembling* and *Sickness unto Death* (both, New York, Anchor, 1954) and if you want more *The Concept of Dread* (Princeton, NJ, Princeton University Press, 1941). I alternate him with Camus to maintain morale. Camus is such a stylist that he must not be missed. *The Rebel* (New York, Vintage, 1956; Harmondsworth, Penguin, 1974) is his great polemic, see also *The Myth of Sisyphus* (New York, Knopf, 1955; Harmondsworth, Penguin, 1975); and his

essay 'Neither Victims Nor Executioners' published as a *Liberation* pamphlet in 1961.

MAP 13
Here my 'bible' is *The Meaning of Anxiety* by Rollo May (New York, Norton, 1977). It was Rollo's PhD thesis for Paul Tillich. A moving tribute to the latter is in *Paulus* (New York, Harper & Row, 1973; London, Collins, 1974) a book of unfashionable fidelity to a teacher. Other books by May referred to are: *Love and Will* and *Power and Innocence* (New York, Norton, 1969 and 1972; London, Collins, 1972 and 1976). Paul Tillich's *The Courage to Be* (New Haven, Yale University Press, 1959; London, Fontana, 1962) was a response to *The Meaning of Anxiety* in thesis form. 'Oh whistle and I'll come to you' by M. R. James can be found in *Ghost Stories of an Antiquary* (New York, Dover, 1971; Harmondsworth, Penguin, 1960). The conformity studies by Richard S. Crutchfield reported in Map 13 are from 'Conformity and Character' *American Psychologist* 10, 1955.

MAP 14
There is no substitute for *The Divided Self* (New York and Harmondsworth, Penguin, 1965); *Self and Others* (New York and Harmondsworth, Penguin, 1965) is nearly as good. For R. D. Laing's debt to Jean-Paul Sartre read Laing and David Cooper's *Reason and Violence: A decade of Sartre's philosophy* (New York, Random House, 1971; London, Tavistock, 1964). Sartre's *Being and Nothingness* (New York, Citadel Press, 1965) is also essential.

MAP 15
Becker 'made it' with *The Denial of Death* (New York, Free Press, 1973), after which some of his earlier books were reprinted by Free Press: *Angel in Armour* and *The Structure of Evil*. Unfortunately, *The Lost Science of Man* is out of print but *Escape from Evil*, his last (unfinished) book is in print (New York, Free Press, 1975).

MAP 16
'Left and Right: A Basic Dimension of Ideology' by Silvan Tomkins appeared in *The Study of Lives: Essays on Personality in Honour of Henry A. Murray* edited by Robert W. White (New York, Atherton, 1963). I explored it extensively in *Radical Man* (New York, Doubleday, 1971; London, Duckworth, 1971).

MAP 17
'The Great Ravelled Knot' by George W. Gray appears in *Physiological Psychology: Readings from Scientific*

American (San Francisco, W. H. Freeman, 1975); see also 'The Brain' in *Scientific American*, September 1979.

MAP 18
'Specializations of the Human Brain' by Norman Geschwind and 'Brain Mechanisms and Movement' by Edward V. Evarts, both in *Scientific American*, September 1979; see also *Programs of the Brain* by J. Z. Young (Oxford, Oxford University Press, 1978). Karl Pribram's research is discussed in 'Problems concerning the structure of consciousness' in *Consciousness and the Brain* edited by G. G. Globus (New York, Plenum, 1976). Colin Blakemore's statement is from his Reith Lecture printed in *Mechanisms of Mind* (Cambridge, Cambridge University Press, 1978). *The Purposive Brain* by Ragnar Granit was published in 1977 (Cambridge, Mass, MIT Press; London, Allen & Unwin).
The map illustrations are adapted from W. Penfield and T. Rasmussen *The Cerebral Cortex of Man* (New York and London, Macmillan, 1950).

MAP 19
'The Reticular Formation' by J. D. French in *Physiological Psychology*, op. cit. Map 17. See also John C. Eccles *Understanding the Brain* (New York, McGraw Hill, 1977; Maidenhead, Harper & Row, 1977) and Stephen Rose *The Conscious Brain* (New York, Knopf, 1973; Harmondsworth, Penguin, 1976).

MAP 20
This map and the illustrations are taken from *Fact and Fiction in Psychology* by H. J. Eysenck (New York, Gannon, 1965; Harmondsworth, Pelican Books, 1965). He is an immensely prolific writer. I found that the book he edited, *Behaviour Therapy and Neuroses* (New York and Oxford, Pergamon Press, 1960), to be the most convincing portrayal of his viewpoint, his popular books seem dogmatic and preoccupied with establishing his authority while denouncing that of enemies.

MAP 21
Paul D. Maclean puts his position well in 'The Paranoid Streak in Man' in *Beyond Reductionism* edited by Arthur Koestler and J. R. Smythies (Boston, Beacon Press, 1969). See also his contribution to *Astride the Two Cultures* edited by Harold Harris (London, Hutchinson, 1976). Arthur Koestler expounds his theme ably in *The Ghost in the Machine* (New York, Macmillan, 1968; London, Hutchinson, 1967).

MAP 22
I'm indebted to Karl Pribram for the idea of the instability of the limbic system, see *Emotion: The Search for Control* (New York, McGraw Hill, 1968); this is also a part of the Papez–Maclean thesis, see Map 21. The functions of the limbic lobe are well summarized in *The Mitchell Beazley Atlas of Body and Mind* (London, Mitchell Beazley, 1976). 'Runaway' is a cybernetic concept, see Maps 45–51.

MAP 23
The Psychology of Consciousness by Robert E. Ornstein (San Francisco, W. H. Freeman 1975; Harmondsworth, Pelican, 1975) is the basic reference on the split-brain. See also R. W. Sperry 'The Great Cerebral Commissure' in *Scientific American*, January 1964. See also Michael S. Gazzaniga 'The Split Brain in Man' *Scientific American*, August 1967. *The Mind–Brain Bulletin*, Los Angeles, is a good way of keeping up with development. But beware of the large number of evangelistic books treating the right hemisphere as a gateway to Eastern religion. I find J. E. Bogen the most profound commentator on the implications of his own surgery; see his 'Educational Aspects of Hemispheric Specialization' in *UCLA Educator*, Spring 1975.

MAP 24
Julian Jaynes's *The Origins of Consciousness in the Breakdown of the Bicameral Mind* (Boston, Houghton-Mifflin, 1976) says it all!

MAP 25
K. H. Pribram's *Languages of the Brain* (Englewood Cliffs, Prentice Hall, 1971) is essential reading. This map comes largely from 'The Neurophysiology of Remembering' in *Physiological Psychology*, op. cit. Map 17. It was updated by some recent papers: 'Mind: does it matter?' *Philosophical Dimensions of the Neuro-Medical sciences* (Dordrecht, D. Reidel, 1976); 'Holonomy and Structure in the organization of perception' in *Images, Perception and Knowledge* (Dordrecht, D. Reidel, 1976); see also 'Problems concerning the structure of Consciousness' in *Consciousness and the Brain*, op. cit. Map 18. For pictures explaining holographs I am grateful to Itzhak Bentov's *Stalking the Wild Pendulum* (New York, Dutton, 1977; London, Fontana, 1979) and to Peter Russell's *The Brain Book* (New York, Hawthorne, 1979).

MAP 26
I owe much to conversations with Stephen

Nachmanovitch and some to his doctoral thesis 'Job's Return: William Blake's Maps of the Deep'; but my chief guide in this map was *Milton* itself edited with a commentary by K. P. Easson and R. R. Easson (New York, Random House, 1978; London, Thames and Hudson, 1979).

MAP 27
Arthur Koestler's *The Act of Creation* (New York, Macmillan, 1964; London, Hutchinson, 1976) was my chief inspiration. A summary is found in *Janus* (London, Hutchinson, 1978) while Koestler's supporters rally in *Beyond Reductionism*, op. cit. Map 21, and *Astride the Two Cultures*, op. cit. Map 21. I am grateful to Arthur Koestler for answering queries.

MAP 28
Creativity and Intelligence: Explorations with Gifted Students by J. W. Getzels and P. W. Jackson (New York, Wiley, 1962) began the whole divergent–convergent debate. Liam Hudson took it up in *Contrary Imaginations: A Psychological Study of the English Schoolboy* (New York, Schocken, 1966; Harmondsworth, Penguin, 1968). In the English setting it inevitably became entangled with C. P. Snow's *The Two Cultures* (Cambridge, Cambridge University Press, 1961). For Hudson's 'theatrical' memories of Cambridge see *The Cult of the Fact* (New York, Harper & Row 1972; London, Cape, 1972) and more recently *Human Beings: An Introduction to the Psychology of Human Experience* (London, Cape, 1975).

MAP 29
De Bono's books are confusing because their American and British titles vary. I found the American publication *Lateral Thinking: Creativity Step by Step* (New York, Harper & Row, 1970; London, Ward Lock Educational, 1970, under the title *Lateral Thinking: A textbook of creativity*) most interesting; the illustrations are adapted from the latter with the publisher's permission. The story of the merchant's daughter comes from *New Think* (New York, Avon, 1971) called *The Use of Lateral Thinking* (Harmondsworth, Penguin, 1967) in Britain. *Future Positive* (London, Maurice Temple Smith, 1979) is also cited.

MAP 30
Barron's major book is *Creativity and Personal Freedom* (Princeton, NJ and London, Van Nostrand, 1968); an earlier version was entitled *Creativity and Psychological Health*. See also, Jay Ogilvy's book *Many Dimensional Man*, op. cit. Map 1. Barron has a tribute to Koestler in *Astride the Two Cultures*, op. cit. Map 21.

MAP 31
The text and illustration are adapted from 'Traits of Creativity' by J. P. Guilford in *Creativity and its Cultivation* (New York, Harper & Row, 1959); it is reprinted in *Creativity* edited by P. E. Vernon (New York, Macmillan, 1976; Harmondsworth, Penguin, 1978).

MAP 32
This is adapted from Chapter 11 of *Client-Centered Therapy* by Carl R. Rogers (Boston, Houghton-Mifflin, 1951; London, Constable, 1975). See also his *On Becoming a Person* by the same publishers (1961, 1974).

MAP 33
Abraham Maslow's *Motivation and Personality* (New York, Harper & Row 1954) is essential reading. This particular interpretation of the hierarchy is in *The Individual in Society* by D. Krech, R. Cruchfield and E. L. Ballachey (New York, McGraw Hill, 1962). For Maslow's later work see *Towards a Psychology of Being* (New York, Van Nostrand, 1962) and *The Psychology of Science* (New York, Harper & Row, 1966).

MAP 34
This chart comes from 'Interpersonal Diagnosis' by Timothy Leary and Hubert S. Coffey in the *Journal of Abnormal and Social Psychology* 50, 1955. It is reproduced in *Personality: Readings in Theory and Research*, E. E. Southwell and Michael Merbaum (eds) (Belmont, Cal., Wadsworth, 1964). They appear to have been most influenced by Sullivan's 'Multidimensional Coordination of Interpersonal Data' in *Culture and Personality* (New York, Viking, 1949). Sullivan wrote little, his *Conceptions of Modern Psychiatry* (Washington DC, William Alanson White Foundation, 1949) is generally regarded as his basic position. The research of my own I refer to is in *Sane Asylum: Inside the Delancey Street Foundation* (San Francisco Book Co., 1977; New York, William Morrow, 1978).

MAP 35
Martin Buber: The Life of Dialogue by Maurice Friedman (New York, Harper & Row, 1960) influenced me, as did Friedman's *To Deny our Nothingness* (New York, Delacourt, 1967). Two of Buber's books are now published in paperback by Charles Scribner's *I and Thou* (New York, 1970) *Good and Evil* (New York, 1970).

Also important is *Between Man and Man (Boston, Beacon Press, 1955; London, Fontana, 1961) The Knowledge of Man* edited with introduction by Maurice Friedman (New York, Harper & Row, 1964). A good students guide to existentialism in general is *The Worlds of Existentialism: A Critical Reader* edited by Maurice Friedman and available from University of Chicago Press, 1973.

MAP 36
I find Lewin difficult to read. However *A Dynamic Theory of Personality: Selected Papers* by Kurt Lewin (New York, McGraw Hill, 1935) is the basic source of the map. On putting Lewin's ideas to work I recommend *The Healing of a Nation* by David Loye (New York, Delta, 1971) and Alfred Marrow's appreciation *The Practical Theorist* (New York, Basic Books, 1969).

MAP 37
Erik Erikson's chart originated in *Childhood and Society* (New York, Norton, 1963; London, Hogarth Press, 1964). Probably his best exposition is in 'Identity and the Life Cycle' on *Psychological Issues*, vol 1, no 1, 1959. *Identity: Youth and Crisis* (New York, Norton, 1968) is also worth reading. For an excellent appreciation of Erikson see *Generative Man* by Don S. Browning, op. cit. Map 4. Richard Sennett in *The Uses of Disorder* (New York, Knopf, 1970; London, Allen Lane, 1971) and in *The Fall of the Public Man* (New York, Knopf, 1978; Cambridge, Cambridge University Press, 1977) makes excellent use of identity as a concept in sociology.

MAP 38
Jean Piaget's *The Moral Judgment of the Child* (New York, Free Press, 1965; Harmondsworth, Penguin, 1977) is Kohlberg's starting point while Piaget's *Origins of Intelligence in Children* (New York, Norton, 1963; Harmondsworth, Penguin, 1977) includes most of the structuralist assumptions Kohlberg shares. Kohlberg's clearest statement of his position is 'Stage and Sequence: The Cognitive-Developmental Approach to Socialization' in *Handbook of Socialization Theory and Research*, David A. Goslin (ed.), (Chicago, Rand McNally, 1969). Plato's cave comes from his 'Education for Justice: A Modern Statement of the Platonic View', The Ernest Burton Lecture on Moral Education, (Harvard, 1968, mimeo). His research protocols were applied by Norma Haan, Brewster-Smith and Jeanne Block in 'Moral Reasoning of Young Adults', *Journal of Personality and Social Psychology*, vol. 10, no. 3, 1968. I applied Kohlberg's stages to various philosophies of

science in 'Radical Man and the Hidden Moralities of Social Science' in *Interpersonal Development 2*, 1971–2. A trenchant critique of Kohlberg is by Elizabeth L. Simpson in 'Moral Development Research' *Human Development*, 17, 1974. The studies on obedience to cruel commands reported in Maps 38 and 47 are from Stanley Milgram's *Obedience to Authority* (New York, Harper & Row, 1969).

MAP 39
Science and Sanity: An Introduction to Non-Aristotelean System and General Semantics 4th edition, 1958, is Korzybski's great opus, available from the Institute of General Semantics, Lake Shore, Connecticutt, USA. He was popularized by S. I. Hayakawa in *Language in Thought and Action* (New York, Harcourt Brace, 1964). C. A. Hilgartner is an effective modern exponent, reprints of his articles are available from him at 307 Berkeley Street, Rochester, New York, 64607.

MAP 40
I cannot pretend to have read *Principa Mathematica* (Cambridge, Cambridge University Press, 1913) and have relied on explanations by Gregory Bateson in 'Logical Categories of Learning and Communication' in *Steps to an Ecology of Mind* (New York, Ballantine, 1975; London, Paladin, 1976). Paul Watzlawick, J. H. Beavin and Don Jackson also provide an excellent discussion in *Pragmatics of Human Communication* (New York, Norton, 1967). The idea of using the story of the Sphinx came to me while reading Edmund Leach's *Lévi-Strauss* (London, Fontana, 1976).

MAP 41
For this map see *The Structure of Magic* by Richard Bandler and John Grinder (Paolo Alto, Cal., Science and Behaviour Press, 1975). Noam Chomsky is difficult for non-linguists to understand without a mediator. *Chomsky* by John Lyons (London, Fontana, 1975) is some help. *Psycho-Linguistics: Chomsky and Psychology* by Judith Greene (Harmondsworth, Penguin, 1979) is useful. Noam Chomsky's *Reflections on Language* (New York, Pantheon, 1976; London, Fontana, 1976) is the most suitable for the general reader who insists on going to the source.

MAP 42
The illustration is redrawn with permission of Macmillan Publishing Co. Inc. from *Synergetics* by R. Buckminster Fuller (New York and London, 1975); © 1975 by R. Buckminster-Fuller. 'Synergy in Society and

the Individual', Abraham Maslow's presidential address to the New England Psychological Association in Boston, November 1963 explores Ruth Benedict's interest in synergy. Earlier discussions of synergy are found in his *Motivation and Personality*, op. cit. Map 33. The idea for the dual-axis diagrams is from *The Managerial Grid* by Robert Blake and Jane Mouton (Houston, Gulf Publishing, 1965).

MAP 43
Mark Twain's 'The War Prayer' can be read in full in *The Portable Mark Twain* selected by Bernard de Voto (Baltimore and Harmondsworth, Penguin, 1977). I discuss how values split in more detail in *From Poverty to Dignity: Strategy for Poor Americans* (New York, Doubleday Anchor, 1975).

MAP 44
I confess to finding Jacques Lacan unintelligible. Here I relied on *Psychoanalytic Politics* by Sherry Turkle (New York, Basic Books, 1978; London, André Deutsch, 1979). Those with a strong tolerance for ambiguity may try Lacan's *Ecrits: A Selection* (New York, Norton, 1977; London, Tavistock, 1977). The work of Ferdinand de Saussure is essential background reading; I recommend *Saussure* by Jonathan Culler (London, Fontana, 1976).

MAP 45
See *Robots, Men and Minds* by Ludwig von Bertalanffy (New York, Braziller, 1967); *Problems of Life* (New York, Harper & Row, 1951). For up-to-date developments in general systems see *General Systems Yearbooks*, Anatol Rapaport (ed.), (Washington DC, Society for General Systems Research).

MAP 46
This map is taken from Salk's *Survival of the Wisest* (New York, Harper & Row, 1973) and from hearing Jonas Salk himself speak. See also his *Man Unfolding* (New York, Harper & Row, 1972).

MAP 47
See Koestler references in Maps 20 and 27.

MAP 48
See Gregory Bateson's 'The Cybernetics of Self: A theory of Alcoholism' in *Steps to an Ecology of Mind*, op. cit. Map 40; also *Mind and Nature: A necessary unity* (New York, Dutton, 1979). A discussion of the governor occurs in 'Mind/Environment' by Gregory Bateson in *Social Change*, no 1, (New York, Gordon & Breach, 1972).

MAP 49
See the whole of Part III in *Steps to an Ecology of Mind*, op. cit. Map 40. See also *The Pragmatics of Human Communication*, op. cit. Map 40, and *How Real is Real?* by Paul Watzlawick (New York, Vintage, 1976).

MAP 50
See Part II of *Steps to an Ecology of Mind*, op. cit. Map 40, *The Authoritarian Personality* by T. W. Adorno *et al* (New York, Harper & Row, 1950), and *Freedom in a Rocking Boat* by Sir Geoffrey Vickers (Harmondsworth, Penguin, 1972). An excellent discussion of fascism in a manner recognizable as schismogenetic can be found in Peter Viereck's *Metapolitics: The Roots of the Nazi Mind* (New York, Capricorn, 1948). *The Origins of Totalitarianism* by Hannah Arendt (New York, Harcourt Brace, 1966) similarly evokes splitting especially in chapter 13. Visual treatments of the Third Reich make the point most clearly, see *Seig Heil!* by Stefan Laurent (New York, 1974). 'The Second Coming' by W. B. Yeats is from *The Oxford Book of English Verse* Helen Gardener (ed.) (New York and Oxford, Oxford University Press, 1972).

MAP 51
My source here is my own *Radical Man*, op. cit. Map 16. See also Marie Jahoda's *Current Concepts of Positive Mental Health* (New York, Basic Books, 1958).

MAP 52
Marx's Concept of Man by Erich Fromm (New York, Ungar, 1961) was my principle source; this edition also includes Marx's *Economic and Philosophical Manuscripts. Marx/Engels: Selected Works in One Volume* (New York, International Publishing Co., 1952; London, Lawrence & Wishart, 1952) is also recommended. Essential reading to balance the humanistic emphasis of Fromm is *The Communist Manifesto* by Karl Marx and Frederick Engels (New York and Harmondsworth, Penguin, 1967). The most famous critique is *The Open Society and its Enemies* by Karl R. Popper (New York, Harper & Row, 1962; London, Routledge & Kegan Paul, 1962). See also, Maurice Cornforth's reply *The Open Philosophy and the Open Society* (New York, International Publishers, 1968; London, Lawrence & Wishart, 1977). On the issue of dialectics see *The Dialectics of Nature* by Frederick Engels (New York, International Publishing Co., 1940;

London, Lawrence & Wishart, 1977). I am also indebted to Richard Lichtman's 'The Marxian critique of Christianity' in *Marxism and Christianity* edited by Herbert Apthecker (New York, Humanities Press, 1968). For the catastrophe befalling both ideological extremes see also *Plays* by John Galsworthy (New York, Scribner's, 1964).

MAP 53
Marcuse's four principle books discussed here are: *Reason and Revolution, Eros and Civilization, One-dimensional Man* and *An Essay on Liberation* (New York, Beacon Press, 1960, 1955, 1964, 1969; London, Routledge, 1964, 1966, 1964, 1969). See also 'Repressive Tolerance' in *A Critique of Pure Tolerance* by Robert Paul Wolff and Barrington Moore Jr (Boston, Beacon Press, 1965). A good critique of Marcuse can be found in *The Freudian Left* by Paul A. Robinson (New York, Harper & Row, 1969). An able history of the Frankfurt School is *The Dialectical Imagination* by Martin Jay (Boston, Little Brown, 1973; London, Heinemann Educational, 1973).

MAP 54
The Structure of Scientific Revolutions by Thomas S. Kuhn (Chicago, Chicago University Press, 1970) is a marvellously lucid thesis and needs no interpreters. Allan R. Buss has been the most successful in applying Kuhn to psychology, see *A Dialectical Psychology* (New York, Irvington, 1979).

MAP 55
Varela is quite new to the United States. I have only encountered the one article from which this map was adapted: 'Not One, Not Two' in *Coevolution Quarterly*, Fall 1976 (Sausalito, Cal.).

MAP 56
I discovered catastrophe theory as this book was going to press and would never have done so but for Denis Postle's *Catastrophe Theory* (London, Fontana, 1980). Another competent treatment is *Catastrophe Theory: A revolutionary new way of understanding how things change* by Alexander Woodcock and Monte Davis (New York, Dutton, 1978; London, Penguin, 1980). But these are popular books, those who wish to immerse themselves in science must read René Thom's *Structural Stability and Morphogenesis* (Reading, Benjamin, 1975) and Christopher Zeeman's *Catastrophe Theory: Selected Papers 1972–7* (Reading, Benjamin, 1977). See also *Catastrophe Theory and its Applications* by Tim Poston and Ian Stewart (London, Pitman, 1978). For a fascinating application of CT to drama see Nicholas Mosley's *Catastrophe Practice* (London, Secker & Warburg, 1979).

MAP 57
I found this by reading *Lévi-Strauss* by Edmund Leach, op. cit. Map 40. It is also discussed by Anthony Wilden in *System and Structure*, op. cit. Map 40. Lévi-Strauss's views on the Oedipus myth are described in his *Structural Anthropology* (New York and London, Penguin, 1979) and in 'The Structural Study of Myth' in the *Journal of American Folklore*, vol. 68, no. 270.

MAP 58
I was much influenced here by George Thomson's *Aeschylus and Athens*, op. cit. Map 2. Many of the observations are his, although his final conclusions are Marxist and mine are not. I was also helped by 'Myth and Culture: Their death and transformation by Rollo May in *ARC Directions*, no. 4, Summer 1967 and by sources cited in Maps 1 and 2.

MAP 59
King by William Johnston (New York, Warner, 1978) is a good dramatization of his life. 'Letter from a Birmingham Jail' is in *Why We Can't Wait* by King (New York, Harper & Row, 1963). *Martin Luther King Jr: A Profile* (New York, Hill and Wong, 1970) is mostly excellent; see especially Lerone Bennett Jr 'When the Man and Hour are met'. See also *Martin Luther King Jr* by W. R. Miller (New York, Avon, 1968). I'm grateful also to John E. McClusky for his conference paper 'Beyond the Carrot and the Stick' at the Midwest Political Science Association in May 1975.

MAP 60
My debt to Bateson is more evident than ever in this summary. See *About Bateson*, John Brockman (ed.) (New York, Dutton, 1976; London, Wildwood House, 1977) and *Our Own Metaphor* by Mary Catherine Bateson (New York, Knopf, 1973). *Mind and Nature: A necessary unity*, op. cit. Map 48, is also crucial.

Index